T0317038

Workers, Unions, and Global Capitalism

Workers, Unions, and Global Capitalism

LESSONS FROM INDIA

ROHINI HENSMAN

Columbia University Press   New York

Columbia University Press
Publishers Since 1893
New York   Chichester, West Sussex

Library of Congress Cataloging-in-Publication Data
Hensman, Rohini, 1948–
Workers, unions and global capitalism : lessons from India / Rohini Hensman.
p. cm.
Includes bibliographical references and index.
ISBN 978-0-231-14800-9 (cloth)
ISBN 978-0-231-51956-4 (e-book)
1. Labor—India. 2. Labor movement—India. 3. Globalization—Economic aspects.
I. Title.

HD8686.5.H46   2011
331. 880954—dc22   2010018408

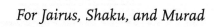

For Jairus, Shaku, and Murad

Contents

viii

Contents

Preface

This book started life as a rather unorthodox thesis presented to the University of Amsterdam in 2006: unorthodox because it was based not on one or two years of fieldwork but on more than three decades of research conducted as a participant in the labor movement, mainly but not exclusively in Bombay. I then rewrote it as a book for Columbia University Press, but while the manuscript was waiting for approval, there were many new developments, including the global crisis of 2008. Fortunately, my main argument—that deglobalization was neither possible nor desirable but that the dominant neoliberal model of globalization was both unjust and unsustainable—was vindicated by the crisis and its aftermath. Hence there was no need to rewrite the main body of the book or to change my conclusions. However, a major update was necessary, and I waited until a year had passed and the situation had settled down somewhat before completing it.

I would like to thank my promoter and supervisor at the University of Amsterdam, Jan Breman, whose guidance, patience, and encouragement ensured that I completed the original thesis, and whose work on informal labor inspired me to take up this issue. My thanks also to Marcel van der Linden, whose guidance was most valuable and whose work on labor internationalism helped me to understand this issue in historical perspective.

Jairus persuaded me to work with unions at a time when I thought of them as bastions of male chauvinism, played a major role in setting up and sustaining the Union Research Group, and bought and borrowed books to help with my research. Without him, this book would not have been possible. Much of the research is in fact a collective endeavor that owes a great deal to other members of the URG: Arun Subramaniam and Ammu Abraham in the early period, Jagdish Parikh, Ram Puniyani, Raju Damle, Ravi Shevade, Sujeet Bhatt, and Jagruti Bhatt; I am especially grateful to Sujata Gothoskar, Chanda Korgaokar, and Apoorva Kaiwar.

Committee members and workers from employees' unions have contributed both information and ideas; among them, S. Raghavan (Voltas and Volkart Employees' Federation), D. Thankappan (Kamani Employees' Union and New Trade Union Initiative), C. C. Mendes, Kamala Karkal and V. A. Nayampally (Pfizer Employees' Union), N. Vasudevan (All-India Blue Star Employees' Federation, Trade Union Solidarity Committee, and New Trade Union Initiative), R. G. Michael (Abbott Laboratories Employees' Union), R. R. Mishra (Philips Workers' Union), Kiron Mehta (Philips Employees' Union), Bennet D'Costa and Franklyn D'Souza (Hindustan Lever Employees' Union), Suhas Abhyankar (Hindustan Lever Research Centre Employees' Union), C. G. Chavan and Dilip Kagal (Nicholas Employees' Union), Harish Pujari (Otis Elevator Employees' Union), A. W. Noronha (Hoechst Employees' Union), and A. Bangera (Siemens Workers' Union). I am grateful to all of them, and especially to Thankappan, Vasu, and Bennet, who have shared their wisdom with me on innumerable occasions.

I owe my work on informal workers in the garment industry to Women Working Worldwide, and especially to its founder and former director, Angela Hale; it makes me very sad that she did not live to see the book completed. Others in WWW and the network of groups associated with it contributed a great deal to my understanding of global supply chains and codes of conduct. My thanks to the women garment workers in Bombay who participated in the research, for helping me to see that the biggest obstacle to their getting organized and fighting for better employment conditions was their informality itself; and to Madhavi and Mistrybai for the use of their homes to interview workers and conduct discussions. I would also like to thank Amrita Chhachhi, who has over the years helped me to clarify issues related to women and work and was the first person to suggest that I work on a thesis at all.

Preface

I am grateful to the Economic and Social Research Council for providing funding from 1993 to 1994 for my research on employees' unions; to WWW for supporting my research on garment workers between 1998 and 2003; and to the International Institute of Social History, Amsterdam, for providing a CLARA Fellowship in 2001, which enabled me to construct the outlines of my argument.

Finally, I would like to thank Sonia McKay for helpful discussions and material from the Labour Research Department; Sughosh Mazmundar for his generosity in supplying me with books I would not otherwise have been able to obtain; Savi and Vijayatara for stimulating comments; Shaku and Murad for helping me with tracking down references and for their faith in my work; and, last but not least, Amlan and Zinedine for hours of fun while I was working on this book.

Abbreviations

ABS	Asset-Backed Security
ABVP	Akhil Bharatiya Vidyarti Parishad
ACFTU	All-China Federation of Trade Unions
AFL	American Federation of Labor
AIBEA	All-India Bank Employees' Association
AICAPEF	All-India Chemical and Pharmaceutical Employees' Federation
AIG	American International Group
AITUC	All-India Trade Union Congress
ANC	African National Congress
ASK	Association for Stimulating Know-how
BBC	British Broadcasting Corporation
BGG	Bombay Government Gazette
BGJB	British Group for Justice in Bhopal
BIFR	Board for Industrial and Financial Reconstruction
BIRA	Bombay Industrial Relations Act
BJP	Bharatiya Janata Party
BKS	Bharatiya Kamgar Sena
BMS	Bharatiya Mazdoor Sangh
BPL	Below Poverty Line

BPO	Business Process Outsourcing
BS	*Business Standard*
BSWU	Blue Star Workers' Union
CBI	Central Bureau of Investigation
CCC	Clean Clothes Campaign
CCPD	Citizens' Campaign for Preserving Democracy
CDO	Collaterized Debt Obligation
CEC	Centre for Education and Communication
CEDAW	Convention on the Elimination of All Forms of Discrimination Against Women
CEO	Chief Executive Officer
CEPAA	Council on Economic Priorities Accreditation Agency
CFA	Committee on Freedom of Association
CGHS	Central Government Health Scheme
CGT	Confédération Générale du Travail
CIAE	Central Institute of Agricultural Engineering
CIO	Congress of Industrial Organizations
CITU	Centre of Indian Trade Unions
CNN	Cable News Network
CPI	Communist Party of India
CPI(M)	Communist Party of India (Marxist)
CPI(ML)	Communist Party of India (Marxist-Leninist)
CRC	(UN) Convention on the Rights of the Child
CSO	Central Statistical Organisation
CTBT	Comprehensive Test-Ban Treaty
CWM	Centre for Workers' Management
DA	Dearness Allowance
DFID	Department for International Development
DGAD	Directorate General of Anti-dumping
DGET	Directorate General of Employment and Training
EFPS	Employees' Family Pension Scheme
EGS	(Maharashtra) Employment Guarantee Scheme
EPFO	Employees' Provident Fund Organisation
EPW	*Economic and Political Weekly*
ESIS	Employees' State Insurance Scheme
ET	*Economic Times*
ETI	Ethical Trading Initiative
EU	European Union

FBI	Federal Bureau of Investigation
FDI	Foreign Direct Investment
FII	Foreign Institutional Investor
FMCG	Fast-Moving Consumer Goods
FMRAI	Federation of Medical Representatives' Associations of India
FSC	Foreign Services Corporation
FTZ	Free-Trade Zone
FWF	Fair Wear Foundation
GATT	General Agreement on Tariffs and Trade
GDP	Gross Domestic Product
GKU	Girni Kamgar Union
GOI	Government of India
GNP	Gross National Product
GPRS	Gas Peedith Rahat Samiti
GUF	Global Union Federation
HLEU	Hindustan Lever Employees' Union
HLL	Hindustan Lever Limited
HMKP	Hind Mazdoor Kisan Panchayat
HMS	Hind Mazdoor Sabha
HR	Human Resources
ICC	International Criminal Court
ICDS	Integrated Child Development Services
ICEM	International Federation of Chemical, Energy, Mine, and General Workers' Unions
ICICI	Industrial Credit and Investment Corporation of India
ICFTU	International Confederation of Free Trade Unions
ICLS	International Conference of Labour Statisticians
ICT	Information and Communication Technology
ID Act	Industrial Disputes Act
IFA	International Framework Agreement
IFTU	International Federation of Trade Unions
ILO	International Labour Organization
IMF	International Metalworkers' Federation
IMF	International Monetary Fund
INTUC	Indian National Trade Union Congress
IPEC	(ILO) International Programme on the Elimination of Child Labour

Abbreviations

IR	Industrial Relations
IRENE	International Restructuring Education Network Europe
IT	Information Technology
ITGLWF	International Textile, Garment, and Leather Workers' Federation
ITS	International Trade Secretariat
ITUC	International Trade Union Confederation
IUF	International Union of Food, Agricultural, Hotel, Restaurant, Catering, Tobacco, and Allied Workers' Associations
IUR	*International Union Rights*
KEC	Kamani Engineering Corporation
KEU	Kamani Employees' Union
KMA	Kamani Metals and Alloys
KT	Kamani Tubes
LARIC	Labor Rights in China
LDCs	Least Developed Countries
LF	*Labour File*
LNP	Lal Nishan Party
MBS	Mortgage-Backed Security
MFA	Multi-Fibre Agreement
MGG	Maharashtra Government Gazette
MIC	Methyl Iso-Cyanate
MMM	Mahila Mukti Morcha
MNC	Multinational Corporation
MP	Madhya Pradesh
MRTP	Monopolies and Restrictive Trade Practices
MRTU and PULP Act	Maharashtra Recognition of Trade Unions and Prevention of Unfair Labour Practices Act
MSN	Maquila Solidarity Network
MSP	Minimum Support Price
MT	Metric Tons
NAFTA	North American Free-Trade Agreement
NCL	National Centre for Labour
NDA	National Democratic Alliance
NFE	Nonformal Education
NGO	Nongovernmental Organization
NIDL	New International Division of Labor

NPS	New Pension Scheme
NPT	Non-Proliferation Treaty
NREGA	National Rural Employment Guarantee Act
NSSO	National Sample Survey Organisation
NTUI	New Trade Union Initiative
OBC	Other Backward Classes
PDS	Public Distribution System
PF	Provident Fund
PFI	Public Financial Institution
PFRDA	Pension Fund Regulatory and Development Authority
PPR	Pinault-Printemps-Redoute
PROBE	Public Report on Basic Education
PSU	Public-Sector Unit
PT	Partido dos Trabalhadores
R&D	Research and Development
RBI	Reserve Bank of India
RPG	R. P. Goenka
Rs	Rupees
RSS	Rashtriya Swayamsevak Sangh
SA 8000	Social Accountability 8000
SAARC	South Asian Association for Regional Cooperation
SAL	Sociedad Anónima Laboral
SICA	Sick Industrial Companies (Special Provisions) Act
SC	Scheduled Caste
SEWA	Self-Employed Women's Association
SJM	Swadeshi Jagran Manch
SSS	Sarva Shramik Sangh
ST	Scheduled Tribe
SLS	Sthanik Lokadhikar Samiti
TCS	Tata Consultancy Services
TGWU	Transport and General Workers' Union
TICL	Transnationals Information Centre, London
TIE	Transnationals Information Exchange
TOMCO	Tata Oil Mills Company
TRIPS	Trade-Related Aspects of Intellectual Property Rights
TU	Trade Union
TUJAC	Trade Union Joint Action Committee
TURF	Trade Union Relief Fund (for Gas Victims of Bhopal)

Abbreviations

TUSC	Trade Union Solidarity Committee
UCIL	Union Carbide India Limited
UNITE	Union of Needletrades, Industrial and Textile Employees
UNCTAD	United Nations Conference on Trade and Development
UP	Uttar Pradesh
UPA	United Progressive Alliance
URG	Union Research Group
USAID	United States Agency for International Development
UTUC	United Trade Union Congress
VHP	Vishwa Hindu Parishad
VRS	Voluntary Retirement Scheme(s)
WCC	World Corporation Council
WIEGO	Women in Informal Employment: Globalizing and Organizing
WRC	Workers' Rights Consortium
WSF	World Social Forum
WTO	World Trade Organization
WTUL	Women's Trade Union League
WWW	Women Working Worldwide

Workers, Unions, and Global Capitalism

Introduction

The Politics of Globalization

Globalization has had a profound impact on labor worldwide, but what, exactly, has this impact been? Enthusiastic proponents of globalization in its heretofore dominant form argue that it levels the playing field between developed and developing countries, creating employment in the latter and enabling them to pull themselves out of poverty (cf. T. Friedman 2005). Diametrically opposed to them are the passionate proponents of deglobalization, who see globalization as synonymous with inequality and oppression and who advocate disabling the World Trade Organization, International Monetary Fund, World Bank, and transnational corporations (cf. Bello 2000).

The economic crisis that started in the United States in September 2008 and swept through the world left the first camp in disarray. With financial institutions collapsing, millions of jobs being lost, GDPs shrinking, and world trade contracting (Wade 2009), even Thomas Friedman (2009) had to admit that the market was "hitting the wall." The opposite camp, predictably, was triumphant: "The current global downturn, the worst since the Great Depression 70 years ago, pounded the last nail into the coffin of globalization," proclaimed Walden Bello (2009).

However, there is a third position, which represents the majority of workers throughout the world. They have been fighting a losing battle for jobs, better employment conditions, and social security for over three decades, a struggle that has become more desperate since the downturn. While it is clear that the model of globalization pursued so far has been a disaster for them, deglobalization would mean a further loss of jobs for workers in exporting countries and would raise both costs of production for companies using their products and the cost of living for consumers. Dissatisfied with both of these positions, international unions have advocated building workers' rights into the new global order (cf. ICFTU 1999), but this has yet to emerge as a concrete alternative.

This book argues that it is not globalization as such but the dominant neoliberal model of it alongside traditional authoritarian labor relations that have exerted downward pressure on labor standards. It attempts to put flesh on the bones of the third alternative by looking at workers' responses to globalization: responses that indicate that labor is "a social force which is central to the development of the international political economy and international relations" (Harrod and O'Brien 2002a, 8).

One year after the bankruptcy of Lehman Brothers, there were superficial signs of recovery, but a closer look at unemployment, poverty rates, and foreclosures in the United States showed that there was no end in sight for the suffering of "regular people," while the banking sector and Wall Street continued to act in a manner that ensured that "the causes of the financial crisis continue unabated and in some cases have worsened" (Weissman 2009). The EU economy was shrinking. While the prognosis in other countries might not have been so dire, the downturn was far from over. The crisis has made it more urgent for the labor movement to craft a viable response to globalization, but paradoxically, it has also made it easier to question the previously dominant model, given that it led to such a catastrophe.

The effect of globalization on labor has been complex and even contradictory. Trade union movements firmly anchored in national history and legislation found it difficult to cope with global integration and the vastly increased mobility of capital; one consequence of this was the decline in the proportion of the labor force organized in unions over the last three decades of the twentieth century, which weakened the bargaining power of workers (Harrod and O'Brien 2002, 10–11). Yet between 1975 and 1995, the global labor force doubled (Munck 2002, 8), making it potentially much stronger as a social force. This book argues that recovery from the crisis *depends*, to a large extent, on the judicious use of this power by workers worldwide.

The secular expansion in employment coexisted with drastic declines in some sectors, including highly unionized ones. Large-scale industrialization in some of the former colonies and the end of the cold war resulted in key East European and developing countries emerging as attractive markets and investment destinations for global capital, thus intensifying competition for jobs among workers who were formerly insulated from such competition. Yet these same events removed obstacles to solidarity between unions in former colonies and imperialist states and between unions on opposite sides of the Iron Curtain. Convergence between employment conditions in different parts of the world made it easier for workers from widely different backgrounds to identify with one another, potentially making global solidarity an achievable goal. Technologies that facilitated the mobility of capital and global competition for jobs at the same time provided workers with a means of spreading the consequences of a local dispute around the world at rapid speed (Herod 2002).

Thus the negative fallout of globalization for workers is accompanied by developments that create the potential for counteracting those disadvantages and, indeed, building an even stronger labor movement. But that would require, first, a rigorous definition of globalization so that the effects of the changes in the nature of capitalism—such as the revolution in information and communication technologies—can be disentangled from the neoliberal assault on workers' rights. Second, it would entail a drive to reverse the decline in union density, either by undertaking a drastic overhaul of existing unions or by creating new models of unionism, such as social-movement unionism in South Africa, Brazil, and South Korea (Moody 1997, 201–226; Munck 2002, 122–125) and employees' unionism in India (chapter 5 of this book). This drive would have to include special measures to tackle the rapid spread of informalization, which creates employees without legal status or rights. The extralegal character of this sector breeds child labor, slavelike conditions, and all manner of abuses, which are exacerbated by the preponderance of disadvantaged workers in it: women, ethnic and religious minorities, migrants, indigenous people, and so on.

The third task would be to formulate a global strategy for labor. This does not mean abandoning the local or national as an arena for struggle. But it does mean thinking globally even when acting locally, because local action—or inaction—that allows workers' rights to be undermined in some distant part of the world results in an assault on one's own rights. For example, protectionist policies aimed at protecting and expanding domestic employment at the expense of workers elsewhere ultimately have a negative effect everywhere (Stevis 2002, 146). Global solidarity in this sense has become a condition for survival, and it demands a much greater knowledge of developments in other countries than ever before. It also demands a fundamental change in the strategic orientation of unions, which has hitherto been centered on the nation-state. Even the largest international confederation, the International Confederation of Free Trade Unions (which merged in 2006 with the World Confederation of Labour to form the International Trade Union Confederation), was "a confederation of national trade union centres, which means that its governing bodies are composed of representatives of organizations accustomed to think and act within the confines of the nation-state" (Gallin 2002, 238). The alternative is not necessarily a monolithic global *organization* but, rather, a global *movement* unified by its goals and developing its strategies through debates across all the borders that divide workers.

The central argument of this book, then, is that globalization itself cannot be reversed any more than the industrial revolution could have been reversed, but the *politics* of globalization constitutes terrain that can and must be contested by workers and unions if the world economy is to emerge from deep crisis. Therefore a global strategy for labor would require that workers not oppose globalization but fight for their own politics, a politics based on global solidarity and democracy, to shape the process.

The Importance of the Local

It is a paradox of globalization that "the greater interconnectedness of the global economy . . . which high-speed telecommunications and transportation technologies have augured means that the consequences of any particular event can be transmitted much further and much faster than ever before" (Herod 2002, 87). Consequently, local events become global ones. In other words, "the growing *extensity*, *intensity*, and *velocity* of global interactions may also be associated with a deepening enmeshment of the local and global such that the *impact* of distant events is magnified while even the most local developments come to have enormous global consequences"

(Held et al. 1999, 15). If this is true of a particular event, it is even more true of labor relations in a whole country: the lowering of barriers to trade and capital movements not only exposes a country's labor force to influences from the global economy but also exposes the rest of the world's labor force to the influence of a particular country's economy. Recognition of this on the part of trade unions resulted in the campaign for a social clause in WTO trade agreements upholding core labor rights. China has understandably received a great deal of attention because of the size of its labor force, the ubiquity of its products, and its authoritarian political system, which bans independent unions. But there is a curious lack of such interest in India, given that it follows closely on the heels of China in terms of the size of its labor force and its growing importance within the global economy.

One reason for this difference could be the perception that labor relations in China constitute a bigger threat to workers in other countries than do labor relations in India, but this is not necessarily true. In China, the preliberalization social contract, which guaranteed job security and extensive welfare benefits for workers, created a strong sense of entitlement among Chinese workers. The government was forced to replace it in the postliberalization period with a labor law promising workers' rights and social security in order to counter massive social unrest, which from 2003 through 2005 led millions of workers to riot or demonstrate (Lee 2007). In India, by contrast, the overwhelming preponderance of informal workers in the labor force facilitated the absence of either social or legal contracts promising workers' rights; the sense of entitlement and thus scale of protest were correspondingly much smaller.

Both Chinese and Indian workers have gained employment from offshoring and outsourcing. But the Chinese model of the attempted denial of workers' rights cannot easily be replicated in countries with a different legal system, whereas the Indian model, where the bulk of the labor force is not even registered or accorded legal status as workers, is far more insidious and has spread rapidly to countries where it was rare or unknown before. On the other hand, India has suffered less from the crisis than the United States or European Union. Although India's stock markets plunged as foreign institutional investors withdrew their funds, its well-regulated banking sector, with a negligible exposure to toxic assets, stood firm (Ram Mohan 2009). And while tens of thousands of jobs were lost in sectors producing for export, the overall increase in unemployment and consequent loss of consumer spending power were mitigated by the National Rural

Employment Guarantee Scheme (see chapter 8), which was up and running *before* the crisis and was allocated more funds after the crisis began. Furthermore, the decline in membership among traditional trade unions was offset by the establishment and growth of a dynamic new federation of independent unions. Thus there are both positive and negative lessons to be learned from the Indian experience, and workers and unions in other countries cannot afford to ignore them.

In July 1991, the Congress Party government, headed by Narasimha Rao, was faced with foreign-exchange reserves sufficient for just a fortnight's imports. To deal with that crisis, it began to implement the stabilization and structural-adjustment programs that had already been recommended by the IMF and World Bank in the late 1980s. This included the abolition of licensing procedures for manufacturing investment (which had popularly come to be known as a corruption-ridden "license-permit raj"), a reduction of the high import tariffs on most goods (but not consumer goods), liberalizing terms of entry for foreign investors, and liberalizing capital markets. Although Rajiv Gandhi had initiated a process of piecemeal liberalization in the mid-1980s, the changes introduced in 1991 were much broader in scope and scale (Balasubramanyam and Mahambare 2001).

When the WTO was established on January 1, 1995, India was a member from the start. This involved new pressures, for example, to eliminate quantitative restrictions on imports, simplify and reduce tariffs, reduce export constraints, reduce the number of activities reserved for the public sector and small-scale sector, further liberalize the Foreign Direct Investment regime, and address the fiscal deficit. India's close integration into the world economy has been more or less continuous since 1991, despite changes of government. This book examines how it is has affected workers and how they have responded, especially in one of India's biggest industrial centers, Bombay,[1] and makes numerous comparisons with examples from all over the world, drawing lessons, both positive and negative, for a global strategy for labor.

Chapter 1 outlines the background that led to this research and discusses the research method used,[2] explaining why the method of emancipatory action research is more appropriate in this case than the attempt to be "objective." My theoretical approach is presented so that it is clear where I am coming from and why this analysis was undertaken. Chapter 2 arrives at a working definition of globalization by examining existing definitions and making a critique of some. The merit of my definition is that it allows for a more nuanced response to globalization than either embracing it in its neoliberal form or rejecting it altogether. Chapter 3 examines four sources of the economic crisis of 2008 and suggests how three of them can be counteracted. The fourth—the widening gap between rich and poor—can only be redressed by a strong labor movement, and chapters 4 to 9 look at ways in which this can happen. Chapter 4 looks at the trade union movement in India against the background of the worldwide labor movement, examining in particular its relationship with the state. It argues that globalization reduces the power of individual states to protect labor rights but creates the conditions for member states of the WTO to protect workers' rights collectively. Chapter 5 discusses the importance of trade union democracy for the learning process in the labor movement and defines and examines an important experiment in union democracy, the "employees' unions" that have been formed spontaneously as an alternative to the party-affiliated national unions in India.

Chapter 6 takes up informal employment, definitions and debates around it, and the conditions of informal workers, arguing that informal labor constitutes the single biggest problem facing the global labor movement in the early twenty-first century. I examine strategies to confront the problem of informal labor suggested by trade unions, informal workers, and the ILO. Chapter 7 examines the adverse effects of sexual harassment on women workers and analyzes the gender division of labor at the workplace and in the home. I also discuss strategies to defend the equality and dignity of working women. Chapter 8 argues that massive resources are needed to create employment and support social-security and welfare programs if the world is to emerge from recession, and a struggle by unions against the narrow vested interests promoting militarism can release them.

Chapter 9 looks at international efforts to deal with the effects of globalization on labor, including international agreements between trade unions and employers, international solidarity action, codes of conduct, and the proposal for a social clause protecting workers' rights in WTO agreements. I examine the way in which employees' unions and informal workers in Bombay have used, reacted to, or participated in them, emphasizing examples of international solidarity. Their potential for improving workers' rights globally is evaluated. Finally, chapter 10 draws out and puts together conclusions arising out of the preceding chapters, which suggest strongly that only a truly global strategy for labor is capable of confronting the challenges of globalization and crisis.

My hope is that this analysis of global labor from the perspective of a crucially important section of it will contribute to a better understanding of globalization, and especially to a realization that workers can and do play a role in shaping the process. This role could be much greater—and indeed *must* be greater—if the global economy is to recover from the crisis. My argument is that realizing this potential depends on the ability of workers throughout the world to build bonds of solidarity across existing divisions and elaborate a strategy synthesizing the interests of all sections of the global labor force.

[1]

Emancipatory Action Research
Into Workers' Struggles

This book is an account of emancipatory action research, which is "collaborative, critical, and self-critical inquiry by practitioners . . . into a major problem or issue or concern in their own practice" (Zuber-Skerritt 1996, 3). The problem or issue or concern in this case was the quandary in which the labor movement found itself in the early twenty-first century, both worldwide and in India: large numbers of unionized workers were losing their jobs while the overwhelming majority of the labor force consisted of informal workers subjected to extremely oppressive employment conditions. Emancipatory action research has been seen "as a way of bringing together social science theory and practice" (Weiskopf and Laske 1996, 123). As a Bombay-based participant in the labor movement who has been involved in labor research since the mid-1970s, I felt the need for a deeper and more extensive critical enquiry into the practice of this movement, one taking into account changes in the overall context resulting from globalization. My objective was to investigate our shared experience in a manner "which link[s] practice and the analysis of practice into a single productive and continuously developing sequence"; thus this book "is about the nature of the learning process, about the link between practice and reflection, about the process of attempting to have new thoughts about familiar experiences, and about the relationship between particular experiences and general ideas" (Winter 1996, 14).

My starting point was the practice of two sections of workers in India—formal workers in employees' unions and informal workers—who had been affected by globalization in opposite ways: the former losing jobs while the latter gained them. The democratic functioning of the employees' unions could in some ways be seen as "best practice" in the trade union movement, yet the fact that the bulk of the labor force remained unorganized posed a problem both for employees in these unions, whose jobs had been transferred in large numbers to informal workers, and for the informal workers themselves, most of whom were unable to bargain collectively in order to improve their employment conditions. The assault on labor rights was already evident by the mid-1970s and intensified with globalization, and even the most combative unions were hard pressed to defend the gains they had made in earlier periods.

This impasse resulted in considerable hardship for many workers who lost their jobs in the formal sector. While unions resisted in various ways, initially they tended to focus their struggle on an opposition to globalization and a defense of members' jobs rather than attempting to fight for the rights of the informal workers to whom work was being transferred. A broader view revealed that a similar perspective inspired many unions in other countries, who were fighting to retain jobs through protectionist measures rather than looking for ways to defend labor rights globally. This is why I found it necessary to engage in a critique of union practice, which, like all practice, was informed by certain theoretical presuppositions that were open to question.

In this case, I will try to argue that a mistaken understanding of globalization and a failure to identify the real roots of the onslaught that the labor unions faced constituted obstacles to developing a more effective strategy. Developing a better analysis became all the more urgent in the wake of the global economic crisis, which led to massive job losses and strong downward pressure on labor standards worldwide (ILO 2009). The purpose of this "theoretical reflection with respect to practical action is . . . to question the reflective bases upon which the practical actions have been carried out, to offer a reflexive and dialectical critique whose effect is to recall to mind those possibilities that practice has chosen on this occasion to ignore" (Winter 1996, 25), and to help workers in different parts of the world to learn from one another.

Social-science research should not be based upon

> the aspirations for objectivity which should more rightfully apply to natural science. Some of these are: reification—treatment of people and events as objects; researchers attempting to adopt a neutral, disinterested position; and researchers avoiding admission that they are constitutive of their data. These aspirations for objectivity are pursued on the grounds that to be subjective by revealing the self in research is self-indulgent or, at worst, even narcissistic.
>
> (Hall 1996, 37–38)

In reality, on the contrary, the result of such attempts to be "objective" is that the constitutive role of the researcher remains hidden, affecting the data and analysis but making it impossible for others to assess in what way it has done so. If emancipatory action research is to have any credibility, therefore, is must adopt a reflexive approach which attempts to

> account for researcher constitutiveness. This process begins with being self-conscious (to the extent that this is possible) about how one's doing of the research as well as what one brings to it (previous experience, knowledge, values, beliefs and a priori concepts) shapes the way the data are interpreted and treated. An account of researcher constitutiveness is completed when this awareness is incorporated in the research report.
>
> (Hall 1996, 30)

These conclusions then have to be tested in practice.

Reflexivity is especially important in action research, which by its nature is the opposite of "neutral" or "disinterested." However, it should be emphasized that a commitment to a goal does not necessarily militate against a commitment to the truth: even in a situation of conflict, no purpose is served by misrepresenting or demonizing one's opponent. The rest of this chapter will be an attempt to summarize the experience, knowledge, values, beliefs, and concepts underlying my research.

The first important influence on my approach to the research and interpretation of data is Marxism, understood here not as a body of doctrine but as a method and theoretical approach. Marx's method is perhaps best summarized in his *Theses on Feuerbach*. According to the first three theses, there is a contradiction in conceiving of social reality as an object, as something to be contemplated, since we ourselves are part of that reality; regarding it as an object therefore amounts to dividing society into two parts, one of which (the researcher, in this instance) is outside of and superior to society. The alternative is to conceive of social reality as human activity or practice, including our own. This has the added advantage of allowing for a resolution of the dispute over whether truth can be attributed to human thinking. "The dispute over the reality or non-reality of thinking that is isolated from practice is a purely *scholastic* question": it can never be resolved. While it is true that circumstances shape people, this cannot by itself explain historical change, which requires us to recognize that human beings in turn change circumstances. The only way of proving the "reality and power, the this-sidedness" of our thinking, therefore, is through practical-critical activity, which is the "coincidence of the changing of circumstances and of human activity or self-changing" (Marx 1975a, 421–423).

From the standpoint of the overwhelming majority of the European working class in Marx's day or the global working class in ours, motivation for changing the world appears to come from the desire to escape from starvation wages, long working hours, and unhealthy conditions of work, which lead to misery, illness, and premature death. But that is not all: working-class struggle continues even when workers are relatively well paid and their working conditions reasonably healthy. There is something about the labor relations of capitalist production that produces conflict even when workers are not struggling for mere survival. Marx begins his explanation by saying that concealed behind the categories of political economy, which seem to describe relations between things—commodities and money, for example—are relationships between people. When we buy a commodity, what we acquire is the objectified labor of the workers who have labored to produce it, including those who produced the instruments of production and extracted the raw materials that went into the commodity's production: people whom we have probably never seen and who may be living in countries thousands of miles away. Conversely, the commodities we produce as workers might include inputs from workers in other parts of the world and may then be consumed by people we have never met. There is a relationship between workers and consumers, but it is not immediately visible, because it is mediated by the market, by money. This causes problems: others may be in desperate need of what we are producing—for example, food or medicines—yet be unable to get it because they have no money to buy it.

The scandal of starvation deaths in early twenty-first-century India, which was happening while warehouses overflowed with grain that was rotting and being eaten by rats, is an apt illustration of this aspect of capitalism (see chapter 8).

However, the market is not the only barrier between workers and consumers. Most people do not themselves sell the commodities they produce; instead, they work for employers who do the selling. It looks as if the workers are selling their labor to the employer, but according to Marx, what they actually sell is their labor *power*, or capacity to labor, and the capitalist, having bought it, sets about making them produce more value than they will get back as wages, i.e., surplus value. The workers not only have to produce a saleable commodity in order to survive; they have to produce it under someone else's command and work longer and/or harder than they would need to if they were simply supporting themselves and their dependants. For the capitalist, there is also a compulsion to succeed in the competitive struggle with other capitalists, which entails a constant effort to increase profits and accumulate capital (Marx 1976, 283–339). In Marx's view, this relationship of compulsion and exploitation, the "alienation" of workers from their own labor (Marx 1976, 990), explains the conflict between workers and employers as well as the source of capitalist profit. In other words, at the heart of the class struggle under capitalism is the fact that for capital, labor power is merely a factor of production and source of profit, whereas for workers, it is inseparable from themselves as living human beings.

It is true that Marx's work has flaws and needs to be developed and updated. But in my opinion, his basic framework still stands and is confirmed by my research. Nor is it Marxists alone who hold this view.

In October 1997, the business correspondent of the *New Yorker*, John Cassidy, reported a conversation with an investment banker. "The longer I spend on Wall Street, the more convinced I am that Marx was right," the financier said. "I am absolutely convinced that Marx's approach is the best way to look at capitalism." His curiosity aroused, Mr. Cassidy read Marx for the first time. He found riveting passages about globalisation, inequality, political corruption, monopolisation, technical progress, the decline of high culture, and the enervating nature of modern existence— issues that economists are now confronting anew, sometimes without realising that they are walking in Marx's footsteps.

(Wheen 2005)

And according to George Soros (1998, xxxvi):

> Capitalism needs democracy as a counterweight because capitalism by
> itself shows no tendency towards equilibrium. The owners of capital
> seek to maximize their profits. Left to their own devices, they would con-
> tinue to accumulate capital until the situation became unbalanced. Marx
> and Engels gave a very good analysis of the capitalist system 150 years
> ago, better in some ways, I must say, than the equilibrium theory of clas-
> sical economics.

This is an important insight. I will try to argue that one of the key contributors to the crisis of 2008 was a democracy deficit: government policy
was shaped by the interests of a tiny minority and not by those of the vast
majority of working people in their countries, and consequently the situation became "unbalanced." After the crisis hit, Marx's *Capital* became a best-
seller: "In his native Germany, copies of *Das Kapital* are reported to be flying
off the shelves as failed bankers and free market economists try to make
sense of the global economic meltdown" (Suroor 2008). And the foreword
to the UN Report on Reforms of the Monetary and Financial System named
Marx as among the greatest economic philosophers (UN 2009, 9).

In his early writings, Marx proposes a model of work that is satisfying
both because it allows for the free exercise of the worker's skill and cre-
ativity and because it is seen to satisfy another's need (1975b, 277–278).
However, Marx did not reject everything that capitalism had achieved: he
saw the vast increase in the productivity of labor due to large-scale production and technological advances as laying the basis for his vision of the
future, when the associated producers would control the means of production for the collective good, with people contributing in accordance with
their abilities and receiving in accordance with their needs (Marx 1974a,
347). The working-class struggle for this vision is what he described
as "communism."

Marx produced neither a blueprint of this utopia nor a roadmap for
arriving at it. Some of his writings, especially on the Paris Commune, suggest that workers would have to discover the pathway and goal for themselves (Marx 1974b, 212); this would accord with his view in the *Theses on
Feuerbach*. Inevitably, workers make mistakes when they embark on this
journey into unknown territory. One example cited by Marx is Luddism:

The large-scale destruction of machinery which occurred in the English manufacturing districts during the first fifteen years of the nineteenth century, largely as a result of the employment of the power-loom, and known as the Luddite movement, gave the anti-Jacobin government . . . a pretext for the most violent and reactionary measures. It took both time and experience before the workers learned to distinguish between machinery and its employment by capital, and therefore to transfer their attacks from the material instruments of production to the form of society which utilizes those instruments.

(Marx 1976, 554–555)

This example of learning by the working class exemplifies a process going on all the time. E. P. Thompson's *Making of the English Working Class* (1966), which gives a more detailed account not only of Luddism but also of many other working-class struggles during the late eighteenth century and first half of the nineteenth century, looks at the multiplicity of ideas and practices that existed within the working class and the process of discussion and debate out of which particular strategies emerged and were tested in practice. Michael Vester's analysis of his account (1975) showed that this process could be resolved into phases of activity followed by phases of reflection, which together constituted cycles of learning. As Gramsci noted, the process of reflection could be carried out by new "organic" intellectuals emerging from the working class, as well as by traditional intellectuals who threw in their lot with the workers (Gramsci 1971, 9–10). In many ways, this cycle of struggle, reflection on experience, trying out new strategies, and once again reflecting on them resembles emancipatory action research in its dialectical interweaving of thought and practice.

One of the lessons learned by workers very early on was that in isolation they could never resist domination by capital: the only hope of improving their lot lay in combining into a workers' union that eliminated competition among the workers who belonged to it. This resulted in a powerful movement—the trade union movement—which exists on a much wider scale today and has been responsible for major improvements in wages, working hours, and working conditions as well as legislation that upholds workers' rights. It was then the capitalists who had to learn a lesson. They had been unsuccessful in opposing the right of workers to form combinations or shorten working hours, but they found other ways to increase the extraction of surplus value, through the introduction of more machinery and the intensification of labor (Marx 1976, 534).

Paradoxically, the net result of the successful struggle for the ten-hour day was that it compelled employers to make technological and organizational changes that altered the entire system and propelled industry forward at a much more rapid rate (Marx 1976, 542). Thus the actual development of capitalism is the outcome of this complex interaction between action, reflection, and learning on the part of workers and a similar process of learning among capitalists, the outcome of which might in some cases make working-class struggle easier (for example, legislation protecting the right to organize and bargain collectively) and in other cases make it more difficult (for example, casualization and informalization).

This view contrasts with a more deterministic interpretation of Marx's critique of political economy, according to which the driving force in capitalist society is the logic of capital and the most the working class can do is to respond to this logic. It has been pointed out that many Marxists appear to make the assumption that under no circumstances do workers take the initiative in bringing about changes in capitalism (Herod 2001). But such a reading would be at odds with the *Theses on Feuerbach*. Even in *Capital*, which is most prone to this interpretation because it sets out to lay bare the logic of capital as an impersonal compulsion on both workers and owners of capital, the presence of an opposing logic of working-class struggle is evident. Indeed, from Marx's time to our own, major changes in capitalism, such as the introduction of new technologies, reorganization of the labor process, and relocation of facilities to new sites, are often a *response by capitalists* to workers' success in controlling the labor process or imposing their own rules on production in other ways (cf. Edwards 1979). Even globalization, a prime example of what is seen as a capital-driven process, is not a monopoly of capital: given the formation of organizations like the International Working Men's Association (First International) in the 1860s, "it might even be suggested that the formal transnationalization of labor in many ways predates that of capital" (Herod 2001, 131).

Marx's work concentrates on the logic of capital, and the logic of working-class struggle can only be glimpsed from time to time, although it is more evident in his political writings. Generalizing from his work, that of other labor historians, and my own experience, I would say that the driving force of working-class struggle, analogous to capital's drive to accumulate, is a desire for dignity, recognition, and control over one's own life and work rather than a struggle for mere biological survival. The conception of workers as human beings capable of making mistakes and learning from experience seems much more realistic than conceptions that see them either as born revolutionaries or as incapable of achieving a consciousness of their common interests without enlightenment from outside. Only a tiny minority of workers consciously set themselves the goal of abolishing capitalism and putting an alternative society in its place, yet wherever principles of autonomy and solidarity guide their practice, they may fight for objectives—such as information and consultation rights or social-security and welfare systems—whose rationale is the satisfaction of people's needs as workers and consumers, as opposed to the capitalist logic of accumulation.

Unionization may eliminate competition between workers in one particular union, but competition with nonunionized workers and workers in other unions remains. And even if all the unionized workers in one country belonged to a single federation, competition with nonunionized workers in that country as well as workers in other countries would persist—the disadvantages of which have become much clearer with globalization. Divisions within the working class based on gender, race, caste, religion, nationality, and so on are all obstacles to success in this struggle, fostering competition instead of solidarity. Thus transformation of the social relations of production from exploitative capitalist relations to cooperative egalitarian ones requires that workers forge wider bonds of solidarity with other workers.

This conception of communism—which I would call "anarchocommunism," as it does not involve taking state power—is very different from what prevailed when I was a student at Oxford in 1967 through 1970. At that time, the left was fairly neatly divided into First Worldists (mostly Trotskyist), who expected the socialist revolution to be achieved first in the advanced capitalist (imperialist or former imperialist) countries, Second Worldists (mostly Stalinist, even if critical of Stalin), who believed that the socialist revolution had already taken place in the Soviet Union and Eastern Europe, and Third Worldists (mostly Maoist), who thought it was actually taking place in the Third World.[1] All of these camps saw the seizure of state power as a crucial step in the revolution, and none of them seemed to feel it was a problem to conceive of a socialist country or group of countries embedded in a capitalist world economy. In this they were partly following in the footsteps of Marx and Engels, who also saw communism as being established in one part of the world (Europe) while capitalism was still developing in others.

I had problems with this conception of communism, problems that I am far better able to articulate now, after a small group of us in various parts of India engaged in a process of intensive discussion in the mid-1970s during the repressive regime of Indira Gandhi's Emergency and after decades of involvement in the labor movement. Despite the upheavals of 1968, the prospect of workers in the United States (at that time embroiled in the war in Vietnam) and Europe (where racist politicians such as Enoch Powell could appeal to sections of the working class) making a communist revolution seemed remote. The Third World, where the majority of working people were the rural poor whose main aspiration was to own a plot of land and where the proletariat was mostly uneducated if not illiterate, seemed equally distant from socialism. The Soviet Union and Eastern bloc seemed furthest of all from communism, with workers deprived even of rights enjoyed in the First World and some Third World countries. In all these cases, the assumption of revolutionary actuality or potential rested on the claim that various parties could *represent* the working class by taking state power and carrying out a transformation of social relations.

This notion is modeled on the bourgeois revolution, which is indeed national in form, where the seizure of state power is a critical step and where the bourgeoisie can be represented by one or more parties. But it is completely unsatisfactory as a conceptualization of communist revolution, where the whole point is that the *working class itself* carries out a simultaneous transformation of itself and its circumstances. It also raises the problem pointed out by Marx in the *Theses on Feuerbach*: who will educate the educators, the so-called representatives of the proletariat, who see themselves as being superior to society but are actually embedded in it and have their own interests—interests that may well depart from those of the working class? Finally, even supposing the proletariat in one country or group of countries could carry out a socialist transformation of relations of production, how would it relate to the capitalist world around it? It would have to insulate itself economically and compete militarily, which could only occur if there were an authoritarian state as there was in the Soviet Union, or its own relations of production would be contaminated by the capitalist ones with which it interacted; in neither case would it be truly communist.

In fact, the interdependence between national economies, which was already a feature of capitalism in the nineteenth century and has been intensified by globalization, rules out the possibility of any such circumscribed communist revolutions. In my opinion, activity directed toward taking state power belongs firmly in the realm of bourgeois politics. It may be progressive as part of a struggle against feudalism, imperialism, or fascism, since struggles for *democracy*, by winning rights such as freedom of expression and association, give workers an opportunity to organize themselves and debate issues democratically. But a serious problem with the nation-statist conception of revolution is that in order to defeat the existing state and take over state power, it is necessary to create institutions that mirror the state apparatus: political party, bureaucracy, and, in the case of groups that envisage the capture of state power through armed struggle, armed forces. Those who construct and control this apparatus have a vested interest in maintaining it after coming to power. If communism is seen not as something other than democracy but as an extension of democracy into areas—such as production—that continue to be governed autocratically even under the most democratic bourgeois state, then the process of creating an alternative state apparatus in order to engage in armed struggle, or gaining control over the existing one through parliamentary politics, cannot be part of it.[2]

The idea of the development of the working class as a learning process was the basis of the activities of a small group of about ten of us who formed the Union Research Group in Bombay in 1980. Bombay was chosen as the arena of our activities because it is "arguably the premier industrial metropolis of the country. The city compels attention with the sheer size and range of its industry and the colour and vitality of its labour movement. Bombay must undoubtedly be central to any study of contemporary trade unionism in India" (Ramaswamy 1988, 17). The group emerged after the Hoechst Employees' Union approached three researchers among us who were collecting data on collective agreements and asked for comparative information that would help them to formulate and argue for their charter of demands. Having compiled the information on pay in pharmaceutical companies for them, it occurred to us that the same information would be useful to other unions, so we put it together in the form of our first *Bulletin of Trade Union Research and Information*. Trade unions in India—even the large national federations—do not have research departments, and this puts them at a disadvantage when engaging in collective bargaining with employers. The purpose of the series of bulletins was to redress the balance by providing unions with information comparable to what was available to managements, and we succeeded so well that managements too started approaching us with requests for our bulletins!

We collected the information by moving from factory to factory and office to office, meeting union leaders and in some cases interviewing workers or visiting shop floors. We made our research available to all unions but found that it was mainly employees' unions, which were free from domination by an external leadership, who made use of it, and this was the beginning of a close and long-standing association with them. Over the course of this, we were drawn into organizing workshops and discussions or participating in conferences organized by them on a wide range of issues that went far beyond those directly connected with collective bargaining, for example subcontracting and union rivalry. The Union Carbide India Limited Employees' Union was one of the unions that subscribed to our bulletin and attended our discussions, so when the Bhopal disaster took place, we went at once to investigate and were appalled not only at the flouting of basic safety measures but also at the dreadful suffering of the victims of the disaster. We subsequently helped to create the Trade Union Relief Fund for the Bhopal gas victims, set up a relief program in Bhopal, and participated in the campaign to get justice for the survivors.

When some of the employees' unions set up a coordination called the Trade Union Solidarity Committee in 1989, the Union Research Group became a nonvoting member of it: nonvoting because not being a union, we could not undertake to mobilize members or collect funds for the activities that were decided upon. But we could participate in the discussions and present our point of view, and we did so quite freely. There were many disagreements, not only between URG members and some of the unionists but also among the unionists and among URG members; I see this not as a weakness but as a strength. It meant that decisions took much longer to be made and that the TUSC could not act in the disciplined manner of party-affiliated union federations, but these drawbacks were an acceptable price to pay for freedom of debate and democratic decision making. In this account, as in TUSC discussions, I present my own point of view but also try to summarize the content of discussions as taken down in notes at numerous meetings.

Another major change occurred after the establishment of the WTO in 1995. The focus of URG research, which had up to then been local (although always with an awareness of developments in the international labor movement), became much more global in an attempt to work out a strategy to defend workers' rights in a more globalized world economy.

Among the most serious crises we faced were the massacres of Muslims in Bombay in 1993 and in Gujarat in 2002, the latter carried out with the collusion of the BJP, which was in power in Gujarat and headed a coalition in the national parliament. The scapegoating of minorities, combined with an explicit hostility to unionized formal workers and attempts to change labor laws so as to take away rights that had been won in an earlier period, made us fear the worst. As a trade unionist in the TUSC remarked in 2002, if the BJP-led coalition retained power after the next general elections, the trade union movement would be wiped out for a long time to come. So for the next two years, we were occupied not only in trying to combat the ideology and politics that split the working class and even allowed some workers to endorse the killings but also in trying to ensure that a different government was returned to power.

Long-term research and activism provides a unique vantage point from which the agency of workers can clearly be seen: the fact that workers are the makers of their own history, albeit in circumstances not of their choosing. It is also the only satisfactory way to understand the context in which the labor movement takes shape. For example, for anyone who has not grown up in India (myself included, since I come from Sri Lanka), it is extremely difficult to understand the all-pervasive influence of caste in Indian society, including the labor movement, except over a long period of time. Second, it is always illuminating to know the ways in which important figures in the labor movement have been shaped by their own past. Sustained contact with them over a period of decades allows some of this history to be observed directly; glimpses of the rest can be obtained through interviews and informal conversations. Third, if the impact of globalization is being investigated, it is important to establish the conditions that prevailed prior to it: "one cannot determine an impact unless one knows what existed before" (Krishnaraj 2005, 3010). Finally, it is important for some enquiries into the effects of globalization on the global labor force to be anchored in an in-depth knowledge of a particular segment of it, so as to counteract sweeping generalizations that may not capture the real complexity of the process.

The second important influence on my approach to the research and interpretation of data is feminism. While the brand of feminism that I espouse could be described as socialist or Marxist, there are also elements of it that involve a critique of the theory and practice of most Marxists. This, of course, is something I share with many other women with a similar history. Feminism influenced my research, which, even before the URG was formed, was focused on working-class women, both as wage workers and as unwaged domestic workers (cf. Prieto 2002; Krishnaraj 2005). As a consequence of one of these research projects in a slum, we were asked by the women we had interviewed to help them set up an income-generating project, and we did so for a while, although there was virtually no capital, and marketing too was a problem. This research showed very clearly that the problems of women as wage laborers could not be separated from their subordination in the family and broader social oppression, and therefore a labor movement that neglected these latter concerns (domestic violence, sexual harassment, and gender discrimination, for example) was not genuinely representative of the working class as a whole.[3]

Studies on women workers in employees' unions undertaken by the URG confirmed that even in the most advanced unions, women could be at a disadvantage. In most of the union meetings I have attended, the number of women could be counted on the fingers of one hand or, at most, two. For me, this constitutes a problem. It goes along with a notion of the working class that ignores the work done in the home (mostly by women) and with a notion of class struggle that marginalizes working-class women and children and fails to challenge the gender division of labor and relations of domination and subordination between men and women.

A feminist critique of mainstream left politics also challenges the nation-statist conception of revolution, which advocates the creation of institutions that are inherently hierarchical and authoritarian and implies a violent revolution. A feminist movement for which violence, authoritarianism, and inequality are the main enemies cannot with any consistency accept that a process steeped in these values could liberate women. Moreover, the perspective of armed struggle involves buying arms and ammunition and thus supporting the military-industrial complex. This conception too marginalizes working-class women and children and devalues the caring work that has traditionally been done by women.

My research on women workers brought me into contact with Women Working Worldwide, a small NGO based in Manchester, which was the center of a network of groups working with women workers in various countries. As part of my work with WWW, I researched responses to the proposal for a labor-rights clause in multilateral agreements of the WTO, led consultation and education exercises with women garment workers in Bombay and Sri Lanka on codes of conduct, and looked into subcontracting chains. The URG had hitherto worked with unionized formal workers, whereas most of the workers in this sector, both women and men, were informal and not unionized. Informality had already emerged as a problem for workers in the employees' unions, many of whom were losing their jobs as a consequence of their work being transferred to informal workers, but for these garment workers the problem was seen from another angle: that of underprivileged workers who had never enjoyed the rights taken for granted by formal workers. One response was that of the women slum dwellers I had worked with earlier: attempts to set up workers' cooperatives. Another was to try to form unions, despite the formidable obstacles. One of the research projects on which I worked investigated the various ways in which informal as well as formal women workers had organized in order to solve their multifarious problems.

Through my work with WWW, I came into contact with groups working with women workers in many other countries, and I myself was able to work with women in Sri Lanka and India. Working together on supply chains was a wonderful way to understand the interconnections between workers spread out across the globe, retail and brand-name companies, and consumers. There were moments, to me very moving, when these links suddenly became visible to the women. One was an educational exercise in which women workers from free-trade zones in Sri Lanka, some working for Gap suppliers, read an account of a campaign to support workers from a Gap supplier in El Salvador whose union had been smashed (see chapter 9). There was a palpable sense of wonder when these young women realized that women workers halfway around the world suffered from the same problems: not being allowed to go to the toilet when they needed to, forced to do long hours of overtime, being dismissed when they tried to form a union. Many were also touched by the idea that consumers in distant countries were concerned about their problems.

WWW's membership of the Clean Clothes Campaign (CCC) through its British affiliate The Labour Behind the Label, and of the Ethical Trading Initiative (ETI), a tripartite organization consisting of companies, trade unions, and NGOs, allowed me to participate in meetings of these organizations and meet actors in the globalization process that I might not have been able to meet otherwise. Participation in their discussions enabled me to gain a different perspective on globalization.

Apart from interviews with workers and union activists and my own notes of discussions, I have consulted material produced by the TUSC and its member unions, such as leaflets, circulars, newsletters, journals, and correspondence (translating into English wherever necessary). The same is true of the proceedings of WWW, the CCC, and ETI. Legal documents—legislation, court judgments recorded in the *Bombay Government Gazette*[4] and *Maharashtra Government Gazette* as well as High Court and Supreme Court judgments—and government policy documents have been used wherever relevant. I have used articles in financial newspapers, journals, and online publications, which, as Baran and Sweezy (1966, 195) once remarked, often identify trends in capitalism earlier and more accurately than Marxist analyses; indeed, the conclusions of good Marxist and non-Marxist analyses are often strikingly similar. The research can be considered as belonging to the category of "new international labor studies," with its interdisciplinary approach (Cohen 1987; Munck 1988).

We often forget that the overwhelming majority of the world's poor are workers and their dependants and that what they need most desperately is justice, not charity. The purpose of this book is not simply to describe this depressing situation but to propose realistic ways in which workers themselves can change it: not by dismantling the emerging global economy but by using the power of solidarity to redirect it in a more equitable and sustainable direction.

[2]

Defining Globalization

What Is Globalization?

Developing a viable strategy for labor in the twenty-first century depends on having a correct understanding of globalization. Supporters of neoliberal policies assume that free trade always leads to a reduction in poverty: "trade is good for growth, growth is good for the poor and so trade is good for the poor" (Dollar and Kraay 2001a, 2001b; cit. Lee and Vivarelli 2006, 8). For these advocates of globalization, it cannot possibly pose any problems for human rights at work because "rising real incomes and greater openness to trade tends to promote human rights" (Sykes 2003, 4; cit. Alston 2004, 471); in other words, the advantages of free trade trickle down automatically to benefit everyone. On the other side, those who either oppose globalization or are anxious about its potentially detrimental effects on employment and poverty encompass a broad political spectrum. The extreme right opposes it from the standpoint of economic and cultural nationalism, and liberals might deplore the loss of national sovereignty because it reduces the effectiveness of state intervention to regulate capital and labor, alleviate poverty, and so forth. Even among left-wing groups claiming some relationship to a Marxist tradition, there are widely differing theoretical approaches to globalization, resulting in diametrically opposed responses to it.

Underlying most of these responses is a lack of clarity about what is meant by globalization. Prima facie, it would appear that a globalized world is one in which there are no barriers (other than purely natural and technological ones) to the movement of people, products, money, and ideas around the world. But globalization in this sense predates capitalism and the formation of nation-states; clearly, this is not the subject of current debates about globalization, although it is not irrelevant to them. It is, no doubt, to clarify this point that various adjectives are used to describe globalization, such as "capitalist," "imperialist," and "neoliberal." However, this creates new problems, because these adjectives have their own meanings. When they are combined with "globalization," where do those meanings end and the meaning of globalization begin?

Globalization as Capitalism

That capitalism is inherently global was taken for granted by Marx. In the graphic words of the *Communist Manifesto*, "the need of a constantly expanding market for its products chases the bourgeoisie over the whole surface of the globe. It must nestle everywhere, settle everywhere, establish connections everywhere" (Marx and Engels 1973, 71). Moreover, the survival of capitalism depends on its extraction of surplus value from wage workers: thus exploitation of workers too is part of the definition of capital. The expropriation of small producers, ruin of small capitalists, and job losses—all seen as characteristics of globalization by its critics—are also inherent in capitalism (Marx 1976). The overlap between globalization and capitalism seems more or less complete.

However, if globalization is capitalism by another name, why not simply call it capitalism? Substituting "globalization" for "capitalism" implies that the real enemy is *international* capital—and that is dangerous. Opposition to global capital has been a defining feature of fascism since Hitler wrote that "the development of Germany was much too clear in my eyes for me not to know that the hardest battle would have to be fought not against hostile nations but against international capital" (Hitler 1943, 213; cit. Henwood 1993, 303).

In India, right-wing opposition to globalization is spearheaded by the "family" of Hindu nationalist organizations (the "Sangh Parivar") associated with the Rashtriya Swayamsevak Sangh,[1] such as the Swadeshi Jagran

Manch, Bharatiya Mazdoor Sangh, and Akhil Bharatiya Vidyarti Parishad. Other members of the family are the Vishwa Hindu Parishad and Bajrang Dal; the Shiv Sena is a slightly more distant relation. These organizations have on various occasions protested against "handing over the nation's consumer market to foreign companies" (BS 1994), "globalisation and foreign investment" (BS 1995), India's accession to the WTO (BS 1998a), and, more generally, liberalization and globalization (ET 1999a). Their alternative, originally put forward by Deen Dayal Upadhyay in his *Integral Humanism*, envisages "small traders and small industry flourishing in a mythical, Hindu-only pastoral paradise" (Upadhyay 1965; cit. Barman 1998).

Right-wing opposition to globalization is not confined to India. Islam and Christianity have their own equivalents of the Sangh Parivar. In the United States, the right-wing politician Pat Buchanan declared that "what is good for General Motors is no longer good for America if General Motors is shutting down plants in Michigan and opening them in Mexico City" (ET 1996). In Europe, right-wing politicians such as Joerg Haider "make opposition to the WTO, globalisation and immigrant workers the main issues in their campaign to 'save' their Aryan way of life" (Sakai 2000). At best, selective opposition to international capital propagates the illusion that capitalism can solve problems of poverty and unemployment so long as it remains national. At worst, it condones barbaric oppression and exploitation by indigenous capitalists and encourages racism and xenophobia. Globalization may be a phase of capitalism, but antiglobalization can never be anticapitalist, because genuine opposition to capitalist oppression and exploitation does not distinguish between "national" and "international" capital nor support the former against the latter. The Dutch antiracist group *De Fabel van de Illegaal* is right when it concludes that "ideologically separating or criticising international or foreign capital simply does not fit into left-wing politics" (Krebbers and Schoenmaker 2000).

Globalization as Imperialism

A large section of the left identifies globalization with imperialism and opposes it from this point of view (e.g., Mathew 2001). Their definition of imperialism relies on Lenin's *Imperialism, the Latest Stage of Capitalism*, written in 1916 and published in 1917. This is usually mistranslated as *"Imperialism, the Highest Stage of Capitalism,"* but as the editors of *Monthly*

Review point out, "historical materialists are not prophets; they do not predict the future course of history. They are concerned rather with the present as history . . . Lenin's 1917 work *Imperialism the Latest Stage of Capitalism* is itself a perfect example of this historical-materialist principle at work" (*Monthly Review* 2004). The distinction between "highest" and "latest" is not a trivial one. The latter implies that it was the latest stage at the time Lenin was writing but could be superseded by another stage at a later date, while "highest" implies the last or final stage, which can only be superseded by something other than capitalism.

Lenin did not claim *Imperialism* to be a fully worked-out theory nor the last word on the subject but, rather, an attempt to explain World War I (which was raging at the time he wrote it) and the collapse of the Second International (Kemp 1972, 26–27). It drew heavily on Hobson's *Imperialism*, first published in 1902, and Hilferding's *Finance Capital: A Study of the Latest Phase of Capitalist Development*, which first appeared in 1910. According to Lenin's definition, imperialism was characterized by (a) the dominance of international capitalist monopolies, (b) the merging of bank capital with industrial capital to create "finance capital," (c) the export of capital rather than the export of commodities, and (d) the territorial division of the world among the biggest capitalist powers. The driving force of imperialism is the fact that

> An enormous "surplus of capital" has arisen in the advanced countries. . . . As long as capitalism remains what it is, surplus capital will be utilized not for the purpose of raising the standard of living of the masses in a given country, for this would mean a decline in profits for the capitalists, but for the purpose of increasing profits by exporting capital abroad to the backward countries. In these backward countries profits are usually high, for capital is scarce, the price of land is relatively low, wages are low, raw materials are cheap.
>
> (Lenin 1964, 241)

Lenin based his theory on Marx's explanation of the general tendency of the rate of profit to fall, resulting in crises. The most powerful and effective way in which this tendency can be counteracted, he said, is to export the surplus capital to countries where rates of profit are high. As a result of the equalization of rates of profit to form an average rate of profit (Marx 1981, chaps. 9 and 10), the overall rate of profit rises and a crisis is postponed.

One problem with this theory is the interpretation of "export of capital" as the net transfer of money capital overseas (Lenin 1964, 242), whereas in fact, throughout the nineteenth century and up to 1914, income from British overseas investment was in excess of the outflow of capital (Barratt Brown 1972, 54). Furthermore, at the time he was writing, it was the industrial latecomers, especially Germany, which were most marked by the development of "finance capital"; in Britain, which had the dominant empire of the time, "competitive individualism was still pronounced in industry where old-established family firms, well provided with capital, resisted amalgamation" (Kemp 1972, 23). These problems merely exemplify a more general one: a definition of imperialism that pulls together two phenomena coexisting at the time that Lenin was writing—finance capital and colonialism—rather than going into the separate dynamics of each. The assumption of a necessary link between imperialism and finance capital is contradicted by the empirical evidence, which suggests, on the contrary, the importance of seeing "the territorial and the capitalist logics of power as distinct from each other" and recognizing that in the early twenty-first century "there appears to be a deep inconsistency if not outright contradiction between the two logics" (Harvey 2003, 29, 204).

Luxemburg's theory of imperialism and crisis in *The Accumulation of Capital*, first published in 1913, takes off from volume 2 of *Capital*, where Marx looks at the circulation of capital. Her central argument is that surplus value produced in Department I (producing means of production) and Department II (producing means of consumption) cannot be realized—that is, sold and converted into money capital—without noncapitalist societies to buy them; thus the existence of noncapitalist countries is crucial for the accumulation of capital, which will come to a halt once all of them have been converted into capitalist societies. Luxemburg insisted the problem was not the availability of money with which to buy the surplus (which could be solved in a number of ways); "the real issue is the effective demand, the use made of goods, not the source of the money which is paid for them" (Luxemburg 2003, 128). Marx's diagram assumed that the surplus products of Department I would be used to expand the productive capacity of both departments, while the surplus products of Department II would be the means of consumption for additional workers hired to work in both departments, thus expanding production and producing even more surplus value in the next cycle. Luxemburg was incredulous, asking, "and what do they do with this increasing surplus value? The diagram replies:

they use it for an ever greater expansion of their production. These capitalists are thus fanatical supporters of an expansion of production for production's sake" (Luxemburg 2003, 315). Bizarre though this may sound, so long as surplus value is being produced and profits are being made on an expanded scale, expansion of production for the sake of production is indeed the aim and end of capitalism: "Accumulate, accumulate! That is Moses and the prophets! . . . Accumulation for the sake of accumulation, production for the sake of production: this was the formula in which classical economics expressed the historical mission of the bourgeoisie in its period of dominance" (Marx 1976, 742). "The production of surplus value, or the making of profits, is the absolute law of this mode of production" (Marx 1976, 769).

Luxemburg responded to the numerous critiques of her work by reiterating: "That is not capitalist accumulation, i.e. the amassing of money capital, but its contrary: producing commodities for the sake of it" (Luxemburg 1972, 57); instead, she insisted, "capitalism expands because of its mutual relationship with non-capitalist social strata and countries, accumulating at their expense. . . . As it approaches the point where humanity only consists of capitalists and proletarians, further accumulation becomes impossible" (Luxemburg 1972, 60). In reply, Bukharin pointed out that the amassing of money capital is not the same as capitalist accumulation (Bukharin 1972, 179–180). Bauer's critique of Luxemburg made the point that

> Accumulation is not impossible in an isolated capitalist society, but it is placed within limits. Imperialism in fact serves to expand these limits. . . . Imperialism increases the number of workers who are forced to sell their labour power to capital. It accomplishes this by destroying the old modes of production in colonial areas and thereby forcing millions either to emigrate to capitalist areas or to serve European or American capital in their native land, where the capital has been invested. Since with a given organic composition of capital the amount of accumulation is determined by the growth in the available working population, imperialism is in fact a means to enlarge the limits of accumulation.
>
> (Bauer 1913, 873–874; cit. Luxemburg 1972, 139, 141)

Trotsky, influenced by the German-Russian Marxist Parvus (Alexander Israel Helphand), also explained imperialism and World War I by capital's need for rapidly expanding markets, but his emphasis was on the contradiction between the inherently global character of capitalism and the limitations of the nation-state. He argued that "with the emergence of a world economy the state could no longer exist as 'an independent economic arena. . . . The future development of the world economy on capitalist foundations will mean an uninterrupted struggle for newer and newer divisions of the same world surface as an object of capitalist exploitation'" (Trotsky 1923, 75–76; cit. Day 1973, 13).

Marx's own work encompasses all the elements emphasized by Lenin (the export of capital), Luxemburg and Trotsky (the export of commodities), and Bauer (the expansion of the wage-labor force), as well as a subsidiary theme in their work, the drive to secure sources of raw materials. He called it "the colonial system" rather than "imperialism," but what he was referring to was the establishment of capitalist empires. In this conception, imperialism starts in the earliest stage of capitalist production, which he calls "primitive accumulation":

> The discovery of gold and silver in America, the extirpation, enslavement and entombment in mines of the indigenous population of that continent, the beginnings of the conquest and plunder of India, and the conversion of Africa into a preserve for the commercial hunting of blackskins, are all things which characterize the dawn of the era of capitalist production. These idyllic proceedings are the chief moments of primitive accumulation.
>
> (Marx 1976, 915)

After describing the "devastation and depopulation" resulting from Dutch slavery in what is now Indonesia; the "inexhaustible mines of wealth" exploited by the English East India Company through its monopolies of the tea, opium, salt, and other trades; the "frightful" treatment of the indigenous population in the plantation colonies; and the various premiums offered by the Puritans of New England for scalps of the men, women, and children who were the region's original inhabitants, he concludes: "The colonies provided a market for the budding manufactures, and a vast increase in accumulation which was guaranteed by the mother country's monopoly of the market. The treasures captured outside Europe by undisguised looting, enslavement and murder flowed back to the mother country and were turned into capital there" (Marx 1976, 916–918).

All this is part of a chapter entitled "The Genesis of the Industrial Capitalist." In the next stage, the "colonial system, public debts, heavy taxes, commercial wars, etc., these offshoots of the period of manufacture swell to gigantic proportions during the period of infancy of large-scale industry." After "Liverpool grew fat on the basis of the slave trade . . . the veiled slavery of the wage-labourers in Europe needed the unqualified slavery of the New World as its pedestal. . . . If money comes into the world with a congenital blood-stain on one cheek, capital comes dripping from head to toe, from every pore, with blood and dirt" (Marx 1976, 922–926). As large-scale industry developed, capital's thirst for markets and raw materials altered the global division of labor.

> By ruining handicraft production of finished articles in other countries, machinery forcibly converts them into fields for the production of its raw material. Thus India was compelled to produce cotton, wool, hemp, jute and indigo for Great Britain. . . . A new and international division of labour springs up, one suited to the requirements of the main industrial countries, and it converts one part of the globe into a chiefly agricultural field of production for supplying the other part, which remains a pre-eminently industrial field.
>
> (Marx 1976, 579–580)

Thus, "India, the great workshop of cotton manufacture for the world, since immemorial times, became now inundated with English twists and cotton stuffs. After its own produce had been excluded from England, or only admitted on the most cruel terms, British manufactures were poured into it at a small and merely nominal duty, to the ruin of the native cotton fabrics once so celebrated" (Marx 1969b, 106). Land rights were changed in order to extract taxes to pay for governing the colony; Bengali peasants were forced to cultivate opium poppies and the opium was smuggled into China, with opium wars waged to overcome the resistance of the Chinese emperor, and as a result of the salt tax, it was sold for three times its mercantile value (Marx 1969c, 128–131; 1969f, 345–348). Resort to torture in order to extract revenue was common (Marx 1969e, 228–234), and famines in which millions of Indians died were created by the English "buying up all the rice and refusing to sell it again, except at fabulous prices" (Marx 1976, 917).

Clearly, Marx was aware of the brutal and exploitative character of colonialism, yet his prognosis was optimistic.

I know that the English millocracy intend to endow India with railways with the exclusive view of extracting at diminished expenses the cotton and other raw materials for their manufactures. But when you have once introduced machinery into the locomotion of a country which possesses iron and coals, you are unable to withhold it from its fabrication. You cannot maintain a net of railways over an immense country without introducing all those industrial processes necessary to meet the imme-diate and current wants of railway locomotion, and out of which there must grow the application of machinery to those branches of industry not immediately connected with railways. The railway system will there-fore become, in India, truly the forerunner of modern industry. . . . The Indians will not reap the fruits of the new elements of society scattered among them by the British bourgeoisie, till in Great Britain itself the now ruling classes shall have been supplanted by the industrial prole-tariat, or till the Hindoos themselves shall have grown strong enough to throw off the English yoke altogether. At all events, we may safely expect to see, at a more or less remote period, the regeneration of that great and interesting country.

(Marx 1969d, 136–137)

Marx expected the end result of imperialism to be the development of capi-talism in the colonies. Was his prognosis justified?

Neocolonialism, Underdevelopment, and Dependency Theory

From the standpoint of the victims of imperialism, the picture looked less promising. Accumulation at the imperialist pole meant depletion at theirs, in terms of money wealth, land (through settler colonization), other natural resources (mineral as well as agricultural), and labor power (through slavery and indentured labor). The expansion of markets for the industrial products of imperialist countries meant the destruction of markets for theirs. Whereas the former could rely on the resources and markets of the whole world for their industrialization, the latter could not even rely on the resources and markets of their own countries. All this, combined with what Marx had referred to as "a new and international division of labour," was the starting point for theories of underdevelopment, neocolonialism, and dependency.

In 1962, the Mexican novelist Carlos Fuentes outlined the problem succinctly: "Those capitalists turned us into single-product countries, exporters of raw materials to the occidental marketplace," and the result was *"continuous monoproductive dependence"* and *"continuous underdevelopment,"* among other things (Fuentes 1963). This was not an original undeveloped state but underdevelopment created by colonialism and maintained even after the colonies attained political independence, due to the division of labor established during the period of direct colonial rule and other distortions fostered by the imperialist powers (Frank 1966, 1969a, 1969b).

The concept of "neocolonialism" was very similar. As the Moroccan Ben Barka wrote in 1962, a couple of years before he was murdered, "the independence acquired by some countries is only nominal. We must understand from that the fundamental characteristic of neo-colonialism, its meaning and inner mechanism, in order to foil its manoeuvres" (Ben Barka 1969, 407). And the Cairo Conference of the heads of state of non-aligned countries explained in 1964, "Racial discrimination, economic pressure, interference, subversion, intervention and the threat of force are neo-colonialist devices against which the newly independent nations have to defend themselves" (Cairo Conference 1969, 131).

What is common to both conceptions is the idea that imperialist domination did not end with the political independence of the colonies. Economic domination persisted and resulted in the continued draining of wealth away from the ex-colonies or Third World to the imperialist countries. One mechanism was through "unequal exchange." Given the dependence of former colonies on the labor-intensive production of primary products (while their former rulers produced capital-intensive manufactured products), and given the relative mobility of capital internationally (while labor was relatively immobile, so that substantial wage differences between developed and underdeveloped countries persisted), more value would be embodied in the exported primary products than in the manufactured products imported in exchange. Inequality thus grew rather than being reduced (Emmanuel 1969).[2]

Another mechanism by which wealth was drained out was by means of foreign investments. For example, of U.S. foreign investments in 1963,

probably the majority . . . was acquired without any outflow of capital from the US. . . . Even in cases where substantial sums of capital are exported, subsequent expansion commonly takes place through ploughing back of profits; and the return flow of interest and dividends (not to mention remittances disguised in the form of payment for services and the like) soon repays the original investment many times over—and still continues to pour capital into the coffers of the parent corporation in the United States. . . . One can only conclude that foreign investment, far from being an outlet for domestically generated surplus, is a most efficient device for transferring surplus generated abroad to the investing country.

(Baran and Sweezy 1966, 111–113)

Finally, aid was also used as a device for boosting capital accumulation in Europe and North America. The loans made under this heading were tied heavily to purchases from the country providing the aid, even if cheaper substitutes were available from elsewhere, and they had to be repaid with interest, which again became a mechanism for extracting more value than the original loan (Hensman 1971; Hayter 1971).

Third World countries, it seemed, were caught in a vicious circle. With their own resources depleted, they had to rely on exports from their distorted economies, foreign investment, and aid in order to industrialize, but all these strategies simply resulted in further outflows of wealth and continued dependence (cf. Sutcliffe 1972, 187–189). The bulk of capital exports went not into Third World countries but consisted of "a kind of cross-investment of giant manufacturing firms in each other's markets" (Barratt Brown 1972, 55). Consequently, "with the outstanding exceptions of Japan and more recently of China, economic development has been limited to the lands of Europe and of European settlement (including Israel)" (Barratt Brown 1972, 65).

Such assessments were based partly on the perception that even where Third World industrialization did occur, for example in Africa, it "merely increased the structural dependence of independent Africa upon the advanced capitalist centers" (Arrighi and Saul 1974, 68). A radical response to this dilemma, articulated most consistently by Samir Amin (e.g., Amin 1964, 1990, 1998), was that Third World countries had to delink from the world economy and become autocentric national structures if industrialization was to become possible. A major premise of this position, implicit or explicit, was that the Soviet Union and China constituted an alternative model in which industrialization, economic nationalism, and socialist revolution were inextricably entwined (e.g., Baran and Sweezy 1966, 205; Petras 1999). One critique of this conception pointed to the substantial degree of industrialization that had actually taken place in many Third World countries following independence from the imperialist powers, questioned the relevance of the notion of "dependence" in an increasingly interdependent world, and concluded that imperialism declines as capitalism grows in the Third World (Warren 1973, 1980).

In evaluating positions in this debate, it is useful to distinguish between two different meanings of "imperialism" that are conflated in theories of underdevelopment and neocolonialism. One refers to political and military intervention in Third World countries through covert actions (the overthrow of Mossadegh in Iran in 1953 or Allende in Chile in 1973), military and other assistance to authoritarian regimes (Suharto in Indonesia, the apartheid regime in South Africa), or overt military attack and occupation (in Palestine, Afghanistan, and Iraq). These can certainly be classified as imperialism. But the other meaning—an assumption that once colonialism had reshaped the social and economic institutions of the colonies, economic forces by themselves would perpetuate and even intensify the relationship of domination and exploitation between the mother country and former colony (Magdoff 1972, 164)—is more difficult to sustain.

There are wide differences among Third World countries, but some were able to industrialize to a level where they could compete with the First World. Their colonial history created enormous difficulties, and most of them remain characterized by high levels of poverty, which is one reason why it is still meaningful to refer to the "Third World." But this does not rule out the possibility of capitalist development. India is a good example. The Indian railways constituted the largest investment within the British empire in the nineteenth century and made other developments—for example iron and steel production—possible. Despite the earlier destruction of its indigenous textile industry, by the late nineteenth century Indian capital had made Bombay into a major base of the textile industry (Chandavarkar 2003, 26). By World War II, India was self-sufficient in the production of cotton textiles and had even become a major exporter of them. Modern industries such as steel and cement had emerged, and there was large-scale production of consumer goods employing modern methods (Bagchi 1972, 433–444). Machinery and machine tools did not fare so well, however. Marx described the extraordinary wastage involved in transporting cotton to Britain to be fabricated and returned to India (Marx 1969a, 86), and although this policy was subsequently modified, the production of cotton-textile machinery in India was blocked until World War II had begun (Bagchi 1972, 44).

These capital investments, both Indian and British, created a proletariat and thus the conditions for a labor movement to develop. Between 1850 and 1900, more than twenty-five thousand miles of railway track had been laid, requiring the labor of tens of millions of Indians, hired largely through Indian contractors who fit Marx's description of petty capitalists (Kerr 1997, xii, 1–8). Around 80 percent were estimated to be unskilled workers, with a high proportion of women and children, many of them "from the lower margins of Indian society," that is, *Adivasis* and *Dalits* (Kerr 1997, 85–88, 104).[3] The skilled workers included carpenters, masons, stonecutters, builders, drillers, ironsmiths, riveters, and erectors. Collective action over nonpayment of agreed wages and abuse by contractors took the form of strikes, riots, and petitions to the government (Kerr 1997, 113–15, 176–80). At the Tata Iron and Steel Company in Jamshedpur, where construction began in 1907 and production in 1911, the various occupations were grouped into skilled, semiskilled, and unskilled categories, with women workers represented only in the last category. (There were no children.) A more stable workforce allowed for the formation of two major unions—the Congress-linked Jamshedpur Labour Union and the nonparty Jamshedpur Labour Federation—which engaged in a complex process of struggle and bargaining involving the Indian employers, the European and American managers and technical staff, the British administration, and the Congress Party. One conclusion that emerges is that the common interest that Indian employers and workers had in obtaining independence from colonial rule did not by any means rule out bitter class conflicts between them (Simeon 1995).

After independence in 1947, the state employed a variety of means to encourage both Indian and foreign investment in industry. Foreign investment in technologically advanced sectors such as chemicals and electrical goods expanded greatly, largely as a result of state licensing policy, while the Indian private sector expanded rapidly in less capital-intensive manufacturing industries. The state itself took over many of the services formerly provided by foreign capital, such as electric power, transport, banking, trading and life insurance, and production of key industrial inputs such as coal. Protective tariffs, import restriction, and currency control led to a withdrawal of British capital and Indian takeover of their concerns (Kidron 1965, 31–57). With the Second Plan, the state moved into heavy industry and began building it up in a concerted fashion despite U.S. opposition, obtaining collaborations with German and British private capital and substantial support from the Soviet Union and East European countries. After the drastic import controls imposed during the foreign-exchange crisis of 1957–1958, foreign companies in modern, technologically advanced sectors of industry moved in to take advantage of the protected market by way of joint ventures with Indian companies (Patnaik 1972, 216–218).

Empirically, therefore, the proposition that capitalist industrialization cannot take place in Third World countries is not sustainable; in the absence of political and military intervention from outside, it is entirely possible. Theoretically, moreover, the idea that capital will go on accumulating in a few countries ad infinitum rather than spreading to the rest of the world seems inconsistent with its constant drive to expand the production of surplus value. Lenin's description of export of capital to the colonies was simplistic, in the sense that it did not take account of the indigenous accumulation of capital in Third World countries, but he was right to think that at some point investment in countries with higher rates of profit would become a compulsion, because without it, "the spatial fix is negated and global crises are inevitable" (Harvey 1982, 435).

Russian "State Capitalism"?

The notion that Russia and China offer an alternative to capitalist industrialization also requires critical scrutiny. The character of the Russian revolution was disputed even before it took place. The Mensheviks saw it as an antifeudal bourgeois-democratic revolution; the Bolsheviks saw it as an anticapitalist proletarian-socialist one. The October revolution in 1917 seemed to confirm the Bolshevik point of view. Later, when Stalin took power, Trotsky maintained that while he had carried out a political counterrevolution, state ownership of the means of production and centralized planning meant that Russia, though not a socialist society, was still a workers' state, albeit a degenerated one. He continued to maintain this position even after the Stalin-Hitler pact and invasion of Poland in 1939 led others in the Fourth International to proclaim that the Soviet Union was no longer in any sense a workers' state and was following an imperialist path (Hansen and Warde 1970; Trotsky 1970, 3–20).

In the case of China, divergent views were present in the writings of Mao himself. Around 1940, he asked, "what, after all, is the character of the Chinese Revolution at the present stage? Is it bourgeois-democratic or pro-letarian-socialist?" and he answered quite categorically: "Obviously, it is the former, not the latter . . . even if the big bourgeoisie betrays the revolution and becomes its enemy, the spearhead of the revolution will still be directed at imperialism and feudalism rather than at capitalism and capitalist private property in general" (Mao 1969a, 229–230). In 1950, he repeated, "the view held by some people that it is possible to eliminate capitalism and introduce socialism at an early date is wrong" (Mao 1969b, 343). Yet just five years later, referring to the formation of agricultural cooperatives, he said, "this is a huge socialist revolutionary movement" (Mao 1969c, 344).

While the dissidents in the Fourth International in 1939 suggested that Russian society was "bureaucratic collectivist" and neither capitalist nor socialist, some Trotskyists as well as other analysts later characterized it as "state capitalist" (Kuron and Modzelewski 1969; Cliff 1974; Bettelheim 1978; Kulkarni 1994), its economy driven not by internal competition between private capitals nor by attempts to satisfy the needs of people within the country (who suffered from chronic shortages of basic necessities) but by external competition (more military than economic) with U.S. and West European capitalism.[4] Moreover, the use of Russian tanks in suppressing the uprisings in Hungary in 1956 (Lomax 1979–1980) and Czechoslovakia in 1968 (Pelikan 1972), Russian backing for the repression following the Polish uprisings in 1970–1971 and 1980–1981 (Ascherson 1981, 233–244, 278–281), and the exploitative relationship with the Central Asian Republics and invasion of Afghanistan in 1979 (Ticktin 1979–1980) all belie the claim that links with these countries were voluntary on their part and instead suggest imperialist domination.

Finally, if the Soviet Union and China really were socialist societies, the disintegration of the Eastern Bloc and the Soviet Union itself and their absorption, along with China, into the capitalist world economy would make no sense from a Marxist point of view: that socialism, which by definition is economically more advanced than capitalism and politically more democratic than bourgeois society, should collapse in this manner without any military conquest by the advanced capitalist countries is inexplicable. These developments, more than any others, are probably what account for the increasing incoherence of Amin's calls for delinking (Nederveen Pieterse 1994).

The most convincing characterization of what happened in Russia in 1917 is that it was an anti-Tsarist revolution followed by an antifeudal social transformation (what Marx called the "primitive accumulation of capital"), and what occurred in China in the 1940s was a liberation struggle against Japanese imperialism followed by a social transformation eliminating pre-capitalist relations of production. The plebeian masses had played a key role in earlier bourgeois revolutions, only to be reined in when bourgeois power consolidated itself (cf. Soboul 1977), and it is not surprising that their role was even more crucial in these countries where the bourgeoisie was weak. Furthermore, the role of the state, always important during the primitive accumulation of capital, would be even more so in these countries due to the weakness of the bourgeoisie as well as economic blockades and military threats by the Western powers. Russia's exploitation and oppression of the Central Asian republics and plunder of Eastern and Central European countries after World War II played the same role in its case as imperialism played in the primitive accumulation of Western Europe and its settler-colonies. Thus the disintegration of the Eastern Bloc and Soviet Union can be seen as part of a global process of decolonization, and the reintegration of Russia and China into a capitalist world economy, no longer as tributaries but as powers to be reckoned with, could be seen as inevitable. Russia and China therefore exemplify different strategies of capitalist industrialization, not alternatives to it.

Imperialism and the State

From the standpoint of the colonies, it appears quite arbitrary to say that the depredations that took place before the 1870s were not capitalist imperialism (Lenin 1964, 256). However, Lenin was right in one sense: the "new imperialism" that took shape in the latter part of the nineteenth century was different from the earlier model, because "after 1860, political leaders within and outside Europe rapidly extended their project of making nation-states" (Bayly 2004, 206). The new imperialism, which depended critically on military conquest and competition, was driven by the aggressive nationalism of the European powers and Japan as they scrambled to snap up territory throughout the world (Bayly 2004, 228–233). As a result of nationalist ideology in imperialist countries, there arose "a sudden community of interest between capital and the proletariat, which finds expression in an identical inclination of both classes to imperialism. What the economy divided, the idea of national power and glory unites" (Adler 1978, 131). The key characteristics of the new imperialism were the all-important role played by the state, both domestically and abroad, and the ideology of nationalism, which created a "community of interest" between workers and their rulers.

Even in Marx's time, the state was involved in protectionism, export promotion, national and international debt, expropriation of peasants and artisans through heavy taxation of essential commodities, commercial wars, and so on (Marx 1976, 918–922), but the dependence of capital on the state increased under the new imperialism. Colonialism required the imperialist power to set up an administrative apparatus in the colony and also to maintain a substantial military presence to deal with uprisings, but less traditional forms of imperialism also relied heavily on extensions of state power outside the imperialist country: for example, the ubiquitous CIA and U.S. military bases all over the world. Even the function of containing class struggle at home, either by extending welfare benefits to the working class or by whipping up war fever and hatred of an external enemy, was carried out by the state.

Globalization, on the contrary, is marked by the emergence of advanced sectors of capital, both productive and financial, which rely on porous rather than impervious national borders and do not need backing from a nation-state. Globalization is not imperialism; indeed, "imperialist globalization" is a contradiction in terms.

Globalization as Neoliberalism

The classical political economists argued that the working of the market, if left to itself, would result in a matching of production and consumption, supply and demand; by working for their own benefit, individuals would achieve satisfaction of social needs (e.g., Smith 1776; Ricardo 1821; cit. Marx 1976). It followed that liberal free-trade policies were universally desirable. This doctrine was undermined by crises that caused untold hardship to large numbers of people and was criticized theoretically by Marx, some of whose followers concluded that a centrally planned economy was the solution to these problems. Later, Keynes, in a less radical critique, felt that in capitalism there was a need for "some coordinated act of intelligent judgment to manage saving and investment and their distribution between domestic and foreign uses," although the state should only "do those things which at present are not done at all" (Keynes 1932, 318; cit. Barratt Brown 1974, 45). Followers of Keynes thus justified and practiced state intervention in capitalist economies.

However, the Keynesian model of capital accumulation was suffering from falling profit rates and stagnation by the 1970s, and the term "neoliberalism" was used for the model that replaced it. This was imposed on many Third World and East European countries in return for loans by the Bretton Woods institutions set up in 1944 (the International Monetary Fund and the International Bank for Reconstruction and Development, or World Bank). The short-term stabilization measures included cutbacks in government expenditure, high interest rates, and currency devaluation, and the longer-term adjustment measures centered on deregulating the economy, liberalizing trade and investment, and privatizing state enterprises. These measures went much further than the free-trade policies envisaged by the classical economists. Giving the repayment of loans priority over employment and expansion contradicted the purposes for which Keynes had argued for the Bretton Woods institutions, which was to provide a supply of money that would enable governments to "deal with balance of payments problems through expansionary rather than deflationary measures, and . . . invest in the infrastructure and industries required for full employment" (Elson 1994, 514). The fact that the currency most in demand was the U.S. dollar gave the U.S. government, influenced by U.S. business, disproportionate power in the Bretton Woods institutions (Elson 1994, 516).

Thus the regime of the IMF and World Bank, sometimes called "the Washington consensus," reinforced U.S. dominance over the world economy and held back the industrialization of developing countries by prohibiting state intervention—in the form of policies such as protectionism and subsidies—which all the industrialized countries had used to nurture their infant industries (Chang 2007). The effect was heightened by the increasingly significant role of private financial institutions and multinational corporations in the working of the system. That in the overwhelming majority of cases their policies failed to stimulate growth, employment, and investment in Third World countries and led instead to economic decline and stagnation is not surprising. The IMF played a key role in the East Asian crisis and collapse of the Russian economy (Stiglitz 2000). Here, at last, in the "market fundamentalism" of the IMF and World Bank, we seem to have a definition of globalization, popularly expressed by clubbing together the IMF, World Bank, and WTO.

It is true that international trade liberalization is an important element of both neoliberalism and globalization. But there are significant differences between the IMF/World Bank on one side and the WTO on the other. At the UN Conference on Trade and Employment in Havana in 1948, a charter for the International Trade Organization, the forerunner of the WTO, was blocked by the U.S. Senate, leaving world trade to be governed by the much weaker General Agreement on Tariffs and Trade (GATT). This arrangement, combined with control over the IMF and World Bank, allowed the United States to impose on other countries policies—such as removal of tariffs and export subsidies—that it did not practice itself. In striking contrast to the Bretton Woods institutions, the WTO, set up in January 1995 at the conclusion of the Uruguay Round of GATT negotiations, was a one-country-one-vote, multilateral institution whose decisions applied equally to all members.

Second, the emphasis on "deregulation," which is characteristic of the IMF and World Bank and resulted in its privatization efforts being marked by corruption and the creation of private and often criminal monopolies (Stiglitz 2002, 54–56, 71), is not shared by the WTO; on the contrary, the avowed purpose of the WTO is to *regulate* the world economy, and this makes it possible to contest the question of whose interests its regulations should serve. A careful reading of the World Bank's 1995 *World Development Report* reveals that behind the façade of deregulation lurks "the notion that the main task of government is to create a climate and environment that is conducive for capital to flourish" (Breman 1995, 2299). In other words, neoliberalism embodies a procapitalist political intervention. It is certainly compatible with globalization, just as fascism is compatible with a national capitalist economy, but it is no more inevitable in a globalized economy than fascism is inevitable in a national one. Whether the neoliberal model of globalization wins out or not depends on the degree and scale of the opposition it faces.

The Twilight of Imperialism

In the first decade of the twentieth century, Hilferding noted the rise of the joint-stock company or corporation and its revolutionary significance for industrial capital: the fact that unlike the individually owned enterprise, it "is independent of the size of individual amounts of capital. . . . Not only does it broaden the circle of those involved (anyone who has money can be a money capitalist), but every sum of money above a certain minimum (which need only amount to a few schillings) is capable of being combined with other sums in a joint stock company and used as industrial capital" (Hilferding 1981, 122). As a consequence,

An ever-increasing part of the capital of industry does not belong to the industrialists who use it. They are able to dispose over capital only through the banks, which represent the owners. On the other side, the banks have to invest an ever-increasing part of their capital in industry, and in this way they become to a greater and greater extent industrial capitalists. I call bank capital, that is, capital in money form which is actually transformed in this way into industrial capital, finance capital.

(Hilferding 1981, 225)

A similar revolution was taking place in the United States in the 1890s: "The specific institutional form that the new property took was corporate capital—capital organized and administered through the specific institutions of investment banks, stock markets, and brokerage houses," which "changed ownership into a more liquid form that was more fungible and more easily transferred from one person to another" and also "mobilized new capital from outside the party of owners and promoters, from other individuals and organizations" (Roy 1997, 248). Here too a bond was forged between industrial and banking capital:

John D. Rockefeller epitomized the movement of an industrialist into the core of the corporate class, a move solidified by his close alliance with the National City Bank and the numerous corporate boards the Rockefeller family and partners sat on. J. P. Morgan led the financial community into the industrial realm, underwriting and controlling the formation of General Electric, International Harvester, U.S. Steel, and other corporate giants.

(Roy 1997, 272)

When Hilferding first published *Finance Capital* in 1910, imperialism had almost reached a point where it had to fight wars to repartition the world between existing and would-be imperialist powers, whereas corporations and financial markets were in their infancy. He and Lenin argued that there was a necessary link between imperialism and finance capital, yet the latter part of the twentieth century saw them moving in opposite directions.

Reorientation of the World Economy?

Financial markets grew massively during the twentieth century. Its last two decades saw the emergence of institutional investors, "commonly defined as financial institutions that invest their clients' money on a longer-term basis, such as insurance companies, pension funds and investment funds. They are distinct from banks, which take short-term deposits from clients," but the distinction was blurring, with banks providing insurance policies and investment vehicles (Lannoo 1998, 316). The rapid growth of this sector was demonstrated by the fact that institutional ownership of the listed UK equity market grew from 29 percent in 1963 to 60.6 percent in 1994 (Stapleton 1996, 19), and pension-fund assets alone amounted to 57.1 percent of the GDP in the United States and over 87 percent of the GDP in the Netherlands at the end of 1995 (De Ryck 1998, 267). With the growth of well-regulated capital markets in some Third World countries, a portion of these funds began to be invested in them. Pension funds in particular were highly prized in India, because they were believed to be "extremely methodical investors," unlikely to pull their money out suddenly, as other investors did during the Asian crisis (ET 2004e). This can be seen as an export of capital, but in a form Lenin could never have envisaged: the capitalized savings of wage earners. It was surmised that a further development of similar institutional investors in Third World countries would help to stabilize domestic capital markets in general and stock markets in particular (Fischer 1998), and Indian corporations began entering this field (Sabarinath and Sriram 2005).

Up to 1946, most of the giant U.S. corporations were "domestically oriented enterprises with international operations," but during the next decade and a half, "in industry after industry, US companies found that their overseas earnings were soaring. . . . As earnings abroad began to rise, profit margins from domestic operations began to shrink. . . . This is the combination that forced development of the multinational company" (*Business Week* 1963; cit. Baran and Sweezy 1966, 195). With a growing feeling that the U.S. market was "saturated," foreign direct investments (FDI) of U.S. corporations shot up from $7.2 billion in 1946 to $40.6 billion in 1963 (Baran and Sweezy 1966, 196–198). Most of this investment was in other developed countries, just as the preferred destinations for *their* FDI were the United States and one another's countries, although a small but significant portion came to Third World countries such as India. Following on from this period was what came to be characterized as the "New International Division of Labor" (although Marx might have seen it as a partial reestablishment of the "old" precolonial division of labor!), during which there was large-scale relocation of labor-intensive production of textiles, garments, and electronics from First to Third World—mainly East Asian—countries (Froebel et al. 1980). This was production exclusively for export, much of it located in free-trade zones, and the vast majority of the workers were women (Elson and Pearson 1981). In India, economic liberalization had a dual effect, on the one hand attracting a large volume of new FDI and on the other spurring major Indian companies to become globally competitive. In both cases, the primary attraction was the domestic market rather than outsourcing (Banaji 1996).

By the beginning of the twenty-first century, sweeping changes had taken place compared to the early or even mid-twentieth century. Cartels, whose development Hilferding and Lenin had made much of, were outlawed in a hundred countries, with vigorous efforts being made to ensure competition (Kolasky 2002). In India, multinational giants such as Hindustan Lever (now Hindustan Unilever) and Proctor & Gamble competed with local brands such as Nirma and Ghadi, to the detriment of profit margins (Vijayraghavan and Chakravarty 2004). At the same time, a growing number of crossborder mergers created multinationals no longer closely bound to a parent country (Edwards 1998; Groendahl 2003). While the vast majority of mergers and acquisitions were between companies based in developed countries, there were also acquisitions by developed-country multinationals in Third World countries, a form of FDI that was becoming more popular than starting new production facilities (ILO 1996a). Developing countries replaced developed countries as the most preferred FDI destinations.

> As 2007 turned into 2008 . . . several years of bullish recovery from an early twenty-first century recession ended abruptly as the subprime market crisis pummeled the world's leading financial markets. . . . Despite

significant obstacles, foreign direct investment (FDI) continued to rise in 2007, and global investors are optimistic about opportunities in the developing world. China and India continue to rank at the top of the FDI Confidence Index.

(Global Business Policy Council 2008, 1)

In trade, too, a revolution was taking place, with products from China, India, and other Third World countries increasingly dominating the world market (Sinha 2004). Most of them were not traditional Third World exports, and even where they were, their volume caused alarm among developed-country producers. An increasing proportion was by way of outsourcing or offshoring, as companies in North America and Western Europe gave up the struggle to compete and instead used the more competitive production in Third World countries to their own advantage. One of the more labor-intensive Third World export sectors that took over most of the world market was textiles and garments (Williams 2004). Engineering raw materials and intermediate products, such as steel, dyes and chemicals, and electronic and automobile components were also increasingly sourced largely from countries such as China and India (Kelkar and Das 2003; Datta 2003; *ET* 2003a; Philip 2004).

The sector where outsourcing caused the most heated debate was the service sector: business process outsourcing (BPO) of functions such as call centers, telemarketing, finance, and accounting (Kachru 2004); human-resource services such as providing pension and benefit schemes, running employee help lines, and handling payroll and stock-options administration (D. Roberts 2004; Mukherjee 2004); and information-technology (IT) jobs such as customer and technical support, software development and testing, network administration, hardware development and testing, quality assurance, help desk and application support, and enhancement (*ET* 2005b; *BS* 2005a).

The trend is from less sophisticated, elementary work to increasingly sophisticated business processes—from code-writing and system maintenance to co-development and design of products; from medical transcription to reading of X-rays to sophisticated surgery and hospitalisation services; from call centres to processing of personal loan applications and insurance claims, to sophisticated financial analysis; the list is long.

(Rajwade 2004a)

A. T. Kearney ranked India as the most attractive offshore location for IT services, followed by China, Malaysia, the Czech Republic, Singapore, the Philippines, Brazil, Canada, Chile, and Poland (Subramanyam 2004).

Subcontracting/outsourcing and FDI both aimed at boosting profits by making use of cheaper labor. Economists in the United States argued that outsourcing was not only good for business but was also good for consumers (because it reduced prices) and the economy (which would otherwise have become uncompetitive), and thus ultimately good for employment, which in the absence of offshoring would have declined much more steeply (Swann 2004; De Jonquieres 2004; Chakravarty 2004). U.S. Federal Reserve Chairman Alan Greenspan warned that a ban on outsourcing would lower the standard of living and lead to more job losses by spurring protectionism in other countries (*ET* 2004a). Yet the perception in the United States that outsourcing was the cause of job losses persisted (Alden 2004).

The export of capital was not all in one direction. Flows of FDI from India to First, Second, and other Third World countries in the 1990s were small but increasing (Kumar 1995). Subsequently, they took the form of acquisitions such as Tata Tea's takeover of Tetley, Ranbaxy's purchase of the France-based generic-pharmaceutical company RPG Aventis SA, Bharat Forge's acquisition of the German firm Carl Dan Peddinghaus GmbH, Sundaram Fasteners' deal to acquire UK-based Dana Spicer, and Dabur's acquisition of UK-based Redrock Ltd. (BBC News 2000; *ET* 2003b; *BS* 2003a; see also *BS* 2005b, 2005c). Like the Brazilian Companhia Vale do Rio Doce's acquisition of most of the Canadian nickel company Inco Ltd., Tata's acquisition of the Anglo-Dutch steel firm Corus, making it one of the world's top five steel makers, epitomized the growing trend (Khanna 2007). Jubilant's acquisition of a U.S.-based clinical-research organization was an example of expansion into R&D (*BS* 2005e). Setting up joint ventures in other Third World and Second World countries was another route (*BS* 2005d). And India too started outsourcing back-office jobs, both to countries with English-speaking white-collar workers, such as the Philippines and Sri Lanka, and to non-English-speaking countries such as the Czech Republic and Mexico (*BS* 2004a). Finally, the decades-old "brain drain," whereby qualified professionals from Third World countries migrated to Europe and North America in search of jobs, was beginning to be reversed by a tiny trickle of qualified European and American professionals seeking jobs in countries such as India (Chatterjee 2004).

The global economy that was created during the heyday of imperialism was constrained first by the protectionism practiced by imperialist countries; then by the emergence of the Soviet Union, which remained outside the system and later took out the countries of the Eastern Bloc; and finally by late industrializers, both among imperialist nations (Japan) and Third World countries emerging from colonialism (such as China, Korea, and India), which used protectionism to nurture their infant industries. At the end of this period, a significant number of Third World nations emerged as powerful industrialized countries. The barriers erected in the old world order became a constraint on the most dynamic sectors of capitalism, which required the whole world as their field of operation. Consequently, the largely decolonized world economy that began to take shape in the latter part of the twentieth century was one in which there was a conscious effort to bring these barriers down, creating a capitalist world integrated not by colonialism, as before, but by relationships of greater (though by no means equal) mutual dependence.

The only area where national boundaries grew stronger, not weaker, was in the case of immigration barriers to the movement of people. "A world market for labour just does not exist in the same way that it does for goods and services. . . . In many ways, the world's underprivileged and poor have fewer international migratory possibilities nowadays than they had in the past" (Hirst and Thompson 2003, 338–339).

The transition from the Group of Seven (G7) First World countries, established in 1976, to the G8, which included Russia (a Second World country) in 1998, to the designation of the G20, consisting of First, Second, and Third World countries, as "the premier forum for our international economic cooperation" in September 2009 (Pittsburgh Summit 2009) is a striking indication of the sweeping changes in the balance of economic power brought about by globalization. The transformation made some of the foremost dependency theorists argue that it represented a shift in the center of gravity of the world economy back to the East (Arrighi 1994; Frank 1998). But was this the only change taking place?

Economic Globalization and the Nation-State

Those who claim that "capital is no less dependent on territorial states than it ever was" and see "globalization as a form of imperialism," with the United States as "the first, and so far the only, truly capitalist empire, relying on its economic hegemony" (Wood 2004; 1999), seriously underestimate the changes in global capitalism that have taken place over the past half-century and ignore the bloody history of U.S. imperialism's reliance on military/political intervention (Sakai 1989; Andreas 2004). Conversely, early suggestions that "there was no necessary link between a capital and its state in the area of extension, that capital was rather a political opportunist, and that existing states often suffered a decrease in their powers as a result of internationalization" (Murray 1971) have been borne out.

Capital relies on the enforcement of contracts in the areas where it operates, and colonial domination was one way of achieving this. But if a firm has operations in ten, twenty, or thirty countries, it becomes increasingly difficult for the nation-state in which its headquarters is located to exert its power directly in these countries, especially since companies from other countries too would wish to operate in them. Outsourcing or subcontracting reduces the need for enforcement, since production is carried out by local companies and could be shifted around over forty, fifty, or sixty countries, each of which would be eager to attract more production. Yet dependence on contracts remains. Obviously, a world economy where basic norms are commonly accepted becomes much more convenient for globalized capital than the unwieldy and politically less feasible method of extraterritorial political or military intervention. It also allows competitive firms from nonimperialist countries to expand globally. Achieving this kind of multilateral system is what the WTO was set up to do.

This created a divergence of interests, not so much between companies based in different countries as between companies with different levels of competitiveness and different business strategies in the same country. Governments had to choose which strategy they supported: a multilateral system that would allow their own competitive global companies to expand but would be a threat to the companies that depended on state support, or the opposite.

This is the conflict that surfaced in the case of outsourcing. "US corporations are picking up the pace in shifting well-paid technology jobs to India, China and other low-cost centres, but they are keeping quiet for fear of a backlash, industry professionals said" (Zielenziger 2003). The backlash was indeed on the way. In early 2004, "the US Senate approved an Omnibus Spending Bill that bans US companies which are in charge of executing federal projects in certain departments from subcontracting the work to overseas companies" (Chanda 2004), an action at odds with the stated U.S. objective of liberalizing trade: "it is the US and other developed countries that had pressed developing countries to negotiate liberalisation of trade in services, not the other way. Therefore, why are they backtracking now?" (Bhaumik 2004). When Gregory Mankiw, chairman of the Council of Economic Advisers, "argued that normal rules of trade apply to services as well as manufacturing; and that just as it makes sense to buy cell phones from Finland if they are cheap and excellent, it makes sense to buy call centre services or software programming from India, if these are the best on the market . . . he was forced to retract the statement the very next day" (Rajwade 2004b).

The BPO conflict was only the latest in a long series of disputes. In early 2000, the Appellate Body of the WTO confirmed that the Foreign Services Corporation (FSC) law in the United States, which gave tax concessions to U.S. corporations such as Microsoft and Boeing for exceeding certain export levels, constituted an export subsidy that was incompatible with WTO rules (Mathrani 2000). The United States replaced the FSC Act with the Extraterritorial Income Exclusion Act, but in January 2002 the WTO upheld an appeal by the European Union, backed by India, Australia, Canada, and Japan, that this too was illegal, and it gave the European Union the authority to impose trade sanctions against the United States unless the tax break was eliminated (De Jonquieres 2002a). Although the U.S. trade representative pledged to abide by the ruling, there were complaints by U.S. lawyers that the WTO was overstepping its limits by intervening in domestic tax policy (Wolffe 2002).

In August 2002, the WTO ruled that the European Union could go ahead with $4 billion worth of trade sanctions against the United States, to match the amount that companies in the European Union claimed they were losing as a result of the U.S. tax concessions (Waddington 2002). The European Union imposed sanctions on imports from the United States in March 2004 and only lifted them when Bush signed a bill repealing the export subsidies in October (*ET* 2004b). Bill Thomas, who drafted the bill, and Phil Crane, who opposed it, were both from the Republican Party.

> The split between Mr Crane and Mr Thomas mirrors divisions among US corporations over the WTO ruling. A coalition of large electronics, oil, retail and consumer companies, including Wal-Mart, Coca-Cola and General Motors, released on Friday a letter endorsing Mr Thomas's bill,

saying it would end what is, in effect, double taxation on the overseas operations of US companies [whereas] the big beneficiaries of the current FSC tax break are companies that manufacture in the US for export, including Boeing, Microsoft and Kodak.

(Alden 2002)

When the United States introduced up to 30 percent tariffs on steel imports in early March 2002, the European Union, Australia, and New Zealand swiftly filed complaints with the WTO; the heads of the IMF, World Bank, and WTO issued a statement criticizing the move; and Japan decided to slap 100 percent retaliatory tariffs on imports of steel and steel products from the United States (*BS* 2002a, 2002b; Alden and De Jonquieres 2002). Faced with the threat of EU retaliatory tariffs as well, the United States excluded 224 steel products from the new tariffs (*ET* 2002a). The WTO's Dispute Settlement Body had already ruled that duties imposed two years earlier on steel piping from South Korea violated trade rules— the seventh time in six years that the United States had been taken to the WTO over safeguard measures, losing every time (*BS* 2002c). Another highly contentious U.S. legal measure was the Byrd Amendment, introduced by Congress in 2000, whereby dumping duties levied on imports were distributed to the U.S. companies that had initiated the dumping charges, a measure that the WTO ruled was an illegal subsidy. It was estimated that the government had doled out about $710 million to U.S. companies under the program over three years. In January 2004, the European Union requested the go-ahead to impose retaliatory sanctions and was joined by eight other countries: Australia, Brazil, Chile, India, Indonesia, Japan, Korea, and Thailand; in September, the request was granted by the WTO (*ET* 2004c).

Perhaps the most bitter dispute was over U.S. and EU agricultural subsidies. The ministerial declaration by the WTO meeting at Doha in 2001 suggested that the Doha round of negotiations would be about "putting development back on the agenda of multilateral trade negotiations such that trade is able to fulfill its role of bringing about all-round prosperity" (Verma 2003), yet huge subsidies to agricultural producers in the United States and European Union, which hurt poor farmers in the Third World, remained untouched (De Jonquieres and Williams 2002). Unfair competition from heavily subsidized cotton produced in the United States was wreaking havoc on the economies of African countries such as Chad,

Burkina Faso, Mali, and Benin, which were dependent on cotton production, and it was the failure to address this issue, more than anything else, that led to the collapse of the WTO talks at Cancun in September 2003 (Subramaniam 2003a).

Subsequently, there was an interim WTO ruling in favor of Brazil's complaint against U.S. subsidies to its cotton growers in April 2004 (Rajagopalan 2004). In July 2004, a framework agreed upon by the WTO in Geneva included the elimination of export subsidies and a cut in domestic support to agriculture by developed countries, while developing countries could continue to provide *de minimis* support to resource-poor farmers and protect some products to address food security and livelihood concerns. This addressed one of the major concerns of Third World countries and helped to restart the Doha round of negotiations (Kumar 2004). In March 2005, the WTO's appellate body made a final ruling on the petition by Brazil, supported by some West African cotton-growing countries, confirming that most of the U.S. subsidies to its cotton growers were illegal under WTO rules (Waddington 2005). The process inched forward at the Hong Kong WTO Ministerial Conference in December 2005—although the phaseout of agricultural-export subsidies in developed countries was postponed to 2013, and no commitment was made to eliminate trade-distorting domestic subsidies (Muralidharan 2005)—only to collapse again at Geneva in June 2006 (Khor 2006). A year later, a meeting of the United States, European Union, Brazil, and India in Potsdam also collapsed because the United States and European Union were willing to give very little by way of cutting agricultural subsidies, while demanding cuts of 60 to 70 percent more in industrial tariffs from developing countries, leading the Brazilian and Indian negotiators to comment that this would turn what was supposed to be a development round into its opposite (Khor 2007).

It was not only producers in the United States and European Union who demanded subsidies and protection; Indian companies that had established oligopolies during the "license-permit raj" were equally unwilling to face competition. A popular form of protectionism was to demand antidumping duties on cheaper imported products, claiming that they were priced below their price in the domestic market of the exporting country and caused injury to domestic producers in the importing country. A study showed that the overwhelming majority of such claims were baseless (Singh 2005). Thus Sterlite Industries, a major Indian producer of optical fiber, demanded that an antidumping duty be slapped on optical fiber imported from Korea (*BS* 2000a); the Directorate-General of Anti-Dumping passed orders imposing dumping duties on soda ash and sodium ferrocyanide imports from China in order to protect Indian producers (*BS* 2000b); domestic manufacturers of dry-cell batteries wanted a dumping duty to be levied on cheap batteries imported from China (*ET* 2001); dumping duties were levied on sodium ferrocyanide, theophylline, and caffeine from the European Union, 3.4.5 trimethoxy benzaldehyde from China, and sodium cyanide from the United States, Czech Republic, European Union, and Korea, despite a lack of convincing evidence that domestic industry was being injured (Goyal 2001); garment companies wanted dumping duties levied on garment imports from Bangladesh and Sri Lanka (Sabarinath and Iyer 2001); Rahul Bajaj, a domestic producer of two-wheelers, asked for an increase in duty from the prevailing 35 percent to 105 percent on two-wheelers coming in from China (Kumar 2002); and by mid-May 2001, over a hundred Indian companies, including some of the largest corporate houses, including Reliance Industries (itself fighting more than a dozen cases), had managed to get dumping duties imposed on sixty-four products and were trying for many more (Subramaniam 2001a).

This protectionism had an adverse effect on other domestic industries, leading to pleas that it should be ended.

The government . . . must take immediate and unilateral steps to ensure competitive pricing in steel. It should slash the import duty on it which, at 30%, is embarrassingly high. A substantial cut is also merited since steel (like cement) falls within the core sector: sudden upward price changes can otherwise hold the whole economy hostage, with huge costing upsets in the downstream user-industries.

(*ET* 2003c)

Again:

It may be recalled that the domestic copper industry led by Sterlite and Birla Copper has been pushing the government to stop the import [of copper] from Sri Lanka. . . . The government has responded to the demand for protection . . . by slapping port restrictions. . . . The users of copper in the electrical industry complained that the handful of producers in India are exploiting the protection of 20% duty on winding wires. The Sterlite-

Birla copper duopoly . . . take advantage of the protected domestic market to milk consumers.

(Goyal 2004)

Plentiful evidence that antidumping policy had a negative effect on consumers and user industries (and hence on employment) led to the plea that the WTO's Anti-Dumping Agreement needed a public-interest clause (Aggarwal 2004).

These cases demonstrate a clear division between producers who benefit from the patronage of their own nation-state and those who operate best in a globalized world. The former category includes producers backed by the neoconservative coterie around George W. Bush: "since many of the interests supporting Bush are not subject to the market, they regard the free market and free trade as no more than rhetorical weapons that are deployed against external competitors and not taken seriously as an operating principle" (Bello 2006, 2). The latter category includes Indian companies that had invested overseas, an expansion strategy that had been more difficult under a regime of tight foreign-exchange controls (*BS* 1999a). This was not a matter of size: some of the corporations that relied on government support were among the biggest in India and in the world, while many of those whose operations were global were much smaller companies linked into a global network (Rajanala 2003; Padmapriya and Balasubramanian 2004).

The contrast with imperialism and the early period of decolonization, during which nation-states played a critical role in enabling capital to expand, could not be clearer. Now, on the contrary, the borders between nation-states become an obstacle to the expansion of the most competitive capitals, for whom the global mobility of commodities, capital, jobs, information, and ideas is crucial. The *Communist Manifesto* had declared that

constant revolutionizing of production, uninterrupted disturbance of social conditions, everlasting uncertainty and agitation distinguish the bourgeois epoch from all earlier ones. All fixed, fast-frozen relations, with their train of ancient and venerable prejudices and opinions, are swept away, all new-formed ones become antiquated before they can ossify. All that is solid melts into air.

(Marx and Engels 1973, 70)

The dependence of capital on the nation-state was one of those newly formed relations that was becoming antiquated before it could ossify.

Technological, Political, and Cultural Correlates of Economic Globalization

Outsourcing of manufacturing—of garments or automobile components, for example—would not be possible without information and communication technologies (ICT) to coordinate production in several different countries contributing to the manufacture of a single product or implementation of an integrated business strategy. A fortiori, the outsourcing of services depends on information technology—indeed, the IT industry itself is one of the hallmarks of globalization. If machinery was the technological starting point of the industrial revolution,[5] ICT was the technological starting point of globalization: in both cases, technological innovation was the condition for a wide-ranging transformation of social relations, which in turn reacted back upon that technology and developed it further.

> While capitalism is characterized by its relentless expansion, always trying to overcome limits of time and space, it was only in the late twentieth century that the world economy was able to become truly global on the basis of the new infrastructure provided by information and communication technologies. [For example,] capital is managed around the clock in globally integrated financial markets in real time for the first time in history.
>
> (Castells 2003, 311)

The possibility opened up by ICT for collaboration by people all over the globe in making a product has created links between workers that are often hidden but that could be revealed and used to build solidarity. In an even more far-reaching development, it creates new potential for collaborative production that goes beyond the logic of capital. Open-source software, the Wikipedia project, and the Firefox Internet browser are all examples of products where people in different parts of the world contribute their work without remuneration so that global consumers may enjoy a product without paying for it (Wall 2005, 187–189). According to an advocate of free software, the development of "goods with zero marginal cost" allows for free culture without depriving artists of remuneration (Moglen and Kumar 2007).

In the constitution of a nation-state, "a two-fold process of interaction is at work: 'internally' with regard to society and 'externally' with regard to other states and actors" (Clarke 1999, 57). Conventionally, sovereignty is seen as the authority of the state over what occurs within its territorial space—its "entitlement to rule" (Held and McGrew 2003, 11)—and recognition of this authority in its external interaction with other states. Internationally, the system has never been able to prevent large-scale violence, despite the adoption of the Geneva Conventions to regulate the conduct of nations during war. The horrific carnage of World War II, including the slaughter of millions of civilians by nuclear bombs dropped on Hiroshima and Nagasaki and conventional bombing elsewhere, led to the foundation in 1945 of the United Nations, whose foremost purpose, as proclaimed in its charter, was "to save succeeding generations from the scourge of war" and for this purpose "to unite our strength to maintain international peace and security." This could be seen as a pooling of sovereignty in order to regulate relations between sovereign nations so as to prevent violent conflict between them, thus modifying the "external" dimension of sovereignty.

The horror of the Nazi genocide created a crisis for the "internal" dimension of sovereignty, too, leading to the Nuremberg trials, which questioned the authority of a state to do as it pleased within its territorial space. The adoption of the Genocide Convention by the United Nations on December 9, 1948, and the Universal Declaration of Human Rights the following day articulated the belief that the most basic rights of human beings cannot be different in different countries but must be common for all peoples. In subsequent decades, the United Nations would pass many covenants and conventions applying to the world as a whole. For example, in 1966 two covenants codifying the rights in the Universal Declaration were adopted by the General Assembly: the International Covenant on Civil and Political Rights and the International Covenant on Economic, Social, and Cultural Rights.

The International Labour Organization, founded in 1919 to promote social justice and internationally recognized labor rights, became the first specialized agency of the United Nations in 1946, and its International Labour Code is a large and growing document. The Convention on the Elimination of All Forms of Discrimination Against Women, 1979, is often described as an international bill of rights for women. The International Criminal Court came into force in June 2002, with the mandate to prosecute perpetrators of four core crimes—war crimes, crimes against humanity, genocide, and aggression—whose scope encompasses both the internal and external dimensions of sovereignty. These "international . . . institutions have both linked sovereign states together and transformed sovereignty into the shared exercise of power. A body of . . . international law has developed which underpins an emerging system of global governance" (Held and McGrew 2003, 11).

Both ICT and international human-rights law impinge on culture. While it is true that commercialization popularizes the commodities of those who can afford to advertise them widely, the availability of free information and culture counteracts this development. The nightmares of those who "deplore the loss of distinct national communities to the homogenizing influence of McDonald's, Disney and Cable News Network (CNN)" (Norris 2003, 287) have not come true. In India, despite globalization, traditional fast foods continue to be more popular than McDonald's, and the latter is losing its appeal even in its country of origin (Tomkins 2002). Bollywood films not only remain more popular than Disney in India but "are becoming more and more popular around the world" (Rosenberg 2005). Indian news channels have a large following, and during the second Gulf War, when Indian reporters were unable to gain access to Iraq, people turned to the Internet and Al Jazeera for alternatives to the news presented by "embedded" journalists working for CNN and the BBC (Banaji and Al-Ghabban 2006). Furthermore, it must be remembered that the creation of "distinct national communities" often involves a violent process of homogenization, and attempts are being made to use human-rights law to protect diversity by providing redress to national minorities who are victims of genocide and ethnic cleansing.

What is emerging, then, is a global order where nation-states pool their sovereignty in institutions of global governance such as the United Nations, WTO, and ICC. Is this, however, merely "a new imperial form of sovereignty" in which the "United States does indeed occupy a privileged position" (Hardt and Negri 2000, xiii–xiv)?

The Decline of the United States as an Economic Power

This argument of Negri and Hardt depends on the proposition that the U.S. project of world domination is fundamentally different from earlier European imperialisms. Superficially, this appears to be true. Consolidating itself at a time when decolonization was well under way and a multilateral world order was emerging, U.S. imperialism was forced to operate under cover, initially of the fight against communism, later of the war on terror.[6] Wherever it could use the new multilateral institutions of global governance for its own purposes, it did so, subverting and corrupting them in the process. An example of this was the use of the United Nations to legitimize wars against Iraq (1991) and Afghanistan (2001) (cf. Hardt and Negri 2000, 12–13).

However, whenever multilateral institutions impinged on its national sovereignty, the United States fought against them. Thus the Chemical Weapons Convention, Biological Weapons Convention, and Comprehensive (nuclear) Test-Ban Treaty, all of which depended on a monitoring regime to ensure that forbidden activities were not taking place, had not been ratified by the United States even while its leaders used the pretext of nonexistent weapons of mass destruction to invade and occupy Iraq in 2003. The excuse was that these international treaties would subject the United States to the same inspection regime as other member states, which, it was felt, would violate its national sovereignty. The United States withdrew from the 1972 Antiballistic Missile Treaty in 2002, rejected the 1997 Land Mine Treaty, and was the only nation to oppose a UN Agreement to Curb the International Flow of Illicit Small Arms in 2001; it refused to ratify the Kyoto Protocol on Climate Change on the grounds that cutting greenhouse-gas emissions was inimical to its national interest (Du Boff and Herman 2002). It not only refused to ratify the Rome Treaty of the ICC but took the unprecedented step of *unsigning* it, thus signaling its intention to sabotage it actively (Lewis 2002).

In its relationships with Third World countries, the United States used military power to establish political and economic control in a similar fashion to European imperialism. Allies in the war against communism, such as Osama bin Laden, would later become the "enemy" in the war on terror, showing how unimportant these pretexts were. When the United States could not use the United Nations as a rubber stamp, it did not hesitate to bypass the authority of the multilateral body—for example, by vetoing every move to enforce UN resolutions on Israel or starting the second war against Iraq in 2003. On closer examination, there was nothing new about this "imperial form of sovereignty." This was not a multilateral empire in which the United States occupied pride of place but rather U.S. imperialism pitted against an emerging multilateral world order. The only multilateral body that could force the United States to surrender part of its sovereignty was the WTO. It was able to do this because it wielded the weapon of economic sanctions against the imperial power, showing that an empire cannot impose its will on other nations purely by virtue of its military might. Economic power is also essential, and that was where the United States had been waning.

The dominance of the dollar underpinned U.S. financial dominance as well as the apparently limitless spending power that allowed it to keep hundreds of thousands of troops stationed all over the world. The strength of the U.S. economy after World War II enabled the U.S. dollar, backed by gold, to become the world's reserve currency. After the United States abandoned the gold standard in 1971, the dollar remained supreme, and its position was further boosted in 1974 when the United States came to an agreement with Saudi Arabia that the oil trade would be denominated in dollars (Spiro 1999). Most countries in the world import oil, and it made sense for them to accumulate dollars in order to guard against oil shocks. Third World countries had even more reason to hoard dollars so as to protect their fragile economies and currencies from sudden collapse. With everyone clamoring for dollars, all the United States had to do was print fiat dollars and other countries would accept them in payment for their exports. These dollars then flowed back into the United States to be invested in Treasury bonds and similar instruments, offsetting the outflow (Clarke 2004).

By the early twenty-first century, the dollar hegemony was creating problems for the world economy (Liu 2002). It allowed the United States to build up debt on a scale that would have wrecked any other country's currency (P. C. Roberts 2004): in 2007, the national debt breached $9 trillion (Johnson 2008). It also allowed the United States to pass on the costs of its empire to the rest of the world. Other countries were compelled to accept fiat dollars because they had no choice. It was the world's only reserve currency—until the euro came into being. The first few countries to shift from the dollar to the euro did so for political rather than economic reasons. In late 2000, Saddam Hussein switched to the euro and converted Iraq's $10 billion reserve fund at the United Nations to euros (Recknagel 2000); in 2002, Iran converted more than half its foreign-exchange reserves to euros (*Iran Financial News* 2002); and North Korea officially shifted to the euro for trade in December 2002 (Gluck 2002). Chavez too began moving Venezuela's trade out of dollars, using barter deals with other Latin American countries as well as euros (Henderson 2002).

As the dollar steadily lost value due to the massive U.S. debt—falling from 86 cents per euro in January 2002 to $1.32 in November 2004, a loss of 35 percent (*Economist* 2004)—others too began to find it prudent to reduce their dollar holdings. George Soros pulled his money out of dollar assets (Hughes 2003), and other U.S. investors followed suit (*ET* 2004d). OPEC countries reduced the dollar assets in their reserves from 75 to 60 percent, and only about 15 percent of China's additional foreign-exchange reserves acquired in the first three quarters of 2004 were in U.S. Treasury holdings (Rajwade 2004c). The Japanese government indicated it would diversify its reserves portfolio, and the Reserve Bank of India started buying euro-denominated securities (*ET* 2005a). In March 2005, the Bank for International Settlements in Basel announced that Asian central and commercial banks held only 67 percent of their deposits in dollars in September 2004, compared with 81 percent three years earlier. Indian banks were down from 68 to 43 percent, and Chinese dollar holdings were down from 83 to 68 percent, with the euro and yen being the most popular alternatives (Johnson 2005). Holdings in more exotic currencies also grew rapidly, albeit from much lower levels: Chinese renminbi (yuan) by 530 percent, Indonesian rupaiah by 283 percent, and Taiwanese dollars, Korean won, and Indian rupees by 129, 117, and 114 percent respectively (Nayak 2005). In July 2005, the fixed exchange rate of the yuan to the dollar was abandoned, followed closely by the Malaysian ringgit, with both currencies being allowed to float in a tight band against a basket of foreign currencies (Goodman 2005; *Dawn* 2005). By the end of 2005, euro-denominated securities had overtaken dollar-denominated ones as a medium for international investors (Cripps et al. 2005). Data released by the U.S. Federal Reserve showed that between late July and early September 2007, foreign central banks reduced their holdings of U.S. Treasury bonds by $48 billion (Evans-Pritchard 2007).

As the Chinese central bank vice director Xu Jian stated, the dollar was "losing its status as the world currency" (Lovasz and White 2007), and "Stephen Roach, the reputed chief economist at Morgan Stanley . . . has begun to write America's obituary as an economic engine of the world. Roach's long view is that the US economy is in terminal decline" (Venu 2004). Putting the U.S. economy back on track would involve "the US having to tackle its current account deficits, having to tackle its debt problems and ending a situation where it relies for its own investment upon sucking in finance from the rest of the world," all of which would be impossible so long as massive military expenditure on maintaining U.S. global dominance remained on the agenda (Gowan 2001). According to Chalmers Johnson (2007), the choice for the United States was between relinquishing its empire in order to survive as a democracy and save its economy or clinging to its empire, becoming a dictatorship, and eventually going bankrupt.

Globalization: The Latest Phase of Capitalism?

I would therefore define globalization as an emerging phase of capitalism, marked by

    a. a capitalist world economy covering more or less the entire globe;

    b. large-scale decolonization and the emergence of some Third World countries as powerful players in the world economy;

    c. a changing relation between capital and the state such that the most advanced capitals do not need protection and support from a nation-state but instead need porous national borders and global regulation;

    d. the emergence of ICT both as a new and increasingly dominant branch of production in itself and as a factor affecting other branches of production, services, and finance;

    e. the emergence and increasing importance of new institutional investors—i.e., new forms of finance capital—including pension funds; and

    f. new institutions of global governance based on the understanding that actions taken in one country can have serious consequences in another: thus greenhouse-gas emissions in one country can result in submergence of large tracts of land in others, agricultural subsidies in the United States can ruin small farmers in Africa and Latin America, labor-rights violations in one country can undermine workers' rights in others, and financial deregulation in some countries can catalyze a global crisis.

Taken together, these changes signify an ongoing transition from the epoch of imperialism to a new phase of capitalism.

[3]

Four Sources of the Global Crisis of 2008

The report of the UN Commission on Reforms of the International Monetary and Financial System (UN 2009a) mentioned three sources of the global crisis of 2008: (a) "neoliberal policies that promoted the growth of national and international inequalities, accelerated global imbalances, and exacerbated volatility through selective and asymmetric globalization—especially the greater liberalization of capital than of labor"; (b) "undue deference being given to financial interests" and the fact that "growing financial markets were held to be a desirable end in themselves rather than a means to ensuring a productive economy"; and (c) the use of the U.S. dollar as the international reserve currency, which was "squarely implicated in the development of global imbalances and the transmission of this crisis as well as previous financial crises" (Jayadev 2009, 27, 28, 30). A fourth source of the crisis, excessive military expenditure, was not mentioned in the report but has been analyzed extensively elsewhere.

Marx on Capitalist Crises

Marx's analysis of crises was unfinished, but we can discern in his work three points at which capitalist accumulation can be disrupted, leading to crises. The process can be broken down into three steps: the production of surplus value by workers, embodied in the commodities they are producing; the sale of those commodities in order to realize the expanded value in the form of money; and the reinvestment of that money in production on an expanded scale, which will produce yet more surplus value.

The first step can be disrupted by the tendency of the rate of profit to fall. Under capitalism, increases in the productivity of labor are reflected not just in a larger *mass* of machinery and raw materials being put into motion by the same number or a smaller number of workers but also in a rising ratio of the *value* of means of production to the value of the wages of the workers (the "organic composition of capital"). Since surplus value, and therefore profit, is created only by living labor, there is a tendency for the rate of profit—the amount of profit gained from a given amount of capital—to fall (Marx 1981, chaps. 2 and 13). This tendency is exacerbated by rising wages, which reduce the amount of surplus value. Marx refers to this as "overproduction of capital" (1981, 359), but it can also be seen as an underproduction of surplus value (profit) in relation to the existing amount of capital (Grossmann 1992, 79, 87). Since the purpose of capitalist production is to produce profit, when the rate of profit falls below a certain point, production ceases and there is a crisis. By devaluing and destroying existing capital, by creating unemployment and pushing down wages, such crises restore the rate of profit and thus reestablish the conditions for investment and accumulation to resume—but at enormous social cost (Marx 1981, 262–264).

There are various ways of counteracting the tendency of the rate of profit to fall, the most obvious being to increase the rate of surplus value (the ratio of surplus value or profit to the value of labor power or wages) by increasing the intensity of labor, lengthening the working day, and/or reducing real wages. But the fall in the rate of profit can also be counteracted without an adverse effect on workers if increases in productivity cheapen raw materials and machinery (so that their value does not rise as much as their volume) and/or cheapen wage goods (so that the value of wages can be reduced while the quantity of commodities bought with them stays the same or even increases). However, within a given society there are limits to how much these factors can counteract the effect of the huge productivity increases resulting from capital accumulation. The most powerful counteracting factor suggested by Marx is foreign trade (which reduces the cost of raw materials and wage goods) and foreign investments in less developed countries where wages are low, both of which serve to inhibit the fall in the rate of profit, although this effect declines as capitalism develops in these countries (1981, 339–347). This was seen as the driving force of imperialism by Lenin, among others.

There is no suggestion in the UN report that a fall in the rate of profit was responsible for the crisis. The rapid pace of globalization would have acted as a powerful counteracting force to that tendency, both through the cheapening of raw materials and wage goods imported from developing countries and through the higher rate of profit obtained from investments in them. The ICT revolution too would have counteracted the tendency of the rate of profit to fall by reducing costs. The strong warning in the UN report that "the introduction of additional protectionist policies to improve domestic conditions at the expense of trading partners . . . has negative externalities that will impede the recovery from the crisis" (UN 2009a, 17) suggests that deglobalization, far from helping to resolve the crisis, would constitute an obstacle to recovery.

Disruption can take place at "the second act in the process" too, if capitalists cannot sell their products and thereby realize the original value plus surplus value embodied in them. This does not necessarily mean that there is no social need for the products, since consumption in capitalism is determined "by the power of consumption within the framework of antagonistic conditions of distribution, which reduce the consumption of the vast majority of society to a minimum level" (Marx 1981, 352). This contradiction between capital's drive to expand production to the utmost while restricting consumption of the vast majority of the population within narrow limits is a constant theme in Marx's analysis (e.g., 1981, 615) and is the basis for Luxemburg's theory of imperialism. While her claim that capitalism must collapse once there are no markets remaining outside the system may be wrong, it is hard to deny that accumulation demands constantly and rapidly expanding markets and that this poses a problem once capitalism covers more or less the entire world.

The UN report suggests very strongly that undue restriction of "the consumption of the vast majority of society" through both national and international policies was an underlying source of the crisis:

> National economic systems which give rise to high levels of inequality pose problems, not only for social and political sustainability but also for economic sustainability, i.e. excessive increases of household and

public debt. They may also contribute to an insufficiency of global aggregate demand . . . the failure to provide adequate assistance to developing countries without inappropriate conditionalities may contribute to the global imbalances, another major contributing factor to this crisis.

(2009a, 44)

This diagnosis suggests that policies aimed at deunionizing and informalizing workforces and dismantling social security and welfare measures, which were put in place both by governments of various countries and by the IMF and World Bank about a decade after rates of profit started falling in the mid-1960s, meant that "sufficient purchasing power was not created in the new regime. The solution to the profitability crisis created a crisis of realisation" (Vakulabharanam 2009, 147). Demand not only for consumer goods but also for production inputs fell dramatically, resulting in millions of job losses around the world.

The third step in the process of accumulation—reinvestment in an expanded scale of production that will produce yet more surplus value—can also be interrupted. In volume 2 of *Capital*, Marx draws up schemas for the social reproduction of capital, and they comprise only two departments of capital: one producing means of production (Department I) and the other producing means of consumption (Department II). He subdivides the latter into IIa, which produces the necessary means of consumption, and IIb, which produces luxury items (1978, 478–487). However, it is significant that luxuries are mentioned only in simple reproduction, when the entire surplus value is consumed by capitalists and there is no accumulation; there is no mention of them when Marx looks at extended reproduction (when accumulation does take place), which is what defines a capitalist economy.

Marx defined labor as either "productive"—in the sense that it produces surplus value/profit—or "unproductive," in the sense that it does not produce a profit (Marx 1976, 1040–1041). However, this definition of productive labor is relevant only from the standpoint of individual capital: labor is or is not productive according to whether it does or does not produce profit for the individual capitalist. A problem arises when we look at production from the standpoint of the total social capital, as Marx realized when he considered the capitalist production of articles of luxury consumption. "This sort of productive labour produces use-values and objectifies itself in products that are destined only for unproductive consumption. In their reality, as articles, they have no *use-value* for the process of reproduction," and hence, if there is "disproportionate diversion of *productive labour* into unreproductive articles, it follows that the means of subsistence or production will not be reproduced in the necessary quantities," and capitalist accumulation will suffer (Marx 1976, 1045–1046). We could therefore make another distinction, one between "socially useful production," the output of which reenters production, and "socially wasteful production," which contributes nothing to social reproduction.

Articles of luxury consumption do not reenter production either as means of production or as necessary means of consumption for workers who engage in production. From the standpoint of the total social capital, they are a dead loss, even though the individual capitalists producing them make a profit. Militarism constitutes an even more important branch of socially wasteful production. Luxemburg came close to suggesting that military production belongs in a third department, since it constitutes the production of neither means of production nor consumption goods and services (2003, 439). Military products do not reenter production: at best they are wasted; at worst they destroy human life, the environment, and the products of human labor. We could therefore put capitalist enterprises engaged in military and luxury production into a Department III. The more surplus value is diverted into Department III, the less there will be for Departments I and II, resulting in a crisis due to a shortage of surplus value for accumulation. This was certainly one of the sources of the 2008 crisis.

Rising Inequality and Poverty

The impact of neoliberal policies on wages from the mid-1970s onward was striking.

> There is a secular decline in the labour share across the globe ranging from developed countries to major emerging economies of Latin America, Asia, as well as Eastern Europe, who have all shared the neoliberal policy guidelines. . . . Although this global trend is very striking, these numbers hide another important fact: the very high wages of the top 10% or even top 1% of the wage earners, among which the CEOs as well as other top managerial income earners are located, are also regarded as part of labour's share.
>
> (Onaran 2009, 172)

In the United States, "the chief executive officers of large US companies averaged $10.8 million in total compensation in 2006, more than
364 times the pay of the average US worker [compared with 42 times in
1980]. . . . As of February 2008, the average top executive received overall
total compensation of $18,813,697" (AFL-CIO 2008). If this is factored in,
the share of ordinary workers goes down even more. Indeed, there was an
absolute fall in wage rates: "In 2000–07, productivity growth in the US
was 2.2 percent, while median hourly wage growth was –0.1 percent" (Foster and McChesney 2009).

One consequence of this widening gap between rich and poor was rising
household indebtedness. Low interest rates and the pressure of funds needing a profitable outlet fueled the housing bubble that peaked in 2005. Bor-
rowers were approved for so-called subprime mortgages and were induced
to accept them by incentives such as low introductory rates, no demand
for evidence of ability to pay, reduced or no down payments, and interest-
only loans. This, in turn, increased the demand for housing and led to a
housing boom, with house prices rising rapidly. Heavy borrowing—in the
twenty-first century mainly against their homes—enabled working-class
households to maintain or raise their living standards despite falling or
stagnant wages. This, combined with cheap imports from China and other
developing countries, postponed the realization crisis for several years but
was clearly an unsustainable situation. The debts had to be repaid with
interest, which could only be done by taking on more debt. At some point,
the mountain of debt would have to collapse. That point was the subprime-
mortgage crisis. It broke in early 2007 but had been brewing since 2005,
when increased interest rates began to push down demand for houses, and
consequently house prices declined. Other developed countries also had
real-estate bubbles that collapsed.

The polarization of incomes created another problem: what was to be
done with the surplus value that accrued to capital? Restriction of demand
for both mass consumption and capital goods meant that investment in
expansion of production would exacerbate the realization problem. So a
much smaller portion of surplus value was reinvested in production, and
a much larger portion was paid out as dividends. Statistics provided by
the Bureau of Economic Analysis of the U.S. Department of Commerce
show that the average ratio of net dividends (dividends paid less dividends
received) to corporate profits in nonfinancial corporate business for the
four years from 1976 to 1979 (inclusive) was 20.6 percent, whereas the

average for the four years from 2004 to 2007 inclusive was 42.5 percent, more than double the ratio in the late 1970s. The average for the first two quarters of 2008 was 57 percent (Bureau of Economic Analysis 2008). The reduction of investment in production meant fewer jobs and rising unemployment, which in turn exacerbated the lack of demand for mass-consumption goods. At the other pole, higher dividends and executive pay added to the problem of excess liquidity. One outcome was the luxury consumption that so outraged American taxpayers when it continued after the AIG bailout (*The Gavel* 2008). But there is a limit to how much a small elite can consume, hence the flooding of financial markets.

The following chapters of this book examine the ways in which the labor movement (primarily in India but also elsewhere) attempted to oppose policies that push down wages and social security and suggests how improved labor strategies as well as a shift in government policies could aid recovery from the crisis, since "policy responses designed to ensure a robust and sustainable recovery from this crisis must address the question of how growing inequality of wealth and income might be reversed" (UN 2009a, 27).

Financial-Market Deregulation

"The financial sector is supposed to manage risk, allocate capital, and mobilize savings, all at the lowest possible transaction costs. In many countries, including the US, the financial system failed to perform these vital functions" (UN 2009a, 47). What accounts for this failure?

Investing in an asset—a mortgage, for example—is done on the expectation of returns that exceed the funds invested. Those returns do not exist at the time of investment, and their realization depends on what happens in the future: for example, that the person taking out the mortgage will keep paying the interest due on it. If that person defaults, then the house (which acts as collateral) can be repossessed, but its value will not include the interest. If there was a housing bubble when the mortgage was extended that subsequently bursts, even the original investment will not be retrieved. At this point, it becomes apparent that part of the price of the house, as well as interest still due on the mortgage, is merely "fictitious capital," as Marx called it. Although financial markets (which he called "the credit system") were relatively undeveloped in his time, and his language now seems archaic, many of Marx's observations could well apply to the contemporary world.

The risk created by this fictitious capital is multiplied when "all capital seems to be duplicated, and at some points triplicated, by the various ways in which the same capital, or even the same claim, appears in various hands in different guises" (Marx 1981, 601). This process was carried to inordinate lengths by the creation of asset-backed securities (ABSs), including mortgage-backed securities (MBSs), and derivatives, including collateralized debt obligations (CDOs).

> Several thousand mortgages may go into a single MBS and as many as 150 MBSS can be packaged into a single CDO. A CDO squared is a CDO created by using other CDO tranches as collateral. Higher power CDOS are particularly difficult vehicles because the many mortgages appear in more than one of the underlying CDOS. Synthetic CDOS use credit default swaps (or other credit instruments) as their collateral, [credit default swaps being] derivatives that allow one party to insure against loss from loan defaults by paying insurance fees to another party. However, since the value of credit default swaps hit $62 trillion in December 2007 while the maximum value of debt that might conceivably be insured through these derivatives was $5 trillion, it was evident that massive speculation, by banks and others, not just hedging, was taking place.
> (Crotty 2009, 128, 131)

While the banks sold many of these products to investors, large quantities remained with them. The invention of structured investment vehicles (SIVs) allowed banks to hold risky securities off their balance sheets with no capital required to support them: these formed part of a huge "shadow banking system," which included hedge funds and private equity funds, from which the banks were supposedly insulated but in fact were not. The purely fictitious character of most of the capital embodied in these derivatives is revealed by the fact that according to Bank for International Settlement estimates, contracts in the various derivatives markets amounted to $600 trillion at a time when global GDP was only around $50 trillion (Vakulabharanam 2009, 150). The whole system was rife with moral hazard, with incentives to make money by destabilizing it. The proliferation of subprime mortgages was a striking example. "Why were these toxic mortgages peddled, originated and distributed after being sliced and diced? Because everyone in this securitization food chain was making a fee and transferring the credit risk to someone else down this food chain" (Roubini 2008).

The bubble was inflated even more by dangerously high leverage ratios throughout the financial system. The risks posed by this were already evident in the 1998 collapse of Long Term Capital Management (LTCM), a hedge fund. With capital of around US$5 billion,

> LTCM borrowed US$125 billion from banks and securities firms to achieve a leverage of equity of 25:1. . . . In addition, LTCM used derivatives extensively. . . . In August [1998], it is estimated that derivatives contracts increased to as much as US$1500 billion. . . . But . . . following the Russian crisis of August 1998, investors stampeded to "quality," unloading high-risk, illiquid securities and moving into low-risk, liquid securities. . . . By mid-September, LTCM's equity had dropped to US$600 million.
>
> (Steinherr 2000, 88)

A Federal Reserve bailout was arranged because it was felt that a default by LTCM would have caused enormous losses to its creditors and other market participants and could have had negative consequences for several national economies, including that of the United States, reminding us that "what the speculating trader risks is social property, not his own" (Marx 1981, 570).

The lessons of LTCM's collapse were not learned; on the contrary, leverage rates were allowed to rise even higher:

> According to one recent estimate, the total leverage ratios (on- and off-book assets and exposure divided by tangible equity) for the two biggest US banks were 88:1 for Citibank and 134:1 for Bank of America. The bursting of the property bubble caused such ratios, which were already too high on the eve of the crisis, to explode as off-balance-sheet commitments and pre-arranged credit lines came home to roost.
>
> (Ferguson 2008)

Thus it is even more true today than in Marx's time that "the greater part of banker's capital is therefore purely fictitious" (Marx 1981, 600). As he pointed out, "in a system of production where the entire interconnection of the reproduction process rests on credit, a crisis must evidently break out if credit is suddenly withdrawn . . . in the form of a violent scramble for means of payment. At first glance, therefore, the entire crisis presents itself as simply a credit and monetary crisis," as it becomes clear that a

tremendous number of the "bills of exchange . . . represent purely fraudulent deals, which now come to light and explode; as well as unsuccessful
speculations conducted with borrowed capital, and finally commodity capitals that are either devalued or unsaleable, or returns that are never going
to come in" (1981, 621).

There were plenty of "purely fraudulent deals," and this, again, was not
something new: they had been implicated in the savings-and-loan debacle
of the 1980s.

> In the financial world we suffer from epidemics of accounting fraud
> when there is a strongly "criminogenic environment." Common factors
> that make an environment strongly criminogenic include non-regulation
> and non-prosecution, assets that lack readily verifiable market values,
> and "market" dynamics (that is, compensation systems) that create per-
> verse incentives. The vectors of such epidemics can include rating agen-
> cies, accounting firms, and appraisers. The symptoms include bubbles,
> but bubbles are also criminogenic. They aid accounting fraud by making
> it easy to create fictional income and hide real losses.
>
> (Black 2009, 80)

Again, the lessons were not learned. A criminogenic environment was
created, and no action was taken against the emerging epidemic of mortgage fraud despite the FBI warning against it as early as 2004. Another
example: the Securities and Exchange Commission was tipped off about
Bernard Madoff's fraudulent fund as early as 1992—and five times thereafter—but took no action until the crisis revealed that he had robbed count-
less victims (Clark 2009).

In his drafts for *Capital*, Marx refers to some "very influential parties of
the capitalist society" seeking to "subordinate the real movement of production and accumulation" to the accumulation of fictitious capital (Krätke
2001, 42),[1] and that is what was happening from the mid-1970s onward
as a result of the failure to regulate this sector in the United States. As
the UN report points out, given the effects of the failure of large banks
on the public, governments cannot commit themselves not to bail them
out (UN 2009a, 50), and given the connections between different financial
institutions, economic efficiency requires that they all should be regulated.
However, "while there is a clear case for government regulation of financial markets, governments often fail to adopt the appropriate regulatory

structures. . . . Even when appropriate regulations are adopted, they may not be effectively enforced. Regulators may be 'captured' by those they are supposed to regulate. . . . The design of regulatory institutions should take into account these risks" (UN 2009a, 51). In response to the allegation that tighter regulation might slow the pace of innovation, the report replies: "There is little evidence that the innovations in the financial sector in recent years have enhanced the overall performance of the economy, though to be sure it may have increased the profits of the sector. . . . These 'innovations' had a negative social return" (UN 2009a, 53).

Some of the elements of a new, comprehensive regulatory regime that have been suggested are increased transparency, the prohibition of over-the-counter trading of financial instruments, and insisting that derivatives be traded only on exchanges; extending regulatory oversight to the "shadow banking system," restricting or eliminating off-balance-sheet vehicles, and instituting a Financial Products Safety Commission to inspect, test, and monitor financial products, prohibiting those that are too risky or opaque; changing incentive structures to discourage excessive risk taking and short-sighted behavior, including severe penalties for CEOs and other operators whose institutions have to be bailed out; eliminating predatory lending; eliminating moral hazard and conflicts of interest such as those that arise when ratings agencies are paid by those whom they rate; restricting leverage ratios; countercyclical capital adequacy and provisioning requirements that call for an increase in capital as the rate of growth of the assets of a bank increases, to help dampen credit booms and ensure that a bank sets aside more funds as it lends more; capital-account management in developing countries to reduce risk and encourage development; and a no-tolerance policy toward financial centers that provide banking secrecy and facilitate tax evasion, with equal treatment for developed and developing countries (UN 2009a; Crotty and Epstein 2009). In order to regulate the financial sector effectively, central banks would have to be state owned and managed in the interest of the public.

While better regulation of financial markets is essential to prevent similar crises in future, it will not work by itself. The deregulation that enabled this massive accumulation of fictitious capital was part and parcel of the neoliberal policies that resulted in huge income disparities, and unless this problem is fixed, lack of demand will continue to restrict the expansion of productive investment. Marx suggests that "the credit system" has a dual character: on the one hand, it "accelerates the material development of the productive forces," but on the other, "it develops the motive of capitalist production, enrichment by the exploitation of others' labour, into the purest and most colossal system of gambling and swindling" (1981, 572). The precrisis regulatory regime facilitated the latter aspect, and a new one should facilitate the former. As significant players in financial markets, pension funds could play a role not only in demanding better regulation but also in following better guidelines themselves, instructing their fund managers to refrain from investing in fictitious capital and instead invest in productive capital that expands employment. It is immaterial where in the world employment is created, because in a globalized world, employment for Chinese workers is good for American workers and vice versa; what is important is investment in the expansion of socially useful production, jobs, and working-class incomes.

The Global Reserve System

The role of the U.S. dollar as the global reserve currency was one of the sources of the crisis and a key mechanism by means of which it was transmitted to developing countries. The crises of the 1990s and early 2000s in Asia, Russia, and Latin America had demonstrated how vulnerable the currencies of Second and Third World countries were to capital flight, and an understandable reaction was to build up foreign-exchange reserves in periods of booming capital inflows as a safeguard against such crises. Countries with export-oriented economies did the same, seeking to insure themselves against balance-of-payments crises and adverse movements in the terms of trade. "The fact that the only 'collective insurance' is IMF financial assistance, which is highly conditional, often imposing pro-cyclical policies during crises, reinforced the view that self-protection in the form of reserve accumulation was a better strategy"; consequently, reserve accumulations doubled between 1997 and 2007, and the bulk of them were in U.S. dollars (UN 2009a, 112).

The most spectacular example of this, and the one which best illustrates the hazards of this system, is the relationship that developed between China and the United States, or the growth of what has been dubbed "Chimerica." The massive buildup of U.S. debt was accompanied by the accumulation of huge Chinese export surpluses invested in dollar assets: "China surpassed Japan for the first time to become the largest holder of

US Treasury securities, with $652 billion in October 2008, compared with Japan's $573 billion. China's State Administration of Foreign Exchange (SAFE) held $370 billion in debt issued by the then struggling US mortgage giants Fannie Mae and Freddie Mac" (Fabre 2009, 301). This surplus was achieved by holding down wages: from 1995 to 2007, the per capita disposable income of Chinese urban residents rose by 1.6 times, while that of rural residents rose by only 1.2 times, compared with an increase in government fiscal revenue by 5.7 times (Fabre 2009, 306). The net result was a substantial weakening of global demand compared with what it might have been if incomes in China had risen more.

As Stiglitz (2009) explains, this situation created several problems:

> in a globalized economy, why should the entire financial system depend on the vagaries of what happens in America? The current system is not only bad for the world, it is bad for the United States, too. In effect, as other countries hold more dollar reserves, we are exporting T-bills rather than automobiles, and exporting T-bills doesn't create jobs. . . . Like it or not, out of this debacle a new and more stable global reserve system is likely to emerge, and for the world as a whole, as well as for the United States, this would be a good thing. It would lead to a more stable worldwide financial system and stronger global economic growth.

While the final shape of a "truly global reserve currency" (UN 2009a, 115) could take years to emerge, moves away from the dollar were already underway prior to the crisis, as we saw in chapter 2, and accelerated after it. By June 2009, China had set up currency swaps with several countries, including Argentina, Belarus, and Indonesia, and allowed institutions in Hong Kong to issue bonds denominated in renminbi, a first step toward deepening the domestic and international market for its currency (Reisen 2009). In May 2009, China, Japan, South Korea, and the Association of Southeast Asian Nations announced a US$120 billion regional currency stabilization fund; in June, the BRIC nations (Brazil, Russia, India, and China) met in Russia to discuss settlement currency options other than the U.S. dollar; and in July, when the IMF issued $150 billion in SDR (Special Drawing Rights) bonds, Russia and Brazil purchased $10 billion each, while China bought $50 billion (Brahm 2009).

Creating regional currencies for regional transactions was seen as another way to reduce dependence on the dollar. In April 2009, representatives of the Bolivarian Alliance for the People of America (ALBA), consisting of South American and Caribbean countries, signed a decree for a new ALBA currency, the sucre, which would not only be used for regional transactions but also function as a regional reserve and emergency fund (Fox 2009). Four Gulf Cooperation Council countries, Saudi Arabia, Bahrain, Kuwait, and Qatar, pushed ahead with earlier plans for a currency union by 2010 with assistance from the IMF (*Emirates Business* 2009). Meanwhile, the U.S. trade deficit fell by 3.6 percent in August 2009 and by 49.6 percent over the course of the previous year (Rappaport 2009), showing that a weaker dollar also had benefits for the U.S. economy.

Militarism

The Changing Role of Militarism

From the time of Marx and Engels, militarism and war were seen as having a negative effect on workers, but during the heyday of imperialism, militarism contributed to the expansion of capitalism (Luxemburg 2003, 446), and the destruction wrought by war, like crises, could reestablish conditions for accumulation. Luxemburg and other Marxists also suggested that the market for military production assured by the state could serve to boost employment temporarily, thus smoothing over business cycles. Initially, the huge expenditure on R&D in this department also spilled over into other industries, leading to major innovations that increased overall productivity, such as the use of computers (Kidron 1967). In an epoch when capital depended heavily on the state, militarism was seen as an asset even in Third World countries such as India, which absorbed smaller South Asian countries such as Sikkim and waged border wars with Pakistan and China. Here the struggle was for redivision of territory between capitalist states.

However, globalization makes it possible for capital to dispense with militarism. With capitalism encompassing the whole earth geographically, there is no necessity to spread it by using guns, bombs, and missiles. And with capital depending on porous rather than impervious borders for its expansion, productivity rather than backing by the military might of a particular nation-state ensures victory in the competitive struggle, and productivity depends on investments in infrastructure, civilian R&D, and the labor force. Far from being an asset, military expenditure becomes a drain on the economy.

The use of taxes to fund military expenditure has always been at the expense of social spending, and the consequences have been especially dire in the Third World. As a placard held up in demonstrations against the nuclear tests in India and Pakistan in 1998 commented sarcastically: "NO FOOD, NO WATER, NO JOBS, NO PROBLEM: WE HAVE THE BOMB!" Ten million dollars spent every day by India and Pakistan in patrolling the icy wastes of the Siachen glacier, where more soldiers have died of exposure than in combat, would have gone a long way toward assuring food, water, housing, health care, and education to the people of these countries (Bidwai and Vanaik 1999, x–xi). Millions of U.S. refugees left stranded in the wake of Hurricane Katrina in 2005 demonstrated that even in the richest country in the world, the government could not endlessly expand military spending without having a disastrous effect on infrastructure and the social sector (Lal 2005).

As R&D in armaments production became more specialized, there were fewer and fewer spinoffs to other industries, and it became a deduction from government investment in civilian research and infrastructure that could increase efficiency and productivity in capitalist production as a whole; as it became more capital intensive, its capacity to absorb labor and reduce unemployment also declined (Kidron 1967, 1970). In the United States in 1993–1994, 55.3 percent of government R&D funding went to defense (compared to 6 percent for Japan and 8.5 percent for Germany), and for every hundred dollars' worth of civilian capital assets created during 1989–1990, forty-eight dollars were spent on military assets (compared to four for Japan and sixteen for Germany). Furthermore, the cost-plus pricing of government armament purchases removed the incentive to increase productivity, which consequently lagged far behind that of Japan and Germany (Melman 2001, 110–114, 124–126).

The perverse consequences of cost-plus pricing—which means that the higher the cost, the bigger the profit—is highlighted in this devastating report:

> Operation Iraqi Freedom, it turns out . . . was an invasion of the federal budget, and no occupying force in history has ever been this efficient. . . .
> Is it really possible to bilk American taxpayers for repainted forklifts

stolen from Iraqi Airways and claim that you were just following orders? It is, when your commander in chief is George W. Bush. . . . According to the most reliable estimates, we have doled out more than $500 billion for the war, as well as $44 billion for the Iraqi reconstruction effort. And what did America's contractors give us for that money? They built big steaming shit piles, set brand-new trucks on fire, drove back and forth across the desert for no reason at all and dumped bags of nails in ditches.

(Taibbi 2007)

By 1990, the value of the weapons, equipment, and factories devoted to the Department of Defense was 83 percent of the value of all the plants and equipment in U.S. manufacturing. In the four decades between 1947 and 1987, the expenditure of the Department of Defense would have been enough to replace and modernize the entire capital stock of the United States; instead, the failure to modernize resulted in its manufacturing base being decimated by the turn of the twenty-first century (Johnson 2008). This, not globalization, was the primary cause of the decline of the U.S. economy. As militarism undermined the U.S. economy, its productivity fell behind that of other First World countries such as Japan and Germany, and production was shifted to Third World countries where, on the contrary, productivity had been boosted by globalization. By diverting resources from socially useful production, military spending slowed economic growth and reduced employment in the United States.

The "permanent arms economy" thesis (Kidron 1967) suggested that military spending, by reducing the reinvestment of surplus value, slows down the tendency for the organic composition of capital to rise and the rate of profit to fall and therefore postpones crises. But carried to its logical conclusion, this argument suggests that consumption of the entire surplus value in socially wasteful production would enable capitalism to go on forever, whereas of course this would mean a complete cessation of accumulation in Departments I and II—and thus the ultimate crisis! The fallacy in the notion of "military Keynesianism," a policy going back to the cold war, is that it treats "military output as an ordinary economic product, even though it makes no contribution to either production or consumption," whereas, in reality, "military industries crowd out the civilian economy and lead to severe economic weaknesses. Devotion to military Keynesianism is, in fact, a form of slow economic suicide" (Johnson 2008).

A State Within a State

The state is the buyer of the products of the arms industry, and

> the state has only taxes and borrowed funds at its disposal, which gives
> rise to a growing national debt, which in turn can be financed and paid
> off only through taxes. . . . In international trade too it is governments
> who buy the weapons, paying for them out of taxes. . . . It is certainly
> true that the arms industry makes profits and accumulates capital and
> appears in no way different from other businesses. But its profits and
> new investments derive from . . . state expenditures, which are drawn
> from a part of the realized value and surplus value of other capitals.
>
> (Mattick 1981, 215)

Thus militarism constitutes not only an *indirect* deduction from capitalist
accumulation by competing with state expenditures on infrastructure, the
social sector, and civilian R&D, but it is also a *direct* deduction from capitalist accumulation because it is financed by taxes on profits and wages. It is
"economically parasitic," as Melman called it, and as it grows, socially useful production shrinks.

How can this happen in a nominally democratic state? According to
Melman, "the state-management has, in fact, become a para-state, a state
within a state" (2008, 3). In this "military state capitalism, the . . . economy
is largely regulated by a system of subsidies. . . . In the case of military
state capitalism the subsidy is largely rendered on behalf of economically
parasitic activity, that yields no return to society" (2008, 6). Allowing this
military state within a state to expand, to the detriment of the economy and
outside the scrutiny or control of the public, involves an assault on democracy (Johnson 2007). The massive escalation of military spending entailed
by the "global war on terror" played a major role in creating the conditions
for the crisis of 2008, pushing U.S. military expenditures ($623 billion) up
to more than the military expenditures of the rest of the world put together
($500 billion) (GlobalSecurity.org 2007). If one adds military spending not
included in the defense budget, "This brings US spending for its military
establishment during the current fiscal year (2008), conservatively calculated, to at least $1.1 trillion" (Johnson 2008).

Militarism constituted a drain on the rest of the world economy in
two ways. One was the dollar mechanism discussed above: since other

countries used the U.S. dollar as their reserve currency, their dollar deposits, created by withdrawing resources from their own economies, subsidized U.S. military expenditures. The other mechanism was their own military expenditures. In India, pursuit of nuclear weaponization resulted in a significant expansion of military budgets. The Indo-U.S. nuclear deal signed in July 2007 was seen by antinuclear activists as an attempt to obtain international endorsement of India's status as a nuclear-weapons state and to accelerate the pace of nuclear weaponization by using imported nuclear fuel for the production of nuclear power, thus releasing domestically produced nuclear fuel for the production of weapons (Abolition 2000 2007, 52). In 2009, India launched a $2.9 billion nuclear submarine and had plans to build four more, buy two more from Russia, and buy six from France (GlobalSecurity.org 2009; Kakatkar 2009). Enormous resources poured into military production constituted a deduction not only from the social sector but also from investments in infrastructure and civilian R&D, which would have made the economy more productive.

Militarism is a hangover from the twentieth century, an anomaly in a globalized world. But there are immensely powerful interests opposing any reduction in military spending, such as those involved in the military-industrial complex in various countries, the arms trade, and imperialist and nationalist forces that seek to expand their power and sphere of influence within and beyond their national territory. This is why opposition to war and military spending has to be a crucially important element of working-class struggle. Clara Zetkin ended her speech at a conference of the Socialist International in 1912 by declaring "war on war" (*Krieg dem Krieg*), and in 1915 she helped to organize the International Women's Peace Conference in Switzerland, attended by women from countries at war with each other as well as women from neutral ones. The conference set up the Women's International League for Peace and Freedom, the oldest peace organization still in existence, which stands for total and universal disarmament. Other prominent socialists, including Lenin, Luxemburg, and Karl Liebknecht, broke with the Socialist International because its constituent parties supported their bourgeois nation-states in World War I.

Following World War II, a wide array of antinuclear action groups were formed, including those of the *hibakusha* (survivors of the atomic bombs dropped on Hiroshima and Nagasaki), the Campaign for Nuclear Disarmament, the Greenham Common Women's Peace Camp, the Plowshares

Movement, and many others, which came together to form Abolition 2000, a network of over two thousand organizations in more than ninety countries working for a global treaty to eliminate nuclear weapons. There is a diverse and vibrant global movement against war and militarism. Its connection with the labor movement is weaker and less explicit than in Clara Zetkin's time, but this is changing. For example, U.S. Labor Against the War, with 184 affiliates in August 2009, ran an active campaign based on international solidarity to end the wars in Iraq and Afghanistan and reorient foreign policy, pointing out also the detrimental effects of militarism on the U.S. economy.

In India, for many decades the issue of militarism was taken up only by a tiny section of the labor movement. Recognition of the danger posed to the people of both India and Pakistan by the hot-cold war between them resulted in activists setting up the Pakistan-India People's Forum for Peace and Democracy in 1994, but it was only the dire threat of nuclear war, following the Indian and Pakistani nuclear tests in May 1998, that galvanized large sections of people in both countries, including union activists, to form the broad-based Coalition for Nuclear Disarmament and Peace in India and the Pakistan Peace Coalition in Pakistan. Employees' unions such as the Nicholas Employees' Union organized discussions on the nuclear tests for their activists, helping to create a consensus against nuclear weaponization. The antiwar movement resulted in popular support for peace by the majority of people in both countries (Bidwai 2004). The Blue Star Workers' Union, as well as some women's groups, were active in creating and maintaining crossborder contacts with Pakistani counterparts, issuing joint statements of solidarity at times when war fever was whipped up in both countries, but these actions were on a relatively small scale.

Obstacles to Demilitarization

A major obstacle to demilitarization is the assumption that militarism makes a nation strong. This is reflected, above all, in the fact that the five permanent members of the UN Security Council (the P5—the United States, Russia, Britain, France, and China) are all nuclear-weapons states and have veto powers, implying that the power derived from nuclear weapons gives a state the right to blackmail the rest of the world into going along with its agenda. This situation urgently needs to be changed. At least five non-nuclear-weapons states should be added to the permanent members, and no state should have veto powers.

A second obstacle is the argument that armaments are needed for "defense." The most bizarre instance is the doctrine of nuclear deterrence, according to which nuclear weapons are needed by a state because fear of retaliation by it would deter another state from attacking it with nuclear weapons. Nuclear weapons, including so-called tactical weapons and depleted uranium weapons, are by their nature weapons of mass destruction, killing and injuring civilians not only in the present but far into the future. It should be obvious that using them under any circumstances whatsoever would be immoral. As for their legality, the International Court of Justice made the unanimous decision that "a threat or use of nuclear weapons should also be compatible with the requirements of the international law applicable in armed conflict particularly those of the principles and rules of international humanitarian law" (ICJ 1996), which prohibits attacks on civilians. This implies, without explicitly stating, that the use of nuclear weapons is always unlawful. Only criminal states would threaten to attack innocent civilians of another state with nuclear weapons in retaliation for a nuclear attack on their own civilians, just as only criminals would threaten to kill another person's baby in retaliation for that person killing their own baby. In a moral universe where the killing of innocents is unlawful, nuclear weapons, even for "deterrence," would certainly be banned.

However in today's world, it is not impossible that nuclear deterrence works in some cases, just as among gangsters the threat to kill a rival's baby if he kills one's own baby might conceivably deter the rival from committing that heinous crime. This is the primary reason why nonproliferation has failed: nation-states that fear nuclear attack if a hostile state has nuclear weapons seek to develop their own weapons to "deter" such an attack. Hence, as the Declaration of the International Meeting of the 2009 World Conference Against Atomic and Hydrogen Bombs in Hiroshima argued: "The elimination of nuclear weapons is the only way to prevent further proliferation." The declaration welcomed President Obama's statement that the United States would seek the peace and security of a world without nuclear weapons and welcomed the agreement by U.S. and Russian leaders on the reduction of strategic nuclear weapons, but it also called for much more: the early ratification and entry into force of the Comprehensive Test-Ban Treaty (CTBT), which would ban nuclear tests and thus the development of new weapons; the conclusion of a verifiable Fissile

Material Cutoff Treaty (FMCT), which would ban the production of fissile material that could be used for nuclear weapons or explosions; the renunciation of the first use of nuclear weapons; and a ban on the use or threat to use nuclear weapons against states lacking nuclear weapons. "These partial and specific measures of nuclear disarmament should be . . . explicitly linked with the goal of the elimination of nuclear weapons" (World Conference Against A & H Bombs 2009).

The monitoring regime for the CTBT and FMCT, which should apply equally to states with nuclear weapons (including Israel, India, Pakistan, and North Korea as well as the P5) and states without nuclear weapons, would prepare the way for a total elimination of nuclear weapons (including depleted-uranium weapons). President Obama broke with the patently racist assumption that some nation-states have the right to possess nuclear weapons while others have not; this change in U.S. attitude, along with the adoption of Resolution 1887 by the UN Security Council on September 24, 2009, which resolved "to create the conditions for a world without nuclear weapons" (UN 2009b), could provide a window of opportunity for the agenda of global nuclear disarmament. If this is combined with the abolition of chemical and biological weapons, along with a monitoring regime to ensure that these weapons of mass destruction are not produced anywhere in the world; the abolition of land mines and cluster bombs, which likewise harm mainly civilians; the adoption of a UN Agreement to Curb the International Flow of Illicit Small Arms, thus preventing arms producers and traders from making profits by selling arms to both sides in a conflict; the acceptance that the invasion and occupation of other countries constitutes aggression; and agreement that both internal and international disputes should be resolved by negotiation rather than war, significant steps toward demilitarization will have been achieved.

The nuclear-power agenda creates problems, however, and should be reconsidered. It received a boost both from the outcry against global warming and from rising oil prices, yet it has enormous problems of its own, quite apart from the danger that it could be used as a cover for developing nuclear weapons. The production process is by no means carbon neutral, it is extremely hazardous to workers and local residents, and its negative effects on the environment through the creation of nuclear waste that remains radioactive for hundreds of thousands of years is no less damaging than the production of greenhouse gases. Costwise too, nuclear power is prohibitively expensive if all the subsidies are taken into account, and it would get more expensive with time. The same investment in achieving greater energy efficiency and decentralized production using safe and renewable sources of energy (solar, wind, ocean wave, small hydro) would yield far better results than nuclear energy, and this is what the National Alliance of Antinuclear Movements (NAAM) in India called for in a rally on October 2, 2009. In addition to demanding an end to India's nuclear-weaponization program, NAAM stated: "Nuclear energy is not cheap, safe, clean or sustainable. It also does not offer a solution to our energy problems" (NAAM 2009). A truly democratic response by policymakers to popular movements opposing uranium mining and nuclear-power plants should rule out even the so-called peaceful uses of nuclear energy, except for medical treatment.

Finally, what makes the transfer of resources out of military production more difficult to implement from the standpoint of workers and governments, especially in countries that depend heavily on armaments production, is that the immediate effect is large-scale job losses. The end of the cold war resulted in 150,000 jobs lost in Britain between 1990 and 1992–1993 and an overall reduction in defense employment of 47 percent compared to 1980 (Grimshaw 1997). Even in countries that do not produce military hardware on a large scale, the armed forces may offer employment to many people from the poorer sections of the population, as in India. Achieving the shift of human and other resources from military to socially useful production without leading to large-scale unemployment is a challenge that was confronted in a creative manner in Lucas Aerospace, whose main products were fighter planes. When the workforce was faced with large-scale redundancies in 1976, they not only formed a Combine Committee to fight the redundancies but also came up with a corporate plan suggesting 150 socially useful products that could be made with their existing machinery and skills, including kidney machines, a life-support system to keep heart patients alive until they reached the hospital, and a range of energy-saving and nonpolluting power-generation products (Cooley 1980, 67–74; Wainwright and Elliot 1982; Workers' Solidarity Movement 1988).

This demonstration that the full range of skills of the workforce could be redeployed from military to socially useful production led to the establishment of the Arms Conversion Project, which by the mid-1990s had contacts worldwide (Melicharova 2000). Conversion could also be used to transform auto plants "into producers of solar panels, windmills, electricity-producing buoys, highspeed trains, electric buses and cars, etc." (Cooke

2009b), while demobilized soldiers could be employed to build railways and erect solar panels and windmills. Countries that now export military hardware, death, and destruction could instead export socially useful technology, goods, and services. The entire conversion could be carried out without a loss of jobs. Indeed, ending the diversion of resources to military spending would enable huge investments in upgrading infrastructure, capital stock, and the labor force, simultaneously creating employment and implementing social-welfare programs. The enormous quantity of greenhouse gases created by militarism could be replaced by energy-efficient and green technologies. In the wake of the global crisis of 2008, this is not only a moral imperative but also an economic compulsion.

Facilitating a Robust Recovery

Globalization was not the cause of the crisis; on the contrary, it offers a crucially important means of overcoming the crisis by making it possible to clear away the toxic legacy of a period dominated by militaristic imperialism and nationalism. However, the dominant model of globalization imposed on the world was implicated in the meltdown and urgently needs to be changed. The crisis was a wake-up call, alerting citizens of the world to the multiple emergencies facing them. Failure to respond adequately could have catastrophic consequences. But a sufficiently vigorous corrective response would ensure a safer, fairer, more peaceful, democratic, sustainable, and productive world.

[4]

Capital, the State, and Trade Union Rights

Globalization, Workers' Rights, and the Crisis

In India, as in most other countries, there is a widespread belief that globalization deprives the state of the power to protect workers' rights. There is also an assumption that prior to globalization, labor was in a much stronger position. These ideas need to be scrutinized carefully, both in the particular case of India and more generally. In India, attacks on labor rights predated globalization and were rooted in ideologies hostile to labor. In other countries, governments used the excuse of increased competition resulting from globalization to justify antilabor policies. Each government justified its attacks on workers' rights by referring to attacks carried out by others, and often these arguments were based on a misrepresentation of the actual situation in other countries.

In the wake of the crisis, it becomes all the more urgent to examine these arguments critically. If attacks on trade union rights and the consequent reduction in working-class incomes were partly responsible for the crisis, continuing or intensifying these attacks could only deepen it. Conversely, a sustainable recovery would be aided immensely by a reversal of antilabor policies. But is this a realistic prospect in a globalized world?

Unions and the Labor Movement

Workers' organizations that bargain collectively with employers over employment conditions—(trade) unions—have been the most universal and stable form of workers' mass organization. However, they take a wide variety of forms, have not always confined themselves to wage issues, and are not the only component of the labor movement.

Workers' Unions

Unions were formed in India for the same reason that they were formed everywhere else: "The only social power of the workmen is their number. The force of numbers is, however, broken by disunion. The disunion of the workmen is created and perpetuated by their *unavoidable competition amongst themselves*. Trade unions sprang up from the *spontaneous* attempts of workmen at removing or at least checking that competition" (Marx 1974c, 91). In Britain, secret associations of workers followed the establishment of modern industry, and when workers "received in 1824 the right of free association, these combinations were very soon spread over all England and attained great power" (Engels 1975, 504).

What is the role of unions? According to Marx, the immediate object of trade unions was confined to questions of wages and hours of work, but, "on the other hand, unconsciously to themselves, the trade unions were forming *centres of organization* of the working class" (Marx 1974c, 91). In the future, he felt, "they must look carefully after the interests of the worst paid trades, such as the agricultural labourers, rendered powerless by exceptional circumstances. They must convince the world at large that their efforts, far from being narrow and selfish, aim at the emancipation of the downtrodden millions" (Marx 1974c, 92).

However, alongside this optimistic vision of what unions could be, Marx also had a less positive assessment:

> Trades Unions work well as centres of resistance against the encroach-ments of capital. They fail partially from an injudicious use of their power. They fail generally from limiting themselves to a guerilla war against the effects of the existing system, instead of simultaneously trying

to change it, instead of using their organized forces as a lever for the final emancipation of the working class, that is to say, the ultimate abolition of the wages system.

(Marx 1987, 95)

While it is possible to envisage unionism becoming more and more inclusive, both in terms of its membership and in terms of the issues it takes up, as recommended in the first vision, it is difficult to imagine the entire membership taking up the objective of abolishing wage labor itself, although a few workers certainly have entertained this dream (cf., Thompson 1966, 912). Thus the latter evaluation of unions suggests that a separate political organization of the working class must supplement unionism; it also implies that trade unions could play a conservative role in circumstances where revolutionary change is possible.

This ambivalence toward unions has plagued Marxists ever since (Hyman 1971). Evidence can be provided supporting both views of unions: as agents of social transformation in some situations and agents of conservatism in others. However, Marx's first approach is more compatible with the theoretical standpoint of this study, which sees the development of the working class as a learning process.

There is plenty of evidence in working-class history of the extension of unionism to wider layers of the working class as well as the adoption of new demands and goals. In Britain, one of the earliest lessons to be learned was that unions of separate trades could be defeated, leading to attempts to form a General Union of All Trades in 1825 (Thompson 1966, 855). When unions of unskilled workers were formed, Engels commented that "these new Trades Unions of unskilled men and women are totally different from the old organisations of the working-class aristocracy and cannot fall into the same conservative ways" (Engels 1987, 149). In the United States, when Taylorism undermined the power of the craft workers and their control over work from World War I onward, new forms of organization developed with new demands: unions comprising skilled, unskilled, and clerical workers in their membership; trades councils coordinating the struggles of different trades; and demands for the regulation of layoff and recall by seniority. The industrial unions of the 1930s institutionalized this rule yet were willing to modify it so that black workers, who had gotten jobs for the first time during World War II, should not be dismissed selectively after the war. Organizing the unemployed and keeping them in the union was another innovation (Montgomery 1979).

Making union membership more inclusive was linked to the broadening of union goals. The "aristocratic and exclusive craft unions" in Britain (Drake 1984, 3) and some affiliates of the American Federation of Labor in the United States (Kennedy 1981, 24) excluded women from the union as well as the occupation. In both countries, women were forced to organize separately, forming a Women's Trade Union League (WTUL) in Britain in 1874, followed by a WTUL in the United States in 1903 and the National Federation of Women Workers in Britain in 1906 (Drake 1984, 11; Kennedy 1981, 47; Boston 1980, 60). Apart from opposing discrimination against black workers and women, the American WTUL put forward demands for day-care centers for children of women workers and for low-rent housing; when the Congress of Industrial Organizations was formed in 1937 with the backing of two powerful unions with largely female memberships, it demanded equal-pay legislation and maternity benefits (Kennedy 1981, 162, 174). In Britain in the 1890s, the WTUL played a leading role in pushing through legislation to help homeworkers and others who had difficulty building unions (Lewenhak 1977, 81).

More recently, equal opportunities in employment has widely been accepted as a union goal (Ball 1990). Women's activism within unions has been accompanied by the extension of union goals to encompass broader feminist issues—for example, not only sexual harassment in the workplace but also more general violence against women—as well as other antidiscrimination and equality issues such as disability, race and racism, and sexual orientation and homophobia, thus enabling union activists to link up with social movements outside the union (Briskin 1993; Leah 1993; Cunnison and Stageman 1993).

A high rate of participation of women in unions has been associated with the linking of workplace, family, and community concerns, as in the case of the Food and Canning Workers' Union in South Africa (Berger 1992, 209) and the Chhattisgarh Mines Shramik Sangh in India (Hensman 2002, 103), leading to the development of what has sometimes been called "social-movement unionism" (Moody 1997, 201–226; Waterman 2001, 12–13). In Brazil, a large-scale introduction of women into the labor force was followed by a "broadening of trade union struggle to encompass basic aspects of citizens' rights, extending their actions from the factory floor to the community level, demanding better healthcare and education facilities, as well as safer and more secure living conditions" (Ramalho 2007, 101–102). This type of unionism in the Third World shares certain goals with European welfare unionism, where "unions rely on social mobilisation to apply pressure on the state to pass laws or implement social policies to benefit the working class as a whole," and social-partner unionism, where unions "participate on national tripartite bodies that hammer out labour and social welfare issues through negotiations" (Phelan 2007a, 12).

Unions confronting a repressive state or imperialist domination have at times been a strong oppositional force. From the late 1970s, unions in Brazil, where they were confronted by a military dictatorship, and in South Africa, where the apartheid state outlawed black unions, played an important role in the struggle for democratic rights (Seidman 1994, 15, 37–38). In both cases, the struggle was also one against institutionalized racism. In South Africa, Africans did not have the vote, and in Brazil, illiterates (mainly nonwhite people) were denied the vote as late as 1962, and other forms of discrimination persisted (Seidman 1994, 22–23). In Korea, unions were part of the independence movement against Japanese rule (Jang 1989, 28–29), and in Iran, a strike of the Teheran Oil Refinery Workers in October 1978 played a decisive role in overthrowing the U.S.-backed regime of the Shah (Bayat 1987, 60–81).[1] In both Korea and Iran, the new regimes also repressed unions (Jang 1989; Bayat 1987), while in South Africa and Brazil, many unionists were disappointed by the African National Congress and Partido dos Trabalhadores (Workers' Party) regimes they had helped to bring in, as they realized that their struggle was by no means over.[2]

Another set of issues concerns control over the labor process: unions pushing forward the "frontier of control" between workers and management (Goodrich 1975). In the United States, the control that craft workers originally had over working practices and the pace of their work was broken over a period of decades in the latter part of the nineteenth century. "Taylorism" or "scientific management" succeeded partially in transferring to management the specialized knowledge that workers had acquired, but it was only with mechanized, assembly-line production, adopted by Ford, that management acquired decisive control over the labor process and the pace of work. The need for high-wage skilled workers was reduced dramatically, and the mass-production semiskilled worker became the norm. In the hands of capital, technology became a powerful means to control workers and the labor process (Braverman 1964), and strategies by workers to make work more tolerable could, paradoxically, strengthen this control (Burawoy 1979). But the new organization of the labor process linked the entire plant's workforce and engendered new forms of struggle: a go-slow, work-to-rule, or minor act of sabotage by a few workers could have a major effect on production; a stoppage at a crucial part of the line could bring the entire plant to a halt. For the new industrial unions, the pace of work and number of workers on a line were still subject to collective bargaining (Edwards 1979).

In the 1980s, there were struggles over the introduction of new technology, and although in Britain the craft unions in the printing industry opposed computer typesetting, photocomposition, and offset printing and were decisively defeated, in the Netherlands unions were able to negotiate agreements on consultation, retraining, and redeployment that gave them some control over the introduction of new technology and its effects on the workforce (Leisink 1993). Health and safety in the workplace also became an important bargaining issue (Banaji and Hensman 1990, 147–148).

Serge Mallet saw the demand for self-management as emanating from a new working class created by continuous-flow technology in oil refineries and chemical plants (Mallet 1975), but this thesis has been questioned from two angles. On the one hand, a study of oil refineries in France and Britain owned by the same company showed that bargaining relationships and the national union culture could be as important as technology or even more so, since the majority of French workers felt that there should be workers' control over financial budgeting and investment decisions, whereas the majority of British workers did not (Gallie 1978, 130). On the other hand, in certain circumstances, demands for self-management might come from workers who did not fit the description of a "new" working class. What is undeniable, however, is that unions have raised demands for control not just over company financial decisions but even over the choice of products, as in the movement for socially useful production (Wainwright and Elliot 1982; Cooley 1985).

It appears, then, that unions can adopt and have adopted a variety of goals: improving workers' lives outside the workplace (through higher wages, shorter working hours, social housing, health care, education and welfare benefits) or in the workplace (through better working conditions and more control over work); democratizing the workplace, society, and state; making work a source of satisfaction for workers; or orienting production toward the satisfaction of need. A combination of these agendas corresponds to Marx's description of communist goals (Marx 1974a, 347) and shows that unions *can* play a revolutionary role. But often their orientation is conservative, seeking to preserve the status quo, and in some cases, especially where union leaderships have links with the state, they may even play a reactionary role: for example, Lenin blamed the "stratum of workers-turned-bourgeois, or the labour aristocracy, who are quite philistine in their mode of life, in the size of their earnings and in their entire outlook . . . *agents of the bourgeoisie in the working-class* movement" (Lenin 1964, 194) for rallying workers behind their respective bourgeoisies during World War I.

Workers' Cooperatives

Mass organizations of workers have also taken the form of cooperatives. They appeared as early as unions, and some have been relatively stable. Marx's assessment of cooperatives, like his evaluation of unions, is ambivalent. On the one hand, he declared that "the value of these great social experiments cannot be overrated" and acknowledged "the cooperative movement as one of the transforming forces of the present society based upon class antagonism. Its great merit is to practically show, that the present pauperizing and despotic system of the *subordination of labour* to capital can be superseded by the republican and beneficent system of *the association of free and equal producers*" (Marx 1974c, 79, 90). Yet in the same breath he warned that

> restricted, however, to the dwarfish forms into which individual wage slaves can elaborate it by their private efforts, the cooperative system will never transform capitalist society. To convert social production into one large and harmonious system of free and cooperative labour, *general social changes* are wanted, *changes of the general conditions of society*, never to be realized save by the transfer of the organized forces of society, viz., the state power, from capitalists and landlords to the producers themselves.
>
> (Marx 1974c, 90)

These two assessments can both be supported by examples. Cooperatives in a capitalist society are subject to the vagaries of the market and may be forced to cut pay or downsize in order not to go out of business—and they may in the end go bankrupt anyway. Yet this does not negate their value as experiments or their transformative potential. Marx was right that state support is essential if cooperatives are to prosper and expand their coverage, as they have in Spain and Italy (Holmström 1989, 1993). On the other hand, state support in a centrally planned economy does not automatically solve all problems, as the case of Yugoslavia demonstrated (Comisso 1979; cit. Holmström 1989, 12). The positive and negative views of workers' cooperatives go with two different models of revolution. The first model is a long, drawn-out process of social change that takes place as the result of workers reflecting upon and learning from their own activity, experience, successes, and failures; the other sees a more cataclysmic overthrow of capitalist state power. Again, this study sides with the former approach.

In Britain, there was a common impression that "co-operatives do not want adversary collective bargaining inside their businesses as they see it as destructive and trade unions do not want co-operatives as they are a waste of time, self-exploiting and/or distracting obstacles," yet "many co-operatives insist on trade union membership," and "several unions, particularly the Transport and General Workers' Union, have helped form co-operatives" (McMonnies 1984, 2). It is true that when traditional trade unionism meets traditional cooperative principles—as in the case of Unilever's Synthetic Resins Ltd., in Merseyside, which was taken over by the Scott Bader Commonwealth—conflicts can occur, and this is consistent with the general opposition to workers' participation in management within the British trade union movement (McMonnies 1984). But such opposition ignores the fact that "collective bargaining itself is a form of participation in management, a 'collaboration' in certain specific if limited areas" covered by the agreement, and therefore, "what is at issue is not the principle of 'participation' (trade unions already 'participate') but the way in which that participation is exercised" (Radice 1972; cit. Purcell and Smith 1979, 160; see also Melman 2001).

While works councils, worker-directors on company boards, and other forms of codetermination have rarely given workers the power to challenge major decisions of the company or get alternative workers' plans accepted, it has at least enabled unions to bargain with more knowledge of company plans for investment and modernization (Banaji and Hensman 1990, 187–193). Thus traditional collective bargaining, codetermination, and workers' cooperatives can be seen not as being in opposition to one another but as being on a continuum, with the area open for workers' control expanding progressively (cf. Purcell and Smith 1979). In contrast with Britain, cooperatives in Italy from the mid-nineteenth century onward had close links with trade unions and local trades councils (Holmström 1989, 23). In Spain, "ideas of self-management and workers' control have a long history, going back to the political and trade union movements of the nineteenth century," and these ideas "affected a small but important minority of trade union officials" (Holmström 1993, 21, 137).

Other Components of the Labor Movement

In addition to unions and cooperatives, there are other working-class organizations that are less common or stable: strike committees; workers' councils; neighborhood committees; organizations consisting of women workers (e.g., the Self-Employed Women's Association), working-class housewives (e.g., Women Against Pit Closures), or both (e.g., the Korean Women Workers' Associations United); mutual-aid groups; consumer cooperatives; housing cooperatives; and many others. Finally, there are groups or individuals who can be seen as providing services to working-class organizations even if they are themselves middle class or predominantly so, by doing research and providing information; running bulletins, newsletters, or newspapers; or organizing public support for workers' struggles (Labor Research Department, International Centre for Trade Union Rights, etc.). All these can be seen as part of the labor movement.

The Trade Union Movement in India

Labor Legislation Under Colonialism and After Independence

The formation of a proletariat in Marx's sense took off in India in the 1850s, with the building of the railways, the beginnings of the modern textile industry, and the growth of plantations. The first form of worker resistance "was to the process of proletarianization itself; it was resistance in the form of refusal to work at all . . . or refusal to work beyond certain amounts, and departure (exit) from the work-site" (Kerr 1997, 170).

Consequently in India, as in Britain, the first labor legislation enacted by the colonial government was directed against workers: the Workmen's Breach of Contract Act (1859) and the Employees and Workmen (Disputes) Act (1860) rendered workers punishable if they walked out of a job during the period of contract; the Transport of Native Labourers Act (1863) of Bengal, amended in 1865, gave plantation owners the power to arrest and punish indentured plantation workers for desertion or indolence (D'Souza 1996, 108). The operation of these laws in the plantations was especially brutal, with planters using their powers to flog workers who tried to resist or escape intolerable conditions. Worker mortality rates were extremely high. It was always workers who were punished, even if employers had committed a prior breach of contract by failing to pay the agreed wages or supply the agreed benefits, miserable as they were (Mohapatra 1998).

This legislation did not prevent conflict, which erupted in numerous strikes, petitions to the government, and occasional riots and violence (Kerr 1997, 176–184). Legislation to restrict the unlimited power of employers can partly be explained as a response on the part of the colonial government to the resistance of workers, which was backed by support from social reformers and philanthropists (Sen 1979; Gupte 1981). However, the workers also received support from unlikely allies: the Lancashire mill owners, who felt themselves at a disadvantage compared to their Indian counterparts. The cotton-textile industry, begun in the 1850s by various business groups in Bombay, was expanding rapidly, and

> the demand for the produce of these Anglo-Indian mills is increasing; cheapness of labour (two pence per day), warmth of climate, cotton from contiguous fields grown at a rate varying from five to six farthings per pound, abundance of coal, to which may now be added increasing means of irrigation, facilities of transit, and available capital, all tend to promote economical production, and to enhance profits; so that even the present generation may witness the Lancashire manufacturer beaten by his Hindu competitor.
>
> (Martin 1862, 280–282; cit. Morris 1965, 25)

In an effort to wipe out this "decisive competitive edge . . . English mill-owners applied pressure on the British government to introduce measures in India comparable to those adopted in Britain," resulting in the passage of the first Indian Factories Act of 1881 (D'Souza 1996, 109), which prohibited the employment of children under the age of seven and restricted the hours of child workers.

In response to continuing struggles over wages and working hours in a situation of labor shortage, the Factories Act was amended several times. The Factories Act of 1891 limited the working hours of women to eleven per day and required all workers to be given a holiday on Sunday unless there was another holiday in the week. The working hours of men were not limited, but agitation for shorter hours continued. Serious unrest among the workers led to riots in 1905. A factory commission was established in 1908 to investigate the long hours, and its recommendations formed the basis for the Factories Act of 1911, which restricted the hours of men to twelve per day. Women's hours continued to be eleven per day, and the employment of women between 7:00 p.m. and 5:30 a.m. was prohibited. In the general strike of January 1920, there was once again a call for shorter hours, and in the Factories Act of 1922, the hours for men were made equal to those for women (Morris 1965, 67, 103–106, 180–181).

The Children (Pledging of Labour) Act (1933) stated that any agreement to pledge the labor of children was void and parents or guardians and employers entering into such agreements would be penalized. However, this practice has continued into the twenty-first century. The Employment of Children Act (1938) prohibited the employment of children under the age of fourteen in hazardous occupations, and this was updated by the Child Labour (Prohibition and Regulation) Act (1986). But even the latter did not prohibit child labor as such and did not apply to informal employment, where children continued to be employed in extremely hazardous occupations. After gaining independence, article 23 of the Indian constitution prohibited debt bondage and other forms of slavery. The Bonded Labour System (Abolition) Act (1976) freed all bonded laborers, canceled any outstanding debts against them, prohibited new bondage agreements, and ordered the rehabilitation of bonded laborers by the state. This act, in conjunction with the prohibition of bondage in the constitution, was used by campaigners to free bonded laborers, especially children. Yet it was never enforced by the state; the number of children in bondage in the early twenty-first century was estimated by NGOs as being over fifteen million, and employers compelling employees to do bonded labor after the act was passed were never convicted or subjected to the stipulated penalties (*South Asian* 2005).

These acts were supplemented by additional legislation, most notably the Workmen's Compensation Act (1923), the Trade Unions Act (1926), and the Payment of Wages Act (1936). The Bombay Industrial Relations Act, enacted in the late 1930s when Congress rule in eight provinces coexisted with British rule over the country, provided for a single bargaining agent for an entire industry in a locality or area. Thus the Congress-affiliated Rashtriya Mill Mazdoor Sangh became the sole bargaining agent for textile workers in Bombay. The labor provisions of the wartime Defence of India Rules were extended by an ordinance in 1946 and became the Industrial Disputes (ID) Act of 1947. It excluded employees who were not classified as "workmen" under section 2(s) of the act, who were defined as follows: " 'Workman' includes any person (including an apprentice) employed in any industry to do any skilled or unskilled manual, supervisory, technical or clerical work for hire or reward whether terms of employment be expressed or implied." Employees not defined as workmen—managers, engineers, workers not employed in an "industry," and so on—were not entitled to raise an industrial dispute and were excluded from any protection for involvement in trade union activities. All this legislation continued in force after independence (D'Souza 1996, 112–115). Indeed, "independence did not usher in fundamental changes in social practices, class relations, state structure, or even legislation" (Anderson 1990, 2).

This continuity between the colonial and postcolonial state has been explained by the Congress Party's uneasy relationship with the trade union movement. The All-India Trade Union Congress (AITUC), whose leaders included Congress members, socialists, communists, and others, remained independent of the party leadership. When Congress leaders were imprisoned after the launching of the Quit India movement in 1942, the Communist Party took over the leadership of the AITUC and presided over a massive strike wave that erupted in 1945. But the Congress leadership was not willing to tolerate an independent labor movement. In 1947, they split from the AITUC to form the Indian National Trade Union Congress, which they could control, and they kept in place labor legislation that would curtail union power (Chibber 111–126). Postindependence, even this weak labor legislation was either not implemented or further watered down by amendments, while concessions to business interests continued to grow (Kidron 1965, 84–94).

Thus labor relations in India retained the marks of their colonial origins in at least two significant ways. One was the discouragement of collective bargaining. At independence, "the laws clearly assumed that unions and bargaining would *not* develop to any appreciable extent and did almost nothing to promote such development. It was government's job to protect the interests of workers and fix the important conditions of employment and, in the process, to maintain industrial peace by preventing strikes and adjudicating disputes" (Kennedy 1966, 48). The Trade Unions Act allowed for the registration of unions but did not require employers to recognize them or engage in bargaining with them, nor did it protect members from victimization by employers. And the ID Act made it mandatory for unions to give strike notice two weeks before embarking on industrial action, during which period compulsory arbitration, which employers could stretch out interminably, could be imposed; the function served by collective bargaining was thus largely taken over by the government.

In 1950, there was an attempt to pass a new Trade Union Act requiring compulsory recognition of representative unions by employers, collective bargaining, and protection from unfair employer practices, along with a new Labour Relations Bill to replace the ID Act. But these were opposed by the ministries in charge of railways, defense establishments, and posts and telegraphs and lapsed in 1951. V. V. Giri, a former trade unionist who became labor minister in 1952, tried to reintroduce the bills but again encountered opposition. In his letter of resignation in 1954, Giri wrote: "It has been my fervent wish that the government should be the model employer, inspiring other employers to follow their example. But I have to confess that the possibility of this hope being fulfilled has become remote" (Kennedy 1966, 46). The Maharashtra Recognition of Trade Unions and Prevention of Unfair Labour Practices Act (1971) extended the rights of recognized unions, but some employees were still excluded. It remained true that

> The IR law in the country gives government virtually unrestricted power to intervene in any labour-management dispute at any stage. The dispute can be brought before a conciliator or referred to statutory adjudication. These legal powers are freely used and not always with a view to securing equitable resolution of disputes. Frequently, the purpose of government is to curb the TU's right to strike, and sometimes to favour one union against another.
>
> (Tulpule 1996, 129–130)

The second way in which labor relations were shaped by colonialism was by the creation of a sharply segmented labor market. Independent India retained the colonial state's assumption that most workers would not be covered by labor legislation, which meant that, for example, the Factories Act (1948)—which covered working conditions, health and safety, basic amenities like toilets, working hours, prohibition of child labor, and workplace crèches and which, most importantly, provided for registration of employers and employees—did not apply to workplaces with electric power that had fewer than ten workers or those without power that had fewer than twenty workers. Thus most labor remained in the informal sector.[3] The Employees' State Insurance Act (1948), providing for accident compensation and sickness and maternity benefits, likewise did not apply to workplaces with fewer than twenty workers without power or fewer than ten workers with power, nor to seasonal factories. The Payment of Bonus Act (1965) and Employees' Provident Fund and Miscellaneous Provisions Act (1972) excluded workers from units with fewer than twenty employees, and the Payment of Gratuity Act (1972) excluded workers from units with fewer than ten employees. Given this legislative discrimination, it is not surprising that government statistics (which probably understate the number of informal workers) suggest that in the decade from 1961 to 1971, the number of informal workers in Bombay was greater than the number of formal workers and growing faster (Joshi and Joshi 1976, 68–71). The proportion of informal workers in the country as a whole would have been even greater if agricultural employment were included.

One way in which the expansion of informal labor occurred was through the shifting of whole establishments into the informal sector. The Report of the (First) National Commission on Labour in 1969 found that the Factories Act "is widely evaded by owners of small workshops, who . . . split a single workshop—sometimes by a sign in the middle of the shed—into two fictitious firms, each employing not more than ten workers" (Holmstrom 1976, 13n). Another method was through ancillarization and subcontracting, where the employer "divides his production in two baskets: the unionized, organized capital intensive sector where, on occasions when the unions get too difficult, he can transfer some of the production to the other basket of unorganized, informal subcontractors or ancillaries" (Mitra et al. 1980).[4] A third method was the time-honored one employed by the British when constructing the railways: the use of labor contractors as intermediaries. This came to be known as the "contract labor system."[5]

The Trade Unions Act (1926) and Minimum Wages Act (1948) did in theory apply to informal labor, but enforcing them was virtually impossible. One piece of legislation ostensibly aimed at protecting informal labor was the Contract Labour (Regulation and Abolition) Act (1970). The title of this act is misleading, as it implies that it provides for the abolition of the *contract labor system*. In fact, it does nothing of the sort; it only provides for the prohibition of the use of contract labor under certain circumstances. Moreover, it contained large loopholes that were exploited by unscrupulous employers, one of the worst of whom was the government itself. First, it applies only to establishments employing twenty or more contract workers and to contractors employing twenty or more workers. Second, although the act forbids the employment of contract labor for work of a permanent or perennial nature, if workers ever complained that this was being done, they would be fired and new workers taken on when the jobs were made permanent. This was a strong disincentive for making such complaints. In an attempt to eliminate this loophole, in December 1996 the Supreme Court ruled in the Air India case that the same contract workers who were working prior to the dispute should be made permanent. The Standing Conference of Public Enterprises, representing public-sector employers, responded by insisting that this judgment be reviewed by a Constitutional Bench of the Supreme Court, which duly reversed the earlier ruling (D'Costa 2006, 43). While this might be attributed to an antilabor trend among the judiciary, the wording of the legislation itself supported such an interpretation.

The Supreme Court has on some occasions upheld the right of informal workers to be made permanent in the face of employers' attempts to use casual or contract labor for permanent jobs (cf. Antony 2001a, 2001b). Thus there is no doubt that government policy could have tilted the balance in favor of formal labor by strengthening workers' rights. Instead, Indira Gandhi's Congress government crushed the railway strike of 1974, and the Emergency—in which workers' rights (especially the right to strike) were severely restricted—followed in 1975–1977. It is worth noting, however, that it was during the Emergency (in 1976) that chapter V B was introduced into the ID Act, stipulating that permission had to be obtained from the government before employers could close down or dismiss workers in a unit employing three hundred or more workers, and this number was reduced to one hundred in an amendment introduced in 1982, when the Congress (I) was back in power. In the early twenty-first century, employers and the government attempted time and again to remove this clause, while unions clung to it as though it were the only measure saving them from destruction.

The Attack on Organized Labor

Although the emphasis in the immediate postindependence period was on large-scale industry, the Industries (Development and Regulation) Act (1951) provided for the development of small-scale and ancillary undertakings—determined by the amount of fixed investment in the unit and number of workers employed—which would enjoy certain privileges, including reservation of production to be done exclusively in such units. Since an exemption from labor laws was on the basis of the number of workers, this meant that these units were effectively exempted from labor legislation (GOI 1951). Thus the government of newly independent India perpetuated the segmented labor market that it had inherited from British rule. In effect, there were two labor regimes within one country, one with high labor standards and the other with extremely low ones. Given the absence of a national border between them, the only thing preventing jobs migrating from the former to the latter was the low productivity in the informal sector and the poor quality of goods produced in it. But all that changed in the late 1970s.

When the Janata Party came to power and the Emergency was lifted in 1977, there was a massive strike wave as workers fought for long-repressed demands. Again, the change in government was seen as an opportunity to strengthen labor rights. But the new government's Industrial Policy Statement, issued in December 1977, declared: "The emphasis of industrial policy so far has been mainly on large industries . . . relegating small industries to a minor role. It is the firm policy of this government to change this approach" (GOI 1977). More than five hundred items—many more than before—were reserved exclusively for the small-scale sector of units, with an investment of up to Rs 10 lakhs, with special assistance for "tiny" units, with investment in plant and machinery of up to Rs 1 lakh.[6] Financial and marketing assistance would be provided to all these informal units, but there was no mention of extending basic rights to the workers employed in them.

When Indira Gandhi came back to power in 1980, her government scrapped the Janata industrial policy and launched a new Five-Year Plan. But instead of abandoning the emphasis on small-scale production, the Industrial Policy Statement of 1980—and thus the Sixth Five-Year Plan that followed—reiterated and expanded it. A policy of "economic federalism" was proposed, with a small number of "nucleus plants" surrounded by numerous ancillaries producing inputs for it; the upper limit for investment in tiny- and small-scale units was doubled to two lakhs and twenty lakhs respectively, while in ancillaries it was raised from fifteen to twenty-five lakhs; the government would ensure the availability of scarce inputs, and "policies regarding marketing support to the decentralized sectors and reservation of items for small scale industries shall continue to be in force in the interest of growth of the small scale industries." In addition, the government "decided to encourage dispersal of industry and setting up of units in industrially backward areas. Special concessions and facilities will be offered for this purpose" (GOI 1980). The Industrial Policy Statement of 1990 raised the ceiling for investment in small-scale units to sixty lakhs and in ancillaries to seventy-five lakhs; resolved to ensure that large-scale units would not encroach on the 836 items now reserved for manufacture in the small-scale sector; and, in response to "persistent complaints of the small scale units" that they were "being subjected to a large number of Acts/Laws . . . particularly in the field of labour legislations," promised that "these bureaucratic controls will be reduced so that unnecessary interference is eliminated" (GOI 1990). In 1999, the definition of "small scale" was expanded to encompass units with an investment of up to Rs 1 crore.

The effect of these policies was to accelerate the transfer of production to the informal sector. In 1977, some companies, including Philips and Telco (Tata Engineering and Locomotive Company), were already subcontracting production (Hensman 1996a, 91), but in general there was not much interaction between the formal and informal sectors—nor much competition between their products, since the quality of production in the informal sector was so poor. With the boost for small-scale units in the new industrial policy, however, they could afford modern technology, and having much lower overheads and labor costs, they could now compete successfully with the large-scale sector.

The consequences were predictable:

The legal requirements binding the factory sector under the Factories Act 1948 are designed mainly for the protection of the consumers by quality control and of the workers by regulating the working conditions. . . . More important still, it gives the workers legal rights to unionize for collective bargaining. As against this, even the Draft Sixth Plan places small units in the unorganized sector, implying that regulations of the factory sector do not apply to these units. . . . If the projected rate of growth for this sector by the planners does materialize, then, by the end of the Sixth Plan period, it should account for about a third of the manufacturing output in the country. Such a large part of the production system will be receiving Government assistance, such as cheap credit, reserved markets, tax concessions, etc. but will not have to accept any regulations as to . . . how it should treat its workers, etc. Do we really want to encourage subminimal wage rates, a weakening of the bargaining strength of the industrial workers, or the very high profit margins which go without taxation?

(Banerjee 1981, 280, 293)

That, it seems, was exactly what the government wanted to do, and it succeeded only too well.

Employers in large-scale industry found themselves unable to compete with the upgraded small-scale sector; Metal Box, for example, justified cost-cutting measures in 1985 by telling workers that they were facing stiff competition from small-scale producers of metal containers and other products.[7] Some foreign companies sold their factories to Indian companies and moved out; others responded by transferring jobs to informal workers and thus reducing the unionized workforce. There were three main ways in which this was achieved. One was to use temporary, casual, or contract workers to do work at the same site; this was done at Pfizer and Abbott, for example. The second was to subcontract production to smaller enterprises employing informal labor. Abbott subcontracted at least 60 percent of its production, Philips a similar proportion, and Hindustan Lever in 1992 was subcontracting 50 percent of synthetic-detergent production, 15.2 percent of soaps, and 69 percent of personal products.[8] The third method was to relocate production to industrially backward areas and hire a completely new labor force consisting mostly of informal workers. Thus CPC International started a unit at Dharwar in Karnataka with fifty contract workers, paying them Rs 45 per day; Boots started two new units, one in Ahmednagar with 105 workers, the other at Jejuri with ninety; Abbott started a new unit in Gujarat with thirty-five formal employees, the rest informal; and all refrigerator production from the Voltas plant at Thane was transferred to a new and fully automated unit at Warora in 1985.[9] Most of these informal workers were paid Rs 2,000 per month or less, roughly 25 to 30 percent of the wages being paid at that time to unionized formal workers in Bombay (Banaji and Hensman 1995, 5).

Having shifted production, the company would then liquidate the existing workforce. The textile industry was the first to do this. The Bombay textile strike of 1982–1983 was followed by the loss of roughly seventy-five thousand jobs due to closures and downsizing, with another twenty-five thousand lost soon after (van Wersch 1992, 234–244). In Ahmedabad, the decline started in 1982 with the closure of fifty private mills and twenty government-owned mills and the loss of almost one hundred thousand jobs over the next fifteen years, the majority in the 1980s (Patel 2001, 6). Other textile centers such as Kanpur and Coimbatore witnessed a similar decline (Joshi 2003, 314; Baud 1983). In every case, weaving was transferred to the decentralized power-loom sector (Baud 1983, 31–32; van Wersch 1992, 40–46). Modern industry was the next target; the pharmaceutical industry in Bombay was virtually demolished (see chapter 5).

How did employers succeed in pushing through these closures and dismissals despite the constraints posed by chapter V B of the ID Act? According to those provisions, everything is left to the government's discretion. The government can, if it wishes, deny permission for a closure, and so long as the prevailing ideology was opposed to making workers redundant, permission was routinely denied or enterprises nationalized. But in an ideological climate that asserted the superiority of small-scale production, it was very easy for the government to reverse its policies and allow closures of units in the formal sector on the understanding that production would be transferred to the informal sector: indeed, this was even rationalized as "creating employment." Moreover, if state authorities did not give express permission for closure or dismissals, the company was still at liberty to go ahead with its plans in the absence of a response from the government within three months.

Informalization of employment was endemic in India, but it was pushed more aggressively from the late 1970s onward. During the latter period, this method of undermining trade unionism spread through much of the world, from South Africa to Latin America to the United States (Webster and Buhlungu 2007, 422; Munck 2002, 115; Clawson and Clawson 2007, 44). Other methods of attacking organized labor were also used. In the United States, where labor law allowed workers to strike in support of their demands on the expiry of their agreement but also allowed employers to hire permanent replacements, employers increasingly used this provision to replace strikers. "Their job rights would then be superseded by those of the replacements who then, typically, heed the employer's call to decertify the union. Strike-busting thus becomes a larger exercise in union-busting" (Clawson and Clawson 2007). In India, a palpable index of increased employer aggressiveness was the fact that in 1985–1986 the workdays lost due to lockouts outstripped workdays lost due to strikes; by 1989–1990, the former were double the latter, at over twenty thousand per year, and although the number fell steeply in subsequent years, it remained consistently above the level of days lost due to strikes (Nagaraj 2004, 3389). Many of these lockouts, sometimes lasting for over a year, were aimed at breaking unions.

Union Organization

The first workers' organization in India, the Bombay Mill Hands' Association, was formed in 1890. N. M. Lokhande, a storekeeper in a cotton mill, was elected as chairman. The organization had no constitution, formal membership, or funds, but it did deal with workers' grievances, held huge meetings of workers, agitated on issues such as shorter working hours and a weekly day off, and made representations on these issues to the viceroy and various government committees and commissions (Gupte 1981, 14–25). The Madras Labour Union was formed in 1918, and the Textile Labour Association was set up in Ahmedabad in 1920 (Janardhan 2007, 35). In 1924 in Bombay, over the course of one of the many strikes sparked off by wage cuts, a textile union called the Girni Kamgar Mahamandal was formed with a weaver at its head, followed in 1926 by the Bombay Textile Labour Union, led by N. M. Joshi, and Bombay Mill-Workers' Union in 1928. However, all of these were overtaken by the Girni Kamgar Union, formed during the textile strike of 1928 and headed by S. A. Dange of the Communist Party of India (CPI), which grew rapidly thereafter and dominated the labor movement (Gupte 1981, 47–53, 67; Chandavarkar 2003, 5). Several other unions were formed in Bombay before and during the 1920s, and by 1929 there were unions of railway workers, seafarers, postal workers, municipal work-ers, and dock workers, unions in engineering workshops, the tramways, match factories, and oil companies, and unions of press, telephone, and clerical workers, peons, shop assistants, and others (Gupte 1981, 70–73).

The earliest union federation to be formed, the AITUC, held its first convention in Bombay in 1920. Its leaders were also leaders of the Con-gress Party, which at that time included Gandhians, socialists, commu-nists, and others (Patel 1999, 3). This initial unity did not last long. In subsequent years, the movement split again and again to form new union federations along party lines. To mention only those still existing by the end of the twentieth century: INTUC was formed by the Congress Party in 1947; various Socialists came together to form the Hind Mazdoor Sabha (HMS) in 1948; Communists linked to the Revolutionary Socialist Party (which was critical of Stalin but did not call itself Trotskyist) split from AITUC to form the United Trade Union Congress (UTUC) in 1949; the CPI (Marxist) split off from the CPI and formed the Centre of Indian Trade Unions in 1964; the Hindu-nationalist RSS set up the Bharatiya Mazdoor Sangh in 1967; in 1969, the CPI (Marxist-Leninist) was formed out of a split from the CPI(M) and later formed the All-India Central Council of Trade Unions; in 1972, the UTUC (Lenin Sarani) split off from the UTUC; and in 1981, George Fernandes split from the HMS to form the Hind Mazdoor Kisan Panchayat. In addition to these unions linked to national parties, there were regional parties and their affiliated unions; the most prominent of these in Maharashtra were the left-wing Lal Nis-han Party and its union, the Sarva Shramik Sangh, and the Marathi and Hindu nationalist Shiv Sena, with its Bharatiya Kamgar Sena and other unions (cf. Patel 1999, 13–19).

Obviously fragmentation was a major weakness of the movement, lead-ing to damaging interunion rivalry and conflict (Tulpule 1996, 130), but this problem was compounded by trade union links with political parties. A par-ticular union might gain from the backing of a party; thus the Congress Party

> has unabashedly used state power to promote the INTUC among work-ers and to give it a pre-eminent position among the various TU orga-nizations. Whenever non-Congress governments came to power, they themselves followed similar policies and promoted those TUs that were politically allied to them. . . . Linkage between the ruling party and a TU organization is, however, not an unmixed blessing. Such links inevitably

compromise a TU's freedom of action and militancy in the pursuit of workers' interests.

(Tulpule 1996, 129)

In short,

Trade union affiliation to political parties had several undesirable consequences for labour. It lost its autonomous power to decide policies and actions. Its politics got subjugated to the so-called larger (electoral) politics with its corresponding ills. It fragmented on party lines. Its leaders could neither understand the aspirations of labour nor understand the dynamics of industry, for example, technological change.

(Janardhan 2007, 36)

The conflict between subservience to the party and fidelity to the interests of their members was a problem also evident in other countries. In China, for example, the leadership of the All-China Federation of Trade Unions (ACFTU) on various occasions attempted to assert its autonomy from the Communist Party and state. In 1950 and 1957, this led to the sacking of union leaders and in 1966, during the Cultural Revolution, to the formation of local Workers' Representative Congresses. After the economic liberalization began in the late 1970s, the demand for autonomy surfaced again and received support from reformers in the top party leadership. The Eleventh National Congress of the ACFTU in October 1988 called for the independence of trade unions from the party and state and for a corresponding reform of the Trade Union Law. But these developments became caught up in the broader democracy movement that culminated in the Beijing Tiananmen Square massacre in June 1989 (White 1995). Subsequently, unions were given a greater role in policymaking at the national as well as enterprise level in order to defend the interests of their members, and the long-awaited Trade Union Law, specifying that trade union leaders should be elected by workers or worker representatives, was enacted in 1992, but the price for these concessions was loyalty to the party. "As such, it was a Faustian bargain in which the unions linked their fortunes and future to those of the Party and it marked a step backwards away from the efforts to achieve greater institutional autonomy" (White 1995, 20).

With the passing of a new labor law in 1994 in China, plant-level collective bargaining between management and unions was being pioneered in foreign enterprises and considered in new-style public enterprises, although this was sometimes opposed by local governments "eager to attract foreign capital and keep foreign investors happy" (White 1995, 27). From the latter half of the 1990s, stories in the Chinese media of employer abuse of workers, horrific mining disasters, and criticism of the ACFTU for its failure to defend workers goaded the ACFTU into "trying to organise as many workers as possible into unions, especially in those sectors where the media were berating the unions over mistreated workers: the foreign invested enterprises and privately-owned (meaning non-state, domestic) enterprises" (Taylor and Li 2007, 500). There were some high-profile successes, such as the establishment of unions in Wal-Mart, a notoriously anti-union employer.

In India too, "refusal by employers to recognise or bargain with unions has been a major obstacle to growth of bargaining" (Kennedy 1966, 106), and governments have often sided with employers. A long struggle for union recognition in Honda Motorcycles and Scooters India in Gurgaon culminated in workers being beaten unconscious by the police on July 25, 2005. Earlier, around fifty union activists were suspended, the president and secretary of the union were thrown from a second-floor window and suffered injuries to their leg and spine respectively, and the entire workforce was locked out (John 2005; Mansingh 2005). Such collusion between employers and the state to deny workers their legal rights has been going on for decades and in several instances has resulted in the death of workers due to police firing (Bidwai 2005; Sehgal 2005; Adve 2005).

The Honda Motorcycles and Scooters Workers' Union had affiliated to the AITUC in order to obtain registration, and this is a strategy that has been followed by other unions that are essentially employees' or workers' unions but are affiliated to national federations. At the ETI conference in 2003, Han Dongfang, a labor activist and editor of *China Labor Bulletin*, suggested that in China, a similar strategy in foreign firms or suppliers of ETI companies—i.e., plant-level unions affiliating to the ACFTU—was one way in which unions could retain a degree of autonomy while conforming with the law (ETI 2003, 38–45). This strategy had successfully been used in Chinese suppliers of Reebok, where plant-based unions with a leadership elected by workers subsequently affiliated to the ACFTU (Maitland 2002). Thus in the sector of party-affiliated unions, there is little difference between India and China, except that in India there are many more party-affiliated unions to choose from. In some ways, Chinese workers are better off; for example, a survey of over six hundred companies found that Chinese skilled production workers earned about 26 percent more than their Indian counterparts (Taylor 2005).

Where Indian workers do have a decisive advantage, however, is in the right to form independent unions. In China, by contrast, the attempt to form independent unions (Workers' Autonomous Federations) in 1989 was crushed after the Tiananmen Square massacre, with unionists being incarcerated for long periods and subjected to brutal treatment. Han Dongfang was one of them. He was jailed without trial for two-and-a-half years, fell seriously ill with tuberculosis, was sent to the United States for treatment, and then was refused reentry to China, whereupon he settled in Hong Kong and continued to support the right of Chinese workers to form independent unions.[10] Others remained in jail. In 1992, workers and labor-rights activists were sentenced to from two to twenty years in jail for organizing the Free Labor Union of China, and in 1994, labor activists running a workers' night school in the Shenzhen Special Economic Zone and publishing a journal devoted to trade union issues were also arrested and kept in detention (ICFTU 1997).

In Russia, thanks to Gorbachev's policies of *perestroika, glasnost,* and workplace democratization, workers obtained the right to break away from the All-Union Central Council of Trade Unions and form independent unions. The miners used their power to support Yeltsin's nationalist call for sovereignty for the Russian republic. This led both to the disintegration of the Soviet Union in December 1991 and to policies that were highly detrimental to the interests of Russian workers, who lost the political leverage they had gained under Gorbachev along with the economic security that the Soviet economy had given them (Christensen 1999, 77–108). In 1993, when the FNPR, the Russian trade union confederation, attempted to oppose Yeltsin's dissolution of parliament, the government froze their bank accounts, cut off their telephones, banned the check-off of union dues, and took away the unions' responsibility for social insurance and health and safety. The FNPR leader resigned, and the new leader adopted a conciliatory stance. The federation's dependence on the government at the national level and on managements at the enterprise level resulted from its lack of support from workers, which in turn was a consequence of its failure to defend workers' rights. This is a vicious circle that could only be broken if FNPR asserted its independence from state and managements or if other genuinely independent unions were formed (Ashwin 2007).

Responses to Globalization by Employers and the State

Globalization increased competitive pressures on Indian companies, especially from other Third World countries. Anticipating that meeting global competition would involve closures and downsizing, the government initiated a National Renewal Fund, primarily for public-sector enterprises, with three purposes: (a) retraining and redeploying workers, (b) compensating redundant workers, and (c) generating new employment. Somehow (a) and (c) got lost subsequently, leaving only (b) to be carried out on a large scale (Nagaraj 2004). This was aided by tax exemption granted for funds disbursed in voluntary-retirement schemes in both public- and private-sector firms.

A small number of well-managed companies welcomed globalization and expressed a readiness to confront its challenges, but employers represented by the RSS-affiliated SJM were opposed to it and demanded that India should leave the WTO, a demand rejected by the BJP (despite its own affiliation to the RSS) on the grounds that it was impractical to remain isolated from the rest of the world (*BS* 2001c). The largest number accepted globalization provisionally, profiting from and even depending on it, but they put forward two major demands. The first was protection from imports and foreign takeovers (Kumar 2002). Thus garment exporters, while opposing protectionist measures by developed countries against their products, urged the government to impose protectionist duties on garments imported from other Third World countries. As Rahul Mehta, the former president of the Indian Clothing Manufacturers' Association put it, "India's commitment to the WTO relates only to countries like America and Europe, and not countries like Sri Lanka and Bangladesh" (Sabarinath and Iyer 2001).

The second major demand from this category of employers was the deregulation of the labor market. Competition from countries such as China exposed the weakness of a strategy based on fragmentation of the labor process in order to evade labor legislation, and they wanted to be able to engage in large-scale production without the inconvenience of complying with labor laws. The demand for an "Exit Policy"—the freedom to hire and fire workers and open and close units without any regulation—came almost immediately after trade liberalization in 1991.

The socialist-dominated United Front government in power between 1996 and 1998 and the BJP-dominated National Democratic Alliance (NDA) government in power thereafter were sympathetic to both demands of employers. Leeway to satisfy the former was restricted by WTO rules, but the latter depended solely on domestic policy, provided labor standards were kept out of the WTO. This explains the opposition of Indian nego- tiators, along with those from fourteen other developing countries, to the inclusion of labor rights in the WTO agenda at the Singapore conference in 1996 (Aiyar 1996). When they finally agreed to labor standards being mentioned in the ministerial declaration at the end of the conference, it was only because it stated that the ILO was the relevant body to deal with labor rights and that protectionist measures would not be taken to enforce them (Bhargava 1996). The purely token nature of this agreement was underscored by the refusal of this group of developing countries to allow the ILO director general, Michel Hansenne, to speak at the WTO meet- ing (BS 1996). Subsequently, any attempt even to discuss this issue was opposed fiercely by the NDA's negotiators. This left both Indian and for- eign employers free to attack workers' rights.

Two concrete proposals for the "reform" of labor laws were made. First, employers, especially public-sector employers, wanted the deletion of sec- tion 10 of the Contract Labour Act, which provided for restrictions on the use of contract labor (Hakeem 2000). Second, employers demanded a revi- sion of chapter V B of the ID Act, to allow employers unrestricted freedom to dismiss workers and close down units with fewer than three hundred workers in one version, one thousand workers in another (Mitra 2001). Exporters wanted special economic zones that would be exempt from the country's labor laws (Raghu 2002), but owners of existing units outside the zones felt this would discriminate against them and argued for the same exemptions outside the zones (Firodia 2003)!

The campaign reached its peak when the NDA government was in power from 1998 to 2004. Full-page advertisements alleging that formal employment was responsible for unemployment frequently appeared in Indian newspapers. In October 2000, the state government of Maha- rashtra proposed revising labor laws along the lines demanded by employers, which would have rendered them virtually useless for pro- tecting workers' rights (Samant 2000; D'Costa 2000). Finance Minister Yashwant Sinha announced, in his budget speech of 2001, that the gov- ernment would liberalize the use of contract labor and permit employers to dismiss employees and close down units employing up to one thou- sand workers with no questions asked. The announcement was greeted with euphoria by the business lobby (Datta 2001; Mitra 2001). However,

the unprecedented procedure whereby changes to labor law were proposed by the finance ministry led to the resignation of the labor minister (Phadnis 2001). In 2002, the cabinet approved the proposed amendment to the ID Act (*ET* 2002b), although no immediate steps were taken
to put it into effect. The second Report of the National Commission on
Labour, which came out in 2002, made recommendations for the formal
sector that followed the lines laid down by employers and the government (Ministry of Labour 2002).

The antilabor crescendo came to a halt after the Congress-led and left-
supported United Progressive Alliance (UPA) government came to power
in the 2004 elections, suggesting that the particularly vicious form that
the antilabor rhetoric and policies had taken during the NDA regime was
inspired not by neoliberalism but by right-wing Hindu nationalism. Under
the UPA, other policies were explored. While export-promotion zones had
existed for decades, the passing of the SEZ (Special Economic Zone) Act,
2005 (GOI 2005), marked a new phase. The act provided for massive state
subsidies, in the form of assistance with land acquisition and exemption
from customs and excise duties and taxes as well as environmental laws, to
firms setting up businesses in these zones. It was estimated by the former
state finance minister Ashok Mitra that the Left Front government of West
Bengal had provided $210 million in subsidies to Tata to set up the Nano
production facilities in Singur (Bidwai 2008). Tata was forced to pull out in
October 2008 due to violent protests against the project, and it moved to
Gujarat, where it received even more subsidies (*BS* 2008).

That this policy should have encountered fierce opposition from agricultural communities dispossessed of their land and livelihoods is not surprising. The worst violence occurred in Nandigram, where armed clashes
and several deaths led to an abandonment of the projected SEZ there (Dhar
2007). Less serious and less publicized incidents occurred elsewhere, for
example in Goa, where protests resulted in the cancellation of all SEZ plans
(Mukherjee 2008). The IMF, World Bank, Asian Development Bank, and
WTO expressed misgivings about a policy that might attract countervailing duties for exports under WTO rules, and within the government, the
Ministry of Finance, which would suffer an enormous loss of revenue as
a result of the policy, had understandable reservations about it (Sen 2006;
Shrivastava 2008). While exemption from labor legislation was ruled out
in the act, by the time it was introduced it was clear that there were plenty
of ways to get around these laws.

The Crisis and Workers' Rights

Returning to the question posed at the beginning of this chapter—does globalization and membership in the WTO restrict or destroy the capacity of a state to defend workers' rights?—the answer is that it would certainly be harder for a state to pursue this goal in isolation, since it might then be faced with capital flight. It would instead have to attempt to use the pooled sovereignty in the WTO and ILO to protect workers' rights in all member countries, and some governments, under pressure from their unions, have tried to do this. But no Indian government belongs to this category. If there were fears that the proposed social clause in WTO agreements could be used in a protectionist manner, they could have proposed amendments, but they did not. It was not globalization itself but the stranglehold over labor policy established much earlier by Indian capital that ensured that globalization would be used as yet another pretext to attack workers' rights.

In the event that an Indian government *did* wish to protect workers' rights, would globalization pose an obstacle by weakening the position of the state vis-à-vis capital? Not necessarily. In fact, globalization *strengthened* the capacity of government to raise the abysmal standards of corporate governance in India, since businesses could not expect foreign institutional investment in Indian equity without improving standards of management integrity, transparency, and accountability. Despite strong resistance to this process from domestic companies, there was an emerging consensus that a substantial reform of governance was necessary in the Indian corporate sector: a consensus that had not emerged earlier despite evidence of large-scale corruption and plundering of public funds on the part of Indian businesses (Banaji 2001b, 2005; Mody 2001).

If globalization could help to raise standards of corporate governance, it could also help to improve labor standards, if they were made mandatory by the WTO. If it wished, the government could fight for the incorporation of workers' rights in the emerging global order. Instead, it fought tooth and nail against such a measure, ensuring the defeat of governments of other countries that attempted to protect the rights of their own workers. It appears that far from depriving the Indian government of the power to strengthen workers' rights in India, globalization conferred on it the power to undermine workers' rights in other countries! That all the party-linked central unions supported the government on this issue is additional evidence of their lack of autonomy from the state.

The negative fallout of this policy contributed to the crisis of 2008. By opposing the defense of union rights, Indian government policy helped to reduce the expansion of global aggregate demand to such a degree that a crisis of realization became inevitable. Other governments also pursued policies that undermined the basic right of workers to join unions and bargain collectively without fearing the loss of their jobs. In the OECD countries, where the thirty-year period following the end of World War II had been a "golden age" for trade unionism, union density levels fell across the board from the mid-1970s, and "all trade union movements in OECD countries now operate in far harsher economic and political environments" (Phelan 2007a, 16–18). The United States featured prominently in this list. "For America's workers, the years since the 1970s have been lost decades. Income has been lost as society's wealth moves upwards, jobs have been lost by the millions, power has been lost as unions decline and retreat" (Moody 2007, 97). Although Third World countries never had a "golden age" of trade unionism, some did have strong trade union movements; however, "in virtually every country where neoliberal reforms and labour market liberalisation has been adopted, density levels have fallen" (Phelan 2007a, 19–20).

In country after country, the period since the late 1970s is a story of attacks on union rights, and there was no sign of this abating in the wake of the crisis. A striking example was the opposition to (or attempts to water down) the Employee Free Choice Act in the United States, which aimed to make it easier for workers to join unions and bargain collectively, on the grounds that such a measure would be inappropriate given the fragility of the economy (Cooke 2009a). Individual employers cannot see the larger picture, nor are they worried about the long-term consequences of their single-minded pursuit of profit, even if these turn out to be disastrous for the economy (cf. Marx 1976, 381). But the role of government should be to look beyond the immediate interests of individual capitalists. Ideally, it should also represent the interests of other sections of society. But even if it fails to do this, it should at least represent the long-term interests of capitalist society as a whole, which are threatened if the consumption levels of workers are held to a bare minimum or pushed below this level. Reversing the widening inequalities that made such an enormous contribution to the crisis would require governments to enact legislation and implement policies that strengthen the labor movement and to do so internationally, in a coordinated fashion. At the same time, workers need to take steps to revitalize their movements and organizations, and that too needs to be done in solidarity with workers in other countries.

Employees' Unions

An Experiment in Union Democracy

How Important Is Union Democracy?

There has been a great deal of debate about the importance of union democracy, both theoretically and among union activists. Does union power depend mainly on the number of members, or is their commitment to the union and active involvement in it equally important? If participation by the membership in union decision making contributes significantly to its strength, what are the structures and procedures that encourage such involvement? If "Union power is built on power on the job" and "the matter of workplace power inevitably leads to the question of the workers' power within the union itself" (Moody 2007, 176–77), then union power is inextricably linked to union democracy. This issue gains urgency in the wake of the crisis, when strong unions could make the difference between the effective protection of workers' rights, leading to a sustained recovery, on one side and mounting job losses, wage cuts, and contraction of demand on the other.

In India, the capacity and desire for self-government within unions manifest themselves in an important experiment in union democracy: employees' unions. There have been studies of the party-linked unions, but hardly anything has been written about employees' unions. Yet their importance is growing. It was suggested that the proportion of total union membership in employees' unions increased steeply, especially from 1980 onward, while the proportion in party-affiliated unions declined (Bhattacharjee 1999, 22, 42), and this trend is accelerating in the twenty-first century. This is therefore an expanding area of unionism.

Centralization, Decentralization, and Democracy in Unions

Shopfloor workers in many countries have created their own forms of organization, sometimes against heavy odds and in overt opposition to the central union leadership. In Britain, the shop-stewards' movement has at various times represented a countervailing force to the central union leadership (Hinton 1973; Hyman 1979; Daniel and Millward 1983), and the democratization of trade unionism was achieved by moving away from centralized bargaining (Undy and Martin 1984, 206). During World War II, a sophisticated system of direct democracy developed in large factories in Argentina, with each shop or department electing a delegate and the delegates forming a *cuerpo de delegados* (shop stewards' plenary), which elected a *comisión interna* (factory committee) that negotiated with management (Munck et al. 1987, 134). Since the 1990s, the number of *comisiones internas* that took industrial action based on the mobilization of workers through participatory democracy has increased (Atzeni and Ghiliani 2007, 110). In Brazil, elected *delegados sindicais* (shop stewards) played a key role in the "strike of four hundred thousand" in 1957, leading the pickets and ensuring the success of the strike (Fontes 2000). In the Netherlands, which has a highly centralized union structure, attempts to establish a plant-level union presence (*bedrijfsledengroep* or BLG) encountered enormous difficulties (Windmuller 1969; Leinse 1980; Banaji and Hensman 1990). In Italy, factory councils challenged the central union leadership at various periods (Gramsci 1977; Clarke 1977); more recently, there were attempts to establish the *rappresentanza sindicale aziendale* (RSA), or "unionized presence in the workplace," as an offshoot of article 19 of the Statuto dei Lavoratori, which empowered workers, whether unionized or not, to establish an RSA (Terry 1993).

Two major problems can arise at the interface between a large centralized union and individual workforces. One is lack of participation by workers in union activities: "The old organizational culture of the unions and the need for control felt by their officials are obstacles to more extensive and more direct membership participation" (Zoll 1996, 86). The opposite problem occurs when organization at the workplace is strong but comes into conflict with the central union leadership. In such circumstances, it may take government legislation such as the requirement to hold strike ballots—usually introduced under the mistaken belief that strikes are engineered by a small minority of militants—to make the organization more democratic (Hyman 1996, 62). In extreme cases, such conflicts can lead to "a strike by the rank-and-file membership against the union leadership" and a situation of dual power, as occurred when the managing committee of the Port Kembla branch of the Federated Ironworkers' Association in Australia removed a shop delegate from his post and the workforce refused to accept his removal (Dickenson 1982, 53–57).

Models of trade union democracy that see it as being similar to parliamentary democracy assume that so long as there is an opposition to the party in power, democracy is assured (cf. Lipset et al. 1956). This may be better than a one-party system, but it cannot ensure that the interests of even the majority of the population/membership are protected. These approaches

conceive of democracy as a system in which members play a passive role, only occasionally being called on to approve the actions taken by their leaders. But as the Webbs demonstrated, an earlier and much more vital concept of democracy in trade unionism based itself on the active participation of the membership at large. As the size of organisations grew and made the practice of "primitive democracy" impossible, a variety of devices such as the referendum, the rotation of office and mass meetings were introduced to retain as much power for the rank and file as possible. . . . Moreover, the emphasis must not simply be on whether members have the right to ratify leadership actions but on whether conditions are such that their participation is actively encouraged.

(Carew 1976, 21–22)

Where a culture of political-party control or bureaucratic control over unions is entrenched, union strength is sapped, because rank and file members are disempowered. For example,

what workers in America face today is not so much a choice between federations, as between types of unionism. There is the old bureaucratic business unionism that exists as the norm in both federations. Whether

it is labelled an "organizing" or "servicing" union, its leaders long ago
surrendered the workplace to management, despite continuing resistance from the members. . . . The second type . . . we call democratic
social movement unionism. It is more a direction to be sought than
either a reality today or a "model" for tomorrow. So far, it is the exception,
the direction in which to look if labor is to regain its power and grow.

(Moody 2007, 184)

In India, by contrast, this type of unionism is a highly significant movement.

The Establishment of Employees' Unions

Employees' unions were able to develop in India because unions have bargaining rights at the workplace (except in the textile industry). Employers too have displayed a preference for decentralized negotiations. Any
discussion of the relative merits of workplace unions as opposed to more
centralized union structures has to be located in the context of the deep
fragmentation of the union movement. In addition to the party-affiliated
unions, there are also unions run by local professional leaders, ranging
from lawyers to characters with underworld links, and employing tactics
ranging from a heavy emphasis on legal battles to the liberal use of violence. Given this wide choice, it is significant that in Bombay, workers
in many of the modern industrial units set up from the 1940s onward
chose to remain independent of all outside leaders and form their own
employees' unions, workers' unions, staff unions, or staff and workers' unions. These unions might retain an outsider as legal adviser or
president or even, in rare instances, be affiliated to an external union,
but in all cases, decisions would be made by the internal leadership and
members. The managing committees of some employees' unions were
undoubtedly dominated or manipulated by management, but most were
fiercely independent and run by extremely conscious and technically
competent leaderships.

Of eleven employees' unions in existence by 1948, ten belonged to companies controlled by overseas firms: two at Lever Brothers, and one each
at ICI, Ford, Goodlass Wall, Greaves Cotton, Volkart, Firestone, East Asiatic, and Indian Oxygen. The sole exception was Tata Oil Mills (Tomco)
Employees' Union, formed in 1946. This pattern continued into the 1950s

and 1960s (Hensman and Banaji 1998). One reason was that unlike most Indian companies, where management doggedly resisted all attempts by workers to unionize, "Many of the foreign firms . . . have had long experience of collective bargaining in their home countries from which both knowledge and attitudes have carried over into the Indian subsidiaries" (Kennedy 1966, 145). This did not mean, however, that there was no resistance to unionization or collective bargaining in foreign firms. In Metal Box, for example, an AITUC union was broken by the company in 1948, and sixty to seventy workers who were active in the union were dismissed. The company introduced a works committee and argued that a union was therefore unnecessary, and in 1961–1962 it tried to bring in two company-sponsored unions. In 1973, the workers brought in the Steel Mazdoor Sabha led by George Fernandes through a court order, but the workers were not satisfied with it, feeling that it agreed to increases in productivity and pressured workers to implement them, did not communicate with workers, and was a *chamcha* (management stooge) union. In response, they formed the Metal Box Workers' Union (MBWU), putting up candidates and winning a majority on the works committee. The company started dismissing MBWU activists, but in 1976 they won a recognition case under the MRTU and PULP Act, and two-thirds of these activists were reinstated.[1]

Similarly in East Asiatic (later taken over by Pfizer) and Hoechst, management formed works committees, which included management representatives, and argued that all workers' grievances and demands could be settled in that forum.[2] In several other cases, union activists or workers trying to form a union were victimized. In Burmah-Shell, the union demanded that "dismissal or disciplinary action should not be enforced either directly or indirectly against any employee for participating in or promoting legitimate union activities." The company responded that "'promoting union activities' is rather a vague term and that Union members or other employees should not engage in Union business during working hours unless they have received sanction to do so from a Departmental Head." The judgment granted the union's demand, subject to the proviso put forward by management (BGG 1949a, 1458). In Blue Star, employees who played a leading role in attempting to form a union were transferred or dismissed, creating an atmosphere of fear that made it hard to resume the effort; even after a lapse of time, it was necessary to use the cover of a cricket club to bring workers together without fear of victimization. The union was finally registered only in 1971.[3]

Forming the union was not the end of the struggle. Burmah-Shell, Stanvac, ICI, British Oxygen, May & Baker, and Union Carbide might have been among the world's largest corporations, yet their subsidiaries litigated tenaciously, resisting union demands every inch of the way. The ICI Employees' Union presented its first charter of demands in 1946, its second in 1953, and its third in 1958, and none of these were settled bilaterally; all had to adjudicated. In Greaves Cotton, the first negotiated agreement occurred in 1974, twenty-eight years after the union was formed, with a series of awards in between. And in Firestone, although workers were unionized in 1948, the first bilateral agreement did not take place until 1969 (Hensman and Banaji 1998, 3). Managements clung to their "prerogative" to fix pay, conditions, and working hours, and unions had to fight for the right to have them fixed by bilateral agreement. The Firestone union complained in 1949 that there were

> no scales or grades fixed by the Company for its employees and that nepotism and favouritism were rampant. The Union, therefore, demands that all employees should be given regular annual increments... The Company . . . contended that the question of increment was one for the Company to decide having regard to the efficiency, regularity in attendance and other factors relating to the work of its employees.
>
> (BGG 1949b, 2473–2474)

The court decided that the union's demand was justified. In Pfizer, likewise, there were no proper pay scales until the union succeeded in obtaining them.[4]

Thus the whole culture of collective bargaining was forced on companies by the employees' unions and other sections of the union movement, largely through the machinery of litigation. It was unions, sometimes but not always backed by the courts, which brought order out of chaos, establishing coherent pay scales and service conditions where management whim had reigned.

There were several reasons why workers preferred this form of union. The most common refrains were: "We don't want 'politics' in our union," or "We may belong to different parties at home, but at our workplace we all belong to the same 'party' [i.e., the union]." This was clearly a reaction against the highly fragmented nature of the union movement and indicated that the formation of employees' unions at the workplace was an attempt to overcome it. Except in those cases where a rival union was established, an employees' union would typically have 100 percent membership. It thus exemplified a high degree of unity.

A second reason cited was that political parties had their own agendas, which would inevitably clash with the interests of the workers, at which point an affiliated union would find its members' interests sacrificed in favor of the party agenda; a common expression of this was the derisive comment that party-affiliated unions had to follow "orders coming from Delhi," that is, party headquarters. A related but distinct reason was the desire to manage their own affairs without being dictated to by an outsider, whether a party or nonparty union leader.

An important factor enabling employees' unions to be independent of outsiders was the presence of salaried staff whose knowledge of English and ability to handle negotiations and legal matters were crucial assets; indeed, their use of research and their sophistication in arguing for demands were much greater than those of external union leaders.[5] For example, the Glaxo Laboratories India Ltd. Employees' Union "annexed to its statement of claim certain information supplied to it by the Labour Research Department, 2, Soho Square, London, about this Company, which information is quite revealing. . . . The Union has also produced before me an extract from the *Economist*" (BGG 1952a, 2819). In this case, wage revision was granted, but equal pay for women was denied. The issue of discrimination against women was a hard-fought one, especially in pharmaceutical plants, which employed a high proportion of women, and the Sandoz Employees' Union "relied on the ILO's Discrimination (Employment and Occupation) Convention, 1958" (MGG 1961, 2759) in arguing against the marriage clause (see chapter 7).

In most cases, staff and blue-collar workers belonged to the same union, and the stability of the union depended on its capacity to secure parity of service conditions between them. In the late 1950s and early 1960s, many struggled for extension of staff conditions to factory workers. For example, the Parke-Davis Employees' Union complained that "there is serious discrimination between the administrative office and the factory" (MGG 1966, 36). Similarly, the Voltas and Volkart Employees' Union stated in their charter of demands that "there is a great disparity between the scales of factory staff and the office staff. The disparity between the white-collar worker and the factory worker is not in keeping with the times and should be eliminated" (Hensman and Banaji 1998, 3). Conversely, where parity was not established, there would be conflict:

At this time [1977], most of the activists were drawn from the staff. . . . At the time of formulating the demands, they'd tell us, "Whatever demands the workers have, we'll include them." . . . But at the time of settling the demands . . . the major share of the benefits went to the staff. . . . A few days before the last agreement, there was a general body meeting to pass the demands. . . . The workers gave such a good fight at this time that all the existing committee members . . . handed in their resignations. . . . The workers put up their own slate. . . . So we got elected, came in and restarted negotiations with the company. Here we got help from one of the committee members from the head office, because the workers didn't have much knowledge of this sort of thing. We didn't know English, and had no idea how to conduct discussions with the company.[6]

By the 1970s, relatively stable union-management relationships and a bargaining culture had been established by most employees' unions. Yet contentious issues could and did put these relationships under strain.

Dearness Allowance: Protecting Wages from Inflation

Dearness Allowance, or DA, was an allowance introduced in the early 1920s to compensate for a rise in the cost of living. Initially, this was a fixed amount (fixed DA) added to the basic salary. Later, the general understanding established by court judgments was that at the lowest level of wages, any increase in the cost of living between agreements should be fully "neutralized" or offset by a "variable DA" linked to the Consumer Price Index. In the words of Justice D. G. Kamerkar, who initiated this system in his award to the workers of British Insulated Callender's Cables Ltd., "I would direct the company . . . to link up the dearness allowance with the rise or fall in the cost of living index number, so that all disputes in future as to dearness allowance can be obviated" (cit. award to Tomco. Ltd.; BGG 1949c, 2123–2125). These schemes were awarded to several workforces, including Lever Brothers (India) Ltd., later to become Hindustan Lever Ltd. (BGG 1952b, 1284–1285). This was an important gain for workers and unions: given that agreements tended to be three years or more apart, it protected real wages from erosion due to inflation. For managements, on the contrary, it meant a loss of control over wages, especially during periods of high inflation.

It seems ironic that Justice Kamerkar should have hoped to obviate all further disputes on DA by linking it directly to the Consumer Price Index, because this, precisely, became a source of bitter dispute between employers and their workforces. In one of the earliest cases of its type, Voltas introduced an absolute ceiling on DA—that is, an amount above which DA *would not rise* no matter how much the cost of living rose—in 1959. This method of breaking the link between DA and the price index was subsequently employed by several other companies, including Hoechst, Glaxo, Searle, Boehringer-Knoll, and Dunlop. Less drastic curbs on DA were introduced by other companies, including Pfizer, Richardson Hindustan, Roussel Pharmaceuticals, Burroughs Wellcome, E. Merck, Sandoz, Bayer, Nicholas, and Abbott Laboratories.[7] All these implied an erosion of real wages over the period of an agreement. In the case of absolute ceilings, the erosion was seldom remedied even with a new agreement. The extent of the damage can be gauged by looking at the wage structure in a Bombay factory where a DA ceiling had not been imposed (Hindustan Lever) in 1996, where starting basic pay for the lowest production grade was just Rs 69.68 per month but DA amounted to Rs 2,867.75 (URG 1996, 30). In other words, DA was by far the biggest component of wages for most workers.

How did managements succeed in imposing these ceilings? A common strategy was to fix the ceiling at such a high level that it did not affect the current wages of any employees, while at the same time tempting them with attractive offers of benefits and allowances that would result in a large immediate wage rise.[8] In such cases, it was lack of information or foresight on the part of union leaders or members that led to the acceptance of a ceiling. In other cases, various degrees of coercion were applied, especially during the Emergency.

Once unions became aware of the dangers of DA ceilings, there was much stiffer resistance when managements tried to impose them. In extreme cases, such as Hindustan Lever and Blue Star, negotiations were deadlocked for ten years or more. In Ciba-Geigy, the court ruled against an absolute ceiling on the grounds that it would be unfair to workers if prices of essential commodities were to rise steeply while wages stagnated (MGG 1981, 1373). Thus unions learned that a wage package that looked generous in the present could rapidly lose its value in the future and that it was therefore necessary to look—and make calculations—ahead.

New Technologies, Job Losses, and Control Over Work

New technologies began to be important in the latter half of the 1960s, when some of the larger companies started modernizing their factories and offices.[9] Some employees' unions were very conscious of the possible effects of computerization on employment. Before 1983, when companies were legally required to get a "No Objection Certificate" from the unions before they could install a computer, a few unions used their veto power, as in the case of Pfizer. This did not deter the company, which got around the difficulty by contracting out the operations it wanted to computerize. In 1967, the union signed a computerization agreement in which the company undertook that there would be no redundancies, no reduction in employment, and no adverse effects on the service conditions of existing employees. A similar agreement was signed at Voltas in 1973, after three years of tense negotiations that included a 135-day lockout. In Glaxo, matters came to a head when the company wanted to replace its old IBM with a UNIVAC third-generation computer in 1979; a major agitation was launched, involving most of the central unions as well as several employees' unions, and a Committee Against Computerization was formed. After over four months of struggle, an agreement was signed guaranteeing that the total number of clerical staff—at that time 481—would not fall below 431 for a ten-year period.

Blue Star was another case of prolonged struggle on this issue. The company demanded computerization in 1981, and when the union refused, it set up a computer operation in the Santa Cruz Electronics Export Processing Zone in 1982. When the union served its next charter, the management too served a "charter," with computerization as one of its demands. In June 1984, it declared a lockout and said it would not be lifted until the computerization issue had been settled. The Supreme Court ordered that the lockout be lifted in February 1985, and the company had to come to a negotiated settlement with the union. The agreement included an undertaking by the company that no one would be retrenched as a result of computerization, the remuneration of present and future employees would be protected, and those displaced would either be provided with jobs requiring the same level of skills or be trained for more highly skilled jobs. Many other employees' unions (for example at ICI, Richardson Hindustan, Roussel, and Boehringer-Knoll) negotiated similar agreements or clauses in agreements.

Factory automation was an even more contentious issue. Automation of the packing lines in Parke-Davis was accompanied by acute problems of overwork: operators were asked to carry out too many tasks at the same time and line speeds were increased to unmanageable levels. Ultimately the workers, mainly women, elected a new leadership to lead a struggle (including tactics such as go-slows) to get workloads reduced. The more common complaint of unions was that workers were being made redundant. The Pfizer Employees' Union opposed automation for this reason and alleged that management had in 1975 encouraged dissident members to break away and join Dina Bama Patil's Mazdoor Congress, whose entry was marked by violence and assaults on its members. Subsequently, Mazdoor Congress members, although not more than a quarter of the workforce, were given extra promotions and a favored bargaining position; with their cooperation, the company was able to bring in new high-speed automatic machinery. Senior workers displaced by high-speed machines were shunted from line to line and asked to do odd jobs, treatment that they experienced as humiliating and demoralizing, which predisposed many to accept voluntary retirement when it was offered. In Richardson Hindustan, where rapid automation beginning in the 1970s had created a pool of surplus workers fearful of losing their jobs, the union put forward a demand for a generous voluntary retirement scheme in 1982; in many other companies, employers took the initiative to introduce such schemes, and insecure workers accepted the "golden handshake." In Hindustan Lever, where the union had used strategies such as go-slows and rolling strikes of a few workers at a time to establish shopfloor control over the labor process, transfer of production to nonunionized workers in subcontracted units and new sites broke this control decisively.

At first, the overwhelming preoccupation of union leaders was to prevent the loss of employment, and this led them to take a Luddite-like stance to new technologies. In every case, they failed in this objective, partly because companies had the option of contracting out the work, and partly because workers were not necessarily opposed to the changes and might even welcome them if they resulted in lighter workloads. The union leaders' second objective was to retain control over the labor process; in this they were more successful. At Blue Star, Hoechst, Pfizer, Voltas, May & Baker, and Ceat, unions succeeded in having some consultation rights included in the agreements. In one of the most detailed and inclusive clauses of this type, the Siemens agreement of 1982 specified that the union should be given details of intended changes at least seven days in advance, that any objections would be discussed, and that workers would have the right to exercise their "collective bargaining power" in case these discussions failed. The Philips Workers' Union used the introduction of new technology as an opportunity to negotiate shorter working hours, and the Hoechst Employees' Union used it as an opportunity to negotiate better health-and-safety regulations and working conditions. All these unions had come to see new technology as an issue over which they could and had to negotiate realistically, rather than putting up a blanket opposition that left no room for bargaining.

Two interunion workshops on modernization, in January and February 1986, were preceded by a workshop of women unionists taking up the same issue, and the discussions at these meetings revealed a sophisticated understanding of what was at stake. For the women workers, the priority was to fight against a speed-up of the line, but they also had constructive suggestions for changes in layout and deployment to prevent bottlenecks and ensure a smoother flow. In all the meetings, it was recognized that although modernization created problems for workers, their fate was even worse where companies refused to upgrade technology, which happened in many textile mills (Tyabji 1998): the factory would ultimately close down, leaving thousands jobless. It was felt that although modernization was currently being used to bolster management control over workers and increase profits, it *could be* of great benefit to workers and consumers. For workers, it could eliminate hazardous and fatiguing operations and increase leisure by making shorter working hours and more holidays possible; for consumers, it could make a larger quantity and variety of better-quality products available at lower prices. At the end of the workshop, a committee was set up to (a) draft a union statement on modernization and campaign for it; (b) draft a procedural agreement on the introduction of new technology, which would ensure full union participation at all stages; and (c) help individual unions faced with this problem to draft specific technology agreements. This committee met several times, and one consequence was that the demand for shorter working hours became the focal point for May Day rallies in 1986.

These employees' unions had learned valuable lessons from their encounter with new technology, and they could have developed a viable strategy for negotiating with management on the issue. Managements too could have learned to recognize this as a bargaining issue, just as they had earlier learned to negotiate with unions on wages. But this process was cut short by the new industrial policy of the Sixth Plan. At the workshop in January, some unions pointed out that government policy was hostile to workers. On the one hand, it prohibited expansion of production on the same premises, thus ruling out the possibility of absorbing the existing unionized workforce when new technology was introduced; on the other, it encouraged transfer of production to nonunionized workers in sub-contracted units and industrially backward areas, where employers could introduce state-of-the-art technology without any need to negotiate with a union. The industrial policy of the Sixth Plan is what ultimately led to the failure of the union initiative.

Health and Safety: The Bhopal Disaster

The Union Carbide (India Ltd.) Employees' Union (UCIL Employees' Union) in Bombay was one of the unions participating in Union Research Group studies of industrial accidents, so when news of the gas leak in Bhopal was reported in the newspapers, a URG investigation was undertaken. What we discovered was a story of government complicity in corporate crime. Everything—from the design of the plant and process to the way it was run—was wrong. And workers and local residents who protested had no way of getting their concerns addressed.

The Bhopal plant was producing highly toxic carboryl pesticides, for which methyl isocyanate (MIC) was an intermediate product. An extremely toxic, unstable, and volatile fluid, it was supposed to be stored at below five degrees Celsius in two large tanks. Even at this temperature, storing such large quantities of a lethal chemical was not safe; the Beziers plant of Union Carbide, which manufactured the same pesticides, did not store MIC but used it up as it was produced. If any MIC leaving the tanks was not absorbed during the production of carboryl, it was supposed to enter a caustic soda scrubber, where it would be neutralized; any toxic gases escaping from the scrubber were supposed to go to the flare tower, where they would be burned by a flame. But the capacity of the scrubber and diameter of the pipe to the flare tower were so small that even if they had been functioning, at least 40 percent of the MIC released on the night of December 2–3, 1984, would have escaped into the atmosphere.

In fact, not one of the safety systems was working on the night of the fatal leak. The refrigeration unit had not been functioning for at least six months, so the MIC in the tanks was at a temperature far higher than was safe. The scrubber was not operating. The pilot flame was off, and the pipeline to the flare tower was disconnected. This state of affairs was the result of a cost-cutting drive by Union Carbide, which included a drastic reduction of staff: the number of plant operators per shift was reduced from twelve to six, and the number of maintenance workers had been reduced from four to two. Even management categories were cut, and a single plant supervisor handled both the carbon monoxide and MIC plants. This inevitably had an effect on work quality. Maintenance suffered. Shortcuts bypassing safety procedures were forced on the workers. According to the most plausible reconstruction of the incident, which conforms with the explanation advanced by the Regional Research Laboratory, a length of pipe leading out of the MIC tank was being washed at 9:00 p.m. on December 2. Slip blinds were supposed to be inserted at each end of it, so that water would not go beyond those points, but this was not done. Thus it was possible for water to leak backward through faulty valves into the MIC tank, setting off the runaway reaction that ended with the discharge of the entire contents of the tank—forty-one metric tons of MIC—into the air.

Accidents had become routine. In 1981, a maintenance worker died after being splashed by liquid phosgene when he opened a pipe that had been declared free of toxic substances by management. In October 1982, a worker was asked to remove coal dust from a moving conveyor, and his hand got trapped in the belt. In the same month, an MIC pipeline burst, causing severe exposure to three workers and panic in the neighboring *bastis* (shantytowns). In early 1984, five workers had to be hospitalized following another leak. Minor leaks were so common that the external siren, which had sounded whenever a leak occurred, was disconnected from the internal alarm system, so that nearby residents would not have their sleep disrupted by "routine" leaks. This was to have fatal consequences on the night of the disaster, when the alarm was not given to the neighborhood until it was far too late (URG 1985a, 1985b).

When the unions demanded safer working conditions and an end to the use of untrained contract workers, management replied that all possible safety precautions were being taken. Those who persisted in their protests were charge-sheeted, threatened, and in some cases dismissed. Local management and the Union Carbide Corporation insisted on the management-rights clause in the agreement signed with the unions on May 14, 1983, which insisted that all planning and control of factory operations were "*exclusive* rights and responsibilities of the management."[10] In contrast with health-and-safety legislation in Britain or the Netherlands, there was no clause either in the agreement or in Indian legislation that empowered workers to take action to ensure the safe operation of their plant. After the disaster, the Factories Act—the only legislation covering health and safety at work—was amended but still did not give workers any rights to ensure safety (Banaji and Hensman 1990, 149–154).

There was, if possible, even greater anger and bitterness against the government than against the company on the part of the gas victims,[11] and indeed, the government was an accomplice from the time it granted the wrong type of license to Union Carbide and allowed it to locate the factory in a residential area, surrounded by *bastis* and sufficiently close to the railway station for hundreds of people to die there on the night of the disaster. Repeated appeals to the government for investigation into previous accidents, action to prevent future ones, and a review of the license given to the plant were ignored. Finally, when workers launched a hunger strike, a tripartite committee to look into their demands was set up; it concluded that the factory was being run in an exemplary manner. When residents, alarmed by the toxic leaks, demanded that the factory be relocated, they were told, with heavy sarcasm: "The factory represents a huge investment, it's not just a stone that can be picked up from one place and put down in another" (URG 1985a, 1985b).

Government complicity with Union Carbide continued after the disaster. In March 1985, the Government of India passed the Bhopal Gas Leak Disaster (Processing of Claims) Act, which gave it the exclusive right to represent the victims. Nasrin Bai and thirteen other victims filed a writ petition challenging the ordinance (*BS* 1985), fearing that the government would not represent the gas victims adequately. That fear proved only too well justified: the final settlement in February 1989 accepted the paltry sum of US$470 million (for several thousands dead and hundreds of thousands seriously injured), dropped all criminal charges against Union Carbide, and dismissed all past, present, and future claims of gas victims. The settlement was greeted with outrage in Bhopal, and thousands of gas victims, most of them women, traveled to Delhi to convey their "shock and anguish at the sudden, shameful and subservient settlement which the government of India and Union Carbide reached" (cit. Hensman and BGJB 1991, 10).

A very different outcome was a real possibility. Following initial URG reports of the appalling suffering endured by survivors of the disaster, around twenty-five employees' unions in Bombay formed the Trade Union Relief Fund for Gas Victims of Bhopal (TURF) and collected funds with which a relief center was set up in Bhopal opposite the Union Carbide plant, run by volunteers (including a doctor) from Bombay and Bhopal. It provided outpatient treatment to victims and taught them respiratory physiotherapy so that they could make the best use of their damaged lungs. It also ran a nutrition program for children (*MP Chronicle* 1985).

As early as December 1984, in discussions between TURF volunteers and workers at the Bhopal factory, the idea of demanding alternative production at the site of the plant emerged. It was obvious that traumatized local residents did not want pesticides to be produced there again (Surya 1985), regardless of whether the plant remained with Union Carbide, was sold to another company, or was taken over by the government. But the workers said that machinery in the formulation plant and fabrication shop could be used to make other products; pollution-control equipment, portable oxygen respirators, and soya products were suggested. The rest of the fifty-three acres, with several buildings and electricity and water supplies, could be used to set up cooperatives for the gas victims to produce items needed locally, and perhaps also a hospital, child-care center, and community kitchen.

While these discussions were going on, the company gave notice for the closure of the Bhopal plant, claiming it was on instructions received from the state government (*BS* 1985). The notice would take effect three months later, on July 11. In the following months, an alternative plan began to take shape, along with the demand that Union Carbide hand over the premises to the workers and gas victims and provide the necessary investment for setting up alternative production. Workers took around copies of a proposal to this effect in the gas-affected areas and collected over ten thousand signatures and thumb impressions in favor of it within a few days. Many of the gas victims too were in need of employment, either because they were no longer able to do the work they were doing before or because their family had lost its breadwinner. A joint organization of workers and gas victims—the Gas Peedith Rahat Samiti (GPRS—Gas Victims' Relief Committee) was formed.

When July 11 came, workers occupied part of the plant, and the TURF organized a demonstration at the Bombay office of UCIL, protesting against the closure of the plant and demanding that the plant, together with a lump sum, be handed over to the workers and gas victims for alternative production (TURF 1985). As a result, the managing director of UCIL, V. P. Gokhale, agreed in principle to hand over part of the plant and arranged for a TURF delegation to be given a tour. Subsequently, others in Bhopal were approached by the TURF. The marketing manager of the Oil Federation was very sympathetic and said that his company would be willing to make deoiled soya cake available for processing. He suggested a possible market-ing outlet could be Modern Bread, a government undertaking producing soya-enriched bread. A survey of the workers' skills was carried out. A simi-lar survey of gas victims, including the disabilities suffered by them as a result of exposure to the gas, was planned (URG 1985c; Jacobs 1985a, 1985b).

One of the four resolutions passed by the General Body Meeting of the GPRS on November 17, 1985, said:

> We feel that a plan for alternative production is quite feasible. There is machinery in the formulation plant which can be used for manufactur-ing food products and animal feed, and the machinery in the fabrica-tion shop can be used for making agricultural implements and other products. There are many buildings which could be used to manufac-ture other useful products. With a relatively small investment, these could provide employment to many gas victims who desperately need an income, as well as producing goods and services which they need.
>
> (GPRS 1985)

The committee reported on its

> first round of discussions with Sri J. Mukund, Works Manager and Sri S. P. Choudhary, Production Manager. . . . Mr Mukund said that he is examining the feasibility of handing over the formulation unit along with its workshop to a co-operative to be run jointly by UCIL workers and gas victims. The feasibility of starting a community kitchen for work-ers and gas victims run by the Samiti was also discussed. Negotiations are in progress. A team of technical experts led by Dr Ojha, Director, Central Institute of Agricultural Engineering [CIAE], visited the formula-tion plants and the Central workshop in the UCIL premises to examine the feasibility of alternative production. Please stand by for their report, which will be made available soon.
>
> (GPRS 1985)

A comprehensive report was produced subsequently, and in February 1986, a meeting was held between representatives of the GPRS, CIAE, and the Department of Industries of the Government of MP, at which the latter pledged to provide work sheds as well as initial investment costs for plant and equipment.

If this plan had been implemented, perhaps gas victims such as Rashida Bi would not have been left feeling that "maybe the people who died were the lucky ones" (Majumdar 1999). There were many reasons why it never came to fruition. First, while there were sections of the left that felt that "Workers' Cooperatives are important forms of self-organisation of workers in industrial and agricultural sectors" (Eashvaraiah 2000, 4), the dominant left ideology saw nationalization as the automatic response to a crisis in any productive enterprise. This demand was raised in Bhopal, despite its inappropriateness in the circumstances, while the demand for workers' cooperatives did not receive support from the mainstream left. Second, with few exceptions, international supporters of the Bhopal survivors hung all their hopes on the court case, and support for alternative production from them, too, was minimal. Third and most importantly, alarmed by these developments and by the occupation of the factory, the government of MP sent workers off to various corners of the state on the pretext of providing them with "alternative employment." Dispersal of the workers destroyed the main organized force in Bhopal that could have carried out a survey of gas victims and spearheaded a struggle for alternative production. Individual government officials were sympathetic to the plan and ready to assist in formulating and implementing it, but it was not acceptable to politicians in either the state government or the central government. The disaster had not changed their hostility to workers' control over production or residents' control over their lives.

Equal Treatment and Opportunities

There have been only a few cases of women organizing separately within formal-sector unions. The All-India Bank Employees' Association (AIBEA) was one. The union had fought for and obtained good employment conditions for women, but they were underrepresented in the leadership. One measure taken was to reserve a few union posts for women, so that they had a chance to gain experience and standing before contesting elections for the general posts. Then, in February 1996, the first All-India Women Bank Employees' Convention was held in Bombay to inaugurate the women's wing of the union, which grew rapidly thereafter. The success of the women's wing in mobilizing women, as well as statements by the women themselves, suggested the importance of separate organizing to help build confidence and leadership skills.[12] Another example was the Mahila Mukti Morcha (MMM), formed in Chhattisgarh in 1981. Women miners in the Chhattisgarh Mines Shramik Sangh realized that despite playing a creative and active role in the union, they were underrepresented in the leadership. More than five hundred women members of the miners' families also became members.[13] Both the women's wing of AIBEA and the MMM saw violence against women, whether inside or outside the workplace, as an issue they had to tackle. But in neither case did separate organizing lead to the union putting forward a demand for equal opportunities for women in recruitment and promotions, despite the fact that women faced considerable discrimination in regular waged work and were routinely relegated to less skilled jobs (Liddle 1988; Hensman 1996a).

The problems of other sections of the labor force who face discrimination have not received even this limited degree of recognition. This is partly because these sections have not, generally, organized themselves *as workers*. Unlike Japan, where marginalized workers have organized themselves into separate unions (Kawanishi 1992, 38–39, 272), or Canada, where they have organized within existing unions to highlight the ways in which discrimination has affected them as workers (Briskin 2002), India has seen no comparable organizing among Dalits and Adivasis (also known as scheduled castes, or SCs, and scheduled tribes, or STs); religious, ethnic and linguistic minorities; people with disabilities; or lesbian, gay, bisexual, and transgender workers. All these groups have organized *outside* the trade union movement but have not succeeded in bringing their concerns into it. Nor has the dominant male caste Hindu section of the formal union leadership taken these concerns seriously, except when they have erupted in violence—and sometimes not even then. This has undermined solidarity and perpetuated divisions within the labor force.

Brutal and widespread violence against Dalits and Adivasis, who have suffered humiliation, exclusion, dispossession, persecution, torture, rape, murder, and the torching of entire villages, led to the enactment of the Scheduled Castes and Scheduled Tribes (Prevention of Atrocities) Act of 1989. The Indian constitution already provided for reservation quotas for

SCs and STs in public-sector employment in order to combat endemic discrimination against them. These policies have had limited effects, and discrimination and violence against these sections persists (cf. *EPW* 1997, 1999; Thorat and Lee 2005). With the reduction of public-sector employment due to privatization, their absence from formal employment becomes even starker. Yet unions have not taken up the demand for equal opportunities for them in employment and education.[14]

Workers from minority communities have been even worse off. There has been no mandatory affirmative action for them. Indeed, Dalits who converted to Christianity or Islam lost their right to SC reservations: this is a case where the state actually discriminated against people on the basis of their religion. The report of the Justice Sachar Committee on the Social, Economic and Educational Status of the Muslim Community of India (Sachar 2006) revealed systematic deprivation and exclusion of Muslims, pointing out that in the case of SC Muslims,

> change in religion did not bring any change in their social or economic status. Because of the stigma attached to their traditional occupation, they suffer social exclusion. . . . Many have suggested that the Order of 1950 [denying them SC benefits] is inconsistent with Articles 14, 15, 16 and 25 of the Constitution that guarantee equality of opportunity, freedom of conscience and protect citizens from discrimination by the State on grounds of religion, caste or creed.
>
> (Sachar 2006, 201)

This anomaly was sought to be addressed by the National Commission for Linguistic and Religious Minorities, chaired by Justice Ranganath Misra, which submitted its report to Prime Minister Manmohan Singh in May 2006. The report suggested deleting the clause of the Scheduled Castes Order of 1950 that denies SC benefits to Muslim and Christian Dalits, but subsequently the government went to extraordinary lengths to suppress it. It was neither published nor tabled in parliament; even when a citizen, Franklin Thomas, filed a right-to-information application asking for copies of the report, the central government objected. The Central Information Commission finally ruled on July 30, 2009, that a copy of the report should be given to Thomas (Kashif-ul-Huda 2009).

Part of the problem is the reservation policy itself, which was originally seen as a temporary measure to protect those who fell outside the caste system from ingrained and systematic discrimination. "It was like a bitter pill for a sick Indian society, a necessary evil, required as long as the disease lasted. There was inbuilt motivation for the society to recover from the disease at the earliest and stop the pills. Since the disease basically referred to the caste system, reservations were the catalyst that would hasten its death" (Teltumbde 2007, 2384). Instead, reservations were extended to caste Hindus on the basis of their caste, thus reinforcing the caste system rather than destroying it. Hence a first step to reform the system would be "reverting to the original conception of reservations for the SCs and STs as a countervailing force against the disability of Indian society to treat its constituents with equity. . . . The system should be worked as a mechanism to end the caste system itself" (Teltumbde 2007, 2385). Working toward antidiscrimination and equal-opportunities legislation, along with the machinery that would be required to enforce such policies (such as an Equal Opportunities Commission, which was, in fact, recommended in 2007 as a follow-up to the Sachar Committee Report), and exploring the possibility of other forms of affirmative action are additional measures that could be pursued (Mehta 2004; Thorat et al. 2005).

The lack of a policy on equal opportunities has had far-reaching effects on the composition of the labor force in Bombay, the employees' unions, and the trade union movement as a whole. The Shiv Sena[15] was formed in 1966 with the goal of securing 80 percent of the jobs in Bombay for Maharashtrians, discouraging migration to Bombay from other states, opposing communists, and upholding Hinduism as the dominant culture in India. Their first campaign was against South Indians, who—although by no means absent from the ranks of unskilled laborers—were better represented than Maharashtrians among white-collar strata because they were, on average, better educated (Gupta 1982, 39–40, 52). Anticommunism has been an enduring theme, and physical attacks were the main means by which Girni Kamgar Union support among textiles workers was broken. In December 1967, the Shiv Sena attacked the CPI office in Parel and hurled stones at a CPI rally. In January 1968, two CPI members had to be rushed to hospital when they were attacked by Shiv Sainiks. The CPI offices were attacked again in May 1970, and the CPI leader Krishna Desai was murdered the following month. Shortly afterward, Shiv Sena leader Bal Thackeray congratulated those who killed Desai, declaring, "we must not miss a single opportunity to massacre communists wherever we find them" (Gupta 1982, 157–159).

Their union, the BKS (set up in 1968), was not popular even with workers who supported the Shiv Sena politically, because of its promanagement stance; indeed, it was brought in by management in some factories to break the power of existing unions (Gupta 1982, 83, 177–178). On the other hand, the Sthanik Lokadhikar Samiti, set up in 1972, soon had branches in numerous offices and factories. Its main demand was that 80 percent of all jobs should be reserved for Maharashtrians (Gupta 1982, 86). Some managements were happy to comply; others did so out of fear. But the net effect was that the ethnic composition of the labor force changed drastically by the 1980s, with younger recruits far less diverse than the older generation.[16]

Leaders of the employees' unions, which reflected this culture of diversity, were worried about the communalization[17] of the labor force as a result of the Shiv Sena's activities. After the anti-Muslim riots of 1984, which were concentrated in Bhiwandi but also affected Bombay, there were interunion meetings to discuss how to meet this threat, and one of the conclusions was that "unions must tackle the arguments spread by communal groups among workers." After the far worse carnage in Bombay in December 1992–January 1993 in the wake of the demolition of the Babri Masjid (Mosque), the TUSC organized a workshop in December 1993 that showed films and discussed the issue, concluding that "communalism and communal divisions are harmful to the cause of the working class and TUs must not allow communal divisions in their ranks." The All-India Blue Star Employees' Federation, at its delegate session in February 1999, condemned a spate of attacks on Christians by RSS-linked organizations. But these were relatively small meetings and educational sessions. Most union leaders were afraid to raise these issues in their own unions, given an atmosphere in which even blood-donation drives for survivors of the violence met with resistance from some workers.

After the massacre of Muslims in Gujarat in 2002, a convention, organized by the left and employees' unions and attended by hundreds of union activists, to condemn the pogrom was finally held. The resolution passed by the convention demanded the "removal of the caretaker chief minister Narendra Modi who acted in support of the communal organisations who were responsible for the genocide in Gujarat" and appealed to workers to "spread the message of communal harmony and . . . work for collection of funds for the help and rehabilitation of Gujarat riot victims" (*New Age Weekly* 2002). Yet even on this occasion, a fundraising drive for the survivors by employees' unions met with strong resistance from some members of their own managing committees. Activists reported some workers saying that the victims deserved what they got: this was evidence of extreme prejudice, given that the victims were helpless innocents who were tortured, raped, and killed in unspeakably brutal ways (Communalism Combat 2002; *Tehelka* 2007). It was after this experience that Vasudevan, as convener of the TUSC, decided that the issue had to be taken up in a more systematic fashion, with a workers' education program that included a variety of inputs.

Problems of Democracy and Responsibility

Employees' unions are generally characterized by participatory democracy. Decisions are made at the workplace level, and leaders are employees who can be—and are—replaced in elections. Some have a "general council" consisting of elected shop or departmental representatives; all have a managing committee, including officeholders who are elected by the entire membership. Many have magazines or news bulletins that publish information relevant to the union. Since there is no status gap between union representatives and ordinary workers, loss of position does not involve loss of pay or prestige (cf. Dickenson 1982, 177). Yet there have been crises in these unions too. Some of the most dramatic incidents of this type occurred during what came to be known as the "Datta Samant wave."

Datta Samant, the leader of the Maharashtra General Kamgar Union, first acquired fame (or notoriety) in 1972, when the workers of Godrej and Boyce called him in to dislodge an unpopular union. He was arrested as a result of the violence that followed, and there was a vigorous campaign for his release. He spent time in prison again during the Emergency and reached the peak of his popularity in the post-Emergency period, when large numbers of workers were attracted by his reputation of being a tough bargainer who won wage increases of magnitudes previously unheard of (Ramaswamy 1988, 22–26). Those cases where an entire workforce went over to Samant were relatively straightforward; cases where some members of an employees' union wished to call him in while others were strongly opposed were more complicated. The consequence, very often, was a bitter, violent conflict between the two camps. It would be easy to see the outcome as purely destructive and negative, but this would be to ignore the learning process that many employees' unions went through as a result of this painful experience. The preparatory research and workshop organized by the URG in 1987 to discuss the problem brought to light the full complexity of the issues involved.[18]

In two of the cases—Pfizer and German Remedies—the employees' union was already having problems with a rival management-sponsored union, and workers brought in Samant, hoping that he might unite the workforce once more. At Wyeth, Burroughs Wellcome, and Hindustan Lever, those who wished to call in Samant either were a majority, or leaders of the employees' union went along with them in order to avoid a divided union situation. At Hoechst, Glaxo, and Siemens, Samant was the first major challenge to the employees' union, and there was stubborn opposition to his entry from the existing leadership and much of the membership.

Before examining the motivations of workers in detail, it is worth looking at management attitudes to Samant. At first, his reputation as a firebrand who was willing to resort to violence in order to get staggeringly large wage increases led to strong management resistance against him. But when they were forced to negotiate with him, there was a subtle change of attitude. "Once the novelty wore off, employers learnt to cope with Samant. Numerous enterprises . . . institutionalized their relationship with him, and some at least . . . found a positive aspect to the relationship" (Ramaswamy 1988, 25–26). While employers might have to pay more with Samant at the head of the union, they could also gain a considerable degree of shopfloor control, which internal leaders had not been ready to give up. Like other external leaders, it was he who decided not only what demands to fight for but also which of management's demands to concede. "What are given up, paradoxically, are the very issues which trouble workers. While workers are concerned about work and employment, it is precisely in these areas that they have conceded the most to management" (Ramaswamy 1988, 74).

For a few workers, the reason for calling in an outsider was the structural weakness of employees' unionism. Real pressure could only be brought to bear by outsiders, they felt, and therefore an outside leader was necessary in confrontations with aggressive or hostile managements. But for most workers, disaffection arose as a result of individual or group grievances. For example, certain jobs might not have been classified or graded properly; an increase in workloads, which affected a particular section, might not have been dealt with in a satisfactory manner by the union; a discriminatory promotion might have gone unchallenged by the union; or the leadership might be biased toward salaried staff, with factory workers not adequately represented and their emoluments allowed to lag behind. In other cases, the criticisms were general but felt more acutely by the dissidents. For example, the union might have agreed to a DA scheme or ceiling that had reduced earnings; wage settlements might not be high enough; or the leadership might be too inclined to solve all problems through negotiations and refuse to take direct action under any circumstances.

It would appear that all these types of grievances could equally well be taken up by a different internal leadership: indeed, that was the method adopted by the Goodlass Nerolac manual workers when they felt that the union leadership was discriminating against them. When URG researchers probed the reasons why others did not do the same, it almost always emerged that an alternative leadership had not been able to muster sufficient support to win an election or, having won, had not been reelected. In such circumstances, many dissident minorities turned to Samant to dislodge the current leadership and solve their problems. Often they felt that they had been denied democratic representation within the employees' union. For supporters of the employees' union, on the contrary, this was either a case of a minority trying to impose their will on the majority by bringing in a powerful outsider or—where Samant supporters were the majority—an abdication of the responsibility to take over the leadership and solve the problems themselves. In either case, it was an undemocratic measure, because it allowed an outsider to make union decisions.

Whether their grievances were justified or not, many of the workers who went over to Samant were disillusioned by the experience. In Wyeth, where in 1981 the whole committee had called in Samant because management rejected their charter of demands, a strike ensued; six months later, finding that they were no nearer to an agreement, they decided to leave him. In 1984, the majority in the Nicholas Laboratories Employees' Union made a similar decision to join Samant because management was not settling a bonus demand, but this was not a unanimous decision. A minority, among whom the medical representatives were predominant, opposed the decision and kept the employees' union alive; after months had gone by without any resolution of the conflict, the majority came back to it. Dissident workers at Hoechst found that Samant was far less concerned about shopfloor problems like classification and excessive workloads than internal leaders; moreover, he took no steps to protect them when management retaliated to their direct action with dismissals and a lockout of the Liquid Orals department, where most of the dissidents were concentrated. Here, as in Glaxo and Pfizer, workers gradually drifted back to the employees' union.

Thus, over the same period that employers were learning to live with Samant, workers were learning that he was not a panacea. There were inherent weaknesses with employees' unions, in that they remained confined to the workplace or company, but their strong point was the degree of control over decision making that their members had, and dissidents who genuinely wanted union democracy realized the superiority of employees' unions in this respect.

However, this did not mean that the problems that gave rise to the crisis had been solved, and the interunion workshop organized by the URG in February 1987 was an attempt to tackle these. The complaint by some groups that the union leadership was monopolized by a few people; the complaint by union leaders that they missed promotions and lost pay as a result of their union posts and got stuck with all the "donkey work" because no one else would do it; the feeling of distance from and lack of communication with the union leaders on the part of some workers; the feeling on the part of the leaders that workers simply brought them a problem and expected them to solve it regardless of the difficulties involved—all these were at some level justified.

When these unions were first formed, the enthusiasm and participation of the members was a condition of their survival, and there was a vitality resulting from the feeling that the union *is* the membership. But once they were established and recognized, members slipped into the habit of leaving most of the thinking and decision making to leaders, feeling that their part was played once they took a problem or grievance to the leader. If the problem was solved, they praised the leader; if not, they blamed him or her. Very rarely did they see themselves as having equal responsibility for finding a solution, and consequently they were unable to appreciate that union leaders might sometimes have genuine difficulties. For example a woman worker, having been told that the union could do nothing about a ten-year award being given to another woman prematurely, said, "we felt very hurt by that. After all, the union being mother and father to us, if it can't do anything, where can we go next?" Again, when dissidents complained about the DA ceiling, union leaders pointed out that they were among the members who had approved the agreement at a general body meeting before it was signed. Many union leaders felt uncomfortable about their role yet had increasing difficulty refusing it, as no one else could match their accumulated expertise.

Another complex of problems arose in the 1970s and 1980s as a result of rapid technological change. The introduction of new machines turned established work relationships upside down and created a hotbed of new dissatisfactions. Increasing workloads, productivity allowances, displacement, and redeployment created conflicts where none had existed before. Promotion and reclassification disrupted the existing hierarchy, and the introduction of shiftworking on some machines created tensions as male workers were promoted over the heads of more senior women. The fact that each of these problems was experienced very acutely by only a section of workers, with others finding it difficult to understand or sympathize, created additional frustration.

Third, the ethnic and gender composition of the workforces changed. As companies stopped recruiting women (see chapter 7) and began recruiting only young Marathi speakers in response to the Shiv Sena's campaign, a kind of generation gap sprang up. The young workers wanted bigger pay increases, while older workers felt that "what the workers are getting presently—forty hours' week, weekly off, bonus, uniform, rest room, canteen, medical treatment—it doesn't occur to them that they have only got this through struggles, they don't bother even to think about all this." Some young workers resented getting less pay than the women and criticized the union for always wanting to solve problems through discussion and negotiation. Union leaders retorted, "in comparing their pay with that of much more senior women employees, they ignore the fact that by the time they reach the same level of seniority, their own pay will be very much higher. . . . They feel this union only believes in discussion, not action, but what kind of methods do they use? One of them used threats of assault against a woman worker to get her to reduce production!"

At the workshop held to discuss this issue, unionists put forward two main strategies to revitalize employees' unions: a greater emphasis on democratic functioning and systematic education and training of existing and potential committee members. One union leader observed that "people think that the committee should be elected unopposed, then management will think that the union is strong, but that is the biggest mistake." However, others observed that it was difficult for a new candidate to stand against an experienced, well-known leader with any chance of success; repeated failure in such attempts was the basis of the charge that the employees' union was undemocratic. Alternatively, there were cases where the old committee members refrained from contesting an election in order to give others a chance, but this could also be disastrous if the new committee signed a bad agreement. This might serve to dispel the charge of undemocratic functioning, but it could also reinforce the feeling of most workers that tried and tested leaders are best and discourage newcomers from coming forward in the future. Another union leader suggested that "one third of the committee should retire at every election, but not lose interest, however. New people should be trained to take their place."

It was felt that training committee members was not sufficient: ordinary members needed education too, so that they could understand the issues being negotiated, have a reasonable idea of the situation outside their company, and make informed decisions when the need arose. They also needed to be involved in processes such as formulating the charter and be encouraged to put forward suggestions that could improve the functioning of the union. Above all, they should be made aware that trade unionism had a role that went beyond simply negotiating for higher salaries.

Even if these measures were implemented, they would not solve all the problems arising from the existence of disparate workforces divided along lines of caste, language, ethnic and religious community, gender, age, skill, and so on; a means of representing the views and satisfying the aspirations of minorities would still have to be incorporated. But confirmed supporters of employees' unions felt that it was essential to safeguard and preserve their one great asset: the potential for truly democratic participation of the workforce in running their own organization.

An Employers' Offensive with State Backing

The agreement dated July 1, 1977, between the Philips Workers' Union and Philips India Ltd. was probably the first to mention a charter of demands submitted by the company to the union in response to the union's charter of demands. This subsequently became standard practice: whenever a union submitted a charter for a new agreement, the company would do likewise and insist that both "charters" be discussed simultaneously. Sometimes, instead of a "charter" it was a "Notice of Change under Section 9A of the Industrial Disputes Act," but the intention was the same: to withdraw rights or terminate benefits that had earlier been won by the union. Thus a management "charter" or "notice of change" was mentioned in agreements between the respective unions and Blue Star Ltd. (April 12, 1978), Britannia Biscuit Company (May 2, 1979), Goodlass Nerolac Paints Ltd. (October 10, 1980), Griffon Laboratories Pvt. Ltd. (February 14, 1982), Merind Ltd. (February 24, 1986), and many others.

It was relatively easy for managements to withdraw facilities, privileges, or benefits that were not part of any collective agreement but had become accepted as a matter of custom and practice. For example, unions were initially denied the right to time off for union work; thus when the Bombay Automobile Employees' Union demanded from the Firestone Tyre and Rubber Company of India Ltd. that "representatives of the Union should be allowed to see the Officers of the Company, Government Representatives, etc., and the time taken by them should not be treated as leave," not only the company but also the Industrial Court rejected the demand (BGG 1949c, 2462). But many unions subsequently established the right for union representatives to take time off for union work without loss of leave or pay. In rare instances—similar to cases in Britain where the convener or one or two senior shop stewards could work full time for the union and might be granted facilities like an office and telephone on company premises (Boraston et al. 1975, 32, 187)—employees' unions established a practice whereby one or two officeholders would be entitled to such facilities.

The Blue Star Workers' Union received such facilities from management. But in 1977, when Vasudevan, a stenographer and founding member of the union, was general secretary of the BSWU as well as the All-India Blue Star Employees' Federation, the company began attempting

to restrict trade union activities during working hours. . . . In 1989, in the context of a prolonged and severe management offensive against the union and the federation, the Company asked Vasudevan to do company work, with the intention of restricting his union activities. He refused to accept this. The company then stopped his wages with effect from 25 October 1989. It was against this that the BSWU filed a complaint of unfair labour practice before the Industrial Court. The Industrial Court decided in Vasudevan's favour, holding that the practice whereby Vasudevan did only union work during working hours (in the years 1983 to 1989) had become an implied agreement. The Bombay High Court . . . reversed this judgement and held that a "concession" had been given to Vasudevan

and this did not amount to an implied agreement. . . . The Supreme
Court refused to intervene in this matter or make any comment.

(TUSC n.d., 1–2)

In the face of attempts by other managements "to project this judgement as if it has taken away all rights of union leaders to do union work
during duty hours," the TUSC emphasized that

the rights of union leaders of recognised unions to attend court cases
either under Section 23 of the MRTU and PULP Act or under analogous
provisions is not even discussed, let alone affected. Secondly, any written
agreement or Standing Order or rule recognising/formalising any rights
of union leaders is still valid. Lastly, the judgement does not rule out the
possibility that in a different set of facts and circumstances, a similar
practice may well amount to an implied agreement.

It also pointed out that "this case comes at a time when there is a general
attack on trade unionism and workers' rights, and many attempts to eliminate them altogether" (TUSC n.d., 2–3).

An increasingly common method of combating or eliminating trade
unionism was to deny sections of workers the right to engage in it. Here
managements were assisted by ambiguities in the ID Act, which protects
only those who are designated as "workmen" from arbitrary dismissal.
Courts interpreted this to mean that there is a "nonbargainable category"
of employees who do not have the right to belong to a union or bargain
collectively: a clear violation of ILO Conventions 87 and 98 on Freedom
of Association and the Right to Organise and Bargain Collectively, not to
mention of the Indian constitution! An important section of employees to
be attacked in this way was medical representatives of pharmaceutical companies. Many employees' unions in pharmaceutical companies included
medical representatives among their members (for example, the Merck
Sharp & Dohme India Ltd. Employees' Union), and in some, such as the
Nicholas Laboratories Employees' Union, these workers played an important role. Most companies negotiated with them, but some agreements,
such as the one dated December 1, 1982, between the Ralli Group Employees' Union and Rallis India Ltd., made explicit "the Company's contention
that Medical Representatives are not 'workmen' as defined in Section 2(s)
of the Industrial Disputes Act."

From the mid-1970s onward, a major attack was launched on them. When a medical representative on the managing committee of the Sandoz Employees' Union attended the first meeting with management to discuss the union's charter of demands in August 1975, the managing director objected to his presence on the grounds that he was not a "workman." A separate charter of demands for medical representatives was then served in November, and in January 1976 the company was informed that a negotiating committee was ready to discuss the demands. But the company refused to negotiate. In June, it forced its medical representatives to sign individual agreements, threatening them with dismissal if they refused. At the same time, it started harassing the medical representative who was on the committee of the Sandoz Employees' Union with charge-sheets and an enquiry, eventually terminating his employment. He took the matter to court, but the court dismissed his complaint on the grounds that the plaintiff was not a "workman" according to the definition in the ID Act (MGG 1981, 195ff.). Since other companies were beginning to do the same, the matter was sufficiently serious for the Sandoz union to take the matter up to the Supreme Court.

The Supreme Court judgment of August 1994 in the Sandoz case, which denied union rights to medical representatives, opened the floodgates to management attempts to push more and more employees into the "non-bargainable" "officer" category. Sales representatives were not the only ones subjected to this treatment. At Goodlass Nerolac, during a prolonged lock-out in 1987, 150 technical staff were forced to sign an agreement converting them to the "officer" category under threat of dismissal if they refused. By 1993, 90 percent of the office staff had been converted to the "officer" category. Previously, the union had struggled to get promotions for subclerical staff ("peons"), and now they had all been converted to "junior officers" without any change in their job! Similar absurdities were perpetrated at Parke-Davis.[19] A circular of Hindustan Lever Mazdoor Sabha dated August 23, 1984, satirized a management move to convert C-4 clerks into officers:

In fact, there may well be some truth in the rumours that while the C-4 Clerks will be designated as Administrative Officers, C-3 Clerks will be Deputy Administrative Officers, and C-2 Clerks will be Assistant Administrative Officers, etc. Even for the Service Staff, the likely designations are Auto Officers for Drivers, Attendant Officers for Sepoys and Sanitary Officers for Sweepers!

The ID Act defines such antiunion activities as unfair labor practices, but once the nonbargainable category had been created, it was impossible to prevent the expulsion of unionized workers into it.

Transferring production to contract workers, subcontracted units, and new facilities in industrially backward areas was another way of breaking unions. An early case was at Boehringer-Knoll, which in 1982 announced the closure of its chloramphenicol plant and the retrenchment of fifty-seven workers after contracting out the plant's production. The union filed an Unfair Labour Practices case, arguing, among other things, that the proposed lockout and dismissals could be classed as victimization. On this occasion, the Maharashtra government refused permission for the dismissals, and its decision was upheld by the High Court.[20] In 1990–1991, Pfizer was having 24.92 percent of Becosule capsules, 53.22 percent of Terramycin capsules, and 100 percent of its Dumasule and Marax capsules manufactured by third parties, and this amount increased the following year even while capacity lay idle in the Thane factory. The union pointed out that by getting drugs produced in the small-scale sector, the company could evade the drug price–control policy of the government as well as payment of taxes, and customers were being cheated because they "do not know whether a tablet or capsule they eat is manufactured in the Company's factory or a shed/hut somewhere."[21] Between 1984 and 1990, Hindustan Lever opened plants in several industrially backward areas, employing state-of-the-art technology and large productive capacities but paying subsistence wages, imposing overly long working hours, and providing abysmal employee facilities (Nair et al. 1999). At the same time, it gradually phased out production in its unionized plant at Sewri in Bombay. Nor was this an unmixed blessing for workers in the new locations, since the company proceeded to close those facilities once the tax holiday was over and move to even newer locations, mainly in the northeast, where a ten-year tax holiday was on offer (Chakravarty 2002).

Having transferred production to nonunionized workers, next these companies closed down their Bombay factories, using a mixture of bribery and fraud backed by intimidation and violence. Usually, the first step was to create an atmosphere of insecurity by "making illegal and arbitrary deductions from our salaries, suspending workers at random on flimsy grounds, issuing memos and charge-sheets indiscriminately, and refusing to negotiate with the union" (Harish Pujari, Otis Elevator Employees' Union); and by keeping workers "idle without work for months so their morale is destroyed, by creating a false impression in the workers' minds that they can take VRS and do business, by trying to get the all-India federation derecognized, by not signing a single major wage settlement since last ten years" (N. Vasudevan, All-India Blue Star Employees' Federation). "Management . . . made workers sit idle without work, tried to reduce paid holidays by almost seven days, attempted to make the five-day week to a six-day week" (Arvind Tapole, All-India Voltas Employees' Federation).[22]

They then offered voluntary retirement schemes, sometimes on very attractive terms. Ciba-Geigy retired its entire workforce of nine hundred in 1993. At Boots, the additional ploy of selling the factory to an unknown company called Neo-Pharma was used to coerce employees to accept a VRS. The employees' union in Abbott Laboratories put up stiff resistance, getting a stay order in court to stop the company from selling the factory to an unknown entity called Suvidha Chemicals. The company—which had refused to negotiate a new collective agreement since 1982, was deunionizing the workforce by classifying medical representatives as nonbargainable, was hiring large numbers of temporary and contract workers, and had locked out the factory for thirteen months in 1987–1988—retaliated by suspending four union officeholders.[23] In the end, fearing that the deal with Suvidha would go through and they would then be left with far worse employment conditions or dismissal without compensation, most workers in Abbott accepted the VRS. In Nicholas, the union gave workers calculations showing how much they would lose by accepting the VRS, held protest demonstrations, and went to court against the scheme (C. G. Chavan, Nicholas Employees' Union).[24] In many cases, once a sufficient number of workers had been induced to leave, bringing the total strength of the workforce down to less than one hundred, employers could close the unit without government permission (D'Costa 1999). The Ciba-Geigy, Boots, Abbott and Nicholas factories were ultimately closed.

As these and many other examples show, the "voluntary" nature of a VRS was often very suspect. A long lockout in 1987 and management sponsorship of a rival union that engaged in physical attacks on supporters of the employees' union were used at Goodlass Nerolac. The Philips Mahaunion (Federation) was broken in the 1980s by a combination of sponsoring rival unions and victimization. The Otis Elevator Employees' Union, which had been resisting the use of contract workers for maintenance jobs since the 1980s, faced a management-sponsored rival union and protracted lockouts in 1994.[25] Meanwhile, the Roche, Hoechst, Boehringer-Mannheim, and

Parke-Davis factories were closed. In Hindustan Lever, where the union mounted a vigorous campaign against VRSs, there was a year-long lockout in 1988–1989, a rumor that the factory was going to be closed, and the victimization of union officeholders. In August 2006, the company sold the Sewri (Bombay) factory to a loss-making subsidiary, Bon Limited, which had a share capital of only Rs 5 lakhs; HLL had to transfer Rs 10 crores to Bon so that it could buy the factory! When Hindustan Unilever applied for permission to close the factory, the labor commissioner first rejected and later accepted the application (NTUI 2007). The union appealed to the High Court, which ruled that if the transfer to the subsidiary was not legally valid, then it followed that the closure was invalid, and even if the transfer was valid, the closure might still be invalid. It directed the Industrial Tribunal to decide both matters within six months. In October 2009, after more than three years of struggle, the union finally accepted a VRS package that included the last drawn salary up to each worker's due date of retirement. Blue Star was one of the few companies where the Bombay factory survived, despite the opening of a third factory in Dadra and a fourth in Himachal Pradesh. This was because its market was expanding, orders were pouring in, the skilled workers were in the union, and the company understood that the union therefore had the power to cause problems for it.

Some companies never reconciled themselves to dealing with unions, but others had accepted a collective-bargaining culture by the 1970s. What possessed the latter to turn on their negotiating partners so ferociously? The standard answer, "globalization," is not compatible with the chronology of the attacks. They started in the mid-1970s and escalated rapidly in the 1980s, when the Indian market was still heavily protected from imports. What it was *not* protected from was products made in the informal sector. Faced with competition from an upgraded informal sector, which enjoyed "fiscal incentives in terms of exemption from excise tax, direct subsidy, price preference, credit, technical and marketing assistance" (Ramaswamy 1994, M-13), a few multinational corporations sold their factories to Indian companies (for example, Roche and Nicholas sold theirs to the Piramal Group), while many concluded that the only way to survive was to subcontract production to small-scale units. But this strategy had disadvantages, especially for pharmaceutical companies, due to the difficulty in ensuring quality control. An even more attractive alternative, given the generous incentives, was to shift production to industrially backward areas where wages were low, the latest technology could be introduced at one stroke, and labor legislation could be avoided by using informal workers.

Employees' Unions Fight Back

From Shopfloor Control to the Struggle for Self-Management

As relocation and subcontracting undermined shopfloor power drastically, employees' unions shifted their struggles to the corporate level. There were numerous examples of this, but the three detailed here will illustrate the range of such interventions. In 1985, the Philips Employees' Union brought out a book with a red cover adorned with the couplet (in Hindi):

> One owl will suffice to send the garden to seed.
> What fate awaits it with an owl on every branch?

The garden was the company, the owls its executives, and the book consisted of more than fifty letters documenting ways in which senior executives and directors were, in the words of the union president, Sudhir Vaidya, milking the company for all it was worth, through massive loans at soft interest rates, interest-free deposits for executives' flats (many owned by the executives themselves), large quantities of electronic goods sold to executives at a tenth of their price, and so on. As a letter to the company's auditors, dated March 18, 1985, and signed by the union general secretary, Kiron Mehta, explained:

> When we started writing these letters in June 1984 it was our earnest wish and hope that in all fairness the Management would look into the matters and would sincerely try to set the matters right. Unfortunately, that was not to be. The shocking apathy displayed by the Management has convinced us that if we do not take the steps in the right direction, these practices will continue and the Company will be in dire financial crisis in a few years.
>
> (Philips Employees' Union 1985; Dubashi 1985)

The second example was the intervention of the Hindustan Lever Employees' Union (HLEU) in the merger of Hindustan Lever Limited

(HLL) and Tata Oil Mills Company (TOMCO).[26] With HLL having around a 66 percent market share for soaps and detergents in India, while TOMCO had around 17 percent, the first of HLEU's complaints was that with the merger and elimination of TOMCO as a competitor, HLL would monopolize 79–80 percent of the Indian market for soaps and detergents. The Monopolies and Restrictive Trade Practices (MRTP) Act states in its preamble that it is "an Act to provide that the operation of the economic system does not result in concentration of economic power to common detriment, for the control of monopolies, for the prohibition of monopolistic and restrictive trade practices and for matters connected therewith and incidental thereto." After liberalization in 1991, section 23 of chapter III, which required companies with a market share of 25 percent or more to seek the approval of the central government for merger or takeover schemes, was deleted. The union argued that with the removal of this blanket restriction, the MRTP Commission had an even greater responsibility to ensure that monopolies did not restrict or distort competition. The company argued that the revision of the MRTP Act meant that mergers and amalgamations were beyond the pale of any anticompetitive laws. The MRTP Commission refused to grant an injunction restraining the merger but agreed that it could indeed inquire whether a merger would result in a monopoly being created or in restrictive trade practices.

The second complaint of the union was that the share exchange ratio of two HLL shares for fifteen TOMCO shares, announced to shareholders without any disclosure of the calculations on which it was based, affected around 78 percent of TOMCO shareholders adversely. The valuation, carried out by a director of TOMCO, devalued TOMCO shares by over 30 percent by excluding the company's holdings in other Tata group companies, as well as its real-estate holdings. However, the Supreme Court ruled that it was sufficient to disclose only the share-exchange ratio without the calculations. This is a far lower level of disclosure than developed countries require. The third complaint was that prior to the merger, Unilever held 51 percent of the shares in HLL, but this holding was diluted to 49.98 percent after it. In order to raise its stake back to 51 percent, HLL had to buy more shares, and on March 16, 1993, it asked the Industrial Credit and Investment Corporation of India (ICICI), a public financial institution, to value its shares. ICICI obliged the very next day, valuing them at Rs 105 per share, but this was far less than their market price. On this issue, the Supreme Court ruled in favor of the union, forcing Unilever to pay Rs 700 per share and thus bring Rs 210 crores of foreign exchange into the country, compared with the Rs 30 crores it would have paid according to the original scheme.

The third example concerns interventions made by the Kamani Employees' Union (KEU), which was formed as the National Staff Association in 1951 but later changed its name.[27] KEC International was incorporated as Kamani Engineering Corporation Ltd. in 1945, and within a few years it had acquired market leadership in the production and erection of electricity-transmission towers in India. By the end of the 1960s, it had entered the global market and added manufacturing facilities in Jaipur to its factory in Kurla, Bombay. By 1974, however, production had come to a standstill, and the company booked huge losses. The Kamani family was torn apart by internecine quarrels. KEU appealed to the central government to intervene, which it did through the public financial institutions, as the Life Insurance Corporation of India was the single largest shareholder in the company and Unit Trust of India was among the ten largest shareholders. The Industrial Development Bank of India and ICICI converted their large term loans into equity, and the public financial institutions thereby acquired a controlling interest in the company. Through their intervention, KEC was turned around. From a loss of Rs 2.90 crores in 1974–1975, it recorded a profit of Rs 2.93 crores in 1975–1976, and by the end of the next financial year it had wiped out accumulated losses of Rs 6.59 crores. In each year between 1975 and 1983, KEC booked a profit before tax in excess of 10 percent of revenue, and by 1980 it had won export orders in twenty-two countries spread across four continents (excluding Europe). Relations with the union were marked by an informal system of codetermination.

In 1982, the R. P. Goenka group acquired a 16 percent stake in the company by purchasing shares from Kamani family members. In the next few years, the RPG group intensified control over KEC, and in May 1984, R. P. Goenka became chairman of the board of directors. From 1993 onward, when the board of KEC ceased to have any representatives from the public financial institutions sitting on it, the company went on an investment spree, as a result of which it incurred huge losses. The only productive investment, made in 1995–1996, was in a new 21,000 metric ton–capacity transmission tower manufacturing plant at Buti Buri, Nagpur, an industrially backward area. Added to the existing capacity of 75,000 metric tons at the Bombay and Jaipur plants, this should have resulted in a total capacity of 96,000 metric tons per year. Instead, the capacity of the two older plants was downgraded, although there was no change in their productive capability. The result was that the investment of Rs 30 crores in the Buti Buri plant resulted in a reduction of total capacity by three thousand metric tons!

The rest of the investments were means by which KEC assets were siphoned into the RPG group, leaving KEC bereft of cash and heavily in debt once again. In 1995, the RPG group acquired shares in another transmission-tower company, SAE India Ltd., and by 1997 it had a controlling interest and renamed it RPG Transmission Ltd. Almost immediately, the same pattern of asset stripping that had characterized the group's dealings with KEC began. This was the context in which the closure of the Bombay unit, through a voluntary retirement scheme offer to its employees and a merger of KEC and RPG Transmissions, was attempted. The productivity of the Bombay plant was the same as that of the new plants, and as it had the most experienced workforce, equipment manufactured at Jaipur and Buti Buri were routinely brought to Bombay for repair or troubleshooting. Only by a manipulation of the accounts was it shown to have lost money in 1995–1996, after having shown a substantial profit the previous year. Given the previous record of the RPG group, KEU realized that the only reason for the closure of the plant was to sell off the valuable land and that the merger would be used to tap the money market in order to divert more funds into other companies of the RPG group. The union therefore opposed both measures. The company responded with large-scale victimizations, dismissing around one thousand workers. (See chapter 8 for the KEU response.)

The common pattern that emerges from these three examples is one of rampant corporate and managerial malpractice, to the detriment of the companies they were managing. The absence of legal requirements for transparency and accountability in corporate governance was glaring, and minority shareholders, who held a large portion or even the majority of shares, were cheated with the blessing of the courts. Even where public financial institutions were major creditors and majority shareholders, they failed to intervene except under considerable pressure from the union, thus colluding in the malfeasance and allowing companies to channel public money into private pockets. In these circumstances, the demand by industrialists that they should be allowed to close down "potentially sick companies" without any scrutiny (De 2001) sounds like a plea for legalized plunder. The final irony is that in each case it was the union that acted in the best interests of the company and the public!

Changes in Legislation

The labor-law changes proposed in 2000–2001 brought unions together in Maharashtra, where the Trade Union Joint Action Committee, a coordination of all left-of-center unions in Bombay, undertook a series of rallies, demonstrations, local meetings, and other actions culminating in the Maharashtra *bandh* (general strike) of April 25, 2001. The complete success of this strike (*BS* 2001a) and the unprecedented unity that enabled it were not achieved easily. It is unlikely that this unity would have materialized if not for the feeling of extreme insecurity among members of all unions and the pressure they exerted on their own leaderships.

On May 10, the Maharashtra government assured trade union leaders that the proposed labor-law changes had been "nullified" (*BS* 2001b). At the national level, however, the campaign for the same changes continued unabated, and proposals to enact them were incorporated into the recommendations of the Second National Labour Commission Report. On February 26, 2003, over 350,000 workers and activists from left-wing and employees' unions throughout India held a rally in Delhi against the antiunion policies of the government (Nicholas Employees' Union 2003). TUSC and NTUI union members campaigned against the NDA before the parliamentary elections in 2004 and pressed opposition parties, including the Congress Party, to include protection for labor rights in their party manifestos (NTUI 2004). Their campaign no doubt contributed to the electoral defeat of the NDA and is probably the reason why the new Congress-led UPA government did not pursue the labor-market liberalization that had been the hallmark of the previous regime.

Thus the trade union movement staved off labor-law changes that would have transformed the remaining 7 percent of workers in formal employment into informal laborers at one blow (see chapter 6). But it was not successful in stemming the more gradual contraction of formal employment that would, over a longer period, lead to the same result. By concentrating their energies on *preventing* any change in labor laws, the central trade unions neglected the task of *proposing and pushing for* changes in legislation that would strengthen the bargaining power of workers and stem the informalization of production. To the extent that such proposals were made, it was employees' unions that made and fought for them. A crucial victory was won by HLEU in 2005, when the Supreme Court ruled in its favor in a case it had been pursuing since 1998. Section 9A of the

ID Act required companies to give employees "notice of change" before making any changes that would affect their conditions of employment, but neither HLL nor any other company complied with this requirement when subcontracting or relocating work. The court ruled that all such changes would have to be reversed, since they did not follow the correct procedure. The court also prohibited voluntary retirement scheme settlements with individuals, saying that the union was the appropriate body to make such agreements and that individual agreements smacked of coercion.[28]

On the all-important issue of union rights, the TUSC had this to say:

> No union can function adequately without a strong organisation at the workplace level, which means that employees at this level must have enough time to participate in union activities. For a number of reasons—transport problem, domestic responsibilities (especially in the case of women), and so on—it may not be convenient or possible for some employees to attend to union activities outside working hours. In other cases, the volume of union work may be so large that it is simply not possible for it to be handled entirely outside working hours. . . . The dominant ethos among employers and some members of the judiciary today is that an enterprise should be run as a dictatorship in which the workers are only expected to carry out orders. But trade unionism is the democratic response to these dictatorial ideas, and time-off for trade union work is an essential component of union rights. . . . We feel that the effective functioning of a union requires not only that leaders should have time-off for union work up to and including full-time union work with pay from the company . . . but also that ordinary members should have time-off to attend meetings, union education and training sessions, etc. . . . The legal recognition of the right to form unions is incomplete without the right to time-off, and measures should be taken to incorporate it in legislation.
>
> (TUSC n.d., 3–4)

The logical place for such a clause would be in a new Trade Union Act, which should also proclaim the right of *every* employee, regardless of the work he or she does or the number of workers in the workplace, to belong to a union of his or her choice, to bargain collectively, and to be protected from victimization for union membership or activities. This would get rid of the arbitrary denial of trade union rights to those classified as not being "workmen" under the ID Act (the infamous "nonbargainable" category) and to employees in small units. This demand was implicit in the protest organized by the TUSC against a Supreme Court judgment denying members of the Mukand Staff and Officers' Association the benefits conferred by an Industrial Tribunal in 1998 on the grounds that they were not "workmen" under the ID Act (Singh 2004). Second, the clauses sought by V. V. Giri, which would make it mandatory for employers to recognize representative unions and negotiate with them, are also overdue by more than half a century and should be incorporated (cf. Kotwal 2000).

Another set of issues was raised by union interventions in corporate governance. As a result of these experiences, HLEU, KEU, and the Centre for Workers' Management (CWM; see chapter 8) proposed amendments to the Companies Act to enable unions and workers to be represented on company boards, so that they would have access to company information and the right to intervene in company decisions (D'Costa 1997; CWM 1997a). Workers are stakeholders in the companies they work for, not only because they are affected by company decisions but also because it is their labor that is objectified in the company. Thus the representation of workers on company boards can in the first place be seen as a democratic measure, giving an important group of stakeholders the ability to participate in decision making. For example, in March 2009, KEU won a historic legal victory when it secured a union presence on the Asset Sales Committee and thus obtained the legal dues of workers prior to liquidation, distributing around Rs 35 crores to nearly 1,100 workers (NTUI 2009, 7). In the second place, however, it is clear from the cases that unions have investigated that small shareholders and the public (through public financial institutions and public-sector banks) have been plundered with impunity by the owners and managers of many companies. The presence of workers' representatives on boards would thus additionally be a measure for safeguarding the interests of small shareholders and the public.

Discussions around the Bhopal disaster revealed the dire state of health-and-safety legislation in India. There is an urgent need for separate legislation covering health and safety at work, instead of having this topic as one among many covered by the Factories Act; it is in any case indefensible that only workers in registered factories should have the right to health and safety at work. A separate act should therefore cover all employees, enable workers' representatives to form safety committees with information and inspection rights, and, in extreme cases where workers apprehend a major accident that could result in serious injury or fatality, allow workers to shut down the production process without being penalized for their actions.

Finally, on January 26, 1995, the TUSC held a workshop to discuss the problems posed by contract labor and subcontracting. This workshop produced a series of recommendations for amendments to existing legislation, which will be discussed in chapter 6.

The Struggle for Solidarity

Once subcontracting and relocation made it possible for companies to continue production even if their Bombay plants were shut down, it became obvious that no workforce could meet this new offensive on its own. The first and most obvious move was to contact workers in the new locations and try to bring them into either the employees' union or a company federation. Bombay-based unions did this for workers in the Pfizer plant at Kalyani, the Blue Star plant at Bharuch, the Hoechst plant at Ankleshwar, the Voltas plant at Warora, the Glaxo plants at Nasik and Ankleshwar, and many others. Some of these accounts of unionization, as in the case of Blue Star, sound as if they come from a fictional thriller, with midnight meetings and membership forms smuggled in and out of factories clandestinely. The HLEU embarked on the daunting task of contacting workers in the numerous new units, as well as those in companies amalgamated with or taken over by Unilever, to form the All-India Council of Unilever Unions.

Making alliances across companies was another logical step. There were a number of attempts to do this, most rather short lived, but two relatively stable formations emerged. One was the All-India Chemical and Pharmaceutical Employees' Federation, formed by pharmaceutical unions in the 1960s. It had become less active in the 1970s, and there were attempts to reactivate it. In 1994, a "Factory Office Field Workers United Front" was formed to work out a plan of action to confront the deunionization of the pharmaceutical industry, and thereafter a series of meetings was held to investigate these problems.[29] The other was the TUSC, initially formed in 1989 to support Telco workers in Pune struggling for collective bargaining rights (Singh and Sebastian 1989). In subsequent years, solidarity and support was extended not only to employees' unions in Bombay but to many others, including textile workers on hunger strike; workers of Nagpur Alloys who had been fired upon by police in 1990 and by management in

1991; workers of the UP State Cement Corporation at Dalla, where around forty people were killed in police firing in June 1991; workers in Bhilai and Rajur in Madhya Pradesh subjected to police firing; and victims of the Marathwada earthquake in 1993, in which tens of thousands of people died (TUSC 1992, 1993). It was obvious that a permanent body was needed to bring employees' unions together and combine their strength, so the TUSC continued to be active and gradually gained considerable standing. Its reputation attracted workers attempting to set up employees' unions in new occupations, where the advice and support of experienced unionists were crucially important; for example, it helped workers in courier services to set up the AFL-DHL Employees' Union in 1999.

One of the most important activities of the TUSC has been the attempt to discuss and find solutions to problems currently facing the trade union movement. The more monolithic and hierarchical structure of traditional unions is inimical to democratic discussion, because once the leaders lay down the line, members have no way of disagreeing. This is damaging even if the leadership is right, because members who have not had a chance to voice opposing views tend to defer to the leaders in public but keep their own views unchanged in private. (Of course, this can and does happen even in employees' unions, but less so.) Even more damaging are situations where the leadership has nothing to offer but slogans and strategies that cannot safeguard workers' rights. In traditional unions, there is very little that dissidents can do to change union policy or outlook. In the TUSC, as in employees' unions in general, more democratic functioning allows minority views to be aired and discussed.

The example of the TUSC inspired the New Trade Union Initiative (NTUI), a national federation of independent unions.[30] In 1999, there were a number of meetings on closures and lockouts attended by fifty to sixty unions. At that time, Ashim Roy left the HMKP (which was linked to one of the parties in the extremely antiunion NDA government), feeling that with more and more unions throughout India becoming dissatisfied with the central trade union federations and looking for an alternative, a national federation of independent unions had become feasible. The TUSC too supported the idea, fearing that without backing from such a federation, it might not survive the employers' onslaught. At a meeting held at the CWM in Delhi in April 2000, a decision was taken to launch the NTUI.

The idea was greeted with considerable enthusiasm at a series of regional meetings. At the meeting in Bombay, Thankappan of the Kamani Employees'

Union pointed out that "one third or more of organised labour belongs to unaffiliated unions," and Yeshwant Chavan of the Sarva Shramik Sangh reiterated that "trade unions are organisations of the working class, not of political parties." Both emphasized the need to organize informal workers. A document, "For a New Initiative," was circulated, discussed, revised to incorporate gender and other equality issues, and finally adopted at a meeting in New Delhi in December 2001. Describing the NTUI as a "national platform of non-partisan left-democratic trade unions created with the objective of forming a trade union federation," it summed up the main difference between itself and existing left-wing trade union federations by arguing that a

> weakness of the trade union movement has been the lack of democracy in its functioning. . . . Democracy has to become a major instrument for building the new federation, for building solidarity, for determining political and bargaining objectives and for deciding policies and strategies. . . . In the policy making bodies adequate representation should be allowed to reflect the diversity of opinions and views. Moreover the federation's key strength should be plant level union organizations. . . . The workplace level union organization should have the residuary powers in the federation and only such powers will be delegated to the higher industrial, regional and national structures as are decided by unions through a democratic and transparent process.
>
> (NTUI 2001)

At a meeting of NTUI in August 2004, a managing committee was formed. Members of the TUSC felt that the formation of such a federation would open up enormous possibilities for linking struggles of formal and informal workers and for achieving representation of employees' unions at a national level. At the same time, they felt it would have to be run very differently from other federations to ensure democracy. If there was consensus on any issue, there would not be a problem, but when there were controversial issues, problems could arise. If the principle of democracy was to be preserved in such circumstances, the secretariat of the NTUI (formed in order to coordinate its activities) should not have the power to enforce decisions on individual unions.

In dealing with collective bargaining, the TUSC has functioned very much like the more democratic British unions, where full-time union officials did not intervene unless the shop stewards' committee called upon them to do so (Boraston et al. 1975). Likewise, in the TUSC the member unions have full autonomy but know that they can call upon senior members for advice and assistance if they need it. The NTUI in addition requires a carefully crafted system of what has been called "articulated" bargaining at different levels (Giugni 1969) to ensure maximum bargaining power without sacrificing democratic control over decision making. One possibility would be for the NTUI to negotiate framework agreements that would lay down minimum standards and maximize the space for member unions to negotiate their own collective agreements.

So far as more political issues are concerned, the TUSC ran up against problems when there were attempts to turn it into a federation in the mid-1990s. One problem related to the issue of communalism. Since many employees' unions had Shiv Sena supporters among their membership and even on their managing committees, there was opposition to any clause in the constitution opposing communalism. Here the NTUI had an advantage over the TUSC: starting from scratch, the NTUI could incorporate equality and solidarity issues in its aims and objectives, whereas the TUSC, having been constituted without the requirement for any such commitment on the part of its constituents, had difficulty getting such a clause accepted.

The other contentious issue was globalization. TUSC members comprised a spectrum, ranging from those who felt that globalizing the trade union movement was the correct response to those who felt that outright opposition to globalization was imperative. The NTUI initially adopted an intermediate position. Its analysis was similar to that of the antiglobalizers, but it also affirmed the importance of international solidarity (NTUI 2001). This became a source of contention during the WSF meeting in Bombay in January 2004. The NTUI secretariat decided to participate wholeheartedly, while the antiglobalizers in the TUSC were part of the rival Mumbai Resistance 2004. Strict adherence to the principle of democracy in this case, where despite debate a consensus had not emerged, required that individual constituents of the NTUI and TUSC—either union members or member unions—should be free to participate in either gathering or both and to affirm their identity as *members* of the NTUI or TUSC, but no one would have the right to represent either the NTUI or the TUSC *as a whole*. More generally, democratic functioning would mean that only those issues on which there was a consensus should be included in public declarations put out in the name of either organization.

On March 5–6, 2006, after a process of broadly based, prolonged, and intensive discussion unprecedented in Indian labor history, the NTUI was launched as a federation at a founding conference in Delhi. Its aims and objectives, as proclaimed in its constitution, included the following:

Article 3.2: to struggle against all forms of economic exploitation, caste, gender, ethnic and other social discrimination and oppression; 3.5: to recognise women's work, both paid and unpaid, in the economy and the family; 3.6: to promote fraternity, solidarity, and unity among diverse sections of international working people on the basis of equality and the self-respect of nations and peoples; 3.7: to oppose aggression, promote peaceful coexistence between countries, and eliminate nuclear weapons and other weapons of mass destruction; 3.10: to build a democratic trade union movement through the education of members: one that contributes to effective participation in and control of unions by members and to developing fraternal relationships between unions and federations; 3.12: to encourage and enable the participation of labour in the local, state, national and international community and the exercising of their rights and responsibilities as citizens to deepen and broaden the democratisation of state and society; 3.16: to ensure the autonomy of each affiliated union and its right to a political viewpoint; 3.18: to secure legislation, policies and practices to actualise internationally accepted human and labour rights, eliminate authoritarian and feudal institutions, practices and values and promote labour rights, democratic values, the dignity of labour and equality at the workplace and in society; 3.21: to promote the organisation of unorganised labour on the basis of the unity of interest at the industrial or sectoral level; 3.22: to build solidarity among working people based on the commonality of interest and tolerance for all beliefs and faiths and strive for ideals of secularism.

(NTUI 2006)

After its inauguration, there was an emphasis on bringing more women into the leadership and on training its organizers, taking into account the fact that knowledge had become much more necessary for union activists. In some areas, the response to the NTUI was tremendous; for example, unions with a membership of 470,000 workers affiliated to it in Jammu and Kashmir, where it was compiling information on democratic-rights violations and livelihoods.

In the wake of the crisis of 2008, employees' unionism retained its dynamism. Despite the fact that the airline industry had been hit badly by the crisis and the pilots of Jet Airways were legally barred from going on strike, they went on mass sick leave when two leaders of their newly registered union, the National Aviators' Guild, were sacked without notice on July 31, 2009. As the dispute continued, two more pilots were sacked (Aggarwal 2009). Their high degree of bargaining power (given that they could hardly be replaced at short notice!) and vocal support from eight national trade union centers (*Deccan Herald* 2009) as well as the NTUI enabled the pilots to win their demands, although they agreed to keep the union in cold storage unless it was needed. TUSC membership had been decimated by the closure of a large number of units in which it once had unions, but it moved into new sectors, and the center of gravity of employees' unionism moved to Pune, where dozens of employees' unions came together in the Maha Union. Most importantly, employees' unions now understood the importance of organizing informal workers, either bringing them into existing employees' unions if they worked in the same workplaces or helping them to form their own unions if they did not.

The Importance of Trade Union Democracy

In tackling each of the issues described above, workers learned important lessons, and this would have been difficult or impossible if they had not been running their unions themselves. When those who make decisions are not the people who are affected by those decisions, there is a break in the learning process, incorrect policies cannot easily be corrected, and the same mistakes can be made again and again. Conversely, those who suffer the consequences of a wrong decision have a powerful motive to change direction in the future, provided that they have the power to do so. Such empowerment is crucial during periods of rapid and unprecedented change, which has occurred due to globalization, when previous experience may not provide answers to current problems. It is even more critical at a time of economic crisis, when failure to respond appropriately could leave workers in a descending spiral of disempowerment, leading to job losses, leading to yet more disempowerment. This does not mean ruling out a role for full-time union organizers, researchers, legal experts, and coordinators, but it does mean ensuring that the union membership has the last word in decision making.

Of course, lessons can be learned from the experience of others, too; for example, unions in India could benefit a great deal from studying ways in which unions elsewhere have tackled issues of equality, nondiscrimination and equal opportunities, health and safety, and trade union rights. But this is an argument for expanding the learning community beyond national borders, not for reducing democracy. Finally, if democracy is seen as a positive value in general, workers cannot be expected to uphold it in society while foregoing it in their own organizations! For all these reasons, the project of building union democracy from the bottom up, which employees' unions in India have been engaged in, is one that is well worth studying both within India and in other countries.

[6]

Informal Labor

The Struggle for Legal Recognition

A Global Problem

Only when informal labor started spreading rapidly around the world, toward the end of the twentieth century, did it begin to figure prominently in international union discussions. But the problem had been incubating for much longer in various countries, especially India, before globalization unleashed it on the rest of the world, and it was partly the failure to tackle it at its source that allowed it to spread. It is perhaps the single biggest threat to workers' rights, and a global strategy for labor cannot hope to be effective without confronting it. The expansion of this sector made an enormous contribution to straitjacketing global aggregate demand, and a robust recovery from the current economic crisis will be impossible if more and more workers continue to be pushed into it. An examination of India's experience of informal labor is important, both because it is so deeply entrenched that a coordinated effort will be required to eradicate it and because informal workers in India, precisely because they have been subjected to its often slavelike conditions for so long, have practicable suggestions about how it could be tackled.

Definitions of Informality and Types of Informal Labor

The "informal sector" (described in India as the "unorganized sector") consists of enterprises that are not regulated by the state. In 1993, the Fifteenth International Conference of Labour Statisticians (ICLS) agreed on a definition of the informal sector, which was adopted in the new System of National Accounting. It included both small enterprises characterized by self-employment and those having employer-employee relations. The latter were distinguished from formal-sector enterprises by "either the size of unit, below a specified level of employment, or non-registration of the enterprise or its employees" (Unni and Rani 2003, 42–43).

However, informal workers are not confined to the informal sector. Many are found in the formal sector, while others—domestic workers, for example—are not employed by enterprises at all; in fact, there is considerable diversity within both sectors (Sethuraman 1998). The term "informal economy" was proposed in order to capture the diversity of informal employment arrangements (WIEGO n.d.), but it is hard to see how this is any improvement on the term "informal sector," since it suggests an even sharper boundary between formal and informal "economies."

At the fifth meeting of the International Expert Group on Informal Sector Statistics in September 2001, the ILO argued for the need to distinguish between informal employment and the informal sector, and this suggests a solution to the dilemma. What I propose to do here is to use three terms: *informal sector*, as defined by the ICLS in 1993, encompassing employers, employees, and self-employed workers in unregistered enterprises; *informal workers*, meaning unregistered workers, both employees and self-employed, working in both formal and informal sectors; and *informal labor* or *informal employees*, referring to unregistered employees in the formal or informal sector or outside both. "Conceptually, a primary attribute of informal employment is the absence of regular or written contracts" (Sudarshan and Unni 2003, 27).

Critiques of the notion that the informal sector is a stepping stone from rural labor to the formal sector, or that it consists primarily of the self-employed, are now well established (Breman 1996, 6–7). If informal workers in India ever had any hope of moving into formal employment, that hope was all but extinguished by the new industrial policy of 1977–1980, after which the traffic in the opposite direction—from formal to informal employment—increased massively. And while it is true that there are self-employed workers in the informal sector, the vast majority are employees. Most of them are rural, but a large number are also found in urban areas, and some migrant workers oscillate between the two.

The distinction between employees and self-employed workers is not always easy to establish, especially in the case of women home-based workers. But there is a difference:

> [self-employed workers] have greater control over the design and marketing of their work: they decide for themselves what goods they will produce . . . and finally sell their work directly to the final customer. . . . It is also important to recognise that not all homeworkers can be categorically assigned to one group or the other. . . . Some, for example switch between piece-work and own account—a weaver may produce goods for a subcontractor when work is available but make items to sell to local customers when it is not.
>
> (Brill 2002, 114)

Even where the self-employed worker and the employee is the same person, it is important to distinguish the different *employment relations* in which he or she is involved at different times, since being an employee implies a dependence on an employer or employers. Making this distinction may not be easy, given that employers are often anxious to pass off employees as self-employed workers. Thus in *beedi* (indigenous cigarette) production, firms responded to labor legislation by reducing the amount of factory production and extending the subcontracting system. "They have cut the official links between firms and contractors, and between contractors and workers. Now raw materials are ostensibly 'bought and paid for' by contractors, and again 'bought and paid for' by workers. In fact, raw materials are supplied on credit to both" (Baud 1987, 71).

Similar stratagems were employed vis-à-vis garment homeworkers, with the collusion of government officials:

> When we first started organising the women garment stitchers, we were told by the employers that these women were not workers but just housewives who were stitching in their "leisure time"; whereas we found that they were working anywhere between eight to ten hours a day. We were also told by the labour commissioner's office that since there was no direct employer-employee relationship between the employer and the

women, they were not covered by any labour laws, although we found
that there was complete control of production by the employers.

(Jhabvala 2003, 260)

These homeworkers were in the same position as workers in nineteenth-
century domestic industry, which Marx described as "an external department
of the factory, the manufacturing workshop or the warehouse. . . . An example: the shirt factory of Messrs. Tillie at Londonderry, which employs 1,000
workers in the factory itself, and 9,000 outworkers spread over the country districts" (Marx 1976, 591). The 1988 report of the National Commission
on Self-Employed Women and Women in the Informal Sector made a clear
distinction between dependent and self-employed workers, explaining that
"the nature of legislative protection that is needed for these two categories of
workers is not the same. The piece-rated workers need better rates of wages,
better implementation of labour laws; on the other hand, own-account workers need remedies that generally lie beyond the scope of labour laws." Yet
documents prepared by the Ministry of Labour in the early twenty-first century deliberately obliterated the distinction (Mazumdar 2007, 180–182).

Contract labor is another component of informal labor. The labor contractor—the *tekhedar, seth, mukadam*, or whatever the person is called
locally—recruits a gang of workers and takes them to the principal
employer. They work on site, under the supervision of the contractor, who
is paid a lump sum for their labor and in turn distributes wages—or does
not, as the case may be—to the workers. Except in rare cases such as the
beedi industry, where the Beedi and Cigar Workers (Conditions of Employment) Act (1966) specifies that the factory owner will be considered the
employer even if the work is distributed through a labor contractor, the
principal employer has no contact with the workers and is not considered
to be their employer; for example, Reliance Energy got a court order stating
that contract workers working for the company were not Reliance employees. Neither is the contractor considered to be their employer, even in cases
where the principal employer is not held to be employing them. In other
words, the paradoxical end result of the Contract Labour (Regulation and
Abolition) Act, which assigns shared responsibility for contract workers to
the principal employer and the contractor, is that these workers are wage
laborers without an employer. Many work in large-scale formal enterprises,
in both private and public sectors. Others are migrant workers, laboring in
both urban and rural areas and moving on when the work is over.

Contract workers are quite deliberately used in hazardous work with a high incidence of serious and fatal accidents—construction, chemical plants, nuclear plants, and so on—because the employer is not held liable for accidents. For example, the construction industry is the second-largest employer in the country, employing over thirty-two million workers, but working conditions are deplorable. Employers make no attempt to eliminate or even minimize hazards, and consequently the number of crippling and fatal accidents is extremely high (Menon 1999). At the Union Carbide plant at Bhopal, one of the complaints of workers prior to the disaster was that untrained contract workers were being employed in the chemical plant, which was a hazard to themselves and to others (URG 1985a). And Otis Elevator used untrained contract workers instead of its own skilled and qualified employees in the erection and maintenance of lifts, at horrific human cost: five fatalities in the space of two years, numerous serious injuries, and increased risks to customers (Lokshahi Hakk Sanghatana 2001).

The bulk of the rural poor engage in informal labor, since even if they own a small plot of land it cannot sustain their families for more than a few months of the year. Therefore at least some members of the family are wage laborers, either in the vicinity or some distance away, and sometimes the whole family migrates for work. The majority are Dalits and Adivasis, who are oppressed socially and economically. For example, sugarcane in South Gujarat is harvested mainly by migrant Adivasis from Khandesh in Maharashtra, recruited through *mukadams*. The work of cutting, cleaning, and bundling the cane is carried out by groups of two or three workers, usually a couple with or without a working child. Sickness and injury from the machetes are common and can result in death; nursing mothers have to care for their babies during the breaks in their workday. Workers receive less than the minimum wage and are often cheated even of that small amount. Payment for the work of a couple or threesome is given to the man: the work done by women and children is not recognized separately (Breman 1990; Teerinck 1995). Extreme poverty and insecurity of employment become means by which employers can enforce forms of bondage, by advancing to workers sums of money that they—and in some cases their children—have to repay many times over. Bonded child labor is widespread in the informal sector, especially but not exclusively in rural areas (cf. Karunanithi 1998).

Informal workers in the formal sector may be casual, "temporary," migrant, or seasonal workers. Some may have been working for the same employer for several years, but they are never put on the payroll of the firm or given appointment letters or pay slips, and they may be subjected to periodic breaks in employment to prevent them from working 240 days in a year, which would legally entitle them to the status of permanent employee. Complicated procedures may be used to account for the work they do without acknowledging their existence or presence in the workplace. A case study of ceramic ware production in Gujarat found that "several units maintained registers which showed their family members, who never worked there, as their employees. Payment of benefits were shown as having been made to these persons while the actual workers, whose names were not in the registers, did not get anything" (Das 2003, 88–89).

Lack of a formal employment status has often been associated with sexual harassment, since women workers who might lose their jobs are afraid of complaining about it. S. Meerabai, a union activist at the Pondicherry Leather Products factory of Hindustan Lever, had the courage to speak openly about the sexual harassment from supervisors faced by women workers in her unit. But when this became known to management, she was called by the factory manager to his office, assaulted so badly by a supervisor that she had to be hospitalized for five days, and finally suspended for "rude and disorderly behaviour"![1] Migrant women workers in the export-oriented fish-processing industry were kept virtually in captivity, forced to work long hours in unhygienic conditions, denied the minimum wage, and subjected to sexual harassment. The processing units technically were part of the formal sector, but the workers remained in the category of informal labor because of their seasonal and migrant status (Sharma 1999).

Homework and contract labor are combined where homeworkers, instead of getting their work directly from an employer, get it through a contractor. In such cases, they usually have no idea who their employer is. The system can tempt workers to become subcontractors. Thus in the garment export industry in Delhi, "in peak seasons, enterprising women workers turned into sub-agents. If they received a large number of pieces, they worked on some and put out others to their women neighbours, retaining a small profit margin . . . for themselves" (Rao and Husain 1987, 60).

Wage workers in informal units are another subcategory of informal labor. Many of the small units that employ them subcontract production from large-scale formal units. "Subcontracting has been defined as a situation in which a parent firm, instead of doing the work itself, requests another independent firm to undertake the whole or part of an order it has received while assuming full responsibility for the work vis-à-vis the customer" (Watanabe 1972; cit. Baud 1987, 69). In such cases, workers in the informal sector may be doing exactly the same work as those in the formal unit but being paid a fraction of the wages and working longer hours under much worse conditions. A good example is "the textile industry, once the biggest employer of labour in the organized sector, and now one of the biggest employers in the unorganized. . . . Weaving has shifted to the unorganized sector, which enjoys the advantage of cheap labour, and profits, in addition, from the evasion of excise duties" (Ramaswamy 1999, 55–56).

Subcontracting has become almost universal in Indian manufacturing, and sometimes the chains have two or more links, with subcontractors in turn subcontracting to even smaller units. Here, too, there is a temptation for workers to become subcontractors, and some companies encourage this, helping to set up former employees as subcontractors carrying out part or all of the labor process that was formerly carried out in the factory. But not all small firms subcontract; some, including many that produce for the large domestic market, are unregistered firms or "registered small firms employing few or no regular workers even though they do not take or give jobs on contract" (Das 2003, 89).

Finally, there are large numbers of informal workers—including children—in the service sector, working to deliver tea, fruit, or vegetables to customers; as security guards, cleaners, or scavengers; plying handcarts or rickshaws; or in domestic service. The dividing line between self-employed workers and employees is even harder to draw here, and the consequences of this ambiguity in their status can be devastating for the workers. In one case,

> SEWA went to court on behalf of a cart-puller with a hired cart, who was involved in a street accident and broke both legs, in the process of delivering cloth from a wholesaler to a retailer. Although the cart-puller had been delivering goods for the wholesaler for more than 20 years, the court ruled that there was no employer-employee relationship, and so no one could be held liable under the Workmen's Compensation Act.
>
> (Jhabvala 2003, 261)

Formal/Informal Employment Statistics

By its nature, informality is hard to document, and the difficulties have been compounded by inconsistent definitions and lack of thoroughness in compiling statistics. Official statistics are often a gross underestimate of the number of informal employees. In the ceramic industry in Gujarat, "the issue of omission in the unregistered sector has been found to be quite serious, with only about 3 per cent of the total number of units getting reflected in the . . . statistics. Similarly, the official data on employment was less than 2 per cent of our estimate," since some employees in registered units were informal (Das 2003, 97–98).

This problem should not arise if the survey is done at the household level, yet even here informal workers, especially women and children, may not be counted. Since informal labor is irregular, it is easy to classify workers as unemployed even if they are working.

> As the definition of the term employment becomes more rigorous the number of unemployed increase for both males and females. Unemployment figures are highest following the daily status concept where a person is unemployed even if only on the day of the interview. It is somewhat lower if a person is considered unemployed only if he has not worked on any day during the previous week. Unemployment is lowest when confined only to people who are usually unemployed, that is, those who have not found work for a fairly long period.
>
> (Banerjee 1985b, 11)

Given the way in which women homeworkers in the garment industry classified their own work patterns—2–3 days per month, 1 week per month, 7–20 days per month, 1 month per year, 2–3 months per year, 4–6 months per year, 7–9 months per year, and 10–12 months per year (Rao and Husain 1987, 58)—it is obvious that only the broadest definition of employment would classify them all as wage workers, and narrower definitions would fail to detect or record the work done by many of them.

Changing census definitions have resulted in apparently wild fluctuations in women's labor-force participation (Liddle 1988, 7–8). Wage systems such as the one employed for sugarcane harvesters, where only the men are counted as workers even though there are as many women, as well as some children, underestimate the total number of informal workers. This is even more likely to occur when women "work as helpers in a family unit for own account work," where "they are often ignored as workers" (Jumani 1987, 255), both by their families and by the government. The same thing might happen with working children.

For all these reasons, it is necessary to keep in mind that employment statistics are not totally reliable, especially with respect to informal labor (Nagaraj 1999a, 1999b; CSO 1999). Despite this caveat, however, there is surprisingly broad agreement on the overall picture:

1. Employment in formal-sector manufacturing, both the private and public sectors, grew at a rate of around 3.8 percent per year between 1970/1971 and 1980/1981, 0.53 percent per year between 1980/1981 and 1990/1991, and 2.69 percent per year between 1990/1991 and 1997/1998. Thus after a sharp drop in the 1980s, the growth rate recovered somewhat in the 1990s (i.e., postliberalization) (Goldar 2000). The CSO made a similar estimate of a 2.26 percent compound annual rate of growth of employment in the organized manufacturing sector during the period 1992–1998 (*BS* 1999b).

2. Total employment (formal and informal) grew by 2.17 percent per year between 1977/1978 and 1983, 1.54 percent per year between 1983 and 1987/1988, and 2.43 percent per year between 1987/1988 and 1993/1994 (Mahendra Dev 2000a, 825).

3. While employment growth in formal-sector manufacturing declined from 1.86 percent per year during 1978–1983 to −0.45 percent per year during 1983–1988 and recovered to 2.31 percent during 1988–1994, employment growth in informal manufacturing changed little, from 3.69 percent per year during 1978–1983 to 3.97 percent per year during 1983–1988, and it declined to 1.08 percent per year during 1988–1994 (Mahendra Dev 2000b, 49).

4. Looking now at the proportion of informal labor, the total labor force was 314.13 million in the 1991 census, while the government's *Economic Survey 1997–98* estimated the labor force as being 397.2 million in 1997. According to the *Statistical Outline of India 1998–99*, formal employment rose from 26.73 million in 1991 to 28.25 million in 1997, which means that formal labor declined from 8.5 to 7.1 percent during the period 1991–1997. The National Sample Survey Organisation estimated that formal labor fell from 8 percent in 1994 to just over 7 percent in 1999–2000 (Soman 2001; Satpathy 2005). Growth in formal employment was rapid in the first half of the 1990s, decelerated after 1996, and reversed after 1997/1998; according to the Directorate General of Employment and Training, the absolute number of formal jobs declined every year from 1997/1998 to 2002, with a fall of 4.2 lakhs in

2001–2002 alone, ending at 27.3 million in March 2002 (Soman 2003; BS 2003c). Combined with the 2001 census data, which estimated the total labor force as being 402.5 million (Soman 2002), this would put the proportion of formal labor at around 6.79 percent in 2001/2002.

5. Formal employment in manufacturing increased by 3.6 percent from 5.5 to 5.7 million between 1980/1981 and 1990/1991 and grew rapidly up to 1996, after which it decelerated until 1998 and declined thereafter; by 2000/2001, it was back at 5.7 million. However, labor productivity grew massively, by 119.1 percent during the former decade and by 80.6 percent during the latter, with output growing at 7 percent per year throughout the entire period (Nagaraj 2003, 3708; 2004, 3389).

While these figures are not directly comparable, since some pertain only to the private sector, some to private and public, some only to manufacturing, and some to employment as a whole, there is agreement on the overwhelming and growing preponderance of informal labor. This impression is confirmed by regional studies, including an analysis of data from the National Capital Territory of Delhi, which found that the size and distribution of the informal labor force had begun increasing substantially in the early 1990s, with the increase in child labor being especially striking (Banerjee 2006, 7).

Interpreting the Statistics

The assumption justifying government policies promoting the informal sector—including its exemption from labor laws—is that it increases employment, and the statistics are touted triumphantly by Indian industrialists as proof of this "fact." The Federation of Indian Exporting Organisations and the All-India Organisation of Employers attribute the decline in the growth rate of formal employment to protective labor legislation, especially the lack of freedom to hire and fire in order to obtain flexibility (BS 2004b), whereas informal employment, they say, is free to grow without this constraint. On the other side, many trade unionists attribute these same developments to globalization. Where does the truth lie?

To take up the second argument first, it is evident from the statistics that there is no clear link between globalization and the preponderance of informal labor, which predated globalization by decades. Nor is there a clear link between globalization and declining formal employment; in the manufacturing sector, for example, formal employment declined sharply in the mid-1980s, grew rapidly between 1991 and 1996, and declined again in the late 1990s.

The temporal pattern of formal sector–employment expansion also casts doubt on the contention that it is the job-security provisions of the ID Act that are responsible for its declining growth. Although it is true that formal employment dropped sharply in the mid-1980s, it recovered despite the absence of any change in the law. The corollary of this argument—that labor-market liberalization encourages employment growth—needs to be examined carefully, because it is based on assumptions about formal and informal employment that do not stand up under scrutiny.

The first assumption is that *there is no relationship between formal and informal employment; therefore all the growth in the latter can be seen as the creation of new jobs.* This is very far from being true. As we saw in chapters 4 and 5, there was a wholesale transfer of jobs from formal to informal labor. This occurred in a range of industries: textiles (Baud 1983, 31–32; van Wersch 1992, 40–46); beedis (Banerjee 1985a); engineering, chemicals, and pharmaceuticals (Banaji and Hensman 1990, 123–125; Hensman 1996a, 90–92); and electronics (Chhachhi 2005, 250–252). The statistics conceal this story. Much of the explanation for the slowdown in growth or absolute decline of formal employment lies in the transfer of jobs out of this sector. Conversely, much of the growth in informal employment is accounted for by this transfer. Therefore, *this is not the creation of new jobs but simply the downgrading of existing ones.*

The second assumption is that *more employment can be generated in the informal sector because it uses techniques of production that are labor intensive.* This is often not the case. Many studies have found that the technology used in decentralized informal-sector production is the same as that used in the formal sector. In other cases, the processes subcontracted to the informal sector are labor-intensive operations that are not automated even in the formal sector. Overall, there is no basis for the assumption that production processes are necessarily more labor intensive in the small-scale sector (Ramaswamy 1994). Capital costs are lower only because so little (in the case of homeworkers, nothing at all) is spent on providing decent conditions in the workplace (Banerjee 1981, 286; Holmström 1984, 151). On the other hand, working hours are invariably longer in the informal sector: for example, twelve-hour shifts in the decentralized power-loom sector as opposed to eight-hour shifts in textile mills, an increase of 50 percent (Breman 1996, 125; Roy 1998, 901). It is therefore likely that the same production, carried out in the formal sector with shorter working hours, would create not less but *more* employment.

The other main justification for informality is the argument that labor legislation, which protects formal workers, undermines global competitiveness and discourages foreign direct investment. The garment industry illustrates the negative consequences of this belief.

The Garment Industry and Its Informal Workers

The economic liberalization of 1991 led to a spurt in the growth of garment exports from India, although the domestic market continued to be relatively stagnant. Thus globalization created a genuine expansion of employment; in the hand-loom sector, there were even opportunities for upward mobility, with craft workers becoming small entrepreneurs (De Neve 2005, 311, 319–320). The value of garment exports rose from US$1,598 million in 1989–1990 to US$3,675 million in 1995/1996, more than doubling within five years and becoming 12 percent of India's merchandise exports and 16 percent of manufactured exports (Unni and Bali 2002, 119). There were expectations that this trend would continue (Roy 1998), but according to the *Economic Survey 2001–02*, by 2000/2001 the value of exports was US$5,577, a drop in the rate of growth due to competition from cheaper and/or better-quality products from other Third World countries (*BS* 2001d). Even the domestic market began to be invaded by these products, some from countries such as Taiwan and Korea, which have considerably higher labor standards (Shah 2001).

According to the director of marketing research of the government's Textile Committee, 95 percent of textile and textile-related production, including garment manufacture, was in the small-scale sector, and this was one reason for its lack of competitiveness (Dayal 2004). Garment manufacturing was taken off the list of industries reserved for the small-scale sector in 2000, in anticipation of stiffer competition resulting from trade liberalization (*ET* 2000a), but companies still failed to invest in large-scale production in time to take advantage of the Multi-Fibre Agreement phase-out at the end of 2004 (Majumdar 2004; Majumdar and Pandey 2005).

Most commentators agreed that the main weakness of Indian textile and garment production was its decentralized character, resulting in low productivity, which put it at a disadvantage vis-à-vis China, despite the fact that wages were 30 percent lower in India (*BS* 2002d). Industrialists kept textile units small in order to evade duty and labor laws, with the result that the quality of their products was not good enough for export (Jaipuria 2001). Government policy too was implicated: "The Chinese textile and clothing sector was a pale shadow of the more vibrant Indian one in the beginning of the 1980s," but "the Chinese set up large scale garment sewing plants to meet the growing global demand for the most cost-effective clothing even as the government of India continued to move in exactly the opposite direction" (Singhal 2003); "Indian government regulations penalise producers that grow beyond a certain size" (Luce 2004). The result of applying differential tax rates to the large-scale and small-scale sectors "has been extensive revenue loss for the government, unequal competition among segments with the odds stacked against the organised sector, fragmentation of capacities and resultant failure of the industry to incorporate the huge advances made elsewhere in the world in terms of technology and organisational upgradation" (Arun 2002).

Consolidation of the industry, with fewer and better suppliers, was suggested as one remedy by Mark Neuman of International Trade and Global Strategies for Limited Brands and MAST Industries; he also recommended higher labor standards and zero tolerance for child labor (*BS* 2004c). A similar strategy of technological upgrading to increase productivity and produce higher-quality products with a well-paid, educated, and skilled workforce had been proposed a decade earlier (Chandra and Shukla 1994). But Indian advocates of garment-industry interests were demanding instead that the denial of labor rights in the small-scale sector be extended to large-scale units. Most garment producers took the advice to consolidate and were "bringing their dispersed factories under one roof to attain economies of scale," but, unable to find Indian managers experienced in running large units, were hiring more expensive First World managers, who were available in large numbers due to the closure of garment units in their own countries (Rai 2004).

The garment industry in Bombay had few large units at the start of the twenty-first century. Most production took place in *galas* (small rooms in multistory industrial estates) employing, typically, ten to nineteen workers, or in even smaller units in slums. The value of the garments was low, by comparison with Delhi, and virtually the only strategy used by employers in the struggle to be competitive was to spend as little as possible on their workers. Thus not only were wages below the minimum in the vast majority of cases, but facilities were also abysmal, with toilets, for example, often in a filthy and unusable condition or absent altogether (Gothoskar et al. 1998; ASK 2001).

Go Go International, employing around 110 workers in 1998, was located in Shah and Nahar Industrial Estate in the old textile area of Lower Parel. The owners, who were big industrialists, had twenty-one other units in the same industrial estate, registered under different company names, and they also owned units in other parts of Bombay and in Bangalore and Tirupur. Nandita, Anjali, and Kamala[2] had been working at Go Go for approximately five years but had not been made permanent; even those who had been working for ten years had no employment contract. Fear of dismissal was used by the employer to establish control over the workers, and there were informers among the workers who were used as a means of surveillance over them. As the women said: "Even if we are seen talking to you, we will be asked questions afterward," and "people are afraid of saying anything in case the next person is an informer."

They were earning Rs 2,500, Rs 2,600, and Rs 2,700 respectively per month (slightly below the minimum wage). Increments were given according to the whim of the employer, and those who were seen to be cooperative—for example, by working overtime—got more, while those who were outspoken got less. They worked forty-eight hours a week, 9:30 a.m. to 6:00 p.m., Monday to Saturday, but there was more or less compulsory overtime of up to two hours a day for women. Men sometimes had to work for twenty-four hours at a stretch; only women with small children were let off. They were unaware of any cases of sexual harassment but did feel there was discrimination against women in pay. The company preferred to employ men, probably because they could be forced to work at night; there were only four women in the workforce. They were penalized if they arrived late, regardless of the problems they might have had with public transport; once Anjali had been sent home for arriving ten minutes late when she was pregnant. Women in the unit were receiving ESIS (that is, state-provided) maternity benefits.

Anjali had formerly been employed in Contessa Knitwear, from where she had been dismissed for trying to form a union. They had heard from other workers that at Go Go and its sister concern Goenka and Goenka there had been an attempt to form a union about seven years earlier, but many workers had been dismissed and the union was broken. The one issue they felt that was of overwhelming importance was formal employment status: "If you could get us just that one thing, then we could get other people together and struggle for everything else. But at the moment, everyone is afraid—even we are afraid. Who wants to go looking for another job after working for five years in one place, starting at a lower salary? And getting a job won't be easy if other employers in the area get to know you're a troublemaker." In 1999, they did try to form a union and were first locked out and then dismissed. At another factory, Prakash Garments, 151 workers who joined the SSS in 2002 were locked out and then dismissed, and their work was subcontracted to small-scale units; the union filed a case against the company but was hampered by the fact that the dismissed workers had no proof of employment. Later, the entire factory closed down.

Tanuja was working at Bombay Modern Garments, producing exclusively for Pepe Jeans. There were fifteen workers, of whom ten were women. The piece rates were Rs 5 per piece for stitching the front of the jeans, the same for stitching the back, and Rs 2.20 for joining back and front, which is what she was doing. She could do about sixty pieces per day, for which she earned roughly Rs 132, but she felt that there was pay discrimination against women: "Women get less increments because they work less overtime." However, women did get ESIS maternity benefits. Thread trimming was being given out to homeworkers at the rate of thirty paise per piece,[3] and Tanuja was bringing work home because her husband had been victimized; he, her mother-in-law, and other members of the family did thread trimming at home. She believed that if workers formed a union in her unit, they would be dismissed. She had formerly worked for a company called A-1 Garments, which closed down when a union was formed. It reopened with new workers plus those from the former workforce who had not joined the union; those who had joined it were left out.

Shalini had worked for three years at Bharat Textile Company, making ladies' trousers and shirts. There were about fifteen women and four or five men working in her unit; formerly sewing had been done in it, but when a union was formed the owner got very angry, dismissed the workers, and removed the machines, after which no stitching was done there. She did "layering" (piling up layers of cloth prior to cutting) and "sorting" (putting the various parts of each garment together), and was getting paid Rs 35 per day for working from 8:45 a.m. to 6:00 p.m., Monday to Saturday. Permanent workers were paid for their day off (Sunday) and received a bonus once a year (one month's pay), maternity benefits, and a medical allowance; Provident Fund contributions were made by the employer and their own contributions were cut from their pay. Informal workers like Shalini received none of these facilities and benefits. There were others working in similar sweatshops, where working conditions were abysmal, some being located in shanties with neither running water nor toilets. Workers in one were being paid Rs 700 per month, less than a quarter of the minimum wage; when they demanded an increase, the employer switched to piece rates, and they ended up working harder for the same wage. In another, where workers were earning Rs 850 per month, the workers formed a union and presented a charter of demands. Instead of negotiating, the employer closed the unit, restarted it after two months, and took the workers back on a wage of Rs 800 per month.

Usha and Manisha were homeworkers trimming threads on shirts and T-shirts they were given from various companies in a nearby industrial estate. They were earning twenty-five paise per piece—Rs 25 for one hundred pieces—which they said could be achieved by one worker in a day only if she worked at it full-time. They were getting no benefits, and said that often children at home, especially girls, were asked to work in order to boost earnings. As this suggests, child labor was often a problem among homeworkers. Some of the older women—factory and sweatshop workers as well as homeworkers—were totally illiterate and could not even sign their names; the younger workers were mostly literate, although some said they had been working since the age of twelve. Vasanthi, also a homeworker, pointed out that there were hidden deductions: women had to buy the thread cutter for trimming and the thread for button stitching and button holing. They also had to carry the heavy bundle of clothing from the factory on their heads and back again when the work was completed, which they were not paid for doing. Irregularity of work was a major problem: "We have to go looking for work from place to place. Some get it, some don't. When we do get work, we often have to work flat out to meet the deadline—if we don't, we won't be given work the next time."

Usha, Manisha, and Vasanthi often worked for Patel Hosiery Mills, which was subcontracting work to over fifty sweatshops ("job work units") as well as homeworkers. They told us that in the factory, where around one hundred workers (mainly men and a few women) were employed on the premises, an earlier attempt at unionization had been broken by dismissing the workers who were responsible for it. Many homeworkers complained that the employer yelled at them if they failed to complete an urgent order and that they had to tolerate such behavior because they were afraid of losing the work. Also, "the supervisors and male workers don't treat us with respect" and made "dirty" remarks, a form of sexual harassment. These workers had direct contact with the factory, whereas some of the other homeworkers, who got their work through a contractor, did not know where it was coming from. Sometimes there was no work for a long time, so they took in other types of homework—anything to make ends meet.

Apart from the consistently substandard employment conditions of these workers, what was striking was their chronic sense of insecurity and the regularity with which attempts at unionization were met by dismissals or closure of the unit. Excel Garments, with 150 formal workers (almost all women), was the exception that proved the rule: it was the only unit where workers managed to form a union and keep it alive. The fact that informal workers—and even formal workers in units with fewer than one hundred employees—could be dismissed with impunity for exercising their right to freedom of association lay behind the demands of employers for "flexibility," which, in their language, almost always meant "union-free workforces." This did not mean that the organization of informal workers was impossible, but such examples were rare; the majority of informal employees who tried to unionize lost their jobs. Most were too terrified even to try.

The Politics of Informality

Was there any basis for the claim by employers that India's labor laws put them at a disadvantage globally? Tips from a garment-industry insider suggested that cheap labor and the lack of workers' rights were *not* important conditions for success: "Forget about cheap labour. Poverty is no longer an asset. . . . Get your government to help. You do not need special subsidies. You need only those facilities that only government can and should supply. Among these are decent schools to train managers and technicians; reliable electricity; reasonable logistic facilities; and most of all, less corruption" (Birnbaum 2001).[4] This is precisely the advice that was not taken in India. According to one report, "leading logistics players complain that stringent customs regulations and lack of infrastructure facilities in India have continued to negate the edge enjoyed by Indian exporters and logistics players" (Joseph 2002). Another study, sponsored jointly by the World Bank and Confederation of Indian Industry, found that the "low labour cost advantage is being whittled away by higher power costs, interest rates and regulatory hurdles," including "delays in customs clearance, which on average takes 15 days" (*BS* 2002e).

Contrary to the widely held view that a dilution of labor legislation was necessary to encourage foreign direct investment (cf. Kuber 2005), A. T. Kearney's survey of over one thousand top international companies in 2001 showed that the two major attractions of India were the potentially huge size of its market and the availability of an educated, skilled, English-speaking labor force at competitive wages. In other words, it was the top end of the labor market that was the main attraction, not the informal sector. China's market was seen as being disproportionately larger—some companies estimated it as being ten times larger—and this was a factor making China a more attractive destination. The list of negative features in India was topped by bureaucracy. Alleged labor-market rigidities due to the ID Act were not even mentioned (Global Business Policy Council 2001). Interviews with executives of UK multinationals corroborated these findings (Banaji 2001a).

The market was so much larger in China because the prices of consumer goods were considerably lower than in India; in other words, a mass market for these products had developed (Vijayraghavan 2000). In India, by contrast, most consumer goods apart from the bare necessities of life were beyond the reach of over 90 percent of the labor force and their families, and thus the market was a mere fraction of the size it could have been. In fact, it was suggested that rather than cutting into the domestic market, cheap imports from countries like China could have been *creating new markets* for domestic producers who were efficient enough to bring down prices while maintaining quality (Zhu 1997). This leads to the interesting hypothesis that far from attracting foreign direct investment, low wage levels make India *less* attractive as an investment destination for both foreign and Indian investors, who might prefer a larger consumer market. The key to success is not cheap labor but "better finance and infrastructure, which requires both more competition and better regulation; and transforming labour market regulation, to foster skills, *while avoiding the counterproductive interventions that so often destroy employment in the formal sector*" (Wolf 2004).

It appears that the huge preponderance and more rapid growth of informal as compared to formal employment was the result neither of globalization nor of protective labor laws but of government policies favoring the informal sector. Employer preference for a minimum of state regulation, or preferably none at all, is understandable (cf. Harriss-White and Gooptu 2000, 89–90). The aversion to and sabotage of state regulation in the informal sector was not confined to labor laws but included tax evasion, illegal use of electricity, evasion of environmental laws, and, in general, establishment of a close relationship with the huge black economy and underworld (Breman 1996, 183). All these measures would enhance profits and reduce or abolish deductions. But given the lack of evidence that informality boosted employment or that India's labor legislation made it uncompetitive globally, what interest did the *government* have in promoting informality?

This question cannot be answered unless it is recognized that although the informal sector is not regulated by the official state, it *is* regulated by traditional social institutions, with rigid hierarchies based on caste, religion, and gender, which interact with the official state to produce a "shadow" state (Harriss-White 2003, 20–21, 88–89; 2005).

> Some roles in the "shadow" state are played simultaneously by the bureaucrats of the official State; for instance, accepting tribute, patronage and/or clientelage. Other "shadow" state livelihoods are a form of self-employment, although they depend on state employees, politicians and other interested social forces for their incomes; for example, private armies enforcing black or corrupt contracts, intermediaries, technical fixers, gate-keepers, adjudicators of disputes, confidants, contractors and consultants. Hence the real State, including its shadow, is bigger than the formal State.
>
> (Harriss-White 2003, 89)

The informal sector—and also a significant part of the formal sector—consists mainly of family firms, which tend to operate under a system of patriarchal gender relations (Harriss-White 2005), while the traditional *varna* system—pervasive among the majority Hindu community—relegates workers either to the bottom of the caste hierarchy or beneath it altogether.[5] These relations are sanctified by religion as belonging to a God-given order, and struggles for women's or workers' rights are seen as a threat to it. Precolonial labor relations were structured by caste. British colonial rule created a thin veneer of state-regulated industrial relations on the surface but left the vast majority of workers to manage as best they could, exploited increasingly by capital while being regulated by traditional caste and gender relations. Successive governments in independent India left the system largely untouched.

The result was a small number of permanent workers in large-scale formal units enjoying a degree of job security that would have been the envy of most workers in First World countries, while for the vast majority, the only thing standing between their families and starvation was their ill-paid, insecure, informal employment. The two sectors reinforced each other. The prospect of being suspended over that abyss made permanent workers cling to their status for dear life, while employers, unable to hire formal workers for temporary jobs even to substitute for workers away on leave or in response to fluctuations in production, made this an excuse to preserve and expand informal employment. Is there any way in which flexibility to vary the number of workers according to the exigencies of production can be combined with workers' rights to unionize and bargain collectively?

Legislative Changes

The View from the Formal Sector

A TUSC workshop on January 26, 1995, to discuss contract labor and subcontracting came out with a draft charter of demands. Its introduction pointed out that

> since the early 1980s, many large establishments have been systematically running down their permanent workforces and replacing them with non-permanent and contract workers in new units in "backward" areas. They have also been subcontracting much of their production to units in the unorganised sector. It is becoming clearer day by day that so long as the substantial disparity in legal rights and employment conditions between the organised and unorganised sector continues, employers will use the labour of unprotected workers in the huge unorganised sector to undermine the bargaining strength and job security of permanent employees in the organised sector.

The proposed amendments to legislation included: (1) Amendment of the ID Act to include contract workers as "workmen," so that they would be covered by labor legislation. (2) Amendments to the Contract Labour Act to (a) compel employers in whose establishments contract labor had been disallowed to treat the existing contract workers as their own employees from the date they started working at the establishment; (b) make the Contract Labour Act applicable to all establishments and contractors, regardless of the number of workers; (c) provide for a hearing to the proposed contract workers as well as regular employees of the principal employer before granting a contract to the contractor; and (d) require the principal employer to give details of the workers needed, e.g., in which department, what category, etc. (3) Amendment of the Maharashtra Contract Labour Rules to state that contract workers should get wages and benefits equal to the average being paid to permanent workers, not minimum wages.

Amendments proposed for the small-scale sector included the following: (1) Removal of exemptions from labor laws based upon the size of the unit, so that all labor laws are applicable to all establishments, regardless of the number of workers employed. (2) Elected representatives of workers in industrial estates to be given the powers of inspectors under various labor laws such as the Factories Act, Minimum Wages Act, ESI Act, etc. (3) Employers in the industrial estate should jointly provide a subsidized canteen, health clinic, crèche, training center, and "fair price shop"[6] to workers of the estate.

These were far-reaching proposals, but before examining them further, it would be useful to look at the proposals made by informal garment workers.

The View from Informal Workers

At workshops on March 18 and 25 and October 2, 2001, informal garment workers formulated their problems and demands. Unlike the employees' unionists, these workers were not familiar with the law and therefore did not make suggestions for specific amendments. Nonetheless, their demands and suggestions could be given a legal form. (1) Many of their demands were for inclusion under existing labor laws covering minimum wages; prompt payment of wages, bonuses, and social security (e.g., Provident Fund); paid days off, holidays, and leave; reasonable working hours; proper overtime payments; and no compulsory overtime. Such demands were made not only by factory and sweatshop workers but also by homeworkers, who insisted: "It should be accepted that we are workers, and have every right to put demands to employers. There should not be any discrimination—in terms of wages or other allowances—between homeworkers and factory workers. We are workers and there should be equal respect for our labor." (2) Another set of demands related to formalization and proof of employment: registration, identity cards, appointment letters, payment slips, welfare cards, and attendance cards or attendance diaries, which the employer would stamp whenever they were given work. (3) Finally, they felt, "we should have a union"; "it is important to have a union, because then we would get our rights, there would be no mental harassment or sexual abuse."

Legislative Reform

There was a large area of overlap between the proposals coming from formal and informal workers, which related to ending the exclusion of informal workers from most of the existing labor legislation. But one problem that loomed large in the minds of the informal workers yet was overlooked by the formal workers was *the need for proof of employment*. How can workers obtain their rights if there is no legal recognition that they are workers? How can they claim unfair dismissal for trade union membership or activities if they cannot prove they were employed in the first place? "The attempt to increase labour's capacity to associate and bargain collectively is futile in a context where large numbers of workers do not even have the minimum recognition as a 'worker'" (Swaminathan 2002, 3). Systematic violation of the right of informal workers to unionize, despite the fact that the Trade Unions Act is supposed to cover them, indicates that "certain employers have found that they don't need to have the law changed; they just side-step it by changing the employment relationship. They vacate the law" (Marin 2003).

This was a practical problem confronting the informal workers, and they proposed various remedies that deserve serious consideration. Their demand for the registration of all workers and employers was suggested by existing legislation for occupations characterized by a high degree of casualization: the Dock Workers (Regulation of Employment) Act (1948); the Maharashtra Mathadi, Hamal, and Other Manual Workers (Regulation of Employment and Welfare) Act (1969); the Kerala Agricultural Workers' Act (1974); the Kerala Head Load Workers' Act (1978); the Tamil Nadu Manual

Workers (Regulation of Employment and Conditions of Work) Act (1982); and the Building and Other Construction Workers (Regulation of Employment and Conditions of Service) Act (1996), which was passed after more than ten years of campaigning by the Tamil Nadu State Construction Workers' Union (Rajesh and Singh 2003).

These acts require the formation of state-level tripartite boards consisting of employer, employee, and government representatives to register all employers and workers and regulate employment (Subramanya 2005, 28). They have enabled workers to organize in extremely casualized and apparently unpromising occupations such as dock labor, handcart pushing, and scavenging (Deshpande 1999; Chikarmane and Narayan 2000).

However, the existing legislation was fragmented in two ways: it differed from one state to another, and there was separate legislation for different occupations, making joint struggles of informal workers across these divisions extremely difficult (Breman 1996, 198). The National Centre for Labour (NCL), a coordination of independent organizations of informal workers, was set up in 1995 as a step toward overcoming this fragmentation. It was founded at a convention on May 28 and 29 in Bangalore and launched with a rally of around seventy thousand informal workers on May 29. It represented over five hundred thousand informal workers from diverse sectors and all parts of the country and announced:

> The structure of NCL shall consist of a General Council, an Executive Committee and a Secretariat. The General Council is the decision making body and shall be democratically elected by member-organizations, who also have the right to recall or replace any representative. Representatives will reflect the actual composition of the NCL membership in terms of gender, caste and community.
>
> (NCL n.d., 6)

When the deliberations of the Second National Commission on Labour were in progress, a letter to the chairman from the Akhil Bharatiya Mathadi Transport and General Kamgar Union testified: "In view of the regulation of employment and timely deposition of wages and levy with the Boards, all the benefits reach these workers in time. The standard of living of these workers has considerably improved. Mathadi workers live with grace and pride and thus their social status has improved." It suggested that "such type of enactment should be made and implemented all over India, in all the states, to cover the large number of unprotected manual labourers who are deprived of their rights." Another informal workers' union, the Nirman Mazdoor Panchayat Sangam of Tamil Nadu, submitted that "with compulsory registration of employers and workers, regulation of employment and wages, management of work records through the Board, the workers will rightfully get the social security benefits and also get liberated from exploitation" (cit. Subramanya 2005, 29). The recommendations of the Second National Commission on Labour (2002) included the proposal for registration of informal workers but not for the compulsory registration of employers.

The draft Unorganised Sector Workers' Bill (2004) also mentioned the registration of workers and registration of the employers of unorganized-sector workers but went on to specify that only workers shall make an application for registration, making it clear that it would not be compulsory for employers to register. This would of course make the regulation of employment impossible. Given that the bulk of the proposed legislation pertained to the setting up of welfare boards for informal-sector workers, it was described as a "truncated social security scheme" (Menon 2005a, 13). The NCL and informal workers' unions had formed the National Campaign Committee for Unorganised Sector Workers and conducted two seminars (in Chennai in May 2001 and in Delhi in August 2001) to formulate an alternative bill, and the final draft was handed to the Lok Sabha Speaker on May 5, 2005, at the end of a rally (Menon 2005a, 15).

The National Commission on Enterprises in the Unorganised Sector was asked to review the proposed legislation, and in the light of suggestions from left-wing parties in the Indian Labour Conference that there should be a separate bill for agriculture, drafted two bills: the Agricultural Workers' Conditions of Work and Social Security Bill (2007) and the Non-Agricultural Workers' Conditions of Work and Social Security Bill (2007). While proposing considerable improvements in employment conditions and access to social security, the bills did not propose the compulsory registration of employers and employees; it suggested that wage slips may be provided to nonagricultural employees, although this was not feasible in agriculture (NCEUS 2007). The Labour Ministry did not accept the necessity for a separate bill for agricultural workers—pointing out, correctly, that most agricultural workers and marginal farmers shifted to other jobs in the off season—and did not agree to other proposed changes either (Chatterji 2008). Finally, the bill was passed in its truncated form in December

2008 as the Unorganised Workers' Social Security Act, failing completely to tackle the issue of regulating informal employment and failing even as a social-security measure (see chapter 8).

This legislative approach to reform has three major problems. One is that it conflates workers who are employees and those who are self-employed, whereas their needs are very different. The second is that without the registration of employers and employees and regulation of employment, neither workers' rights nor social-security provisions can be ensured. Third, this approach "negates the principle articulated by the ILO that 'since the fundamental principles and rights at work and the fundamental Conventions apply to all workers, there should not be a two-tiered system or separate regulatory framework for formal and informal workers'" (John 2005a, 4). The approach of both employees' unions and informal garment workers, which seeks to bring informal labor under the purview of existing legislation, is much more appropriate.

Putting this into practice would require the compulsory registration of *all* employers and employees, and records of all employment would have to be kept. This would result in the formalization of informal employees, in the sense that they would all have proof of employment, however casual it might be. This may sound utopian, but it has been attempted: in Bulgaria, "a new law has very big penalties for employers who don't register, to push employers to employ workers formally" (WWW 2003a, 60). In India, there would be problems due to illiteracy on the part of many workers and some employers, so a great deal of assistance would be required to implement such a scheme. These provisions could be embodied in a new Employment Regulation Act, but a revised Trade Union Act should also emphasize that the right to form unions and bargain collectively depends on the right not to be dismissed or otherwise victimized for doing so, which in turn depends on employees having proof of employment. Employers who contract production out would be responsible for ensuring that the subcontractors are registered; failure to do this would be penalized.

There have been various attempts to regulate contract labor. The National Union of Mineworkers in South Africa included clauses in its August 2003 agreement stipulating that "the primary employer (the mining company) has full responsibility for the contracted worker. Secondly, the secondary employer, that is, the labour broker who provides the services, must be registered (and must show proof of payment of registration fees). Thirdly, the employer must provide basic coverage for such benefits as retirement or death" (Webster and Buhlungu 2007, 422). Legislation along similar lines was proposed in India (Edwin 2003) and implemented in Britain after the tragedy in February 2004, when at least twenty-one Chinese contract workers drowned while picking cockles in Morecambe Bay.

> In July 2004 . . . the Gangmaster (Licensing) Act became law. From 2006, a new authority will be established with powers to issue and withdraw operating licenses to all employers of temporary workers in the agricultural sector. It will become a criminal offence for labour providers to operate without a licence and for labour users to use labour providers who do not have a licence.
>
> (Hawkins 2005, 10)

In fact, labor contractors perform three separate functions, and they should be required to register in only one role if their activities are to be regulated. They could register as recruiting agents, in which case they would be paid a commission by the employer for the workers they supply, but the workers would then become employees of the employer; as supervisors or team leaders, in which case they, along with the workers they supervise, would be registered as employees and paid by the employer; or, finally, as "petty capitalists," like the Indian contractors engaged in building the railways, that is, as employers. In this last instance, the contractor would take on the responsibilities of an employer, and the company, person, or entity (such as a housing society) engaging him (or, more rarely, her) would be responsible only for checking that the contractor was registered as an employer and had a valid license.

Such a system would ensure that contract workers had a clear employer-employee relationship with a single person or company. The system of shared responsibility in the Contract Labour Act simply has not worked, because neither the principal employer nor the contractor takes responsibility for these workers. But under this system, a contractor who did not abide by statutory regulations would have his license revoked and would then face imprisonment for continuing to operate, as would anyone using his services. Regulation of contract labor becomes even more important in the globalized context, where it applies not just to unskilled workers but also to skilled and qualified employees who get jobs through temporary-employment agencies (BS 2004d). It is crucial that it be clear at all times who takes the responsibility of an employer for these employees.

Another demand put forward by the employees' unions—that regular workers should be consulted about the proposed use of contract labor that might affect the employment status or terms and conditions of existing employees—was the focus of a campaign by the International Federation of Chemical, Energy, Mine, and General Workers' Unions, and it was successful in Brazil and Canada (Mather 2005). Such a requirement would help to ascertain that employers were not just trying to cut costs or prevent unionization by using contract labor for regular jobs. Finally, workers could form labor cooperatives, and it has been demanded that these should be given preference when work is given out to contract workers (NTUI 2009, 4).

It should be emphasized that none of these steps would make these workers regular, much less permanent: they would still be casual, temporary, part time, or seasonal. The only difference would be that they would have a formal employment contract, or its equivalent, constituting proof of employment. The next step would be to make all the existing legislation applicable to them, with pro rata benefits and facilities and, most importantly, recognition of their right to unionize and bargain collectively without being victimized. This would entail translating piece rates into time rates in the case of homeworkers, to make it clear how much working time was represented by a certain number of pieces; they should then get facilities such as paid days off, leave and holidays, extra payments for working overtime to complete an order, and benefits—including maternity, retirement, and health-care provisions—on a pro rata basis, thus conforming to the ILO Convention on Home Work (1996), which specifies equal treatment for homeworkers (HomeNet 1999b).

The third step would be to regularize employment as far as possible. While it may not be possible for companies to guarantee permanent, lifelong jobs to their employees, they should certainly employ the same worker for a job so long as it continues in existence, unless incompetence or wrongdoing can be proved against the worker. This would not rule out temporary contracts for work that is genuinely temporary, but it would ensure that irregular workers are not used for regular work. It was suggested that only after working ten years should a worker be entitled to an indefinite contract (Nath 2003), but this seems like an excessively long probationary period. The current requirement of 240 days might be more appropriate, especially since companies themselves often voluntarily make temporary employees permanent within a year (Patel 2005).

The Supreme Court has ruled that "it would be an unfair labour practice if work is taken continuously from daily wage workers for a long number of years without considering their regularisation" (Antony 2001a), yet many employers contrive to do precisely that. Here the proposal by the TUSC that contract, casual, or temporary workers should receive the same wages as permanent workers doing the same work would be important. The judiciary has taken contradictory positions on this issue, with the "Orissa High Court asking the state government to provide 'equal pay for equal work' for casual employees working in its irrigation, power and various other projects," while the Supreme Court set aside the judgment and ruled that minimum wages were sufficient (*BS* 2002f). The Orissa High Court was in principle more correct, since unequal pay for the same work constitutes discrimination against those who receive less. That the Supreme Court could make such a ruling is striking evidence of the system of employment apartheid prevailing in India, where discrimination against the vast majority of employees on the basis of their employment status is seen as being legally justified. Despite the ruling, the NTUI-affiliated contract-workers' union at the Bokaro steel plant continued fighting for equal pay.

If employers genuinely need flexibility, they should be able to have it: hence the need to provide for temporary contracts. However, it is absolutely necessary to rule out the possibility that they use such provisions to employ irregular workers for regular jobs or to deny workers their fundamental rights: hence the need to penalize employers who artificially keep employees irregular or treat irregular workers unequally. Bringing all employment under the purview of the same labor legislation—thus abolishing the two-tier system that denies basic rights to informal employees—and making it mandatory for employers to employ regular workers for regular jobs and pay equal wages to irregular workers would be two essential steps toward creating labor flexibility. A third and equally essential step would be a comprehensive social-security system to ensure that the loss of employment does not mean that workers and their families fall hopelessly into debt or starve (see chapter 8).

Education and Child Labor

In India, child labor is rarely found in the formal sector, but it is rampant in the informal sector. The ILO estimated that there were at least ninety million working children in India at the end of the twentieth century, the largest number in any country in the world (*ET* 2000b). Some NGOs put the figure even higher, while the government figures were much lower, but the ILO estimate is probably reliable if children working in their own homes were included.[7]

Child Labor in India

Three children, Farook, Suresh, and Sahdev, died within three months in 1998 in Gujarat. Farook was cleaning used polythene bags that once contained the highly toxic pesticide Phorat, Sahdev was working on a road construction site and was crushed by falling concrete, and Suresh was crushed to death when part of the bridge he was breaking collapsed on him (Chauhar 1998). Every Diwali, there are reports of children being blown up in fireworks factories (*LF* 1998). A study of match production in the Sivakasi-Sattur belt in Tamil Nadu demonstrated how government policies encouraging informality (by restricting match production in the formal sector, excise differentials favoring the small-scale sector, and exemption from labor laws) actually promoted child labor in this hazardous industry (Chandrasekhar 1997). Similarly, in the Ferozabad glass industry, "it was normal to see six-year-olds running between furnaces with hot iron rods larger than they," and "the boys do not just have bare feet, they have bruised, cut, infected, blistered and burnt feet," yet the industry "gets up to 90 per cent subsidies from banks" (Dewan 1999, 295, 296, 294).[8]

These examples of child labor in hazardous industries would probably be included among the "worst forms of child labor" as defined by the ILO. But supposedly nonhazardous work, the elimination of which is not seen as such a high priority, is by no means safe for children. Fifteen-year-old Banu had been working in the garment industry since she was eleven. In June 1998, her skirt got caught in an unprotected overlock machine at Koshi Garments, Tirupur, throwing her violently to the ground. She died later the same day (John 1998). Eight-year-old Shiva, an orphan, was sold by his uncle for Rs 1,500 to Ganesh Rajput, who put him to work in a small unit making sweets and snacks. The children were made to work long hours and treated with appalling cruelty. When Shiva tried to run away in June 1993, Rajput caught him and beat him to death (Sharma 1998). Employment in the garment or confectionery industries may not be classified as among the worst forms of child labor, but children nonetheless suffer serious injury and death in them. Agriculture, where the majority of boys are employed, has hazardous machinery and toxic pesticides; domestic service, in which the majority of girls are employed, puts a child at the mercy of the employer's family and exposes her to possible verbal, physical, and sexual abuse. Unhealthy working conditions and long hours of work—often nine or more hours per day, six or seven days a week—undermine the children's health (Basu 2000).

The risk of abuse or injury is probably least where children work in their own homes. But it cannot be assumed that working in one's own home is insurance against occupational diseases or injuries. Girls helping to roll beedis at home, for example, sit in an unhealthy position for hours on end, breathing tobacco dust day and night. Young children left alone at home to care for smaller siblings could be at risk from fire and other hazards, especially given the extremely substandard housing in which most informal workers live. Their greatest loss, however, is the denial of an education, which ensures that when they grow up, they will inevitably be confined to the same poorly paid informal work as their parents. This hits underprivileged sections of the labor force hardest. "Together the Scheduled Castes and Scheduled Tribes accounted for about 40 per cent of the total child workers in the country. This share of SC/ST child labour in the country's total child labour in 1993–94 was much higher than their share in the total child population, which was 27.5 per cent" (Thorat 1999, 156–157). By a disproportionate denial of education to SC/ST children, child labor reinforces inequality and caste oppression. Similarly, "According to available statistics, the majority of children out of school are girls. . . . The implications of such unequal treatment result in limiting the opportunities and choices that girl children may have both in the present and in the future" (Burra 2001, 483–484). The resulting female literacy rate of only around 40 percent perpetuates the disempowerment of women.

The Argument Over Rights

Those who advocate the immediate abolition of child labor do so from the standpoint of the ethical and human-rights position that this class of human beings has a right *not* to be workers. It is thus primarily an argument that child labor results in the denial of a child's right to adequate rest, play, education, and childhood itself (Burra 2003; Sinha 2005b) and only secondarily an argument about the effect of child labor on workers' rights. This is the approach taken in the UN Convention on the Rights of the Child (CRC), adopted in 1989.[9]

One counterargument is that there may be "a conflict between the rights of the child to education and the economic needs of the family," including the "need" of the child herself/himself to work for a livelihood (Kabeer et al. 2003, 16). This counterposition of needs and rights has been criticized because it ignores the *need* of children for education "in order to participate in civil democratic society as informed participants" and to gain "the knowledge and skills required to take advantage of the opportunities that modern economies offer" (Burra 2003, 74). Indeed, in this context there is no meaningful distinction between needs and rights; the "need" for children to work can be—and has been—also articulated as a "right." However, it is curious that the "need" for, or "right" of, children to work is never argued with respect to the children of well-to-do families, which it ought to be if it is genuinely universal. It is therefore either an argument that poor children are fundamentally different from richer ones, with different needs and rights, or simply a way of saying that all children need, and have a right to, a livelihood— and that the only way that poor children can secure a livelihood is by working.

Another argument against the universal child-rights approach is that in Third World countries there is "a local social construction of childhood which is somehow more real, more honest, than the global social construction of childhood" in instruments like the CRC (Bissell 2003, 69), and therefore those who oppose child labor in places like Bangladesh should be criticized for implying that "as a result of work and life's hardships, children in the developing world do not experience childhood; and at the very least they are 'unfortunate,' because the opportunities of children in the West have been stolen from them" (Bissell 2003, 57). This argument seems to suggest that children in "the West" and children in "the developing world" have different needs and rights. Yet child labor was widely prevalent in the West in the eighteenth and nineteenth centuries, and there are millions of children in Third World countries who do go to school. If workers in developed countries could fight for an education for their children and get it, why should workers in developing countries not do the same?

It is true that some working-class parents in India are more anxious that their sons should get employment rather than continue their education and that daughters should help their mothers at home rather than go to school (Ramaswamy 1983, 132–133). But do they have a right to put their children to work at an early age? Marx, referring to child labor, said that the parents "sell" their children, and the worker thereby becomes a "slave dealer" (Marx 1976, 516, 519). This sounds harsh, yet how else can it be described when parents in India literally do sell their children into bondage for a few hundreds or thousands of rupees, condemning them to long hours of labor and cruel treatment for the rest of their childhood (Burra 2003, 78–81)? Since children themselves do not have the legal right to enter into contracts, this is a form of slavery.[10] The argument that parents have the "right" to do this is linked to a notion of children as the property of their parents. If the relationship were seen as one of trusteeship rather than ownership, this would not be possible.[11]

In Europe, the transition from a regime where child labor was rampant to one in which children were protected from exploitation was accompanied by democratization of the family and a dramatic change in the way children were seen by their parents, with fathers, especially, becoming less distant and authoritarian (Jans 2004, 32–33). Wherever child labor has been abolished in Indian villages, the change is no less dramatic: "Fathers are drinking much less and are working harder because they have to invest in their children's education. Further, parents have become *parents*, with a lot of pride in the fact that their children are no longer in work but are students. The quality of life in the family has vastly improved" (Sinha 2005b). Love depends on respect for the other as a person, and it is only when children are no longer regarded as a source of income that they can be appreciated as an end in themselves.

In fact, only a small minority of working-class parents in India do not value education for their children. Workers in employees' unions in Bombay did their best to send their children to good schools and colleges, sometimes spending a considerable portion of their earnings to do so. And the informal garment workers agreed unanimously that child labor should be abolished, expressing their determination to give their own children— including daughters—an education. The demand for education from poor parents has been noted all over India:

we find how they are sending their children to overcrowded schools; to schools that lack teachers; to schools without water or toilets; to schools that do not respect their children. . . . Even as it is incessantly argued that the poor cannot and will not send their children to schools, they send them in the hope that one day the school system would learn to respect them and their children. . . . In fact, if the education system is surviving even at the level it is in the country today, it is because of the poor and their battle for schools.

(Sinha 2005b)

It has been suggested that the greater decline in fertility among poor, illiterate women in the 1990s can be explained by their strategy of limiting family size so as to be able to educate their children, both boys and girls (Arokiasamy et al. 2004). The demand for education from poor parents undeniably far outstrips the supply.

However, it is sometimes argued, the children themselves may wish to work; for example: "A young girl working in a factory in Bangladesh . . . may not want to be forbidden to stitch shirts if her only alternative is destitution or even prostitution" (Stalker 1996, 4; cit. Kabeer 2001, 376). Here it is important to specify why the children "want" to work. If they believe that their own survival or that of their families depends on their earnings or that the only alternative is prostitution, it is natural that they would "want" to work. If there are no schools available, or there are no teachers in the school, or they are discriminated against and abused at school (as often happens to SC/ST children), there is no incentive for them to pursue an education. It is only when they and their families are guaranteed a livelihood and when good schooling is available to them that they can *choose* not to have an education. But in India, these are precisely the circumstances in which children *never* choose not to go to school. The reason is not hard to find. Anyone who has cared for a small child has encountered the inexhaustible curiosity of children—their endless questions, which often pose scientific or philosophical challenges to adults. If schooling does not satisfy this curiosity, the remedy is to improve the educational system rather than to deprive children of the wherewithal to satisfy their thirst for knowledge. The Mamidipudi Venkatarangaiya (MV) Foundation, a child-rights organization in Andhra Pradesh, found that children went to great lengths to persuade their families to let them go to school; a fourteen-year-old girl who had been married off even threatened suicide if she was denied this right (Farooq 2005).

There is a valid argument that work in a safe, nonexploitative framework should be seen as a part of education in a broader sense. But it is the *exploitation* of children by their families and/or employers that is referred to when their "right to work" is invoked. The ILO Minimum Age Convention sets fifteen years as the lower limit for employment, but if young people between the ages of fifteen and eighteen take up full-time work, it would be desirable for them to have the option of returning to education later on, as many young people who have left school early wish to do later in life. It would also be good if preprimary education, with a large component of play, could be provided on an optional basis.

The argument for differential rights for children, depending on whether they are born in developed or developing countries or in rich or poor families, comes dangerously close to a racist or class-racist argument that justifies discrimination against poor children in the Third World. In fact,

> independently of culture and time, children share some typical characteristics. . . . Immaturity of children in a certain sense is a biological fact. . . . Always and everywhere children are growing up. They are young and have less experience in comparison to most adults of their environment. There is still a lot to discover. . . . [Moreover,] playing is . . . an important activity in the life of every child. . . . From a psychological perspective play . . . is considered to be essential for a good and healthy development of the child and is viewed as an important method in the learning process. . . . While they are playing, children reveal themselves as meaning-givers that can actively intervene in their environment. While playing they are shaping their environment and social networks. Play allows them to be actors.
>
> (Jans 2004, 35, 37)

The crucial role of play in a child's development accounts for why very poor children are seen playing in the most inhospitable environments: on dangerous building sites, in slums next to open drains, on the roadside with traffic whizzing past. Depriving them of the opportunity to play and learn is far more damaging to their development than poverty alone and is experienced as deprivation by the children themselves (Iyengar 1986).

Practical Arguments

The most common argument against the immediate abolition of child labor is that it is caused by poverty of the country or the child's family.

One variant is that "with very poor countries we cannot use the law to banish it, unless we are insensitive to the well-being of the children." Instead, "we need to limit the amount a child may work and be prepared to vary this according to the country's general economic condition" (Basu 2003, 103, 102). Another variant argues that since the children themselves and their families depend on their earnings, it is necessary to eliminate poverty before child labor can be eliminated (Grote 2000; Kabeer 2001, 373–375; Mehta 1999). According to the World Bank, "in poor households children may contribute a significant proportion of household income, which means that because such households spend the bulk of their income on food, income from child labor may be critical to survival"; strong enforcement of compulsory education "may reduce child labor but also endanger the welfare of poorer households who depend heavily on this income source" (Fallon and Tzannatos 1998, 10). The Indian government has expressed similar sentiments (cf. GOI 1979, cit. Sinha 2005c, 2576).

Yet even from the narrow standpoint of income, child labor has a negative outcome in the longer term. "Contrary to accepted belief, persons who start work at an early age do not, in adulthood, have any advantage in terms of higher productivity or wages over workers who join employment at a later age. In fact, in some cases it is quite the reverse" (ILO 1996b, cit. Burra 2003, 76). Thus among informal workers, adults who had started work as children earned less than those who had received an education; they would, of course, have little chance of getting formal employment, for which educational qualifications would be required.

One solution that has been suggested is part-time education that can be combined with labor. For example, "the Non-Formal Education (NFE) Programme began in 1978 and was later expanded in 1987–88. In 1999, there were 279,000 NFE centres with an enrolment of about 7 million children. . . . The NFE centres run for two hours (mostly at night) for a period of two years, [but] the NFE programme has not been able to provide quality primary education for out-of-school children" (Jhingran 2003, 197). The program was criticized for promoting "a class divide between . . . the children of 'upper' castes who go into the formal school system, and children of 'lower' castes who are forced to work the whole day and who study in the evening" (Burra 1999, 263). The inadequate quality and quantity of the education offered is not the only problem. Children in full-time employment do not get enough time even to rest; they are simply too exhausted to study: "Chitra is 11 years old. She works in DNK, a concern in Thennampalayam, a district in Tiruppur, producing cotton knitwear. . . . When there is a lot of work, she works 1½ shifts, that is 12 hours, from 8 o'clock in the morning till 9 o'clock in the evening, with only an hour's lunch-break in between. She has to work on Sundays too" (Scheu 1999, 228). On the other hand,

> part-time, seasonal work as well as domestic tasks may allow for enrol-
> ment of children in schools. . . . However, irregularity of attendance and
> long periods of absence, which may often result because of the nature
> of such work, as well as the sheer burden of housework, are likely to
> adversely affect children's ability to cope with such schoolwork and their
> interest in studies. Poor performance and discontinuation from school
> are likely to follow.
>
> (Nambissan 2003, 123)[12]

What is the alternative? The contention that the prevalence of child labor in a country is a function of its poverty is not supported by the evidence. A cross-country study of child labor concluded that "poverty is not even a significant reason for child labour when the influence of other explanatory factors for child labour are simultaneously taken into account, whereas unequal income distribution and lack of access to education are much more important reasons" (Ahmed 1999, 1820). This suggests that what is responsible for child labor is a lack of will on the part of the government to provide a good education for every child. Within India, Kerala has long had high literacy rates, in contrast to those of other states. In Himachal Pradesh, where in 1961 there was a high level of child labor and literacy rates were 21 percent for males and 9 percent for females, literacy rates for children aged ten to fourteen went up to 94 percent for boys and 86 percent for girls by 1991 (PROBE team, 1999, 115–116; cit. Burra 2003, 88): "this has obviously been a result of the deep commitment that the state government has to universalising elementary education and this is clearly seen by the high level of per-capita expenditure on education, which is about twice the all-India average. The teacher-child ratio is also twice the national average" (Burra 2003, 88). These examples show that government policy in making quality education accessible to every child has a crucial role to play in eliminating child labor.

Furthermore, a survey conducted by the MV Foundation found that "there is little difference in the economic status of those families send-ing their children to school and those who are not" (Nagarjuna and Sinha

2004, 6). After a campaign by the MV Foundation (Wazir 2002), which resulted in withdrawing 242 children from work and placing them in schools, it became apparent that "a number of families who were relatively better off were, prior to the project, not sending their children to school. Even more significantly . . . no cut off point exists, in terms of economic status, below which a family has no option but to send their child to work" (Nagarjuna and Sinha 2004, 8). Thus even the poverty of the family is usually not the reason why children are sent out to work.

Critics of the poverty argument for the continuation of child labor argue that, on the contrary,

> *the full-time work of children is the cause of poverty.* If poverty has to be eradicated, there has to be a frontal attack on the full-time work of children at the cost of education. . . . *When children start working at a young age they remain illiterate, unskilled and unable to demand their rights for equal wages and better conditions of work.* Working long hours, they burn themselves out and their health is severely impaired. As adults, in situations like these, they are often heavily in debt. The circumstances of unemployment—if not unemployability—combined with their inferior position in the hierarchies of caste and class, predispose them to putting their own children to work. And so the downward spiral of exploitation and poverty is perpetuated.
>
> (Burra 2005)

Therefore, getting children out of employment and into school is a precondition for ending poverty.

One method that has been used to try to combat child labor, especially in carpet production, is social labeling. In the carpet belt of Uttar Pradesh, where 25 percent or more of the weavers were children, the "Rugmark" label was initiated in 1994 to certify that carpets had been made without child labor. However,

> the inspection system is applicable only during the daytime and it is then very . . . obvious that when the car of the inspector enters the villages, the children are immediately taken off the looms and put in the backyards or in adjacent rooms, so that when the inspector reaches the looms under the shed, there are no children working on the looms and only adults are to be seen.
>
> (Khan 1999, 212)

In addition, contractors shifted operations to less accessible villages, and the Rugmark Foundation, with an inspection and certification staff that was much too small to cover these dispersed locations, was unable to verify the voluntary affidavits by companies pledging that they were not using child labor. Subsequently, "random visits to some villages have shown children . . . working on looms, where the majority of looms in the village are supplying to one of the large exporters who claims to be selling all his carpets under the 'Rugmark' label." The "Kaleen" label, introduced by the Carpet Export Promotion Council and Ministry of Textiles of the Government of India in 1995, suffered from the same problems (Gupta 1999, 183–184).

A different approach was to involve the children, their parents, and the community around them in a campaign to get children out of employment and into full-time formal schooling. The MV Foundation, which pioneered this method, started work in 1991 "on the premise that the only way to eliminate child labour is to universalise education and vice versa" (Sinha 2003, 322). Youth activists from the villages played a prominent role in the campaign. Once the community was convinced of the need for their children to be educated, it was able to persuade employers to stop using child workers and press the government to provide enough schooling to accommodate all the children. The MV Foundation organized bridge courses for older children so that they could catch up with their peers instead of joining school at the lowest grade, coached children who needed extra attention, and helped parents with the unfamiliar procedures required to get children admitted to school and keep them there (Sinha 2003). A similar initiative in the carpet belt

> created village-level committees, which are called "Village Child Labour Vigilance Committees." These have been constituted with the initial support of ILO-IPEC. They are responsible for identifying the children on the looms, withdrawing them, putting them in schools, keeping vigil so that no new children replace them, and enrolling potential child labourers in government-run schools or in the schools run by the Centre for Rural Education and Development Action (CREDA). We have also created committees of women, which we call the "Mothers Group." These women's groups are trendsetters and very instrumental in getting their children withdrawn from work and put into schools.
>
> (Khan 1999, 218)

These programs in South and North India were in rural areas, but there have been others started in urban areas as well. CINI-ASHA started a Programme for Child Labourers in Calcutta in the mid-1990s, aimed at moving child workers into formal schools and building community-based support for education. Although the group was successful in getting the children into school, and the families made the necessary adjustments, only a tiny proportion were able to enter municipal schools, which meant that the rest had educational expenses that were high for poor families (CINI-ASHA 2003). Pratham, a group in Bombay that started an "every child learning" program in 1998, succeeded in enrolling almost ten thousand children in six hundred bridge courses within months, but it then found that in some areas the local municipal schools were already overcrowded and had no room for the children, and in other areas there was no school that was easily accessible (Banerji 2003). In both cases, the main constraint was the lack of an adequate provision of free elementary education by the government. There are numerous examples of similar initiatives, in both urban and rural areas, in some cases by NGOs, which provide their own schools.

These experiments put to rest the myth that children from extremely poor families cannot be taken out of work and put into formal education. Not only was enthusiastic support obtained from the children, their families, and local communities for the MV Foundation program, but the bargaining power of women increased with the nonavailability of child labor, resulting in an increase in their wage rates and vast improvement in working conditions. "Regarding male labour, it is noticed that from working for just 16–18 days in a month, they are now finding work for 24–26 days in a month. The terms and conditions of long-term contracts with their employers have also improved" (Sinha 2003, 324–325). This is not surprising. In India, with high rates of adult unemployment and underemployment, children's labor competes with that of adults in the same family or community (Iyengar 1986; Chandrashekhar 1997), so that the purely labor-market effect of the withdrawal of child labor is an increase, not decrease, in family income.

This effect would be magnified enormously if campaigns against child labor were combined with legal measures to formalize informal labor. Child labor has been given a high profile in campaigns to eliminate gross violations of labor rights, and in one way this has been a good thing. When the groups that later grew into the South Asian Coalition Against Child Servitude started working to release bonded child laborers in the 1980s, "phrases like child servitude or child bonded labour were never used in media, judiciary or government circles" (Satyarthi 1999, 270). Largely as a result of their efforts, child labor was widely recognized as a serious problem both in India and internationally, and efforts to abolish it gained strength. A high point of this process was the Global March Against Child Labour in 1998, in which approximately fifteen thousand children and child-rights activists participated (*IUR* 1998).

Yet highlighting child labor also had a negative consequence: it created a widespread assumption that child labor could be abolished while still denying other informal workers their labor and social-security rights. But, "since 92 or 92.5 per cent of the country's workforce are employed in this unorganized segment without getting reasonable wages or social security measures, this is a prime reason why children are drawn into employment" (Thankappan 1999, 66). In other words, child labor and informal labor are linked, and so long as the latter persists, so will the former. If, on the other hand, all the measures proposed earlier in this chapter were implemented, most child labor could be wiped out without hardship to the children or their families.

However, there might still be cases where survival would be threatened if the child stopped working. At very low income levels, the loss of a parent's income due to death or disability could mean that the family might not be able to survive without a child's wages. Where there were preschool children in the family and both parents were at work, child care could be a problem. And in cases where the child had no parents at hand due to death, abandonment, or because he or she had run away from domestic abuse, the child would need a livelihood. Only comprehensive social-security and welfare provisions can solve these problems (see chapter 8).

Article 45 of the Directive Principles of the Constitution of India promised that free and compulsory education would be provided to all children up to the age of fourteen. This was supposed to have been delivered within ten years, but sixty years later it had still not materialized. The eighty-sixth amendment to the Indian constitution (2003) made education between the ages of six and fourteen a fundamental right but was criticized for failing to specify that the quality of education and educational facilities available to all children should be the same, with a discontinuation of nonformal education, drastic upgrading of government schooling, and improvement of government-aided schools (Yasmeen 2004). Activists argued that honoring this promise would entail (a) amendment of the Child Labour Act (1986) to prohibit *all* child labor; (b) legislation providing for free, compulsory, quality formal education for all children aged six to fourteen years (Sinha 2005c); and (c) a major increase in state funds for education. The global need for such measures was affirmed at a two-day workshop in Hyderabad on "Trade Unions and Child Labour" organized by FNV Mondiaal and other trade unions within the framework of an international conference entitled "Out of Work and Into School—Children's Right to Education as a Non-Negotiable," organized by the Stop Child Labour campaign in November 2004 (Kurian 2005).

After years of campaigning, the Right of Children to Free and Compulsory Education Bill was finally passed in August 2009, making education a right for all children between the ages of six and fourteen. It included provisions for 25 percent of places in private schools to be extended to disadvantaged children on a non-fee-paying basis, and it prohibited the vetting of students and parents and arbitrary capitation fees. While some education activists criticized it for failing to tackle the provision of education to children under the age of six and above the age of fourteen and for perpetuating a two-tier model of education, others welcomed it as a major step forward (Education International 2009). As with all legislation, vigorous campaigning for its implementation as well as for the abolition of child labor would still be required to make even its limited provisions a reality.

The persistence of child labor undermines democracy, which requires the participation of all in decision making. It is much harder for those who are illiterate or uneducated to make informed decisions on many issues, and this makes them second-class citizens who are either left out of decision-making processes or made vulnerable to manipulation by those who can feed them disinformation. This is what accounts for the overwhelming demand from the poor that their children should receive an education. A state that does not satisfy this demand cannot claim to be a democracy (Sinha 2005c).

Eliminating Informal Labor

Policy Changes

The policy of encouraging the small-scale sector by various incentives has been responsible for serious and widespread violations of fundamental human rights. Instead, it would make sense to guarantee a level playing field to the large- and small-scale sectors, ensuring that the latter is not discriminated against in obtaining credit and other facilities but also doing away with the reservations, tax concessions, and other incentives it is offered, including exemption from labor laws. This will enable the small-scale sector to do well where it is genuinely as efficient as, or more efficient than, the large-scale sector but will not discourage units from growing by threatening them with the loss of privileges.

The main result of such a policy change would be that large companies, which earlier subdivided their operations in order to evade labor laws and excise duty, would consolidate them instead, as occurred in the garment industry. It might also result in some small-scale employers going bankrupt, but many of their workers, as in the garment industry, would end up employed by larger companies, and the employers themselves would become eligible for social-security provisions until they were able to earn again. Very small subcontractors would probably be able to earn more as workers in large units than they could as contractors. An important outcome would be a major expansion of revenue for the state, which could be used to improve and subsidize the electricity supply and upgrade other parts of the country's infrastructure.

The task of registering employers and employees would become simpler once the plethora of small and tiny units is reduced. Employment regulation and unionization would become easier, the market would expand, and total productivity would improve. The increase in revenue could help to fund a modest but comprehensive social-security and welfare program that would end India's shameful human-development statistics—infant and under-five mortality, maternal mortality, malnutrition, child labor, and illiteracy—all of which are among the worst in the world. It could also be used to provide support for producer cooperatives. The net result of eliminating informal labor by ensuring the registration of all employers and employees, regulating employment, and bringing all employment under the purview of labor laws would be a great leap forward on the road to India becoming a world-class country.

Another policy change that is required would be to outlaw incentives to induce companies to move their operations to industrially backward areas. However desirable it might be to industrialize such areas, subsidizing companies to move out to them is not the best way to achieve this, especially when it involves destroying employment in their oldest units in places such as Bombay, as well as in newer units in other backward areas once their tax holiday ends. It would make far more sense to use the taxes paid by these companies to build up the infrastructure in the more backward areas, thus making it more worthwhile for them to set up new facilities there when they expand production, rather than engaging in the utterly wasteful procedure of relocating the same production from place to place.

Union Organizing

Despite the enormous obstacles facing them, large numbers of informal workers were organizing by the start of the twenty-first century. The verification report released by the Central Labour Commissioner in December 2006 showed a massive increase in membership in the central trade unions, and most of the new members were informal workers (*The Hindu* 2006). Others had joined independent unions, such as the Nirman Mazdoor Panchayat Sangam, which organizes construction workers in Tamil Nadu. There were cases of hand-loom and other informal workers forming unions and engaging in collective bargaining (De Neve 2005, 144–151; Rajesh and Singh 2003). In January 2006, after a worker was killed in a work-related accident and his family was offered a mere Rs 26,000 as compensation, Reliance Energy contract workers contacted the TUSC, which helped them to get the amount raised to Rs 650,000 and to take up demands for bonuses and ESI medical benefits. They subsequently formed the Mumbai Electric Employees' Union, and with TUSC support they commenced a struggle for social-security benefits, which was still going on in 2009. Power-loom and garment workers, and contract workers in steel, oil, gas, coal, refineries, chemicals, fertilizers, and power generation were all being organized by NTUI unions (NTUI 2007a).

There was much more separate union organizing among women workers in the informal than in the formal sector. One of the earliest and best-known examples was SEWA, founded in 1972, but others were formed subsequently. Homeworkers making beedis in Hyderabad went from house to house contacting workers in order to form the Navayuga Karmika Beedi Sangam; the union was registered in 1987, and by 1994 it had a membership of around five thousand (Hensman 2000, 2002). Penn Thozhilalargal Sangam (the Women Workers' Union) was started in Tamil Nadu in 1999 and registered in 2001, organizing women in construction and quarrying, domestic service, and the garment industry. The Domestic Workers' Union, which was started in 2005, had around twenty-six thousand members in Bombay and fifty thousand in Maharashtra by early 2008, a truly impressive rate of organization. This resulted in the Maharashtra Domestic Workers Welfare Board Act (2008), which provided for the registration of workers, the regulation of employment, and welfare and social-security benefits (*The India Post* 2009). Even where women did not organize separately, they were often vocal and active in unions of informal workers.

Global Coordination

It is an irony of history that a system of employment based on traditional caste and gender relations in India was so compatible with the neoliberal agenda that similar forms of labor spread like a pandemic in the late twentieth and early twenty-first centuries, infecting even countries that had never had the problem before (Mather 2005). There were two ways in which informal labor exerted a downward pressure on global labor standards: by allowing employers to shift jobs from formal to informal workers and by creating an incentive for other employers to use similar methods. As with other pandemics, it is vitally important to tackle informal labor at a global level. The only way to ensure safety would be to eliminate it altogether, as was done with smallpox. It should be emphasized that this does *not* mean eliminating the *small-scale sector*. Small-scale enterprises of self-employed workers could continue as before (unless they wished to form cooperatives), and small-scale employers could continue to operate, provided they registered themselves and their employees and complied with labor laws.

Clarity about the nature of informal labor is essential. The well-meaning but dangerous tendency to romanticize informality—appealing for "appropriate regulations, laws and policies . . . that promote it" (WIEGO n.d: 3) or for bringing the "informal economy centre-stage" (Jhabvala et al. 2003)—goes together with a tendency to conflate self-employed and dependent workers and gloss over the superexploitation and denial of human rights suffered by the latter. Once the distinction is made—as the ILO Convention on Home Work does, for example—it becomes much clearer why the only way to cure the ills of informal labor is to eliminate it altogether by formalizing and bringing it under the purview of existing labor laws. This was the conclusion arrived at by the ILO at its General Conference of 2002. Its "Resolution Concerning Decent Work and the Informal Economy" deplores that "unregistered and unregulated enterprises often do not pay taxes, and benefits and entitlements to workers, thus posing unfair competition to other enterprises." It correctly identifies the problem of informality as "principally a governance issue," emphasizing that "the legal and institutional frameworks of a country are key" and that therefore "the government has a primary role to play." The resolution insists that "the elimination of child labour and bonded labour should be a priority goal," pointing out that "child labour is a key component of the informal economy. It undermines strategies of employment creation and poverty reduction, as well as education and training programmes and the development prospects of countries."

Given all these evils of informal labor, the ILO draws the logical conclusion that "programmes addressing the informal economy . . . should be designed and implemented with the main objective of bringing workers or economic units in the informal economy into the mainstream, so that they are covered by the legal and institutional framework" and adds that "in many developing countries, rural development and agricultural policies, including supportive legal frameworks for co-operatives, need to be enhanced and strengthened. Special attention should be given to the care responsibilities of women to enable them to make the transition from informal to formal employment more easily."

However, the most critical goal is to "identify the obstacles to application of the most relevant labour standards for workers in the informal economy" and "identify the legal and practical obstacles to formation of organisations of workers . . . in the informal economy." What are these obstacles? The answer is provided by the informal garment workers and others who point out that the right to organize and bargain collectively means nothing if workers can be dismissed for doing so, which is easy for employers to do, as the workers have no proof of having been employed in the first place. Nor can they enjoy basic rights so long as their identity as workers is not legally recognized. Registration of all workers and employers and some form of legal employment contract are thus absolutely necessary if they are to have the right to organize, among other basic rights; extending labor legislation to cover all employees would also be necessary. Conversely, it is the lack of registration and formal contracts and the exclusion of informal employees from coverage by labor legislation that constitute the most formidable obstacles to their getting organized and obtaining other basic rights.

The ILO could, and should, do something to remedy this problem. At a seminar on informal workers organized by IRENE, the Clean Clothes Campaign, and the Evangelische Akademie in Meissen in September 2004, one of the proposals was that the right to proof of identity as workers and proof of employment should be incorporated in one of the ILO Core Conventions. The most appropriate would be no. 98, on the Right to Organize and Collective Bargaining (1949), which deals (among other things) with protecting workers from victimization for belonging to a union or taking part in its activities. Alternatively, a new convention could be passed and incorporated in the Core Conventions. In the early twenty-first century, if the trend of informal labor spreading worldwide is to be reversed, it would be necessary to incorporate such a provision in a core convention applicable to all ILO members. If it is accepted that "campaigning for the human rights of informal sector workers, and helping them organise into unions, is a crucial contribution to the social movement of tomorrow" (Gallin 2001, 243), then the first step in that direction is to insist that they must have the right to proof of their identity as workers and to proof of employment. If the ILO also offers assistance to those governments that claim they are unable to carry out the task of registering employers and employees, this would provide crucial support to the human rights of informal workers. In the wake of the crisis, such measures would contribute not just to the welfare of billions of workers but also to the health of the world economy.

[7]

Working Women and Reproductive Labor

Globalization has resulted in record numbers of women entering the wage-labor force globally. According to the ILO, "the share of women in wage and salaried work grew during the past ten years from 42.9 per cent in 1996 to 47.9 per cent in 2006" (ILO 2007). The same report noted that women continue to be an underprivileged section of the labor force. This chapter examines two major reasons why this is the case: namely, the gender division of labor and sexual harassment and violence against women. As a result of these practices, the constitution of women workers as a cheap and flexible labor force is almost universal, and this creates serious problems for the labor movement. The very fact that this division between male and female workers exists makes it harder to build working-class solidarity and arrive at a common strategy to improve employment conditions and confront the challenges of globalization. Putting this issue on the agenda and working out ways to tackle it is an important part of a global strategy for labor.

Definitions

As we saw in chapter 3, what is productive labor from the standpoint of individual capital can be unreproductive labor from the standpoint of total social capital. (We are here referring to social, not biological, reproduction, although biological reproduction, without which there would be no new labor power to replace workers who die, is a necessary element of social reproduction). Conversely, labor that is not productive from the standpoint of individual capital—that is, it does not produce a profit—can nonetheless be socially useful from the standpoint of society and also facilitate the accumulation of capital, for example by contributing to the production of essential infrastructure and labor power. Finally, there is a distinction between waged labor and unwaged labor: a domestic worker cooking for an employer's household is waged; a housewife doing the same work in her own home is unwaged.

The labor of waged workers producing means of production or subsistence is both productive in the sense that it produces a profit for individual capitalists and reproductive in the sense that its products reenter production. That of waged workers in state schools or hospitals and unwaged working-class housewives is not productive, as it does not produce profits for any capitalist, but it is reproductive, or socially useful, since its products—educated, healthy, adult workers—reenter production. The work of waged workers in armaments factories is productive, creating huge profits for the companies employing them, but not reproductive, as their products do not reenter production. And that of soldiers in the army is waged but neither productive nor reproductive. The important point to note, especially in the context of a fragile recovery from the crisis, is that shifting labor from unreproductive sectors, even if they are profitable (such as armaments production), to reproductive or socially useful sectors, even if they produce no profit for individual capitals, stimulates overall capitalist accumulation.

Capital and Gender

Most feminists trying to explain the subordination of women under capitalism have concluded that capitalism does not create this subordination, although it certainly uses it to its own advantage (Mackintosh 1981; Himmelweit 1984). Although individual capitalists may have prejudices against women doing particular kinds of work, for capital as such it does not matter whether workers are male or female, so long as they produce surplus value at the maximum possible rate. As Engels observed, in 1839 more women than men were employed as factory operatives in England, with devastating consequences for the family:

> The employment of women at once breaks up the family; for when the wife spends twelve or thirteen hours every day in the mill, and the husband works the same length of time there or elsewhere, what becomes of the children? . . . That the general mortality among young children must be increased by the employment of the mothers is self-evident, and is placed beyond doubt by notorious facts. . . . The use of narcotics to keep children still is fostered by this infamous system. [However,] in many cases the family is not wholly dissolved by the employment of the wife, but turned upside down. The wife supports the family, the husband sits at home, tends the children, sweeps the room and cooks.[1]
>
> (Engels 1975, 436–438)

In other words, capital prefers to employ women if they are cheaper and more flexible than men, but if and when they become more expensive (by winning maternity benefits, for example) and less flexible (winning the right to refuse shiftwork or overtime because of domestic responsibilities), men will be employed for the same occupations, or formal women workers will be replaced by informal ones, because men have no legal claim to concessions for domestic labor, and informal women workers can be dismissed if they demand any. It is not capital that has an interest in sustaining the existing gender division of labor in the workplace: it is comfortable with the situation described by Engels. The two main reasons why there is discrimination against women in waged work (and they are linked to each other) seem to be the domestic division of labor, which is in one form or another almost universal, and the strategies by male workers to exclude women from occupations that are regarded as being more skilled or prestigious (cf. Cockburn 1985). Both these tendencies can be found in India.

Sexual harassment at work is simply one expression of the more general violence against women in society, but its occurrence in the workplace may be aimed at discouraging women from entering employment. This is very evident, for example, in the film *North Country*, a fictionalized account of a real case, *Jenson v. Eveleth Taconite Co.*, where a woman worker brought a class-action lawsuit against a mining company in the United States for failing to protect her and her co-workers from sexual harassment. Even where the aim is not to exclude women from the workforce, sexual harassment makes employment unpleasant or even unbearable for many women. It can thus be seen, at least in part, as a form of discrimination that is almost always directed specifically against women. It has also been described as "the most common and least discussed occupational health hazard for women" and can cause "depression, fatigue, headaches, sleeplessness, hostility, inability to concentrate and deterioration of personal relationships" (LRD 1996, 13). Paradoxically, legislation aimed at protecting women from sexual harassment, such as a ban on night work for women, can become an additional reason for discrimination against women.

The Gender Division of Labor in the Working Class in India

In the words of Dr. S. Radhakrishnan in his inaugural address to the National Committee on Women's Education set up in May 1958: "While the greatest profession of a woman is, and probably will continue to be, that of home-maker, yet her world should not be limited to that relationship" (GOI 1964). If the government of independent India recognized the right of women to enter employment outside the home, the implicit condition for this entry was that they continue to be responsible for running the home and taking care of children. The concern it expressed for the welfare of women workers was genuine enough, but the remedies proposed were aimed at helping them to take up the double burden more effectively rather than relieving them of part of it. The understanding was that men would be the primary breadwinners and women would take sole responsibility for unwaged work in the home. They might also earn, if necessary, but only in a supplementary capacity.

This followed smoothly from a precapitalist division of labor in which women were assigned the role of subordinate workers; for example, they were not allowed to belong to the ancient craft guilds even though they assisted their husbands in their home workshops (Sengupta 1960, 237; cf. Pinchbeck 1930, 2, 125). Thus women entered the capitalist labor force already in a weaker position, and employers took advantage of this fact to pay them less than men for the same work, as the Royal Commission on Labour in India found in 1931 (Subramanian 1977, 93). India's British rulers supported the employers. When the Bombay Strike Committee in the textile strike of 1928–1929 demanded that the wages of all workers should be raised to Rs 30 per month, the Strike Enquiry Committee set up by the government replied that the payment of an equal minimum wage had not been adopted anywhere and that a higher wage was fixed for men because "a large proportion of adult male workers are responsible for the maintenance of a wife and children, whereas the proportion of women who have dependants is comparatively small" (cit. Savara 1986, 85).

Acceptance of the fact that large numbers of women had to work for wages if they and their families were to survive meant that there was no systematic attempt by male workers to exclude women from the wage-labor force or from unions. Union policy was that wherever women were in employment, they should be paid the same as men for doing the same work. Chapter 4, clause 4 of the Equal Remuneration Act (1976) required that "no employer shall pay to any worker, employed by him in an establishment or employment, remuneration . . . at rates less favourable than those at which remuneration is paid by him to workers of the opposite sex in such establishment or employment for performing the same work or work of a similar nature." Although this left out the issue of "work of equal value," and although even the provision regarding "work of a similar nature" was hardly used by unions, women were almost always paid equal wages for the same work wherever unions were active. This contrasted with informal, nonunionized employment, where women earned only 50 to 65 percent of the wages earned by men in the same occupations (Joshi and Joshi 1976, 105).

The Factories Act banned night work for women, which was seen as necessary for protecting them from sexual harassment. The assumption that women had the sole responsibility for running the home was evident in much of the protective legislation. In 1929, the Bombay government, followed by other states, passed an act providing for eight weeks of paid maternity leave. The Employees' State Insurance Act (1948), which applied to the whole of India, extended the period of paid leave to twelve weeks but restricted it to low-paid workers. ESIS benefits were financed by contributions from workers, employers, and the government, whereas the All-India Maternity Benefit Act (1961) required the employer to bear the full cost of twelve weeks' maternity leave on full pay. The Factories Acts of 1934 and 1948 stated that a suitably equipped crèche must be provided for the preschool children of women workers wherever fifty or more of them were employed in one workplace; this was reduced to thirty or more women in 1976. Wherever protective legislation was implemented, it made women more expensive (because of crèche and maternity-benefit expenses) and less flexible (because of the prohibition on night work) than men, and this resulted in the replacement of women by men in the textile industry (GOI 1964, 9; Morris 1965, 66, appendix 2).

Unwaged Work and Formal Employment in the Pharmaceutical Industry

The principle behind the traditional segregation of jobs by gender in India appears to be that women are allotted jobs that are considered less prestigious.[2] In Hindu culture, no prestige is attached to heavy manual labor, and women are employed in such strenuous operations as road building and construction. Conversely, jobs that in the West would be seen as "women's work"—secretarial work, cooking, sewing, cleaning, and "housekeeping" in factories—are routinely filled by men. There is also considerable variation across the different regions of the country, bearing out the proposition that "the assignment of any particular task to one sex or the other varies enormously" (Rubin 1977, 178). In the manufacturing industry, occupations involving a higher degree of education and skill are considered more prestigious, and women are barely represented in them. Since more prestige is attached to working with a machine than to doing the same operation manually, an operation often passes to a man when it is mechanized.

The classification of most women workers in the pharmaceutical industry as "semiskilled," despite the high degree of speed, precision, and dexterity required for their machine-paced jobs (which many male workers admitted they could not match), was almost certainly due to the stronger bargaining power of male workers and their monopoly of "skilled" jobs. The arbitrariness of what are regarded as "masculine" and "feminine" attributes of workers and jobs, as well as what is regarded as "skilled," "semiskilled," or "unskilled" (with the same job sometimes being regarded as one or the other depending on whether it is done by a man or a woman), has been pointed out in many studies (cf. Cockburn 1983; Chhachhi and Pittin 1996; Pollert 1996). Perhaps the most striking example comes from the United States, where engineering jobs traditionally classified as "male" were reclassified as "women's work" during World War II, but only on the understanding that this was a temporary measure (Milkman 1987, 61–63).

The consequences of gender segregation in both waged and unwaged work became very clear in the pharmaceutical industry. The companies that set up operations in and around Bombay from the 1940s onward—

predominantly multinationals—recruited young, single women in large numbers to work on the packing lines. The employees' unions formed in this sector supported women's employment rights as they were then understood: the right to security of employment, equal pay, maternity benefits, and child care. Women were active in the unions; indeed, a few years after the Pfizer Employees' Union was formed in 1950, it had a woman president, Kamala Karkal. And when a federation of pharmaceutical employees' unions was formed in 1960, one of the first major actions it launched was against the marriage bar.

By 1963, as the case of May & Baker showed, fifteen pharmaceutical companies had a clause in their employment contract stating that female employees would resign upon marriage; only four did not (MGG 1963, 2361). The argument of companies such as Sandoz was twofold: first, that the women had agreed to this condition of employment when they signed the contract, and second, "that having regard to the requirements of production of pharmaceutical products the material has to be prepared in conditions of extreme care . . . for which a regular labour force is essential," whereas "married female employees who may have to attend to their household duties and look to the needs and comforts of their husbands and children may not be as punctual and regular as unmarried female employees" (MGG 1961, 2758–2759). The union's plea that "the requirement to resign on marriage is arbitrary, capricious and an unfair labour practice . . . bad in law and in violation of fundamental rights and . . . ILO conventions" was rejected by the adjudicator, who ruled that "the contention of the company that it is in the interests of the efficient operation of the company not to employ married women is *bona fide*" (MGG 1961, 2758, 2759–2761).

In general, the assumption underlying the union claims that the dismissal of women upon marriage constituted discrimination against them was that married women could carry out their domestic responsibilities as well as their paid work without neglecting the latter. On the rare occasions when unions put forward demands for equality on the grounds that men too had domestic responsibilities—for example, when the Bombay Labour Union and Petroleum Workers' Union demanded paid paternity leave from Burmah Shell Refineries Ltd., on the grounds that "at the time of delivery the husband finds it difficult to manage the house and other children, if any in the house, in addition to his job"—they were given short shrift (MGG 1965, 4181–4197).

The demand for paternity leave was not pursued by the unions, but the campaign for abolition of the termination-upon-marriage clause was. When Ms. Desai, an employee of May & Baker, was dismissed upon getting married, unions belonging to the Maharashtra State Pharmaceutical Employees' Federation pooled their resources to appeal against unfavorable judgments in lower courts and pursued the case all the way up to the Supreme Court. While the case dragged on, women workers held factory-gate meetings, organized processions to the Maharashtra Legislative Assembly, and demonstrated outside the homes of directors, shouting slogans like "*Hai, hai! Kya hua? Shaadi karna manaa kiya!*" (Alas, alas! What has happened? They have forbidden us to get married!), embarrassing foreign directors by alleging in front of their neighbors that they were encouraging the "immoral traffic of female employees." On February 20, 1965, the demonstrators went on a one-day fast at Martyr's Memorial, organized a huge procession, ceremonially burned a copy of the marriage clause, and threw the ashes in the Arabian Sea. Final victory was won later that year, when the Supreme Court ruled in favor of the unions: women workers could no longer be dismissed upon marriage, and the employers' practice of doing so, which had been upheld time after time by the courts, was now seen as discriminatory and unconstitutional (Hensman 1988). This form of discrimination was not peculiar to India; no-marriage clauses in employment contracts were at one time common in Europe and the United States: indeed, only in 1968 were such clauses outlawed in France (Glendon 1989, 78).

Battles for equal pay had begun even before the antimarriage-clause agitation and had by and large been won by the time it was over. Subsequently, struggles for maternity benefits and workplace crèches were also generally successful. There can be no doubt that unions launched battles for women's rights and fought them well. Yet the union strategies also had fatal flaws. Without any policy on equal opportunities in recruitment and promotions (although the Equal Remuneration Act covers these issues), women remained in the labor-intensive jobs that were subsequently hardest hit by automation. They were seldom retrenched, but as they retired they were either not replaced or replaced by men. The proportion of women in the workforce fell sharply; at Pfizer, where more than half the workforce originally consisted of women, the recruitment of women stopped in 1969, and at Roche Pharmaceuticals, the proportion of women fell from 56.7 in 1962 to 9 percent by 1983. Managers said that with equal pay as well as protective legislation, women had become more expensive and less flexible than men (URG 1983b, 1984a; Hensman 1988). The same thing was happening in China by the 1990s (White 1995, 7).

The unions did not fight against these policies, partly because the strength of women in the unions had declined. As women got married and had children, their domestic commitments increased, leaving them less time for attending meetings or other union activities (cf. Pollert 1981, 109–126). Many also faced opposition from husbands to being out after working hours doing union work and from male colleagues at work to taking a leadership role in the union. Studies in Tamil Nadu showed that even where unions had achieved the difficult task of overcoming caste prejudice to incorporate Dalits in the leadership, women might be totally absent (Ramaswamy 1983, 106; De Neve 2005, 311). In Tirupur, the reasons cited by women workers for not playing an active part in the union included "lack of time because of other household work; opposition from the employers; resistance from family members; perception that trade union activities are men's affair" (Neetha 2001, 48).

Women pharmaceutical workers who became and remained union leaders shared certain characteristics: relative freedom from child care and housework, supportive families, and male support in the union. The findings of a study in Delhi were remarkably similar (Chhachhi 2005, 192–193, 197, 215). It was rare to find that combination of conditions, and the number of women leaders was therefore small. They were worried about the shrinking number of women workers but lacked support to do anything about it even from other women workers, who, since their own jobs were not at risk, had less motivation to launch a struggle over the declining proportion of women in the workforce. Employers were quick to abandon a strategy—the marriage bar—that had been defeated and to adopt a new one—nonrecruitment of women—that took advantage of weaknesses in the unions they confronted.

The attempt by employers to keep married women or women with young children out of employment in various ways is a theme that recurs again and again in accounts of women's employment all over the world (WWW 1991; Rosa 1994, 95–96; Hensman 1998a). The exclusion of married women might be seen as gender discrimination, since married men are not treated in the same way. But it is not *just* gender discrimination. Women without family responsibilities were originally preferred for some jobs and only replaced by men when they won legal rights that made them more expensive and less flexible than men. It appears that domestic labor poses a problem for formal employment.

In India, the percentage of women in formal factory employment never went above 12 percent, by 1961 had fallen to 10.65 percent, and by 1996 was only 10 percent. Employment of women in the public sector was somewhat higher, but only in plantations, where labor conditions were the worst, did they constitute half the labor force (GOI 1964, 6; Bajpai 1996, 71). Economic liberalization further reduced formal employment for women in traditional sectors, due to the accelerated informalization of employment, privatization of several public-sector enterprises, and decline of the plantation sector. Only in the ICT-dominated service industry was there a large-scale expansion in women's formal employment, especially in call centers, where women constituted around 45 percent of the rapidly expanding labor force. With the government deciding in 2005 to amend the Factories Act to allow night work for women, provided their "dignity, honour, and safety" were protected in the workplace and in transport provided to and from the workplace, it became possible to employ women call-center workers on night shifts. But, as in the early days of the pharmaceutical industry, studies found that all were young, the overwhelming majority were unmarried, and those who were married had no children (Remesh 2004, 24–26; Mazumdar 2007, 288–289). The timing of the shifts also acted as an implicit marriage bar and put women at extra risk of sexual abuse.

Informal Employment: Contrasting Strategies to Deal with Unwaged Work

Informalizing employment in order to avoid accommodating women with family responsibilities has a long history:[3] "A historical examination of women's casualised work questions the assumption . . . that 'flexibility' is a modern invention; the supposedly 'new' forms of production actually have very old precedents" (Rowbotham 1994, 159). In India,

> the annual note on the working of the UP maternity Act during 1938 admits that many women workers were dismissed immediately after the Act was passed. . . . Similar is the conclusion of a . . . study by the International Labour Office: "Women fail to file claims . . . because they fear such an application may be followed by dismissal. In some cases, women workers are unable to prove completion of the requisite period of service because their employers have not kept the requisite records."
>
> (Punekar 1950, 33)

Decades later, employers were using the same methods against women workers in garment factories and sweatshops. They were paid less than men for the same work, dismissed when they got pregnant, and rarely got their jobs back afterward. In the textile industry, women in the informal power-loom sector worked more than eight hours per day, six days a week, working night shifts on alternate weeks (Baud 1983). If this grueling schedule was not compatible with their domestic responsibilities, they had to leave. Not surprisingly, most of the women employed in this sector were young, had no children, and had other women in the family doing the housework. The fact that their employment was informal allowed their employers to ignore their domestic responsibilities.

Homework provided a contrasting model. Here the site of waged and unwaged work was the same, allowing the women to intersperse finishing operations such as thread trimming and button stitching with childcare and other household tasks. Given their living conditions, it was essential that at least one person had to be at home in the daytime. They lived in *chawls* and *bastis* without internal toilets or water supply; in Lower Parel, the water in the shared taps was available only from 3:00 to 5:30 p.m., which meant that women not only had to do as much of their washing as possible in this period but also had to collect and store enough water to last until the following afternoon. Homeworkers and housewives did not suffer the same sense of isolation as they did in Western countries—for example, they could sit on their doorsteps and chat as they did their homework and meet at the water taps when they were on—but their domestic workload was huge.[4]

Homework may sound like an ideal arrangement for women with domestic responsibilities, but it is not. The low piece rates resulted in girls being drawn into helping with the waged work; thus waged work interfered with homemaking, which ideally should provide children with an environment conducive to pursuing their education. Conversely, constant interruptions for household tasks meant that women could do less waged work, and therefore earned less, since the work was piece rated. "It's difficult to make money working at home when you've kiddies. I much preferred the evening shift, when my husband would have the kiddies and I could go to work and get on with the job without being interrupted" (Allen and Wolkowitz 1986, 25). These difficulties were also evident among beedi workers, where taking care of children in a hazardous working environment was an even greater problem (Hensman 2000, 251).

The irregularity of work meant that sometimes the women had no work to do, while at other times, "we have to work flat out to meet the deadline—if we don't, we won't be given work the next time." Thus the idea that homework gave the women more flexibility was largely an illusion, because they could not afford to turn down the offer of work, even if it entailed working "overtime," for fear of not getting work in the future. Nor could it be assumed that their earnings were unimportant for family survival: some had started work when their husbands lost their jobs in the textile mills in the early 1980s and were the main breadwinners. Of course, when there was no work they did get more leisure time, but it came at a price: a loss of earnings. Thus informality offered women two options: either casual outwork or full-time work without any concessions to domestic labor.

Globalization expanded women's informal employment in India: "New opportunities for women have emerged in foreign exchange earning export industries like garment, leather, food processing and electronic goods, but they are subject to occupational health hazards and oppressive work conditions. Export oriented industries . . . are seekers of cheap labour and women do constitute cheap labour" (Bajpai 1996, 72). It was partly women's domestic role that constituted them as cheap labor.

Tackling Sexual Harassment at the Workplace

In 2002, the European Parliament agreed on a legal definition of sexual harassment as "any form of unwanted verbal, non-verbal or physical conduct" with the purpose of violating a person's dignity, in particular when creating a "hostile, degrading, humiliating or offensive environment" (LRD 2003, 83). The situation in India varies widely. In workplaces where there is a well-established union with a strong presence of women and a culture of respect for women, sexual harassment is virtually outlawed. Conversely, it is rampant in the informal sector. Nor are educated and qualified women exempt.

A university professor accused of sexually harassing female college students, escapes institutional censure. A high-ranking police officer publicly slaps a senior IAS officer on her backside and continues to enforce the law unscathed by her complaint. A village level development worker advocating the cause against child marriage is sexually harassed. When authorities fail to heed her complaints she is gang-raped. Female resident doctors are told by an inquiry committee that the sexual affronts made to them by Head of Department were really methods of "discipline"; in short, as the case of *Theresa Lehmann v. Toys 'R' Us* in the Supreme Court of New Jersey, 1993, put it, sexual harassment was routinely used to discredit a woman "by treating her as a sexual object rather than as a credible co-worker".

(Kapur 1996, 95–96)

It was women's rights groups rather than trade unions that catalyzed a breakthrough by helping Bhanwari Devi (the social worker who had been gang-raped in Rajasthan) and her colleagues to pursue the case legally, as a result of which the High Court in 1993 ruled that it was a case of "gang-rape which was committed out of vengeance." Women's groups also filed a petition in the Supreme Court, under the name "Visakha," asking the court to issue directions concerning sexual harassment at the workplace, as a result of which the Supreme Court in 1997 issued guidelines based upon provisions in CEDAW, which the Indian government had signed and ratified. The National Commission for Women, in consultation with women's and civil-rights groups, took up the task of formulating a law on sexual harassment (Desai 2005).

A Sexual Harassment Bill was prepared by 2005 but was then subjected to numerous revisions, and all of its progressive features were diluted or removed in the 2007 version. The clarification in the definition of "sexual harassment" that it was the reasonable perception of the woman that certain conduct was sexually colored and unwelcome was deleted. The section indicating that employers have to take responsibility for ensuring compliance with the law and can be punished for failing to do so was also deleted. However, in the case of the Hewlett-Packard call-center employee Pratibha Srikant Murthy, who was raped and murdered in 2005 by a cab driver contracted by the company, the Supreme Court in 2008 ruled that the director at that time, Som Mittal, was liable and could be prosecuted, since he was responsible for her safety and protection (*ET* 2008). In the section on Rules of Evidence, sensitivity to the complainant, nonpermissibility of evidence based on the aggrieved woman's character and personal/sexual history, and the need to take note of socioeconomic conditions and hierarchy were all deleted. Features such as issuing interim orders to protect the woman and her supporters during the enquiry and afterward, even if the complaint was dismissed, and allowing the woman to take action under other laws, such as those on rape and sexual assault, were also missing. Worst of all, a section was added stating that if the allegation was found to be false, the woman could be punished! Furthermore, there was provision for the woman to withdraw the complaint, thereby providing a space for harassment and pressure on the woman to do so. Justice Verma, the author of the Visakha Guidelines, said that if passed in this form, the bill would "kill the spirit of Visakha" (NTUI 2007b; Bhaduri 2007).

An agreed-on text had not been put before parliament even by late 2009. The struggle to push through and implement legislation that could protect women from sexual harassment in the workplace continued, giving trade unions too an opportunity to intervene. The NTUI felt that "this also provides an excellent opportunity for trade unions to address issues of patriarchy and sexism within their own formations" and to uphold "women's rights and working class unity" (NTUI 2007b).

The Production of Labor Power

Tackling the gender division of labor in the home requires an examination of the production of labor power. Given the centrality of labor power to capitalism—since as the only commodity that can produce surplus value, and therefore profit, it is the sine qua non of accumulation—it is somewhat surprising that Marx nowhere describes its production. He comes closest to it in the chapter on "The Sale and Purchase of Labour-Power":

> Given the existence of the individual, the production of labour-power consists in his reproduction of himself or his maintenance. For his maintenance he requires a certain quantity of the means of subsistence. Therefore the labour-time necessary for the production of labour-power is the same as that necessary for the production of those means of subsistence. . . . If the owner of labour-power works today, tomorrow he must again be able to repeat the same process in the same conditions as regards health and strength. His means of subsistence must therefore be sufficient to maintain him in his normal state as a working individual. . . . The owner of labour-power is mortal. If then his appearance in the market is to be continuous, and the continuous transformation of money into capital assumes this, the seller of labour-power must perpet-

uate himself "in the way that every living individual perpetuates himself, by procreation." . . . Hence the sum of means of subsistence necessary for the production of labour-power must include the means necessary for the worker's replacements, i.e. his children. . . . The costs of education vary according to the degree of complexity of the labour-power required. These expenses . . . form a part of the total value spent in producing it. The value of labour-power can be resolved into the value of a definite quantity of the means of subsistence.

(Marx 1976, 274–276)

Marx gives examples of means of subsistence like food and fuel, which need to be replaced daily, while others, like clothes and furniture, can be purchased at longer intervals. But that is all. Unlike his detailed descriptions of the production of other commodities, here there is no description of a labor process, nor even a mention of instruments of production (such as a stove, pots and pans, broom, bucket, and mop). Just raw materials—means of subsistence—and the finished product: labor power. The implicit assumption is that only a process of individual consumption is required to convert those means of subsistence into labor power. Yet the worker would not be maintained in his (or her) "normal state as a working individual"— nor be replaced when he (or she) could no longer work—unless somebody carried the raw materials and instruments of production home from the market or shops, cooked the food and washed up after the meal, dusted, swept, mopped floors and washed clothes, fed the baby, changed it, gave it a bath, and so on.

The home is therefore a site of both individual consumption and production.[5] *Both* are necessary for the production of labor power, and Marx's failure to identify and analyze the latter has been attributed to his "patriarchal position" (Weinbaum 1978, 43). In fact, Marx's confusion of production with individual consumption leads to bizarre contradictions. For example, he writes of domestic labor that "the largest part of society, that is to say the working class, must incidentally perform this kind of labour for itself; but it is only able to perform it when it has laboured 'productively'. It can only cook meat for itself when it has produced a wage with which to pay for the meat" (Marx 1963, 161). If we generalize this proposition, it would state that until a commodity has been sold, it cannot be produced. But it should be obvious that labor power especially cannot be sold for the first time until hundreds of hours of labor time have been spent on its production. As Marx recognizes elsewhere, "its exchange value, like that of every other commodity, is determined before it goes into circulation, since it is sold as a capacity, a power, and a specific amount of labor-time was required to produce this capacity, this power" (Marx 1976, 1066).

Engels not only acknowledged the existence of domestic work and the gender division of labor within it but even observed that the reversal of gender roles during the industrial revolution, and the distress caused by it, was possible only "because the sexes have been placed in a false position from the beginning" (Engels 1975, 439). He did not carry that analysis further, however, and this theoretical gap was what was sought to be remedied in the debate around domestic labor (i.e., housework and childcare) that raged in the 1970s (Malos 1982). Let us look at the contributions that throw light on the production of labor power.

Most participants agreed that domestic labor is socially useful and necessary; that is, it is useful not just to other members of the household but to society as a whole. It was agreed that domestic labor *transfers* the value of the commodities bought with the wage to the end product, labor power. But does it also *create* value?

Those who said "yes" (Dalla Costa and James 1972; Seccombe 1973 and 1975) were surely correct, while those who said "no" (Benston 1969; Coulson et al. 1975; Gardiner et al. 1975; Himmelweit and Mohun 1977) were wrong. Domestic labor is part of the production process of labor power, a commodity that is sold on the (labor) market. To say that it does not produce value would contradict the whole starting point of Marx's theory of surplus value, according to which

> the value of each commodity is determined by . . . the labour-time socially necessary to produce it. . . . Hence in determining the value of the yarn, or the labour-time required for its production, all the special processes carried on at various times and in different places which were necessary, first to produce the cotton and the wasted portion of the spindle, and then with the cotton and spindle to spin the yarn, may together be looked on as different and successive phases of the same labour process.
>
> (Marx 1976, 293–294)

The denial that domestic labor produces value seems to come from a confused amalgam of two ideas. The first is that labor producing use values that are not themselves sold as commodities but are directly incorporated into another product that is sold as a commodity does not produce value. If this were true, it would result in an absurd situation where the value of the labor power of a male worker who eats his meals at restaurants, gets his clothes and linen washed at a laundry, and pays for a cleaner to clean his flat is much higher than that of another worker, doing the same job at the same workplace and earning the same wage, whose wife does the shopping, cooking, washing up, washing, and cleaning. The second idea is that labor that is not waged does not produce value. This would result in the even greater absurdity that the products of millions of petty commodity producers around the world—farmers and artisans—have the same value as their inputs, since their labor, being unwaged, adds no value to them! It is surely more logical to argue that to the extent that domestic labor performs a function that is necessary for the production of labor power, it produces value, since "the value of labour-power is determined, as in the case of every other commodity, by the labour-time necessary for the production, and consequently also the reproduction, of this specific article" (Marx 1976, 274). This is reproductive labor, because it makes an essential contribution to social reproduction, and "once the interdependence of work and family responsibilities is acknowledged, it becomes harder to attribute value only to paid work" (Conaghan 2002, 55).

Does domestic labor produce surplus value? A housewife is not paid wages, but her subsistence is paid for out of her partner's wage, so his employer pays her indirectly. If the amount paid for her subsistence is the same as or more than what her partner would have to pay to buy the services she performs on the market, then she would not be contributing to surplus value. But if her subsistence costs are less than the value of the services she performs, either her partner is exploiting her by withholding part of the payment for her labor, or her partner's employer is keeping part of what he would otherwise have had to pay out as wages, and thus her labor is contributing indirectly to his surplus value.

Thus although Dalla Costa and James (1973) were wrong to think that domestic labor is always productive, it is true that this labor may allow extra surplus value to be appropriated by subsidizing the production of labor power. The Bolivian women's leader and miner's wife Domitila Barrios de Chungara made a precise calculation of this, comparing the work performed in the home with the cost of the same services bought on the market: "One day I got the idea of making a chart. We put as an example the price of washing clothes per dozen pieces and we figured out how many dozens of items we washed per month. Then the cook's wage, the baby-sitter's, the servant's . . . Adding it all up, the wage needed to pay us for what we do in the home . . . was much higher than what the men earned in the mine for a month" (Barrios de Chungara and Viezzer 1978, 35). Thus if a miner's wife died or stopped working and the man was compelled to buy on the market the services she had performed, his wage would not be sufficient, showing that it was less than the value of labor power. The women's surplus labor allowed the mine owner to appropriate more surplus value than he would otherwise have been able to. But it is impossible to see this effect so long as the production of labor power (and its value) is seen solely as the activity of waged workers. Only if it is seen as the collective product of the working-class household is it possible to calculate the real rate of surplus value.

What happens if there are two or more wage earners in the family? We can examine this by looking at three different situations found in India. Situation A is one in which a male worker in a formal-sector enterprise is able to support his wife and, say, two school-going children. They might rent a two-bedroom flat with running water, use a gas stove, and eat fairly well. The woman is there when the children come home from school and can spend time with them even while she does other chores. In effect, the man's wage is sufficient to pay for the upkeep of another person (his wife) to do all this work (cf. Seccombe 1973).

If it is a woman who is the formal-sector employee, the continuity between her waged and unwaged work is clearer: she must do both, perhaps with some help from others at home, in order to support and sustain the family. The increase in time spent on domestic labor in order to compensate for lower wages is also more obvious. A study in Delhi showed that in response to a cut in real wages between 1994/1995 and 1999/2000 resulting from inflation, the total time expended on waged work and domestic labor by women workers increased from thirteen or fourteen hours to sixteen or seventeen hours a day, as they spent more time shopping around for the cheapest goods, queuing up at the ration shop, and cleaning inferior rice (Chhachhi 2005, 247–249).

If the male breadwinner loses his job and has to take up informal employment in a small enterprise, earning half of what he was earning before (situation B), his family has two options. They could move to a *basti* where his wife has to spend many more hours collecting water from the shared tap, cooking on a kerosene stove, queuing up at the ration shop, cleaning, preparing food, washing up, and so on. Their standard of living would be lower, but by spending much more time on housework—perhaps sixteen as opposed to ten hours per day—she could feed everyone on the lower wage and keep the children in school. Alternatively, she might find a job that pays half or less of her husband's former wage. They can then stay in their flat, but everyone has to help with the housework, even though she continues to do the bulk of it, working perhaps eighteen or more hours a day. In both cases, the rate of surplus value has gone up. If the technology in the small enterprise where the man now works is the same as in the large one, half of his former wage is being taken as additional surplus value. If his wife does not get a job, this is partly compensated for by her increased domestic work; if she does, then her wage may compensate for the loss in his earnings, but now she works even longer hours as well as creating surplus value for her own employer. It now takes two wage earners to support the family.

Situation C is the most tragic: the man loses his job and cannot find another—at most he can find casual work for ten to fifteen days a month. His wife gets a job, but even their combined earnings cannot support the family, so the children are taken out of school and sent to work too. It now takes four wages to support the family. They are all producing surplus value, and their collective working hours have increased substantially. This situation occurred, for example, as a consequence of the closure of textile mills in Ahmedabad (Breman 2004, 203–209). Millions of agricultural and migrant-labor families have always been in situation C, as indeed were most working-class families in Marx's time: "everywhere, except in the metallurgical industries, young persons (under 18), women and children form by far the most preponderant element in the factory personnel" (Marx 1976, 577); even a steel and iron works "employs 500 boys under 18, and of these about a third, or 170, are under the age of 13" (Marx 1976, 371). If we include other permutations—for example, where there are small children in the family and a slightly older girl is kept at home to look after them while her parents go out to work—the bulk of the labor force in India belongs to situations B and C.

The Genesis of the Working-Class Family

Left to itself, capital's "werewolf-like hunger for surplus value" (Marx 1976, 353) pushes down wages and extends the working day to such an extent that all members of the family, excluding only the smallest children, work long hours in wage labor simply in order to survive. If at any time it needs to retrench workers, it dismisses men rather than women and children. The family as a space apart from capital is destroyed. It is workers, through their struggles for higher wages, the abolition of child labor, and the restriction of working hours, who win back time and space for the family. In this they are supported up to a point by the state, acting in the interests of the capitalist class as a whole. At an earlier stage, the state used legislation to force reluctant workers to labor long hours, but after capital extended these hours to such an extent that it "produces the premature exhaustion and death of this labour-power itself" (Marx 1976, 376), the state stepped in again to limit working hours and ensure that labor power was not "maintained and developed only in a *crippled state.*" In such a situation, the price of labor power (embodied in wages) is below its value, since "the value of every commodity is determined by the labour-time required to provide it in its *normal quality*" (Marx 1976, 277, emphasis added).

Thus both wages and working hours enter into the calculation of whether the price of labor power is or is not below its value, since labor power is sold for a specified number of hours; this calculation cannot be accurate unless all the hours worked by all members of the family in order to produce labor power are taken into account. But labor power is not a purely physiological entity. "In contrast . . . with the case of other commodities, the determination of the value of labour-power contains a historical and moral element" (Marx 1976, 275): wages must enable the working class to live at an acceptable standard of living. Setting the value of labor power at an acceptable level and then ensuring that its price does not fall below this value are important goals of working-class struggle. The "moral and historical" element would differ from one society to another, but it seems reasonable to set the minimum at a level where income covers basic requirements of food, water, clothing, shelter, health care, and education; where the minimum age for employment complies with the ILO norm of fifteen years; and where adults get at least eleven to twelve hours per working day for rest and recreation, plus paid weekly days off and annual holidays.

The Working-Class Family in India

In 1890, women millworkers in India were getting up at 4:30 a.m. and working until late at night in order to complete their household chores as well as their wage labor. They had only two holidays a month and even higher rates of sickness than men. Most women took leave for at least one or two months before and two to six months after childbirth. Up to the age of six months, infant-mortality rates were higher among children of mothers who were not employed. But this pattern reversed between six months and one year, when infant-mortality rates went up to 102 per thousand live births for babies of mothers who were employed, as these employed mothers either kept their babies beside them as they worked or left them at home to be fed buffalo milk or brought to the factory for breastfeeding. The administration of opium to these infants was routine (Savara 1986, 38–45). Children as young as seven worked in the factories.

By contrast, the Factories Act of 1948 prohibits the employment of children under fourteen in registered factories and restricts the employment of children between fourteen and fifteen to four and a half hours in the daytime, with paid annual leave of one day for every fifteen days worked, provided he or she has worked for 240 days or more in the previous calendar year. Working hours for adolescents above this age and adults are restricted to forty-eight per week, with one weekly day off and paid annual leave of one day for every twenty worked, with the same proviso as for children aged fourteen. Women were prohibited from working between 7:00 p.m. and 6:00 a.m., but this provision was changed in 2005 to allow women to work at night. There are equivalent provisions for mines, plantations, shops, and other establishments. The statutory work week of forty-eight hours, when combined with travel to and from work and domestic labor, means that even in the formal sector, most women never get enough time for rest and recreation. Women workers in Chennai reported getting up at 4:30–5:00 a.m., working for sixteen to eighteen hours, and being forced to miss meals in order to meet their factory and domestic work schedules (Swaminathan 2002, 9–10). However, for workers in formal employment, there has been a considerable advance in wresting family time away from wage labor and raising the standard of living.

The same cannot be said for informal women workers. At the turn of the twenty-first century, malnutrition and ill health resulted in a maternal mortality rate of 540 per 100,000 live births, with around 136,000 women dying of pregnancy-related problems each year. Maternal malnutrition resulted in 30 percent of infants having "low birth weight," creating health risks that would last the rest of their lives. The infant mortality rate was sixty-seven and the under-five mortality rate ninety-three. Forty-seven percent of under-five-year olds were severely or moderately malnourished. This resulted in a large number of children dying or becoming disabled as a result of contracting preventable or curable diseases (UNICEF 2004, tables 1, 2, 5, 8; Krishnakumar 2004; Pelletier et al. 1995). In other words, the exceedingly low wages, long working hours, lack of health care, and unhealthy living and working conditions of the vast majority of women workers resulted in the production of labor power in a crippled state.

Even if we leave aside considerations of justice and humanitarianism and look at the process from a purely capitalist point of view, this means that there is a considerable waste of productive resources (women) and an appallingly high proportion of defective products (children). Another consequence in India, where traditionally sons stay with their parents after marriage while daughters go to live with their in-laws, is that the devaluation of women has often been associated with the selective abortion of female fetuses by those who can afford it, female infanticide by those who cannot, and the spread of the dowry system and associated dowry deaths. The falling sex ratio (of females to males in the population) reached such an extent in states like Haryana that it led to human trafficking in women, with wives being purchased from other states and treated as bonded labor (Arora 2003).[6] Even from the standpoint of total social capital, this is not a desirable situation.

Unions have demanded equal wages for women doing the same work as men, yet arguments for a "family wage" also reveal an underlying assumption that most women will be dependent on male wage earners who will therefore have to be paid enough to support them. Two union officials in Bengal who were interviewed by the Royal Commission on Factory Labour (1931) argued for a wage that would be sufficient to support female dependants as well as children:

> Although not formulated explicitly as a demand for a "family wage" based on a male-breadwinner/dependent wife conceptualization of the family, the complaints of the Bengali trade unionists over wage levels certainly involved the assumption that the typical worker was a married male with a range of non-employed dependants whom he had increasing difficulty maintaining.
>
> (Standing 1991, 149)

The Delhi Agreement of 1935 between the Ahmedabad mill owners and the Textile Labour Association made this assumption explicit by specifying that married women workers whose husbands were employed in the mills would be dismissed (Chhachhi 1983, 41–42). The fact that unions have not used the clause in the Equal Remuneration Act prohibiting the rampant discrimination against women in recruitment, promotions, and training is eloquent testimony to the nearly universal agreement that a woman has less right to a job (especially a well-paid one) than a man.

Both a Victory and a Defeat

What has happened here? Are these developments a victory or defeat for women in particular and the working class as a whole? The answer to these questions, unsatisfactory though it may seem, is "both." Comparing the living and working conditions of nonunionized informal workers and their families with those of unionized formal workers and their families, no one could deny that men, women, and children in the latter category are vastly better off in terms of living standards, rest and leisure, and access to health care and education. It would be hard to find a housewife married to a formal-sector worker who would want to trade places with an informal woman worker in her hut, *chawl*, or roadside shack; it is indisputable that "the retreat of certain family members from the labour force, in conjunction with an organized attempt to secure a 'family wage'" (Humphries 1980, 157), has resulted in a very welcome rise in the standard of living. Like the miner who was glad she had left her job because she no longer had to do domestic work after coming home exhausted from a day's labor (Pinchbeck 1930, 269), most women workers in India are glad to escape from heavy labor and have more time for homemaking. It is less obvious but also true that compared with women and men living on construction sites or in dormitories supplied by their employers, workers who have homes that are outside the purview of their employers have greater freedom to discuss, organize, and struggle collectively (cf. Humphries 1980, 159–163). These are gains.

Yet the development of the male breadwinner/family-wage norm was also a defeat for women, because it undermined the principle of equality. Some married women, especially if they have no young children, prefer to go out to work and get help with housework rather than stay at home all day (cf. Chhachhi and Pittin 1996, 110). Young women in India, as in China and other developing countries, may see factory work, despite its oppressive character, as offering the possibility of escape from patriarchal family control, "a realm of new-found freedom and experience for personal growth" (Lee 1998, 162). For large numbers of women-headed households, the acute shortage of formal employment for women means there is no alternative to poverty. The assumption that only men have dependants is not sustainable; nor is it true that all men have dependants. Moreover, even when husband and wife are earning, there is no basis for the assumption that his wage pays for basic subsistence while hers is supplementary: indeed, most research shows that in such situations, women's wages are spent entirely on ensuring family survival, while a variable portion of men's wages is spent on alcohol, tobacco, gambling, and other activities (cf. Elson 1995, 183–184; Kottegoda 2004, 137–155).

Thus there is a negative element in the way that the demand for a "family wage" has been posed, fought for, and won. It is directly oppressive to women and disadvantageous to their dependants if they have any (Hartmann 1981, 20–21; Barrett and MacIntosh 1980; Barrett 1980, 26–27). Gandhi's justification for the expulsion of women from the Ahmedabad mills made the patriarchal assumptions behind this decision explicit: "It is not for our women to go out and work as men do. If we send them to the factories, who will look after our domestic and social affairs? If women go out to work, our social life will be ruined and moral standards will decline" (Patel 1988, 380; cit. Breman 2004, 112). This attitude undermines the working-class struggle as a whole by constituting women as secondary wage earners and therefore cheap labor. In formal employment, capitalists may have lost the battle to draw all members of the working-class family (except the very youngest) into the wage-labor force and compel them to produce surplus value, but they have very astutely used male dominance in the working class (which shaped the outcome of this struggle) to their own advantage, by constituting women as a reserve army of cheap labor (Beechey 1977, 1978). In Bombay and Ahmedabad, women's formal jobs in the textile mills were destroyed in the early twentieth century (Kumar 1983, 110; Westwood 1991, 292–295), but when men's jobs were in turn destroyed, women had to enter informal employment to ensure family survival. Their constitution as a cheap and flexible labor force meant that in this latter situation, living standards for the whole family fell drastically.

Moreover, as discussions in the pharmaceutical factories and elsewhere showed, even well-paid formal women workers had difficulty participating actively in the union, due to a combination of domestic labor commitments, objections from husbands, and prejudice in the workplace, thus posing obstacles to united struggles. How can all these problems be overcome?

Demands of Women Workers

The domestic workload of informal women workers would be lightened considerably by the provision of decent housing, potable water, sanitation, and primary health care to all households, which would also reduce illness and death from preventable diseases such as dysentery and malaria. These have all been demanded by informal women workers, along with the formalization of their labor. In India, this constitutes a massive agenda, but unless it is undertaken, labor power will continue to be produced in a crippled form. However, would these changes alone ensure that women are not treated as cheap and flexible labor? The experience of women in the pharmaceutical factories, as well as the experience in other countries, suggests that they would not. The residual problem of the gender division of labor in the workplace and the home, which restricts the earning capacity of women, would still remain.

The demands of the pharmaceutical women workers took over from where those of the informal workers left off. There had been struggles over working hours, which in all the factories had been reduced below the statutory maximum, so that in most cases, women got Saturdays and Sundays off (URG 1986). In the two factories where women were working longer hours, they complained that they did not get enough time at home. Reducing the statutory maximum, at least down to forty hours per week, is an issue that the male-dominated national unions have not taken up, yet these women felt it was absolutely vital for any worker who has to combine waged work with domestic labor. On the issue of job segregation at work, women had different opinions, but most agreed that if a woman felt she could do what was regarded as a "man's job," she should be allowed to try her hand at it. There were no cases where women had tried to get "women's jobs" upgraded on the grounds that they involved more skill than they were credited for; however, there was great anger in one factory where women felt they were doing the same work as men but being allotted a lower grade and pay scale. Most of them felt that they should be protected from having to do night work. If it had been argued that the goal should be to abolish night work for men, too, as in Sweden (Lewenhak 1977, 287), the equality argument could not have been used so easily to remove this protection from women.

On the issue of the gender division of labor in the home, there was a wide diversity of opinions. It was commonly felt that if women were earning, men should help at home. Some women felt that men were not of much use at home, but others said that their husbands took leave and did all the housework after the birth of a child. Most felt that a man should get ten days to two weeks of paternity leave (most were not getting any at all) and have access to crèche facilities for his children if his wife were dead, ill, or worked at a place where there was no crèche (cf. Briskin and McDermott 1993, 10). Male unionists, most of whom had encountered such situations, supported these demands. However, companies flatly refused to consider these arguments, even under extremely tragic circumstances (see Hensman 1996b, 194–200).

Socializing and Sharing Domestic Labor

Moving toward a resolution of these issues requires us to take a closer look at the work performed in the home. It can be divided into work that results in a product that is distinct from a person (such as cooking a meal or washing clothes) and work whose product is inseparable from a person (like childcare). The first kind of production can be mechanized or taken over by capitalism, and in practice this has occurred to some degree. Women workers may buy bread instead of making *chapatis*, use a range of processed and semiprocessed foods, and use a washing machine. There is considerable scope for mass production of these goods and services to proceed further, especially in India, reducing the workload of this type of domestic labor: laundries, take-out restaurants, and community kitchens are all possibilities, and women's cooperatives providing these services have been formed.

Cleaning is a special case. There is not much scope for mass-production techniques here; it is labor-intensive work made more onerous by the fact that its product is noticed only when the work is *not* done. Most upper- and middle-class households in India get this work done by domestic workers, but that is hardly an ideal solution: it is not accessible to working-class families, makes use of cheap labor, and tends to reinforce a social perception that cleaning work, which is socially necessary for hygiene and health, marks out a person as inferior. In most societies it pays poorly (if it pays at all), and in India it has traditionally been consigned to Dalits, who were at one time—and still are in some places—treated as untouchable (Menon 2005c). In cases where people are unable to do their own cleaning, one solution, explored by SEWA, would be to have cleaning cooperatives supplying the service.[7]

Finally, there is caring work, where there can be no mechanization, no substitution of dead for living labor: caring and nurturing is by its nature labor intensive. Although the majority of people needing care are children (since everyone begins life as a child), there are also adults who need it. Many people with disabilities and old people need part-time or full-time attendance, and an accident or stroke can at one blow convert an able-bodied adult into one needing long-term care. In India, this work falls mainly on women, and with the increasing longevity of the population, the care of old people is becoming more important.

One solution to the problem of childcare proposed by Lilina Zinoviev shortly after the Russian revolution was state-run childrearing: "'Our task now is to oblige the mother to give her children to us—to the Soviet State.' The idea was taken up in Kollontai's formulation: 'Children are the State's concern.' She added: 'The social obligation of motherhood consists primarily in producing a healthy and fit-for-life child. . . . Her second obligation is to feed the baby at her own breast'" (Broyelle 1977, 71). A similar suggestion was that "it would . . . be desirable for the child to be left to his parents infinitely less than at present, and for his studies and his diversions to be carried on . . . under the direction of adults whose bonds with him would be impersonal and pure" (de Beauvoir 1997, 539). A logical conclusion following from this approach is that women's liberation requires the application of modern technology to the production of children, in order to free women from the "social obligation" to produce and breastfeed them (Firestone 1970).

However, the practical results of institutionalized childcare were not particularly positive. Small children left in full-time nurseries in Russia were found to be more backward than those looked after at home (Rowbotham 1974, 168), and as a woman lamented in a samizdat publication smuggled out of Russia in 1979: "Kindergartens and crèches are a utopia, which in real life turn out to be anti-utopias. If we send healthy children to such establishments, we get back sick children. Women must constantly report sick in order to be at home with the child. Not with the healthy child, as the case was earlier, but with the sick child" (Malachevskaya 1979; cf. McAuley 1981, 198–99). Another problem, where day-and-night nurseries were tried out in Russia and China, was that women themselves wanted more contact with their children (Rowbotham 1974, 196; Dunayevskaya 1996, 73–74).

The more usual feminist demands are for women to be able to control their sexuality and fertility (Weinbaum 1978, 29–30) and for the development of technologies that would enable them to do so safely, thus ensuring that women have babies only if and when they want them.[8] Advocating the elimination of pregnancy and breastfeeding suggests that the cause of the oppression of women is their biological difference from men. Biological differences such as sex and skin color can certainly be made the pretext for oppression, but it is the social relations under which this occurs that are to blame, not the differences themselves. The biological difference in this case—the fact that women's bodies are adapted to pregnancy, childbirth, and breastfeeding while men's bodies are not—need not lead to the oppression of women. Whether it does or not depends on technological developments and social relations, which in turn determine whether or not women can control their sexuality and fertility safely, whether or not childbearing is a physically safe and socially respected activity, and whether or not there are facilities (like adequate maternity leave and workplace crèches) that provide social support for women who wish to combine childbearing and breastfeeding with paid work.

As for other elements of the gender division of labor, there is no evidence that they have any biological basis, in the sense that all the tasks can be performed either by men or by women, and competence depends not on gender but on inclination and acquired skills. However, given particular social relations, it may well make economic sense to relegate certain tasks to women other than those for which they are biologically adapted. In precapitalist agricultural societies, where having a large number of children was an asset, child mortality was high, and women breastfed each child for one year or more, women might spend over twenty years of their lives in these activities. Under those circumstances, it was more efficient for them to do other household tasks as well, but these relations have been revolutionized by capitalism (Ferguson and Folbre 1981, 321–323). In India, having a large number of children is no longer an asset and may be a liability, with children constituting more mouths to feed and child labor driving down wage rates and causing unemployment by competing with adult labor. Government family-planning programs make birth control relatively accessible and have succeeded in reducing the birth rate; child mortality, while still high, is rapidly being reduced; and a combination of these two developments means that mothers need not spend more than two or three years of their lives breastfeeding infants. On the other side, the interest of capitalism in women as wage laborers provides them with an alternative that is often necessary for the survival of the family. In other words, the material basis for the gender division of labor has changed drastically.

The fact that childcare involves a relationship between carer and child means that if it is passed on to others completely, the relationship is affected, but it does not follow that it cannot be socialized at all. Indeed, at a slightly higher age—five or six years—children routinely go to school, where people outside the family look after them for several hours a day. However, good-quality socialized care requires a high ratio of caregivers to people being cared for, which makes it expensive.[9] This is probably why under capitalism it is not provided without a struggle by both feminists and the labor movement (Zaretsky 1982, 215–217), except as a costly service to the privileged few who can afford it, or in circumstances where a shortage of labor power makes it necessary to induct large numbers of women into the labor force. In India, where millions of children do not even get schooling, much less preschool care, providing high-quality socialized care and education for all children, including residential care for street children, would require a substantial investment. Socialized care of adults is hardly available at all except for the rich; the appalling cruelty with which mentally ill patients are treated in many institutions, as well as the routine appearance of people with disabilities and old people begging on the streets, testify to the disastrous underfunding of this sector.

However, although there is not much formal socialization, a great deal of informal sharing of care does take place. The boundary between the family and the outside world is not as sharp in South Asian cultures as it has become in Western ones. The term "family" would usually refer to the extended family, even where, as in Bombay, there are many nuclear-family households due to migration, and it is quite normal for people who are not kin to be addressed as brother, sister, aunt, uncle, mother, father, son, daughter, and so forth. In traditional families, these honorary relatives would tend to be from the same caste and religion, but in other settings they might simply be neighbors or close friends who could, for example, be asked to look after children on an ad hoc basis. This system has advantages and disadvantages. In traditional families, it means that young women—

and men, for that matter—are more tightly controlled; young women have a heavier workload because they are catering to a larger number of people; and even if there are grandparents around to help with childcare, this comes at a price, in the sense that the children may then be imbued with traditional values such as rigid gender roles. On the other hand, the fluidity of boundaries means that the isolation of mothers with young children is less common, and the small minority of alternative families that are not based on biological relationships and heterosexual marriage are more easily accepted in a metropolis such as Bombay, where traditional communities have partially broken down.

Socialization of some caring work helps to reduce the huge burden now carried mainly by women within the family, but it does not by itself eliminate the gender division of labor. It is quite possible that carers in the socialized facilities are women, that the nurturing that continues to be done in the home is done by women, and that women continue to be treated as cheap labor. Changing this would require challenging the gender division of labor practically and ideologically, because it stunts both those involved in round-the-clock caring work, who never get a chance to exercise other skills and abilities, and those who do not engage in it at all and who never develop the skills and intelligence required for this work. Practical measures to counter it would include eliminating the gender division of labor in employment, working for the equal sharing of domestic labor between men and women, the provision of crèches and nurseries for small children whose parents need childcare, sheltered accommodation or home care for adults who need it, shorter working hours, and regular part-time jobs—if possible with flexible working hours to suit the needs of the employees—for both men and women who have caring responsibilities (cf. Molyneux 1979, 27). But the ideological struggle has priority, because without winning that, the practical struggle will not be won. The fact that, despite decades of feminism and close to two centuries of the labor movement, caring and nurturing continue to be undervalued and seen as "women's work" needs to be explained.

One strand of the explanation can be identified in what has been described as "a great intellectual and cultural ambivalence within feminism," in that it "represented both the highest development of liberal individualism and also a critique of liberal individualism" (Gordon 1982, 45). The bourgeois ideology of individualism penetrated not just liberal feminism but also radical and socialist feminism, leading to a devaluation of caring and nurturing because they constitute, inevitably, a handicap in the competitive struggle for recognition. The other strand of the explanation is constituted by the fact that there have been attempts within working-class movements to eliminate competition between women and men by reinforcing the domination of men over women. Although Marx cannot be accused of advocating such domination, he did help to create the basis for it by ignoring, and thereby devaluing, the socially necessary caring work traditionally done by women.

Excusing oppressive and sometimes violent domestic relationships by attributing them to the all-pervasive ideological influence of capital or patriarchy, as some Marxists and feminists do (see Chodorow and Contratto 1982, 68–69), is a reactionary position. If it is possible to live in a capitalist society and struggle against capitalism, it is equally possible to struggle against authoritarian relationships between men, women, and children; indeed, without this struggle, workers can never escape from subordination to capital. Challenging the domination of capital requires the full involvement of working-class women and children in the class struggle. As Domitila puts it, "the first battle to be won is to let the woman, the man, the children participate in the struggle of the working class, so that the home can become a stronghold that the enemy can't overcome. Because if you have the enemy inside your own house, then it's just one more weapon that our common enemy can use toward a dangerous end" (Barrios de Chungara and Viezzer 1978, 36). Women have an advantage in this struggle to the extent that they recognize "both human needs for nurturance, sharing and growth, and the potential for meeting those needs in a non-hierarchical, nonpatriarchal society" (Hartmann 1981, 33), but it can only be won by the working class as a whole.

Solidarity Instead of Competition or Domination and Subordination

What are the elements of such a struggle, and how far can it progress under capitalism? The first requirement is a battle against authoritarianism in the family; the second is an understanding and acceptance within the labor movement of the value of caring work and the skills and intelligence required for it, followed by the recognition that these need to be fostered in all human beings (Ruddick 1982). Caring conforms to the Marxist ideal of work that is not for profit but directly for the satisfaction of human need; hence recognizing its importance is crucial to the struggle against capitalist exploitation and oppression. Like the Gestalt image of a vase that, when looked at in a different way, reveals two profiles facing each other, whenever we look at a product, we should imagine the faces of its makers *and* the faces of those who cared for the makers.

While the demand for "wages for housework" has the drawback that if met it would eliminate even the limited autonomy enjoyed by working-class women and bring their domestic labor directly under the control of the state as employer (Freeman 1982), the demand that *the value produced by domestic labor* be recognized—for example in statistics such as GDP, in settlements on divorce, and in allocating pensions to women—is an important one, helping to make this vast amount of labor visible. Counting the time spent in domestic labor as part of the working day is also important.

The backwardness of the situation in India, where traditional hierarchies based on gender and age still predominate, could be an advantage if it allows the women's liberation movement to avoid the dead end of liberal individualism. While often confused with the development of individuality, it is in fact as destructive of individuality—the full development of the unique identity of every human being—as authoritarianism and patriarchy, which crush individuality in a more obvious way. Individuality can develop in a child only if he or she is surrounded by the loving attention of other human beings; children completely deprived of this fail to develop their potentialities, and the development of children who receive inadequate interaction of this type is severely compromised. Yet providing this unstinting love and attention inevitably puts the giver at a disadvantage in a competitive market and would therefore be ruled out in a purely market-driven economy.

This contradiction at the heart of bourgeois ideology—the fact that taken to its logical conclusion it threatens bourgeois society with extinction, and therefore the reproduction of competitive individualism depends on its opposite, that is, the reproduction of self-sacrificing women—is what leads to the right-wing insistence on the family as a separate realm from which the logic of capital is excluded (Thorne 1982, 19). However, from the standpoint of the principle of solidarity, according to which the rights and welfare of each individual are linked to those of others, there is no such contradiction; an ethic of care, in which the well-being of the person who is being cared for is seen as essential to the happiness of the carer, is entirely compatible with it. Working for an ideal of nurturance and equal respect for human beings both inside and outside the family (whatever shape or form it may take) is thus an essential component of a labor movement built on the principle of solidarity.

The practical outcome of this understanding would include a struggle for the allocation of vastly more social labor time to this work than occurs currently. For most trade unions in India, which have engaged in collective bargaining exclusively for their own members and have never had a solidaristic policy, the idea of a social wage (including education and health care for all) as a trade union demand would be a new and important departure. Shortening working hours and increasing the number of well-paid part-time jobs with pro rata benefits would improve productivity and expand employment in addition to allowing more time for domestic labor. The Maternity Benefit Act and Factories Act, which require individual employers to pay maternity benefits and provide crèches for the children of their women workers, are direct disincentives to their employing women, as well as being somewhat unfair, since the generational reproduction of labor power is a service to the capitalist class as a whole rather than the individual capitalist. Funding parental leave and childcare from contributions made by *all* employers, workers, and the government removes this anomaly. The final goal of adequate resources for the production of labor power cannot be reached under capitalism, yet it is possible to make considerable progress in that direction even within capitalist society.

Global Initiatives

Ensuring significant progress in combating sexual harassment, socializing the production of labor power, and eliminating the gender division of labor also requires a global movement that would pressure governments to do this. A striking feature of women's lives that emerges from this analysis is the continuity between the oppression that they face inside and outside the workplace. Thus domestic labor puts them at a disadvantage in employment. If they become active in a union they may face disapproval at home. And they may get sexually abused, even murdered, on the way to or from work: indeed, such incidents became so common among female *maquila* workers in Ciudad Juárez in Mexico that a woman activist dubbed it *feminicidio* or "femicide" and set up a coalition to fight against it (Wright 2001). Therefore, unions fighting for women's human rights in the workplace need to make common cause with feminist groups fighting for women's human rights in society as a whole.

The CEDAW Committee, in its General Recommendation no. 19 at its eleventh session in 1992, included a definition of sexual harassment and recommended measures that member states could take to protect women from it (UN 1997–2007). In 2005, the ILO issued a report that begins:

> Sexual harassment is a hazard encountered in workplaces across the world that reduces the quality of working life, jeopardizes the well-being of women and men, undermines gender equality and imposes costs on firms and organizations. For the International Labour Organization, workplace sexual harassment is a barrier toward its primary goal of promoting decent working conditions for all workers.

It goes on to observe that "although it has male victims, sexual harassment is overwhelmingly directed at women, especially those in less-powerful places in the labour market," and that legal measures to prohibit it have been taken mainly since 1995. It concludes by pointing out that "workplace policies and programmes on sexual harassment both reinforce legal prohibitions and play a powerful preventive role" (McCann 2005). However, neither CEDAW nor any of the ILO conventions specifically mention sexual harassment at work; perhaps it might help if there were a separate ILO Convention on Sexual Harassment.

On the other hand, there are numerous instruments dealing with gender discrimination. CEDAW is the main instrument that can be used to oppose gender discrimination, and a number of ILO conventions, including the Equal Remuneration Convention, 1951 (no. 100), and Discrimination (Employment and Occupation) Convention, 1958 (no. 111), can help eliminate the gender division of labor. The Forty-Hour Week Convention, 1935 (no. 47), and Workers with Family Responsibilities Convention, 1981 (no. 156), could help workers trying to combine waged work with caring, and the Part-Time Work Convention, 1994 (no. 175), and Home Work Convention, 1996 (no. 177), could protect the rights of workers who enter into these types of contracts because they are also doing unwaged caring work. The Maternity Protection Convention, 2000 (no. 183), explicitly seeks to protect the rights of women who wish to combine motherhood with paid work. The United Nation's International Covenant on Economic, Social, and Cultural Rights, which stipulates among other things that state parties must provide access to education, health care, and social security for all without discrimination, is another instrument that could be used to combat discrimination against women.

These are issues on which trade unions can work with women's rights groups, to ensure that all countries incorporate these provisions in their legislation and make provisions for their implementation. This would include insisting that all employers have a policy ruling out sexual harassment and discrimination of any sort and working to ensure equal opportunities, which would help other disadvantaged groups as well as women. It would also include educational programs to promote opposition to sexual harassment and abuse both inside and outside the workplace, recognition of nurturing and caring as socially necessary and desirable activities for both men and women, opposition to the gender division of labor both inside and outside the home, and opposition to discrimination against women within unions. In the words of South African women union activists, "gender roles can oppress both men and women. . . . To fight for gender equality is to fight for the right of any person to work, live and love in a way that is not determined by being born male or female" (Kgoali et al. 1992, 48). As in the case of union democracy, this is an issue that unions have to tackle if they are to gain the power they need to confront the challenges of globalization and the economic crisis.

[8]

Employment Creation and Welfare

The Neoliberal Assault on Social Security and Welfare

The past thirty years have seen strong attacks on job security, social security, and welfare benefits. These attacks were most acute in countries that formerly had either welfare states, such as much of Western Europe, or state socialist regimes, such as the former Soviet Union, Eastern Europe, and China. In many of these countries, there was a strong response from workers and unions, who felt that crucial entitlements were being taken away. There were strike waves in France against the withdrawal of job security for young workers, proposed changes in pension entitlements, and job cuts in the public sector (Spiegel Online 2007). Mass demonstrations and riots flared up in China over massive job losses in the public sector and nonpayment of social-security benefits and pensions (Lee 2007). Even in countries with much weaker social-security systems, from developed countries such as the United States to developing countries such as India, cuts were made to the meager welfare benefits that had prevented many poorer families from sinking into destitution.

For both globalizers and for antiglobalizers who defined globalization as neoliberalism, these attacks on state expenditures were inevitable. But, as we saw in chapter 2, attacks on social security and welfare may be elements of the neoliberal model of globalization, but this is not the only model. And as we saw in chapter 3, by making it possible to dispense with militarism, globalization creates the potential for a colossal investment in the labor force, a level of investment simply not possible in an imperialist-nationalist world.

The global crisis of 2008 posed the issue of safety nets in an acute form. The neoliberal assumption that the informal sector could provide a safety net to the unemployed became even more absurd given that hundreds of thousands of informal workers were losing their jobs while the wages of others were pushed down to starvation levels. The notion that these workers could find a livelihood back in their villages was equally absurd, given that they had migrated to urban areas because they could not survive in their villages in the first place (Breman 2009). But the same crisis popularized the notion of "stimulus packages," and this is precisely the context in which measures of employment creation, social security, and welfare must be considered.

Employment Creation

On May 15, 1992, five judges of the Supreme Court of India sitting in a Constitutional Bench upheld the constitutional validity of chapter V B of the ID Act, which prevents firms with over one hundred employees from dismissing workers or closing down their operations without government permission, on the grounds that (a) abysmal poverty had been the bane of Indian society, the root cause of which was unemployment and underemployment; (b) although the state could not be compelled to provide an adequate means of livelihood or work to its citizens, any citizen who was deprived of his right to a livelihood except according to just and fair procedure established by law could challenge the deprivation as offending the right to life conferred by article 21; (c) and therefore the requirement for prior scrutiny of the reasons for retrenchment in chapter V B was to prevent avoidable hardship to employees resulting from retrenchment by protecting existing employment (cit. D'Costa 2001, 8).

While giving comfort to the tiny minority of employees covered by chapter V B, this was grim news to the overwhelming majority of workers left out of its ambit, who would be faced with the prospect of destitution if they lost their jobs. Subsequently, this judgment was challenged from two angles, both of which implicitly criticized its discriminatory implications.

On one side, employers argued against the protection of a "privileged" group of employees; on the other, the Right to Food Campaign, a network of organizations and individuals committed to realizing this right in India, said in its foundation statement (2005):

> We consider that everyone has a fundamental right to be free from hunger and undernutrition. Realising this right requires not only equitable and sustainable food systems, but also entitlements relating to livelihood security such as the right to work, land reform and social security. We consider that the primary responsibility for guaranteeing these entitlements rests with the state.

A major victory of this campaign was the enactment of the National Rural Employment Guarantee Act (NREGA) in 2005. The Right to Information Act (2005) was also the outcome of a massive grassroots campaign of the rural poor demanding transparency in the disbursement of development funds, although its scope was eventually much wider: it was seen as a measure to combat endemic corruption, and it has been used for this purpose. Finally, the Scheduled Tribes and Other Traditional Forest Dwellers (Recognition of Forest Rights) Act, which was passed in December 2006 and came into force a year later, was also the culmination of a huge grassroots campaign. It gave forest dwellers, mainly Adivasis, ownership rights to the land that they cultivated (subject to a maximum of four hectares), rights to minor forest produce, relief and development rights, and forest-management rights. Together, these three acts strengthened the rights of sections of the population who had been neglected by the neoliberal paradigm.

Employment-Guarantee Schemes

NREGA was inspired by the Maharashtra Employment Guarantee Scheme started in 1972 in the midst of drought and famine; the Paschim Banga Khet Majoor Samiti (PBKMS or West Bengal Agricultural Workers' Committee) had been campaigning for the implementation of such a scheme on a national scale for decades. It provided for at least one hundred days of employment per year to each rural household whose adult members volunteered to do unskilled manual work. The minimum wage for agricultural workers, fixed by the state government, would apply, and if the applicant did not receive work within a fortnight of applying, the household would receive an unemployment allowance. Councils at the central and state levels would monitor the scheme, and Panchayats at the district, intermediate, and village levels would be involved in planning and implementation. The objective, apart from providing employment, was to build public works (roads, water management schemes, etc.) and thus boost rural development. In order to ensure transparency and accountability in the use of funds, it was essential that the scheme be linked to the Right to Information Act (Bhaduri 2005).

The final shape of the legislation was the outcome of intense bargaining. The initial draft had restricted the scheme to BPL households (see below), and this was resisted by campaigners on the grounds that it would merely encourage corruption. It was also at their insistence that the minimum-wage norm and a provision for planning and implementation at the Panchayat level were introduced (Papola 2005; Shah 2005). These amendments to the draft were the result of lessons learned from weaknesses in the Maharashtra EGS. However, the suggestion that employment should not be restricted to one person per household or one hundred days per year but should be provided to all adults seeking it for as long as they needed it was not incorporated. Nor were proposals that the scheme be extended to the educated unemployed; to service work, like childcare; and to urban areas, with all workers being paid the same minimum wage (Kannan 2005; Kundu and Sarangi 2005). In February 2006, the scheme came into force in two hundred of India's most backward districts, and in 2007 it was extended to another 130 districts.

Two years after initiation of the scheme—and on the eve of its extension to the whole of India in April 2008—its achievements, shortcomings, and potential were evaluated. The report pointed out the pathbreaking character of NREGA: for the first time in independent India, the right to work was enshrined in law, and this was seen not as a welfare program but as the creation of assets that would enhance rural productivity. Moreover, the specification of minimum labor standards, the ban on the use of contractors, the provision of unemployment benefit, the emphasis on transparency and accountability, and the grassroots involvement in planning and monitoring the scheme were all new. However, there were many shortcomings in the program's implementation. Every state government was required to appoint in each block a full-time program officer with necessary support staff, but nineteen states had not appointed these officers in 70 percent of the blocks surveyed. Twenty state governments had not appointed panels of accredited engineers, and twenty-three had not appointed "Technical Resource Support Groups" as required by the scheme. This had an adverse effect on the preparation of plans, scrutiny, approval, the monitoring and measurement of works, and the maintenance of records. Consequently, only around one-tenth of the registered households received the full hundred days of work, the quality of the projects was poor, and there were delays in the payment of wages and a lack of social mobilizing and grassroots involvement in planning. In many cases, minimum wages were not paid, banned contractors and machines were used, muster rolls were not made available, and social audits were not carried out (Ambasta et al 2008).

Despite these problems,

> in contrast with the scepticism of many economic advisers, most of the sample workers had a positive view of NREGA ... 69 per cent said it had helped them avoid hunger. There were also signs of the NREGA having "helped" in other ways, such as avoiding migration (59 per cent), sending children to school (38 per cent), coping with illness (50 per cent), repaying debt (32 per cent), and avoiding demeaning or hazardous work (35 per cent).
>
> (Drèze and Khera 2009, 11)

Women, especially widows and single women, were appreciative of the chance to earn equal wages in their own name: an average of Rs 85 per day, compared with Rs 35 or as little as Rs 15 per day earned as agricultural laborers. The contrast with previous government schemes like the National Food for Work Programme, where workers earned a pittance of Rs 2 to Rs 4 per day along with two hundred grams of rice, was striking. For these reasons, "the NREGA is also seen by many rural labourers as an opportunity for dignified employment" (Drèze and Khera 2009, 16).[1]

However, there was also a backlash from government functionaries and contractors furious about being denied the opportunity to take a cut of the development funds. One form this backlash took was delayed payments for work performed: "slowing down wage payments is one way of sabotaging NREGA, because it makes workers themselves turn against the programme" (Drèze 2009). The other form was outright violence. When

NREGA workers tried to argue against corruption in the administration of the scheme in West Bengal,

> within minutes, the workers were attacked by a mob of nearly 150 people armed with lathis, axes and chains. The attack was clearly preplanned. . . . It was also very clear that Narayan Mahato, a very popular PBKMS leader who is also an NREGS worker himself, was their main target. Narayan Mahato narrowly escaped being killed, receiving head injuries that required 4 stitches and spinal fracture.
>
> (Patel 2009)

In other cases, the victims were not so lucky; for example, the NREGA activist Lalit Kumar Mehta was brutally murdered after uncovering evidence of large-scale corruption by the contractor lobby and government officials while carrying out an audit of the NREGA program in Palamu District, Jharkhand (Gupta 2008).

Suggestions made for the improved implementation of NREGA included appointment of all the personnel required by the official guidelines plus extra staff to support them, adequate capacity building through training programs, and adequate funding of the scheme. A great deal of emphasis was laid on the critical role of information technology in speeding up processes, ensuring transparency, and eliminating corruption. The full potential of what could be achieved by NREGA was demonstrated in the areas where the National Consortium of Grassroots Civil Society Organisations had been working.

> Door-to-door campaigns for registration of workers and applications for job cards have resulted in significant increases in job card holders. More work is being demanded by people under NREGA. . . . Qualitative changes include an increase in attendance in gram sabhas [village councils], particularly of women, more active local vigilance committees, who question use of poor quality material in construction work . . . better worksite facilities and transparent payment procedures.
>
> (Ambasta et al. 2008, 48–49)

It was suggested that outstanding problems could be solved by creating a dedicated implementation structure, concurrent monitoring using IT, a grievance-redressal mechanism, and an independent, dedicated National Authority to anchor and steer the program (Ambasta 2009).

The importance of the scheme for unions was tremendous. First and foremost, it provided a large new constituency, and unions such as the PBKMS, affiliated to the NTUI, took the opportunity to organize the newly recruited workers. Second, successful struggles for minimum wages, benefits, and facilities strengthened the bargaining power of other rural workers and raised standards accordingly. Finally, the demonstration effect of a scheme where workers are all registered and have job cards, all employment is recorded, and the employer (in this case the state) is forbidden to use contractors is phenomenal. If this can be achieved on such a massive scale under NREGA, it becomes much harder to argue that it cannot be achieved elsewhere. The implications for informal labor are revolutionary and make its abolition a real possibility.

Furthermore, "in the midst of the current economic slowdown, there is enough evidence that this kind of commitment can work to help reduce the slowdown" (Roy and Dey 2009). Programs like NREGA are the ideal stimulus package, because they create employment and boost consumption spending in the present while creating assets that improve productivity in the future. India's employment-guarantee scheme should be expanded to other sectors and could be used as a model for other countries. Of course, the priorities in each country would be different. For example, the German advisory council on global changes has suggested that the most equitable solution for reducing greenhouse-gas emissions is to set a cap of 110 tons per capita of CO_2 emissions over the next four decades. "Schellnhuber, who is the Director of the Potsdam Institute for Climate Impact Research, and winner of the German Environment Prize of 2007 . . . said that an individual emissions cap valid for every single person in the world 'constitutes an elementary principle of environmental justice. Why should a German citizen be allowed to emit more CO_2 than a person in Bangladesh?'" (Godoy 2009). If this is accepted, with the caveat that per capita emissions should be equalized within countries too, it would mean that First World countries would reach their cap very soon and should therefore concentrate their stimulus packages on developing cheap, renewable sources of energy. In South Asia, on the contrary, per capita energy consumption is very low, "primarily due to the fact that a vast majority of the populace does not have access to modern energy sources. Indeed, the region has the largest number of people without electricity relative to the rest of the world" (Chikkatur and Dubey 2009).

Stimulus packages would therefore need to ensure that everyone has access to electricity, even while also developing renewable energy sources.

Microcredit Schemes

Despite the promise held out by NREGA, it was a very different model that grabbed the limelight internationally. "The current consensus, aggressively propagated by some of the leading development organizations including the World Bank, the USAID, and the DFID . . . holds that microfinance based programmes constitute the single most effective development inter-vention that can be universally adapted. . . . This vision emphasizes credit as the most effective weapon against poverty" (Kalpana 2004, 7, 9–10). Women were the favored targets of these programs; in India, they were organized into neighborhood self-help groups, which used peer-group pressure on members to honor the very strict repayment schedules. Yet their usefulness for poor women has been questioned.

> These measures may satisfy what are immediate practical gender needs of women but the short-term relief without a long-term vision that is political, social and cultural will only serve to perpetuate the subordina-tion of women. Women need credit to put their children in schools and pay for private health services but the question of the state's responsibil-ity in providing good education and healthcare free of cost goes unasked.
>
> (Kannabiran 2005)

As a measure of poverty alleviation, microcredit has not worked well. Studies showed that the poorer the recipients, the less they gained, with some even ending up worse off than a control group who did not get loans. Small amounts of around Rs 2,000, on which repayments had to start immediately, were not sufficient for the investments required for a micro-enterprise, especially in the absence of additional support such as busi-ness and technical training and establishment of market linkages; in rural areas with little infrastructure, they were of even less use (Mahajan 2005). Donor pressure to ensure that the schemes were self-sustaining resulted in the Grameen Bank of Bangladesh, which had pioneered the idea of micro-credit in the mid-1970s, moving away from its earlier focus on the poor-est sections to those who were better off. The majority of the poor either excluded themselves or were excluded by the punitive strategies employed against defaulters in this and other schemes, leading to suicides in a few cases and, in many other cases, to loans being taken from traditional moneylenders to pay off installments on loans from microfinance institutions (Kalpana 2004, 15–24).

Given this rather poor record, what accounts for the high profile accorded to microcredit? One explanation suggests that the strategy "manages to appeal to a diverse constituency of aid organizations and commercially motivated private actors within an overarching framework of neoliberalism on account of its stipulation that the poor pay their way out of poverty" (Kalpana 2004, 12). Another explanation is that "at an individual level microcredit instils the ethic of hard work and savings, Weber's 'Protestant Ethic' or Marx's 'Accumulate, accumulate!' . . . The MFIs, in different parts of the developing world, are promoting such secular variants of capitalist economic ethics" (DN 2005).

These explanations are not mutually exclusive. A study of microfinance institutions in Bangladesh confirmed that their policies were not only cruelly coercive—even forcing cyclone victims to hand over relief payments or sell housing materials in order to pay off the loan installments—but also constituted an integration of the poor into financial markets: Muhammad Yunus, the founder of Grameen Bank,

> turned into one of the world's leading businessmen, and became an advocate for foreign corporate investment in Bangladesh. The number of the poor and vulnerable has increased. The GB's spectacular success as a bank in a new form must be acknowledged. But where should we locate its success? Certainly not in poverty alleviation. Its success lies in creating profits by integrating the poor into the market.
>
> (Muhammad 2009)

In other words, microfinance belongs to the neoliberal model of globalization, which was one of the causes of the economic crisis.

Producer Cooperatives

The difference between microfinance and the promotion of workers' cooperatives may seem small, but it is crucially important. The transition from individual to collective production allows for solidarity to be an important ingredient of success, whereas competition generated by microcredit undermines solidarity. Larger loans become sustainable, and projects that cannot be undertaken by an individual yet are crucial for success—like water management—become possible (Mahajan 2005). For the poor, "cooperation is one way of pooling resources and hence increasing control, it is also a way of increasing the bargaining power of those who are weak" (Bhatt and Jhabvala 2004, 5139–5140). This strategy was adopted successfully in India by groups such as SEWA, Sarba Shanti Ayog, and many others, with activities often branching out into the provision of social services (Hensman 2000, 2002). Another case was the Annapurna Mahila Mandal, a women's cooperative started in Bombay by the one-time freedom fighter and mill worker Prema Purao, which provided cooked meals to mill workers and others (Gurung 1999). However, unlike the women's cooperatives in China, which grew to have hundreds or even thousands of members (Broyelle 1977, 18–19), workers' cooperatives in India tended to remain small and technologically backward. An examination of attempts to set up larger and more technologically advanced cooperatives suggests some reasons why this may be so.

The Kamani Cooperatives

Kamani Metals and Alloys Ltd. (KMA) and Kamani Tubes (KT) were set up in the same complex as KEC in Kurla, Bombay, in 1945 and 1960, respectively, and the workers became members of the Kamani Employees' Union (KEU).[2] Up to 1974, KT, which manufactured almost 60 percent of the nonferrous metal tubes and rods in India, was one of the most profitable of the Kamani companies. In 1975, the company recorded a loss, despite showing a growth in revenue. The KEU alleged management malpractice and requested government intervention but was ignored. In 1979, KT defaulted on bank loans, and production slipped to one-fifth of mid-1970s levels. At that point, the KEU leadership went on a hunger strike, demanding a reorganization similar to the intervention by the public financial institutions that had succeeded in turning around KEC (see chapter 5). The government of Maharashtra appointed a committee, which investigated the affairs of KT, found that funds were being siphoned, and recommended nationalization. But the Kamani family blocked this recommendation, and KT continued under the same management. In 1981, production came to a halt, and in 1983, management declared a lockout; although the Bombay Industrial Court ruled it was illegal, the lockout was only lifted four months later. In September 1985, KT defaulted on its electricity and water bills, and the supplies of both were cut off. Management abandoned the plant, and the workers moved in to prevent the machinery and other saleable assets from being stripped. The KEU appealed to the Supreme Court mediator, who had been appointed to mediate between Kamani family members, and he ruled in favor of the union, placing restrictions on the sale of assets and directing management to resume production. The Kamani family expressed its inability to restart KT, and consequently the company was put up for auction. When no buyers came forward, the workers applied to take the company on lease, but the company was not willing to lease KT to them.

Meanwhile, in view of the large and growing number of sick companies, a special department of the Reserve Bank of India had appointed a committee to look into the causes of industrial sickness. The committee found that in the majority of cases, the sickness was caused by mismanagement. In accordance with the recommendations of the committee, the Sick Industrial Companies (Special Provisions) Act (SICA; 1985) was enacted. Its purpose, according to the preamble, was "to secure the timely detection of sick and potentially sick companies owning industrial undertakings, the speedy determination by a Board of experts of the preventive, ameliorative, remedial and other measures which need to be taken with respect to such companies and the expeditious enforcement of the measures so determined." The Board for Industrial and Financial Reconstruction (BIFR) was set up to adjudicate such cases, and SICA became operational in 1987. The KEU seized the chance to approach the Supreme Court, arguing that since KT was a sick company, the case should be taken up by the BIFR, and a workers' cooperative should be allowed to take KT over. The Supreme Court directed the case to the BIFR, which allowed the workers' cooperative to purchase KT shares at a tenth of their face value, in view of the responsibility of management for the sickness of the company. In April 1989, the factory resumed production as a workers' cooperative.

This constituted a departure from the usual demand for nationalization in such cases, which would have resulted in the enterprise being taken over by the government and either being run like any other capitalist enterprise or becoming a black hole into which vast sums of public money would disappear. To the extent that SICA and the BIFR made the cooperative possible, they constituted progressive measures. Yet old attitudes remained. The former owners were compensated for the change in ownership, albeit at a discounted rate, and were not penalized for bankrupting the company by siphoning funds out of it. Nor were the bank officials, who had colluded in the mismanagement, made to pay for their share of responsibility for the failure: all bank loans, including the principal and interest, had to be repaid under the revival scheme. It was the workers, who had already gone without wages for years, who were expected to take a wage cut of 25 percent in the first year and 15 percent in the second year on their pre-1985 wages and thereafter have their wages frozen until the company turned around. It was quite literally a case of the bank robbers, and the bank officials who colluded with them, being rewarded, while the victims who lost their money were penalized.

At this point, workers in dozens of other sick units facing closure started gravitating to the KEU, seeking help in drawing up plans for revival through the BIFR. It was in order to service these unions that the Centre for Workers' Management (CWM) was set up as a KEU initiative. It was located in Delhi, since that was where the BIFR held its hearings. Some of these enterprises were too far gone for revival to be a realistic proposition, but some were potentially viable, and CWM worked on several plans for reviving such units as workers' cooperatives.

In 1991, following a lockout at KMA, management referred that company to the BIFR. A revival scheme for the takeover of KMA by a workers' cooperative, submitted on behalf of the workers by the KEU, was sanctioned two years later. But the former management filed an appeal against the takeover, and the matter dragged on until 1994. Banks did not release working capital until 1995, by which time the interest burden alone had increased by Rs 3.27 crores. The IDBI never released the term loans specified under the scheme for modernization. By this time KT too, which at first had broken even, was facing difficulties. S. R. Gokhale, a former chief executive of the Kamani Metals group who had left to start his own small-scale tube-extrusion plant, explained that "the company cannot hope to survive on the products it had been manufacturing in the last few years before its closure, as these are being made in plenty by small scale extruders and redrawers around the country. Instead, it will have to go in for the more sophisticated import substitution items" (cit. Fernandez 1986, 21). For this, new machinery and technical expertise were required. In 1996, consultants appointed by the IDBI concluded that the plant was inherently viable but needed Rs 4 crores as working capital to raise production levels and capital investment of another Rs 4 crores for modernization. The consultants proposed raising funds by developing and selling surplus property in partnership with a builder, in order to pay off all outstanding liabilities and dues, increase working capital, and carry out modernization. But the IDBI withheld permission until property prices had crashed and the builder had backed out. By then it was too late, and the closure of both units became inevitable. The plans worked out by CWM for the revival of other units as workers' cooperatives did not even get this far.

There were undoubtedly internal problems within the cooperatives. The union was characterized by a gap between its leaders and members and the overdependence of the latter on the former, a flaw that had developed in many employees' unions. This problem was compounded when the cooperatives were set up. Many of the workers were no longer young and were unable to adjust to the idea of being owners of an enterprise; to them, their equity contribution was merely a means of saving their jobs, and they expected management to make decisions for them. At KT, committees set up to encourage workers to discuss and participate in management decisions functioned regularly for a while, and some workers found them useful. But when management started bypassing them, the union did not feel confident enough to intervene, nor did the workers insist on their right to be consulted. At KMA, such committees were not even formed. The shortage of experienced and committed union leaders meant that the two top leaders of the KEU, Yeshwant Chavan and D. Thankappan, doubled as workers' representatives on the board of KT, and Thankappan was also on the board of KMA. This circumscribed their ability to represent the interests of workers in any conflict with management and was one of the factors leading to the formation of dissident unions at both KT and KMA. At KMA, the dissident union, instigated by the deposed owner, Ashish Kamani, took the position that workers' cooperatives were not viable and that the only solution was for the owners to return. As in the case of other employees' unions, the dissidents later returned to the KEU, but by then the damage had already been done.

These problems are not peculiar to the Kamani cooperatives or to India. The problem of having the same people at the apex of both cooperative and union was encountered in the Kirkby Manufacturing and Engineering Cooperative (KME) near Liverpool in Britain, as was the lack of management skills among workers and the reluctance of some to play this role at all (Purcell and Smith 1979, 166, 175). The difference, however, was that at the KME the worker-directors did not have to contend with obstructionist public institutions such as those that constituted the majority on the boards of KT and KMA. Another relevant comparison is with the workers' cooperatives and SALs[3] in Catalonia, which, like the Kamani cooperatives, were formed in order to avoid impending closure. Some of the enterprises in Catalonia, like some of the units from which workers came to the CWM, had no realistic prospect of revival. But many survived and flourished, despite the fact that here too, as in KT and KMA, workers had no experience of running cooperatives, nor any particular desire to do so, and took this path only as a last resort to save their jobs (Holmström 1993, 9–11). It is therefore useful to ask what the critical differences between these cases might be.

The pervasive culture of dependence on the government, politicians, and leaders, and the stranglehold of bureaucracy over the cooperative movement, were two reasons suggested by Thankappan for the difficulties faced by Indian workers' cooperatives. But the greatest difficulty, he felt, was obstruction from government institutions and banks, which were only too happy to lend large sums of money to capitalists but grudged disbursing much smaller sums to workers (cit. Eashvaraiah 2000, 23–27). It is indeed a striking aspect of the Kamani cases that public financial institutions and banks, which never protested while companies siphoned public funds into private pockets, were miserly and unfair in their dealings with workers, passing on the costs of their own dereliction of duty in scrutinizing loans—and their complicity in mismanagement—to the workers, who had no responsibility for the failure of the companies. In another example, the banks and government of West Bengal sabotaged a similar plan for revival of the New Central Jute Mills, despite the fact that workers had already contributed more than Rs 9 crores of their own money (Narayanan 1994, 375–376). This attitude was supported by Rajiv Gandhi, who said that the government could not afford to take over and run sick companies in order to protect the jobs of workers yet seemed quite happy to write off Rs 6,500 crores of public money loaned to the owners of those same companies (Subramaniam 1987, 63).

The same regulatory policy that encouraged corporate misgovernance discouraged workers' self-management. Public funds were squandered on making the rich wealthier and allowing them to make enterprises sick, while workers, who had no social security to fall back on, were prevented from engaging in productive employment, earning a living, and contributing to society through taxes. In fact, "since 1996 there has been a great deal of institutional pressure for reform of the governance culture of Indian businesses," pressure resisted fiercely by Indian business; foreign institutional investors fought for better standards of disclosure and accountability in a less direct form, by dumping the stock of companies that did not conform to them (Banaji 2001b, 12, 19–23). But this would not by itself change the attitudes of the public financial institutions to workers' cooperatives. Pressure for additional policy changes would be required.

CWM attempted to prevent the passage of a new Sick Industrial Companies (Special Provisions) Bill in 1997 and also proposed amendments to the 1985 act. Their analysis of the 1997 bill showed it "suggests that the problem of industrial sickness is a private matter between the management of an industrial company and its secured creditors, and therefore links the whole question of industrial sickness to debt default" (CWM 1997b, 1). However, while a perfectly healthy company might in certain circumstances default on a debt, another company might not default on debts to secured creditors until it had reached a very advanced stage of sickness. The new bill also overlooked the fact that such secured creditors may "have been partners in industrial sickness, often making bad lending decisions (in the absence of adequate project evaluation) and often turning a blind eye to or being partners in mala fide" (CWM 1997b, 7). The second major failing was that "the bill does not have any provisions to protect the rights and interests of workers" (CWM 1997b, 2).

The validity of these criticisms was borne out by a study of 472 cases of industrial sickness, which found that the overwhelming majority were the consequence of either mismanagement, including the siphoning of funds, or bad government policies (such as encouraging companies to set up units in backward areas without ensuring the availability of water, electricity supplies, or even roads). There were very few cases where labor problems led to sickness, yet workers were always the ones who suffered most: "We see plenty of sick industries, but few sick industrialists. The institutions and the banks lose a lot of funds, but it is public money, about which people do not seem to bother very much in our country. It is workers who suffer most" (Narayanan 1994, 365).

Among the recommendations made by CWM, apart from scrapping the new bill entirely, were the following: (1) When a company becomes sick, it should be mandatory for it to be referred to the BIFR. The right to make a voluntary reference should be vested in secured creditors, government agencies, and workers. (2) In assessing sickness and preparing revival schemes, the BIFR must safeguard the interests of all concerned parties, have the right to engage expert assistance to make and assess revival plans and monitor them subsequently, and have the judicial power to enforce its decisions. (3) Workers and trade unions must have the right to be involved at all stages of the proceedings. Outstanding workers' dues must be paid at the outset of any revival scheme, and if a reduction in the workforce is involved, redundant workers must be offered comparable alternatives to their current employment. If the existing management fails to come up with an acceptable revival scheme, workers should be entitled to do so next, and workers' cooperatives should be seen as a serious option. If the scheme involves any financial sacrifice on the part of workers, then all other interested parties must make a proportional sacrifice, and at least 50 percent of outstanding loans from public financial institutions and scheduled banks should be converted into equity, to ensure that they have a stake in the success of the plan (CWM 1997b). Nevertheless, SICA 1997 was pushed through by a United Front government, despite its socialist pretensions, and the situation for workers got worse rather than better.

The amendments to SICA proposed by the CWM, along with the amendments to the Companies Act proposed in chapter 5, would constitute a far superior alternative to chapter V B of the ID Act. The Companies Act would give unions and workers' representatives a role in monitoring the performance of companies, thus providing them with information and consultation rights. SICA would give workers and unions the option of referring a company to the BIFR were there any hint that it was contemplating dismissals or closure as a consequence of mismanagement or siphoning of funds. Workers and unions would have access to the economic and technological expertise required for making an informed evaluation of the company's viability and the feasibility of revival plans, instead of leaving this function to state governments, whose decisions were based solely on political considerations.

Policy on Producer Cooperatives

In contrast to the unhelpful attitude of Indian government institutions, "it is Spanish public policy to encourage the growth of co-ops and SALs, both new starts and takeovers. Government subsidies and effort, and the dedicated work of people in the co-op and SAL federations and the unions, have helped these workers to save their own jobs" (Holmström 1993, 142). In Argentina, too, in the wake of the economic crisis of 2001, workers began to take over factories and other businesses instead of allowing them to close. They were supported by the community in these struggles, and by 2005 there were roughly two hundred of these cooperatives, run by fifteen thousand workers (Dangl 2005). Many were doing better than they had been under their former owners, partly because these were expropriations by the government. The workers did not have to pay their ex-employers nor repay their debts (Lindsay 2002), and they had the support of a new union federation started in 1992, the Central de Trabajadores Argentinos (Atzeni and Ghiliani 2007, 110).

The mainstream left and the trade unions in India are, by and large, opposed to workers' cooperatives. The standard demand put forward by the left when an enterprise is faced with closure is "nationalization." Underlying this is a belief that only the state (preferably controlled by them) can run production and society as a whole; workers are certainly not to be trusted with powers of self-management. On the other hand, the attitude in most trade unions tends to be that if workers take over management, they will be saddled with the problems of the company; they too favor nationalization. The result is that where the government refuses to nationalize, or nationalizes but then runs down and closes an enterprise, there is no alternative to unemployment for the workers.

It is true that restructuring or turning around a failing enterprise may involve sacrifices for workers. For example, in 1965, Hiroshima Dentetsu, the Hiroshima tram company, began running its trams less frequently and ending service at 10:00 p.m. instead of 11:00 p.m. The union realized that the reason behind these changes was to make the trams less attractive to customers so that the company could then be closed on the grounds that it was unprofitable. It proposed an alternative plan to save its members' jobs, restoring the old schedules and even giving up the rest period it had fought for when trams were delayed by traffic. Combined with imaginative innovations, this strategy succeeded in saving around one thousand jobs (Kawanishi 1992, 405–408).

In Portugal, the responses of unions in the nationalized steel and airline industries to liberalization demonstrate the importance of a realistic grasp of the possibilities. Faced with the prospect of restructuring in 1987, the

Communist Party–linked CGTP union in the steel industry refused any form of concession bargaining. The end result was that the workforce was reduced by more than 50 percent and the steel industry was dismembered and put up for sale. By contrast, TAP, the union at Air Portugal, which in 1993 was threatened with the early retirement of over fifteen hundred workers and flexibilized work relations in preparation for privatization, responded with a "Strategic Plan," which included a slower reduction of personnel and maintenance of the company in its integrity, and the union succeeded in getting its plan accepted (Stoleroff and Naumann 1996). For many workers, it is worth making concessions in order to prevent the closure of their plant or company, and this option should be open to the workers instead of being precluded by union policy. One reason for the success of workers' cooperatives in Italy and Spain was that the left and the trade union movement were far more supportive of them than was the case in India (Holmström 1989, 1993; Roy 1994).

The idea of pooling resources to achieve something that individuals cannot achieve on their own is a common one in India, and there are numerous successful consumer cooperatives, marketing cooperatives, and housing cooperatives, in addition to women's cooperatives. Nor is there any reason to suppose that workers in India are not capable of self-management; indeed, a nonprofit erection company started by Kamani workers after more than one thousand of them were dismissed was filling orders and doing well by 2006. However, making this potential for self-management into a reality would involve major changes in government policy. If provided with adequate government support in the form of advice, credit, marketing, and other assistance, cooperatives could provide livelihoods for millions of workers. This would certainly be more equitable than subsidizing petty capitalists to superexploit their employees. It would also help self-employed workers who find it hard to survive on their own in a competitive market.

An even stronger case can be made for agricultural cooperatives, as advocated by the ILO. Writing off bank loans of Rs 60,000 crores to small and marginal farmers in the 2008 budget might have been necessary to stem the flood of farmers' suicides, but it did not help farmers who had borrowed from moneylenders or those owning more than two hectares of land, nor would it help to make farming more viable in the future (*Times of India* 2008). Research on the dilemmas of the widows of farmer suicides in Punjab showed that while some causes of indebtedness, such as dowry payments, might be absent in a more gender-equal society, and others such as medical expenses might be avoided were there inclusive health care, the main cause was ultimately the nonviability of most small-scale farming in India (Padhi 2009). A study of examples in other countries as well as in India concludes that group farming "offers substantial scope for poverty alleviation and empowering the poor as well as enhancing agricultural productivity" (Agarwal 2010, 75). But a significant change in the attitudes of the government, the left, and the trade union movement toward workers' cooperatives would be required to implement such a program.

Social Security and Welfare

The lack of social security or welfare for informal workers is what often precipitates them and their children into bondage: an illness, accident, or loss of employment leads them to borrow from moneylenders, and this debt forces them to bond their own and/or their children's labor to the moneylender. If illiterate, they and their children may carry on working, in conditions resembling slavery, long after the debt and interest on it have been paid (Burra 2003, 78–79). In some cases, even formal workers and their families literally starve when they lose their jobs; for example, after the closure of the UP Cement Corporation factories at Dalla in 1998, around five hundred workers and their family members had died by 2004.[4] In other cases, the male head of the family would commit suicide. A particularly gruesome instance of this occurred when Akhtar Khan and Anant Dalvi, who had been employed by Tata Electric Companies on temporary contracts for periods of nineteen and seventeen years respectively before their employment was terminated in June 1996, immolated themselves in front of company headquarters in Bombay in October 2003.[5]

Only a comprehensive system of social security can ensure that those who are most in need have access to it, yet the tendency—especially during the NDA regime—was to reduce reliance on the state even further; according to former Prime Minister Vajpayee: "We should strengthen and activate all the non-state providers of social security" (*ET* 2002c). Debates on this issue were renewed after the change of government in 2004, with the demand that informal-sector workers should have access to social security. But the Unorganised Workers Social Security Bill, passed in December 2008, was a woefully inadequate measure. Among other shortcomings, it legalized inferior rights for informal workers; excluded the majority of informal workers by specifying that only BPL (see below) workers would be eligible for most of the social-security schemes; did not define what was meant by social security, so that the entitlements covered by it remained vague and nonjusticiable; and made no provision for a grievance-redressal mechanism (John 2008).

Food Security

The Public Distribution System (PDS) had its origin in the rationing of scarce supplies during World War II, but it was retained in the postindependence period as a welfare measure, providing rice, wheat, sugar, and kerosene at subsidized rates in Fair Price Shops. The subsidy was equally beneficial to the farmers who produced the grain, since it guaranteed them a market at an agreed-upon price. Initially, the ration was in theory available to everyone, although even then many households were excluded: for example, migrant workers and the homeless would be excluded by the requirement of an address. Moreover, there was corruption at all levels, and it was common for part of the rations to be sold on the open market at a higher price, while ration-card holders would be given adulterated provisions (Mooij 1999; Jenkins and Goetz 2002). Irregularity of supplies and long queues also meant that a considerable expenditure of time was required to collect rations; for example, when one went to get rice or wheat, kerosene might not be available; when kerosene was available, everyone would rush to get it, the queue would be long, and those at the back of it might be told that the rationed kerosene had run out, leaving them with no choice but to buy kerosene "on the black," at a much higher price.

In 1997, the Targeted PDS (TPDS) was introduced, differentiating between Below Poverty Line (BPL) households, which received rations at a more subsidized rate, and Above Poverty Line (APL) households. Apart from the questionable criteria used to identify BPL households, this also meant additional work in classifying every household and additional scope for corruption in controlling who could get a BPL card. Thus the Shiv-Sena-BJP government, when it was in power in Maharashtra, systematically denied ration cards to Muslims, claiming they were foreigners (Jenkins and Goetz 2002). Over the same period, the farmers' lobby succeeded in raising the minimum support price and amount of grain procured by the government considerably. The government passed on most of the cost to consumers, so that eventually the bulk of the subsidy was going to rich farmers, who were the only ones with enough grain to sell. The excess of the amount procured over the amount distributed meant that another large chunk of the subsidy was spent on storing the grain.

A study in a remote and predominantly tribal area in 2003 found that

> despite acute poverty 73 per cent of the BPL cardholders did not purchase any foodgrains from PDS. As most of such households are casual daily workers and/or collect firewood from the forest to sell in the nearest market they just cannot afford to visit the fair price shop which hardly opens for a few days in a month and even if it opens there may be nothing in the stock. . . . A startling revelation was that such households consumed what is locally called "khudi," i.e. very small broken rice which sells cheaper than PDS wheat or rice.
>
> (Shankar 2004, 2094)

In Bombay, the Rationing Kruti Samiti (Action Committee on Rationing), a federation of around fifty core community groups and other more loosely linked civil-society groups, waged a heroic struggle from 1993 onward to try to eliminate corruption from the PDS, introduce transparency into its workings, and ensure that BPL households got the rations they were entitled to, yet the massive expenditure of time and effort by participants, as well as the risks they took in opposing powerful vested interests, were not matched by its small victories in individual cases (Jenkins and Goetz 2002).

The fact that the PDS was simply not helping those who needed it most became shockingly evident with the widespread occurrence of starvation deaths in 2001. This was not for lack of food, however. "There is so much grain in the Government's reserves that the Respondent No. 2, the Food Corporation of India, has run out of storage space. In some cases, there is barely a distance of 75 kilometres between the location of these godowns [warehouses] and the places where starvation is rampant," stated the petition presented to the Supreme Court by the People's Union of Civil Liberties (*PUCL Bulletin* 2001). The subsidy had become the *cause* of hunger, "a means of transferring public resources to a small section of rich farmers and jacking up food prices to an extent where it becomes unaffordable to the poor. This strategy of ensuring food security resulted in the government having to subsidise grain exports to cattlefeed manufacturers in southeast Asia, so that soaring stocks would not bloat the food subsidy bill further" (*ET* 2004f). "'In effect, animals in other countries get a better quality of wheat than humans here,' said an official of Roller Mills Association bitterly" (Vasudeva 2001).

It has been calculated that only about 2.5 percent of the food subsidy actually reaches BPL families; in these circumstances, proposals that half of the PDS subsidy should be distributed directly to poor households, while the other half is used to fund employment-guarantee schemes, make a great deal of sense (Shankar 2004, 2095–2096). Here India could learn from the *Bolsa Familia* program introduced by Luis Inácio Lula da Silva's government in Brazil in 2004. In 2006, for families below the poverty line of 120 reais per month, it provided fifteen reais per child, up to a maximum of three children, conditional on the children being sent to school and being immunized, and families with an income below sixty reais per month were given an additional fifty reais without any conditions. Given preferentially to the female head of household through a "Citizen Card" mailed to the family, and with payments listed on the Internet, the program reduced hunger, corruption, and child labor and improved school attendance. Replacing the PDS with a similar scheme in India would provide a much-needed safety net and end the scandal of starvation deaths and suicides associated with unemployment and indebtedness. The government would still have to ensure that essential commodities were available at affordable prices in all parts of the country, but the scope for corruption and siphoning would be much reduced.

There are many more food-security schemes in India, but two that could have the greatest effect are aimed at reducing the alarmingly high rates of malnutrition in children. The Integrated Child Development Services (ICDS) program began in a few areas in 1975 and after thirty years covered most of the country. The package of services, dispensed by *anganwadi* workers in *anganwadi* centers, provides supplementary nutrition for preschool children and for women during lactation and the third trimester of pregnancy, as well as health and nutrition education, immunizations, health check-ups, referral services, and nonformal preschool education. However, the program failed to live up to its promise for many reasons:

> Resources meant for the children . . . are routinely siphoned off. . . . Access to services by deprived communities like the SC and ST is restricted if the centre is located in upper caste predominant hamlets. . . .

The centres were located in the main village and sometimes in the house of a forward caste worker, thereby making it out of bounds to Dalit children. . . . Most surveys and studies on the ICDS programme note that the ability of the programme to reach out to children under three remains a problem . . . the growth monitoring data that is fed in the system may well be incorrect.

(Ramachandran 2005)

The quality of the food supplied varied widely. Some centers provided rather unpalatable food, while the meals supplied in others were quite tasty.

Apart from obvious suggestions for improving the program—more centers, better access for SC/ST children, better food, and eliminating corruption—"it may be worthwhile discussing the possibility of splitting the ICDS programme into two: (a) a dedicated home-based programme to promote health and nutrition of children in the 0–3 group; health and nutrition of adolescent girls and pregnant and lactating mothers; (b) a centre-based nutrition and pre-school education programme for 3–6 years" (Ramachandran 2005). All this would require more resources for the ICDS program, but given its importance and the fact that a countrywide administrative framework already exists, it would be worth incorporating the improvements summarized in the study quoted above.

The other major nutritional program for children was launched by the central government in 1995 to provide cooked mid-day meals in all government and government-aided primary schools. As cooked meals still had not been provided by most state governments by 2001, the Supreme Court issued an order in November that they should be introduced in all primary schools within six months. This resulted in a much more rapid spread of the program, but most states did not meet the deadline, and some had not met it even two years later. A survey conducted by the Centre for Equity Studies (CES) in 2003 in three districts in each of three states—Chhattisgarh, Rajasthan, and Karnataka—found that cooked mid-day meals were being provided in seventy-six of the eighty-one schools surveyed, that quantities were adequate, and that the quality varied from an extremely monotonous diet in Rajasthan, to a more varied menu in Chhattisgarh, to the best meals in Karnataka (Drèze and Goyal 2003, 4674).

Results from the CES and other studies showed that school enrollment, especially of girls, shot up after the introduction of cooked mid-day meals, and attendance improved as children started looking forward to going to school. The meal helped to eliminate "classroom hunger" (resulting from children coming to school without having eaten anything in the morning) and malnutrition in general, thus aiding concentration. Among parents, appreciation was greatest among the poorest and most deprived, especially single mothers. While a few upper-caste parents did not like their children sharing a meal with children from lower castes and posed even greater resistance to the appointment of Dalit cooks, in general the scheme tended to weaken caste barriers. But there were many instances where the infrastructure was inadequate: no kitchen in the school; shortage of utensils; lack of plates, drinking water, and fuel; no helper for the cook; inadequate supervision and monitoring; and delays, corruption, and theft in the delivery of supplies. Most of these problems could be solved with bigger financial allocations, and, indeed, this was the case in Tamil Nadu, where an excellent program was being run at a very reasonable cost (Drèze and Goyal 2003).

Health Care

A rudimentary public health-care system does exist in India, and it is at its best in metropolitan centers such as Bombay, where patients who need hospitalization but cannot afford to pay for it can often get the treatment they need. But even in Bombay, informal-labor families spend a large part of their meager incomes on private health care for common ailments, and the situation is much worse in rural areas. Formal workers and their families are better provided for. The Employees' State Insurance Scheme (ESIS) is applicable to all factories except seasonal ones, and it covers temporary, part-time and casual workers, and apprentices (cf. Punekar 1950). It also covers establishments such as shops, hotels, and cinemas that employ twenty or more workers, but it was limited to employees drawing Rs 7,500 per month or less as of April 2004. The scheme is funded by contributions from employers, employees, and the government. The Central Government Health Scheme (CGHS) covers central-government employees and their families and has a lower rate of contributions than the ESIS. Other government departments, such as the railways, have their own schemes. Those earning higher wages in private companies, such as the permanent workers in the employees' unions, usually have company health benefits, which enable them to claim expenses for private health care (Gupta and Trivedi 2005).

There have been many complaints about the poor quality of health care offered by government health-insurance schemes, but the main problem is one of equity: the overwhelming majority of people are not covered by them, and there is disproportionate state expenditure on those who are. For example, 14 percent of public-health expenditure goes to the CGHS, which covers less than 0.5 percent of the population. It has been suggested, instead, that all formal-sector employees should be covered under a single mandatory scheme modeled on the ESIS (Gupta and Trivedi 2005, 4138–4139). If informal labor is formalized and if it is agreed that "minimum wages should satisfy to some extent the need for education, medical aid and other conveniences" (Report of the Committee on Fair Wages 1948, para. 10; cit. Breman 1996, 194), then such a scheme would also cover employees who are currently informal. Self-employed workers could also choose to be covered by paying the same percentage of their earnings as employees. Instead of excluding *employees* earning more than a certain sum, it would be better, as is the case with national insurance in the United Kingdom, to stipulate that only *pay* below that sum would be subjected to mandatory public health-insurance deductions. This would expand the coverage enormously and have a redistributive element.

However, it still would not meet the goal of "Health for All" unless the government expanded its expenditure on health massively compared to the rate of 0.9 percent of GDP in 2005 (Sharma 2005). This would happen only if the government were to provide a modest health-care package to all and spend whatever is necessary to do so out of its revenue. This would look something like the original idea of the National Health Service in Britain, but with all those who are earning, as well as their employers, making compulsory contributions and the government topping up. Such a system could provide universal coverage. It must be emphasized that only a state-run scheme could achieve this; any other form of health insurance would not have sufficient resources to undertake community health and preventive measures and would tend to leave out the poorest, especially women, who would continue not to get health care when they needed it (Gupta and Trivedi 2005, 4132). Contributions by the poorest, even if they were minimal, would enable them to feel a sense of ownership over the scheme and claim the right to representation on the boards running it.

Partnerships with nonprofit organizations could be helpful where the government is unable to provide the service required, but public-private partnerships run the risk of "moral hazard," where doctors overprescribe tests and medicines because they know the patient is insured (Acharya and Ransom 2005, 4149). A study of VimoSEWA, a health-insurance scheme organized by SEWA, found that over 40 percent of the hospitalization claims were for illnesses that were preventable or curable by primary or outpatient care; furthermore, 43 percent of the gynecological claims were for hysterectomies, with the average age of the patients being thirty-seven years and the youngest only twenty-two (Desai 2009). This suggests that unless health insurance is linked to an effective public health system, unnecessary expenditures and procedures could be recommended. Private providers should be tightly regulated. This would still result in a two-tier system—private health care for those who want and can afford it and public health care for all—but at least it would ensure that the latter reaches everyone and is of reasonably good quality. This issue is relevant to both developing countries and developed countries, as the recent heated debate over health-care reform in the United States has demonstrated.

Retirement Benefits

The Provident Fund (PF) is the main retirement benefit for private formal-sector employees in India. It was set up in 1952 by the Provident Fund and Miscellaneous Provisions Act. It includes a schedule that specifies which industries are covered by it, and additions are made periodically. Although workers in the small-scale sector are excluded, it covers contract and casual workers and even homeworkers employed through contractors (Mishra 2005). It requires 10 or 12 percent of a worker's wages to be cut and deposited in her or his account; that contribution is matched by the employer. At retirement, the worker would receive the entire sum, with interest; if a worker dies, the worker's family receives the sum. The Payment of Gratuity Act (1972) required employers to pay a lump sum at the rate of fifteen days' wages per year of service at the time of retirement, disablement, or death. Only government employees receive a pension from a noncontributory, defined-benefit scheme.

In 1971, the Employees' Family Pension Scheme (EFPS) was introduced. It involved the optional transfer of part of the employees' and employers' contribution to the PF—1.16 percent of wages from each—plus a government contribution of 1.16 percent to the new scheme, which would give employees a regular income in the event of disability or give their families an income in cases of death. In 1993, the government proposed to transfer the entire corpus of the EFPS to a new Employees' Pension Scheme. Part of the employer's contribution to the PF, amounting to 8.33 percent of wages, would also be transferred to this scheme, and, unlike the EFPS, it would be compulsory. If the worker died, his or her spouse would receive 50 percent of the benefit until remarriage, and the two oldest children would receive 12.5 percent of the benefit up to the age of twenty-five; thereafter, it could go to a nominee or dependent parent (EPFO n.d.).

The justification for this move from the standpoint of the government was that workers who received their entire retirement benefits in the form of lump sums might not be able to plan adequately for the future and might end up without an income in their old age. Some unions supported the idea, although they suggested modifications, such as linking the level of the pension to the cost-of-living index. However, employees' unions, with the Philips Employees' Union in the lead, waged a campaign against the scheme. Their main criticism was that workers would receive less than the amount they were getting from the existing PF scheme, which they had the option of investing at higher rates of interest or could use to buy a home, and they alleged that the scheme was designed so that a cash-strapped government could lay its hands on workers' savings (*Bombay Journalist* 1993; Shanbhag 1995; Majumdar 1996). Despite stiff opposition, the new scheme was put into effect by an ordinance in November 1995.

This debate has to be seen in the context of the conditions prevailing at the time. First, there was skepticism regarding the working of the PF. Unscrupulous employers deducted contributions from workers but deposited neither their own nor the workers' contributions with the fund, as workers found to their dismay when they tried to claim their entitlements. Moreover, on many occasions officers of the PF were found guilty of gross corruption, demanding bribes to dispose of claims, for example (Menon 2005b). As a result of inflation and the low rate of return due to the requirement to invest in government securities, the amount recovered at retirement was not much more than the amount paid in, and the option of making withdrawals from the fund prior to retirement meant that the amount remaining might be even smaller (Ahya 2001). The process by which industries were added to the schedule of those covered by the PF

Act was uneven and cumbersome, and of course the majority of workers in the small-scale sector were not covered (Mishra 2005). In the absence of adequate transparency and accountability, faith in the government's assurances was low. In addition, this debate raged during a period of high interest rates; those who were at the forefront of the opposition were educated workers who believed that they could invest the money in a more profitable manner.

The New Pension System (NPS), introduced by the government in January 2004 and available to new recruits to central-government employment, was based on defined contributions by the employee and the employer (the government). In December 2004, an ordinance set up an independent Pension Fund Regulatory and Development Authority (PFRDA) to regulate and monitor the new pension system. Four broad categories of pension fund would be licensed by the PFRDA, ranging from those investing in government securities only, with no risk, to those with a higher weighting of equity and therefore higher risk. The employee could choose one or more, and assets could be moved from one fund to another. At the time of retirement, the employee would get 60 percent of the accumulated amount as a lump sum, and the remainder would be annuitized to provide a reasonable pension. Many state governments decided to adopt the same system for new employees (GOI 2005).

If the aim was to solve the problem of the burgeoning pension liability of both central and state governments, given that the number of people above the age of sixty was growing at an annual rate of 3.8 percent between 1991 and 2001, compared with a growth rate of 1.8 percent for the general population (GOI 2005, 2), then the solution could not be faulted. However, the associated and, arguably, more pressing problem—that the overwhelming majority of the population received no retirement benefits whatsoever—was given short shrift. OASIS (the Old Age Social and Income Security project) submitted a report in January 2000 to the Ministry of Social Justice and Empowerment, suggesting that "Individual Retirement Accounts" could be opened anywhere in India by informal workers, that they would be "portable" as workers moved from one place to another or one job to another, and that fund managers would manage the funds and annuity providers would provide the benefit after the worker reached the age of sixty (GOI 2005, 4). There would be no contributions from employers or the government. This might be a suitable scheme for middle-class self-employed people, but for the bulk of informal workers, with below-minimum wages, irregular employment, and chronic indebtedness, and for unwaged workers, the majority of whom were women, it would not guarantee enough funds to live on in old age. The draft Unorganised Sector Workers' Social Security Bill (2005) also proposed a pension fund for informal workers.

The totally unthought-out nature of these ad hoc proposals became clear when the Punjab labor minister pointed out, at the fortieth session of the Indian Labour Conference in 2005, that in accordance with the PF Act, factories and industrial establishments deducted PF contributions from casual workers, most of whom were migrants. "Therefore, any casual worker would move in and out of the definition of unorganised sector worker time and again. This would create difficulty in implementing social security schemes for the unorganised sector workers" (*Tribune* 2005). This objection highlights the dangers of segregating informal workers into a separate category with different rights instead of bringing them within the scope of existing legislation. The final text of the Unorganised Workers' Social Security Bill (2008) merely says that "the Central Government shall formulate and notify, from time to time, suitable welfare schemes for unorganised workers on matters relating to— . . . (c) old age protection" and goes on to specify two such existing schemes in schedule 1, both of which suffer from all the inadequacies specified above.

What are the options, then? There are some on the left, both in India and abroad, who are ideologically opposed to pension funds investing in capital markets (cf. Varadarajan 2005; Minns 2001), but it seems hard to justify the argument that those who wish to invest part of their savings in such funds should be denied the possibility of doing so, nor is it clear that investment in government securities by itself would be able to fund adequate livelihoods for the growing number of people over the age of sixty. On the other hand, the opposite solution, which proposes that retirement benefits be completely privatized, cannot possibly guarantee an old age protected from want and indignity to everyone, least of all in a country such as India, since "defined-contribution schemes only provide participants with what they have put in plus the investment returns" (Minns 2001, 65). Clearly, "a purist strategy—relying only on the market or only on State action—can be awfully short of logistic means" (Drèze and Sen 1999, 29). It follows that some combination of the two would be the most practical. For example, there could be a basic, flat-rate, index-linked, defined-benefit pension available to everyone after retirement age, funded partly by mandatory contributions from employees, employers, and the self-employed and partly by state contributions from general taxation. The rationale for covering everyone by this basic scheme is that (a) those who are well-off early in life might fall into poverty in their old age; (b) even if they do not, their contributions would help to fund the pensions of the poorest, including unwaged workers; and (c) a universal scheme would be more durable. Consolidating the provision of basic pensions into a single scheme, instead of multiplying schemes and dividing them into those covering formal and informal workers, public- and private-sector workers, and so on, would ensure greater transparency and reduce overheads.

The basic pension could be enhanced by optional supplementary pension schemes of the type set up by the government's NPS. Here it would be important to ensure that contributors to the schemes should be well represented on the bodies administering them, which should be public or mutual rather than private, since the latter are more expensive and less accountable; this also opens up the possibility for them to monitor investments so that they conform to modest "ethical" criteria (R. Blackburn 1999, 38, 46). It is paradoxical that the investment of publicly controlled pension funds in the capital market has been criticized not only by the left but also by conservatives, who see it as promoting socialism (cf. M. Friedman 1999; cit. R. Blackburn 1999, 40), which points to its potential as a strategy for socializing capital.[6]

The idea that retirement benefits should be funded solely by individual savings does not recognize that poorly paid or unwaged workers may be doing work that is as socially useful as (or more useful than) the work done by those who can afford to invest large sums for their retirement. Nor does it take into account that after retirement these retirees may "perform other social, voluntary, group and family activities, such as (grand)childcare, community and charity work, all of which are not captured by quantitative measures such as GDP, or which are not set off against the devil of public expenditure, but which are crucial for many social and economic activities" (Minns 2001, 65–66). Given the impossibility that such workers could ever save enough to maintain themselves in their old age, the unspoken assumption behind such plans is that they will be supported by their children—who may be equally destitute or unwilling to support them—or that they will die before they reach the age of sixty, or that they can be left to beg or starve. These assumptions need to be made explicit and rejected. In 2006, India's average age was only twenty-six, which buys the country some time to solve the problem of securing adequate pensions for all. But it will require determination on the part of the government and flexibility on the part of unions if this goal is to be achieved.

Housing

Housing is an element of social security that has received too little attention in India, and the consequences are very visible. More than half the population of Bombay, for example, lives in shantytowns or on the streets. In this context, similar to the situation in many Third World countries, the need for public housing with subsidized rents is particularly important (NTUI 2009, 4). It is becoming equally so in developed countries, where the recent economic crisis has led to the loss of tens of thousands of homes.

Funding Employment Creation, Social Security, and Welfare

The most common argument against a comprehensive social-security and welfare system in India is that it would be unaffordable. This is based on the

> belief that these measures are inordinately "expensive." Several experiences of support-led security (particularly those that have succeeded in spite of a low GNP per capita, as in China, Sri Lanka and Kerala) suggest that this diagnosis is, at least to some extent, misleading. Indeed, the costs of social-security programmes in these countries have been in general astonishingly small.
>
> (Drèze and Sen 1999, 27)

Thus the real costs may be much smaller than envisaged by skeptics.

Abolishing informal labor and setting minimum wages at a level where they can include contributions toward social security and welfare would open up a large new area of funding, namely contributions by the large population of employers and employees who at present pay none. Even if each individual contribution were small, the contributions would add up to a considerable sum. Tax reform that eliminated arbitrary exemptions, imposed progressive taxation on all income above the taxable minimum, and enforced collection would also result in a huge increase of state revenue from taxes (Acharya 2005). There is absolutely no rationale for excluding agricultural income from taxation while taxing urban workers, especially given the emergence of a wealthy rural bourgeoisie:

> The Kanbi Patels have demarcated their domain by placing an access gate at the beginning and end of the street to the village centre. Their houses line the street in between. The new bungalows have two floors, the more recent among them, three. The architecture is incredibly elaborate and garish, but the wealth they radiate is unmistakable. . . . The former stall next to or opposite the house is now used to park a tractor or car. . . . The insides of the houses are . . . as ornate as the facades. Tiled walls, marble floors, settees, carpets, ceiling lights, and kitchens with all kinds of gadgets illustrate the conspicuous consumption of the nouveau riche.
>
> (Breman 2007, 359–360)

The contrast with the one- or two-room huts of their agricultural and domestic workers could not be starker, and to lump them all together in the same "agricultural" no-tax bracket makes no sense whatsoever.

Third, subsidies to capitalists are a drain on the treasury and could be dispensed with. It is true this would lead to the bankruptcy of yet more farmers and small industrial enterprises, but the elimination of petty producers is a law of capitalist accumulation, and to have capitalism while preventing the laws of accumulation from working can only be achieved by large and escalating subsidies that are unsustainable in the long run. The fifty-ninth round of the NSSO found that one-third of farmers did not even like farming, and 40 percent were prepared to give it up provided they could secure another job (Deshpande and Prabhu 2005, 4665). Proper social security and expanded employment-creation programs would let them do precisely that. Support for agricultural cooperatives would help those who wished to stay in agriculture to do so without constantly being threatened with bankruptcy.

Finally, the existence of an excellent social-security system in Costa Rica was attributed partly to the fact that it had the smallest informal sector in the region but also partly to its freedom from defense expenditure, due to its lack of any armed forces (Lago 1994, 42). Diverting a substantial part of India's massive military budget to social security and welfare would help to create an equally good system in India.

Realizing the Potential for Universal Social Security and Welfare Coverage

A progressive reduction of military expenditure has to be a global project. The logic of militarism is inherently competitive: if one state develops or acquires a certain type of military hardware, other states often feel compelled to do the same. It is hard to make headway in arguing against this logic; so long as there is any hint of conflict between states, unilateral or discriminatory disarmament will be hard to achieve. If there were enough pressure to make the United Nations return to its original purpose of saving the world from the scourge of war, and if the International Criminal Court were used to prosecute all military and political leaders guilty of war crimes and aggression, there would be movement toward a global order in which war itself would be outlawed. A global labor movement that pressured states to ratify and implement these treaties and to make progressive reductions in military research and the production and use of military weapons would be a powerful force working for the end of militarism, which would in turn release massive funds and resources for social security and welfare.

Comprehensive social-security and employment-generation programs would protect not only workers but also farmers, artisans, and capitalists driven out of business by the pressures of competition, enabling them to move into other occupations or form cooperatives in their original occupations if they so wished. Such programs would also be preferable to subsidies and protectionist policies, which may save employment in farming and protected industries but do so at the cost of taxpayers and consumers— including industrial consumers—of their products, thus resulting in an overall negative effect on employment (Bhattacharjea 2005). In developed countries, it has been recommended that the state's response to job losses resulting from globalization should be to provide a "form of protection that is not protectionism," by strengthening safety nets and assisting workers to find new jobs (Gould 2003, 96–99). Such a policy is needed equally urgently in developing countries. International cooperation to achieve this end would require workers and unions to make opposition to militarism a key element in their global strategy.

Social security and welfare is primarily an ethical issue: a society in which some people are wealthy cannot be considered humane if it relegates the unemployed and their families to starvation, allows sick people who cannot afford health care to die of preventable or curable diseases, or condemns large numbers of old people to a life of indignity. However, public investment in employment generation and social welfare also pays dividends for capital. In the context of a crisis, it generates employment in socially useful production, thus stimulating the economy. But even after a recovery has occurred, it still makes sense from the standpoint of capital as a whole. If, for example, electricity and health care are provided by the public sector, capitalists have to pay only the cost price of these for themselves and their employees. If they are provided by private suppliers, they have to pay not only the cost price but also the profit of the suppliers; their own costs are elevated and their rate of profit falls, depressing the average rate of profit and helping to push the economy toward another crisis. Governments that take the point of view of individual capitalists who make money out of the misery of the poor and instability of the whole system are both undemocratic and shortsighted.

[9]

International Strategies

How Does Globalization Affect Workers' Rights?

If trade unions throughout the world are to resist downward pressure on employment conditions, it is critical to establish how globalization affects labor rights and to agree on ways of counteracting its adverse effects. This has become even more important in the wake of the current economic crisis. Supporters of neoliberal policies hold that globalization is always beneficial and will automatically eliminate poverty (e.g., World Bank 1995, 47; Lal 2004, 9), and a cross-country comparison, which finds "strong evidence that countries with open trade policies have superior labor rights and health conditions and less child labor" (Flanagan 2004, 26), suggests that openness to the world economy does not undermine workers' rights and may even enhance them.[1] However, the opposite viewpoint is more common in the labor movement.

Antiglobalization protesters claim that globalization undermines labor rights. Efforts by employers and governments in countries such as India to dilute labor legislation, arguing that this is necessary in order to make their products globally competitive, also suggest that high labor standards are a disadvantage in a globalized economy. Both claims rest on assumptions that (a) where protectionist barriers to imports have been removed, high labor costs become a problem in competing with imports from countries where labor is cheaper, and (b) where capital can move freely, it will gravitate to countries where labor is cheaper and workers' rights weaker.

These assumptions should be treated with caution. Cheaper or more flexible labor is only one of the considerations that affect the choice of location for capitalist production. Proximity to markets, productivity, infrastructure, and the availability of a suitably qualified workforce could be equally or more important (Birnbaum 2000). It must also be remembered that even within one country, there can be a segmented labor market, with very different rights in the different segments. However, it seems reasonable to hypothesize that if productivity, infrastructure, and workforce quality are satisfactory, and transport costs are negligible or are more than offset by the lower costs of production, employers will choose a labor market with lower costs and greater flexibility. This is confirmed by experience. Jobs have been shifted from better protected and unionized workers to less protected, nonunionized workers, both within India and internationally. In India, there has been a steady movement of production from formal to informal labor, clearly because the latter is cheaper and more flexible, and one consequence of globalization is that a similar shift of production from developed to developing countries has taken place internationally.

A problem that has been highlighted somewhat less is the plight of migrant workers and the effect that this has on labor standards. Except within economic zones such as the European Union, immigration barriers block the free movement of labor, and thus when workers migrate for work to another country, they are frequently treated as "illegal." This means that they are not covered by local labor legislation and that they seldom join unions or participate in workers' struggles, for fear of being deported. Consequently, their wages and conditions tend to be poor, thus pulling down labor standards in the host country.

All these problems can be traced to the way in which labor law and workers' organizations have developed. Working-class internationalism and working-class nationalism were born at the same time, and this is not as strange as it may seem. When Marx and Engels wrote in the *Communist Manifesto* that "the working men have no country" and that "the proletarians have nothing to lose but their chains" (Marx and Engels 1973, 84, 98), they were stating that at that time, workers had no stake in the nation-state. They had nothing to gain from it and nothing to lose from its dissolution. On the contrary, nationalism and war were a source of loss, as workers in uniform were sent out to kill one another for a cause that was not their own. Thus internationalism made sense, as did the formation of the International Working Men's Association (First International) in 1864. Yet at the same time, workers could not afford to be left out of the regime of rights embodied in the nation-state. Restrictions on working hours, freedom of association, and the right to vote were all associated with citizenship of a particular nation-state. Collective bargaining without legal rights can be a successful strategy only for workers with industrial clout in a tight labor market. If wider layers of the working class are to benefit, and if the benefits are to last, the gains made by struggle need to be inscribed in labor law, and the first pillar on which labor law rests is the nation-state (D'Antona 2002, 33). Thus, paradoxically, as the trade union movement in Western Europe and the United States consolidated itself, the First International declined (van der Linden 1988, 332–333).

Social-democratic or labor parties allied with the trade union movement played a complementary role in assuring a steady improvement in the living standards of workers' families. With the development of social welfare, the fortunes of the working class became even more closely tied to the nation-state. The consequence was that nationalism and internationalism became inextricably entwined in the Socialist (Second) International (van Tijn 1988). "For most French and German socialists, the nation represented the constitutive building block of any internationalism" (Callahan 2000, 54). By the time of World War I, nationalism outweighed internationalism. Nominally working-class parties identified with the imperialist aims of their bourgeoisies to such an extent that they were willing to support them in the war (Adler 1978, 125–135; Lenin 1964, 193–194, 281–285). Those sections of the labor movement for whom internationalism was still a basic principle broke away to form the Communist (Third) International, but by then the labor movement was already firmly anchored to the nation-state. Between and after the world wars, the Trade Union Congress had close links with the British Foreign Office, while the AFL-CIO played a role in promoting U.S. imperialism and crushing democratic movements in the Third World (Thomson and Larson 1978; Spalding 1988; Press 1989a). Through the AFL-CIO, U.S. influence was also exerted on the International Confederation of Free Trade Unions (ICFTU) and International Trade Secretariats (ITSs).

Yet there remained a feeling that national strategies by themselves could not protect groups such as seafarers and migrant workers and that labor conditions in one country could affect workers' rights in another. Between 1889 and 1914, thirty-three ITSs (now called GUFs or Global Union Federations)[2] were formed, bringing national unions together on the basis of a trade or industry. The International Trades Union Secretariat (ITUS) was formed in 1901, becoming the International Federation of Trade Unions (IFTU) in 1913. The reestablishment of the IFTU after World War I and formation of the ILO in 1919 were both crucial to the universalization of the eight-hour working day (van Voss 1988).[3] Yet their role was a subsidiary one; the dominant role was played by national labor movements. This was just as true in the newly emerging nations of the Third World, including India. It is not surprising, then, that workers' rights and labor standards diverged widely from one country to another.

Globalization meant that a growing proportion of production was located in the Third World. Since "the effectiveness of labour-law strategies is undermined where capital has ways to escape regulated and/or unionized labour markets by shifting business or costs to low-wage, uncovered, and non-union labour markets at home or overseas" (Klare 2002, 6), the existence of cheaper labor in the Third World and poor coverage of labor law resulted both in the shifting of production out of First World countries and in downward pressure on workers' rights and welfare benefits in all countries. The inequalities, which had been less visible to First World workers so long as the international division of labor established by imperialism prevailed, now came to be seen as the cause of a "race to the bottom." It became a matter of urgency to "identify, analyse and respond to the conceptual and policy challenges posed by globalization," as scholars who came together under the auspices of the International Network on Transformative Employment and Labour Law put it (Conaghan et al. 2002, xxiii).

This chapter looks at the three broad strategies that emerged and examines the heated debates among trade unions on the issues raised by them. In the shadow of the recession, when protectionism is often seen as a necessary response to job losses and right-wing groups use rising levels of unemployment as a pretext for whipping up hatred and violence against immigrants, it is crucially important that the labor movement should have a principled and well-thought-out position on these issues.

International Union Action

Union responses to the internationalization of production have taken a multiplicity of forms, ranging from international collective bargaining to information exchange. The main impulse for these initiatives has come from unions in Western Europe and North America. In Third World countries, it is mainly the national union federations that are members of international union organizations. However, employees' unions and even informal workers in India have interacted with them on an ad hoc basis.

International Collective Bargaining

A strategy proposed in the 1970s by Charles Levinson, then general secretary of the International Federation of Chemical, Energy and General Workers' Unions (ICEF, now the ICEM), was international collective bargaining (Levinson 1972). The idea was that transnational companies would negotiate agreements covering all their subsidiaries, with ITSs or other international union bodies representing the workers in these plants, thus smoothing out the differences and disparities between them. In theory, this was a logical response to multinational corporations shifting production to subsidiaries in other countries, but in practice it failed to get off the ground. The greatest obstacle, undoubtedly, was employer resistance:

> A major problem in trade union relations with management in foreign affiliates of the multinational corporations lies in the decision-making authority. A number of such companies assert that all decisions relating to manufacturing, finance, capital investment and marketing of products rests wholly with the parent organisation. The field of labour relations, however, is excepted. Management in the subsidiary, according to stated company policy, is responsible for industrial relations, especially collective bargaining.
>
> (Bendiner 1987, 25)

This strategy "effectively insulates the management levels where the major decisions are made from bargaining pressures" and "enables the companies to utilise poor employment conditions and lack of union rights in some parts of the world by appealing to the principle of not interfering with local practices" (Banaji and Hensman 1990, 20).

There were also problems from the union side. Cold-war divisions in the international union movement were an impediment to international bargaining; indeed, "at one point in the mid-1970s Charles Levinson himself attacked rank-and-file leaders in the rubber industry when they organised transnational action in Europe involving the French CGT and the Spanish Comisiones Obreras, both seen as 'communist'" (Munck 2003, 149).

Other problems from the union side were a lack of support for international bargaining from national trade unions due to fear of losing their "sovereignty," a lack of support from union members, differences between national industrial-relations systems, and lack of an international framework (Press 1984, 95). The first of these problems was addressed by International Framework Agreements (IFAs), pioneered in 1989 by the agreement of the IUF[4] with Danone on union rights, equality, and non-discrimination. As the IUF explained, IFAs "do not seek to substitute in any way for local or national collective bargaining. . . . The work of the IUF in this area is best seen as international bargaining aimed at protecting and enlarging the space in which IUF affiliates organise and bargain" (IUF 2000; cit. Wills 2002, 685).

By 2004, there were twenty IFAs in existence. A study of the IFA on trade union rights (TURA) between IUF and Accor, the French-owned hotel chain, showed that there were instances where the IFA had been used successfully to support union organizing in affiliates of the company, although there were also instances where the efforts failed (Wills 2002). Another study of attempts to negotiate IFAs, by the International Textile, Garment, and Leather Workers' Federation, showed that although they solved the problem of encroachment on the "sovereignty" of local unions, they were dogged by all the other problems facing international collective bargaining, especially differences between national industrial-relations systems and the lack of an international legal framework (Miller 2004). In the garment industry, the widespread use of subcontracting posed an additional difficulty.

These case studies demonstrate the serious constraints faced by international collective bargaining. The overwhelming majority of collective agreements are negotiated within the framework of national labor laws, and there is an implicit understanding that if one party reneges, the other can appeal to the state for redress. There is no such mechanism for the enforcement of international agreements; they depend solely on the bargaining power of the protagonists. Yet globalization erodes the bargaining power of labor severely, due to the fundamental asymmetry between the mobility of capital and the relative immobility of labor. Companies can— and do—shop around for labor-law regimes that suit them, whereas even if all immigration barriers were to be removed (and the opposite is occurring), only a small minority of workers would choose to uproot themselves and move away from relatives and friends to an alien environment (cf. Langille 2002, 143). Correcting this disparity requires "a labour law that is no longer identified with the nation-state" (D'Antona 2002, 39). If there is to be significant progress in international collective bargaining, "it is arguable that labour law can no longer rely on the nation-state as the only relevant community . . . it must seek an alternative, or a complementary community" (Mundlek 2002, 282).

The only existing institution that could possibly develop into such a community is the ILO; indeed, the original trade union conception of the ILO was that it would be supported by an International Labour Parliament, which "should not merely adopt international conventions without binding force, but should pass international laws" (Fimmen 1922, 7). The ILO "failed to realize the high hopes of an international labour parliament with legislative and executory powers some socialists had cherished" at its inception (van Voss 1988, 524), but the possibility of pushing it toward that goal has reemerged. A possible step in this direction was the adoption by the International Labour Conference (the annual conference of the ILO) in 1998 of the *ILO Declaration on Fundamental Principles and Rights at Work and Its Follow-up*, in which seven "Core Conventions" were deemed to be fundamental to the rights of human beings at work and a precondition for obtaining all other rights. Whereas previously it was assumed that states were under an obligation to implement only those conventions they had ratified, the declaration stated that "all Members, even if they have not ratified the Conventions in question, have an obligation, arising from the very fact of membership in the Organization, to respect, to promote and to realize . . . the principles concerning the fundamental rights which are the subject of those Conventions," namely, freedom of association and the right to organize and bargain collectively, the elimination of all forms of forced or bonded labor, the abolition of child labor, and the elimination of discrimination in employment and occupation (ILO 1998, 7).[5] This declaration was the outcome of suggestions in a 1994 report by the then director-general of the ILO, Michel Hansenne.

It has been suggested that the vagueness of the wording of the declaration, the failure to name the actual conventions being referred to, the soft monitoring system proposed, and the enthusiastic support for it by the United States (which had previously evinced hostility to the ILO and great reluctance to ratify any of its conventions)[6] indicated that the declaration would be used to further dilute the existing system of protecting workers' rights (Alston 2004). This could certainly occur, but such an outcome is not inevitable. Unions, employers, and governments of the 177 member states of the ILO have accepted these conventions as in principle applying globally to all workers, and this fact can be used to move toward an international labor-law regime that provides the legal foundation for international collective bargaining. It may be a goal that is still far in the future, but if international unions spearhead a global campaign to achieve it, they could eventually be successful.

Successful international bargaining would in addition require global unions to reorganize so as to encourage the active participation of employees' unions and organizations of informal workers in the Third World and initiate a democratic discussion of what the objectives of international bargaining should be. This may not be easy. World Corporation Councils (WCCs), which brought together unions organizing in the same multinational in different countries, were pioneered by the International Metalworkers' Federation, with the purpose of strengthening the bargaining position of local unions and bringing about harmonization of working conditions and regional parity in pay (Press 1989b, 22–23). By 1974, there were WCCs in over forty companies, but they were launched almost exclusively in Western Europe and North America, and union participation in them could have been motivated more by the desire to protect jobs and conditions in the First World than by a spirit of genuine solidarity (Olle and Schoeller 1977). Indeed, a study of European works councils showed that even within the European Union, in a situation of "relocation (or possible relocation) of production and the choice of sites for new investment . . . the urge for survival precluded any interest in forging solidarity between plants" (Wills 2001, 192). Evidently, considerable preparation is needed before genuine international bargaining can take place. Evolving a network structure rather than a top-down one, and using alternative means of communication, including the Internet (Waterman 1988, 2001), would facilitate a discussion of objectives and strategies that are genuinely in the interests of all workers and that cut across national and other differences.

Research, Workers' Education, Networking, and Solidarity Action

Information exchange between workers and unions in different countries, solidarity action, and workers' education on international issues have been pursued both by international unions and by other groups. Unlike transnational collective bargaining, these are activities in which both formal and informal workers in India have participated.

One of the most spectacular successes of international solidarity was support for workers in a Coca-Cola bottling plant in Guatemala City in the 1980s by the IUF, other unions, church groups, human-rights organizations, and solidarity and public-interest groups. Against heavy odds, including a powerful multinational and an extremely repressive state, this support enabled sacked workers to be reinstated, the union to be recognized, and the plant to be reopened when the company tried to close it down to break the union (*International Labour Reports* 1984; Gatehouse 1989). In this case, the global union federation played a decisive role in the success.

In other cases, such as this attempt by Ford workers, the global union was less helpful:

> The IMF has a rule that all contacts between more than two unions . . . must take place through the IMF. So if you want to organise anything, even if you want to get information . . . you must ask your union official; that official goes to the international representative of your union; he sends a letter or telegram to Geneva; Geneva distributes it to the different national unions in the different countries; they ask the convenor or maybe the union official at the specific plant; and the information eventually gets back to Geneva, and from Geneva to your union. . . . We once went through this formal procedure in relation to a strike at the Valencia plant in Spain. . . . It took about six months and even then we got an answer which did not tell us what we wanted to know. . . . In any case, after six months the information was not needed any more.
>
> (Cartier 1989, 61–62)

Not surprisingly, these Ford workers decided to work through informal networks instead.

Most examples of information exchange and solidarity action organized by global unions fall somewhere between these two extremes, demonstrating the potential for internationalism as well as the restrictions posed by bureaucratic structures and procedures. But unlike collective bargaining, this is an area where organizations and groups other than unions can, and do, play a significant role. For example, in the course of its work the URG made contact with the Labour Research Department, Transnationals

Information Centre (London) (TICL, no longer in existence), Transnationals Information Exchange, SOMO (Centre for Research on Multinational Corporations), *International Labour Reports,* (also no longer in existence), *International Union Rights,* Women Working Worldwide (WWW), and the Clean Clothes Campaign (CCC), among others. Research carried out by these organizations and the reports published by the magazines are mainly useful as resources for information exchange and workers' education. However, by forwarding or publishing appeals for help, they also facilitate solidarity action.

In the 1990s, the IUF had a sustained presence in India, funding research into companies in its area of concern and conducting workshops for unions where they could exchange experiences and learn the outcome of the research. This was supplemented by information from foreign participants, including attempts to map the global strategies of major multinationals. The ICEM had a similar program. These programs stimulated information exchange between trade unionists from different companies and different parts of the country and also included an element of workers' education, enabling unions to locate their own experience within the larger picture.

The IUF also extended support to the HLEU, which was attempting to organize an all-India federation of Unilever workers in the face of extreme resistance by the company. Most importantly, it presented instances of anti-union harassment of HLEU unionists to the ILO Committee on Freedom of Association in 1992 and followed these up subsequently. The complaints included (1) police interrogation of the organizers of an IUF seminar and instructions that participants from Pakistan report to the police daily; (2) harassment and dismissal of union leaders from various locations involved in the attempt to form a federation; and (3) forced transfer of six union officeholders from the Bombay factory to other locations (ILO-CFA 1995). As a result of ILO pressure on the government to redress these complaints, some of the dismissed unionists were reinstated, and the six officeholders were transferred back to the Bombay factory.

The WWW project on codes of conduct and subcontracting chains was also essentially an exercise in research, education, and information exchange. Linking up labor activists in nine Asian countries, the United Kingdom, and Bulgaria, it created awareness of the existence of codes among women workers who had never heard of them, stimulated discussion of the pros and cons of codes as a measure to support workers, and organized international conferences where the exchange of information and experience between these different countries could take place. A similar program was carried out by the Central American Women's Network. This encouraged identification of women workers in one country with those in others suffering from similar problems, highlighted global production chains, and helped workers to learn from others who had more experience with codes.

Unfortunately in Bombay, due to the extremely decentralized character of the garment industry, it was impossible to use this knowledge to help local workers to organize. Yet there was an instance of solidarity in the reverse direction: workers in Bombay assisted workers in the United States to organize. The Indianapolis facility of the U.S. catalogue-apparel distributor Brylane was a subsidiary of Pinault-Printemps-Redoute (PPR), one of the largest retailers and distribution firms in the world, which owns well-known brands including Gucci and Yves Saint Laurent. When workers at Brylane faced resistance to their attempt to organize a union, they launched a worldwide campaign against PPR. The basic thrust of this campaign was that PPR was using sweatshop labor in several Third World countries. As it happens, women working for Patel Hosiery Mills, a supplier in Bombay, were involved in the WWW project on subcontracting chains, and information supplied by them, supplemented by interviews with male factory workers, was passed on to UNITE (the U.S. Union of Needletrades, Industrial, and Textile Employees), which was trying to organize the union at Brylane. This information, along with information from other Third World suppliers, was also taken up by campaigners such as CCC and publicized widely, reaching newspapers including the *Independent* (Milmo 2002) and *Libération* (Losson and Pons 2002).

Over the course of the campaign, UNITE produced the glossy *Brylane Sweatshop Holiday Catalogue 2002*, with pictures of Brylane workers displaying clothes distributed by the company. But the text exposed the abuses of workers' rights in suppliers across the world and at Brylane itself. When it was translated for garment workers in Bombay, they listened intently and sympathetically both to the stories of other Third World workers and to those of the American workers. Later, Bruce Raynor, the president of UNITE, wrote to us:

I am excited to announce to you that Brylane workers and UNITE have won official union recognition at Brylane's distribution centers in the state of Indiana. . . . In addition, in response to UNITE's public reports of the working conditions that workers endure at Brylane's sourcing factories . . . Brylane announced that it has adopted a Code of Conduct which incorporates the core labor rights of the International Labor Organization (ILO) and is intended to cover workers at all suppliers of PPR's Redcats division, of which it is a part. We congratulate and thank you for your assistance and solidarity which played an important part in achieving this progress.

The letter went on to observe that the Code of Conduct was not sufficient to address the serious abuses of labor rights at PPR's suppliers, nor were there satisfactory monitoring mechanisms, although they intended to press the company to strengthen them. Yet when the letter was translated for the workers, many women broke into spontaneous applause, thrilled that they had helped workers in another country to win recognition for their union.

As this example shows, information exchange can sometimes cross over into solidarity. The most extended case of this occurred after the Bhopal disaster. In the face of government hostility, and especially after Union Carbide closed down the plant and the workers occupied it, the GPRS in Bhopal and TURF in Bombay (see chapter 5) appealed in desperation to the international community. The response came in many forms. Those who had earlier approached the URG for information wrote articles to publicize more widely the information we provided. For example, Sheril Berkovitch of Australia Asia Worker Links, which had fifteen trade union affiliates, complained that mainstream media reports "grossly underestimated the extent of death and illness," were "less than supportive of the people's point of view," and "hardly mentioned the workers point of view at all and did not talk about the lack of safety precautions." She wrote articles disseminating the information we had provided and helped to publicize the campaign. Michael Jacobs published articles that included a description of the TURF relief center and the alternative plan and appealed for funds to be channeled through TICL (Jacobs 1985a, 1985b).

Letters of solidarity poured in. There were too many to list, but it is worth quoting a few. A branch of the Transport and General Workers' Union wrote, "The 1/128 Branch wishes to let you know that they support your action in trying to keep the Bhopal plant of Union Carbide open producing non-hazardous, cheap and useful goods." The Leicestershire branch of the Community and Youth Workers' Union wrote: "We are writing to offer our support, to let you know that we have today sent £11.50 for your campaign funds. It is only a small amount of money, collected at our Branch meeting, but we hope it will help you in your fight. Although our work is very different from yours, our struggle is the same—for equality and control over our own lives." TICL sent the UCIL Employees' Union a check for Rs 2,940[7] "as a contribution to the union's funds to keep up the fight against Union Carbide. Money is still being sent in and we hope to send on more soon as a small contribution to the struggle."

In 1989, after the Supreme Court had announced a settlement that outraged survivors of the disaster and their supporters, TICL organized a tour of England and Ireland by the activist Satinath Sarangi and three gas victims: Chander Singh, who had lost his job as a cook because his lungs could not stand ordinary kitchen fumes after exposure to the gas; Bilkis Bano, who could not continue working as a seamstress because her eyesight had been affected badly; and Sunil, who had been only twelve at the time of the disaster and had lost his parents, two brothers, and three sisters. During their tour they met, shared platforms with, and demonstrated alongside trade unions and community groups fighting against hazardous production and cost cutting at the expense of health and safety.[8] The visit was an expression of organized international solidarity not in the sense of one-way support for an individual struggle but in the stronger sense of mutual support in a shared cause. This was a striking departure from earlier actions around Bhopal and a clear break with the media image of Third World disaster victims as passive and helpless. In meeting after meeting, the delegation not only requested support for their struggle but also expressed solidarity with local campaigns against health hazards. And the audience, warmly welcoming support for their own actions, in turn pledged their backing to the Bhopal survivors, not simply as victims in need of help but as "fighters in the forefront of a battle . . . demanding international concern and action" (Hensman and BGJB 1991, 12).

These interactions highlighted the need for legal measures to deal with "corporate violence" (Bergman 1993). The pattern of violence in Bhopal, the aftermath in which the government and Supreme Court of India caved in to Union Carbide (see chapter 5), and the Chernobyl disaster, which occurred a few years later, all underscored the necessity for such measures to be international, so as to halt the export of hazardous processes to the Third World and to prevent poor health and safety standards in one country from having devastating effects on others.

An international initiative involving homeworkers was HomeNet, which in the 1990s carried out research, linked homeworkers and the organizations supporting them in many countries including India, and was instrumental in pushing through the Convention on Home Work in the ILO. This led to the formation of the Federation of Homeworkers Worldwide in 2006, with a "common platform of key demands: for social protection including health insurance; the right to organise; decent pay for all work; recognition of their contribution to the economy; education and training, and laws and protection for homeworkers. Organising was seen as the key tool for gaining rights" (Delaney 2007).

Common Goals and Strategies

Successful international collective bargaining may still be some way off, but where workers and unions have common goals and strategies, they can act in a coordinated fashion to push through measures that will benefit workers everywhere. Arriving at such goals and strategies requires the broadest possible discussion. Some of the issues that have arisen are: How can the basic rights of informal workers be protected? What can unions do to ensure that adequate resources are allocated to social welfare and the reproduction of labor power? Is international collective bargaining desirable, and if so, how can it be organized? How can unions take up issues of health and safety on an international scale? Below, two more issues are raised: Can workers make use of voluntary codes of conduct, and if so, how? And should a workers' rights clause be included in WTO agreements, and if so, how should it be framed? All these issues are of vital importance to unions in the epoch of globalization. Organizing discussion around them is therefore another important area of activity for unions internationally, as well as for other labor-rights organizations. The formation of the ITUC in 2006, and the fact that trade unions from most countries in the world, including the former Soviet Union and Eastern bloc countries, are members, would facilitate this activity.

One obvious point is that such a discussion would have to be conducted in a number of languages if ordinary workers are to take part in it. A major strength of the WWW project was the allocation of adequate resources for translation: how, otherwise, could Sinhala-speaking workers in Sri Lanka realize what they had in common with Spanish-speaking workers in El

Salvador, or Marathi-speaking workers in Bombay provide information to support the unionization of American workers in Indianapolis? This is an area where international unions could also provide assistance. Web sites such as LabourStart (Lee 2005), which publish items such as the ILO Core Conventions in many languages, are another way of providing a translation service. Going further, we might ask: should unions be developing an international language, or at least a small number of international languages, which would enable union delegates to communicate directly with each other at meetings? This would certainly be useful. Discussion involves dialogue, dialogue is a process of communication, and having a language in common makes communication faster and easier. This question itself would be one worth discussing internationally.[9]

Codes of Conduct

It was not so much unions as consumer campaigners and development NGOs in Western Europe and North America that took up the challenge posed by large-scale international subcontracting. Appalled at the conditions in which the food they ate and the clothes they wore were produced, they campaigned against large retail and brand-name companies selling products made by workers whose basic rights had been violated, threatening them with a loss of sales. The first response of companies in the garment industry, which was restructuring in a way that "increased the power of retailers and newly emerging brand names and at the same time exposed them more to public scrutiny" (Shaw and Hale 2002, 102), was to deny that they were responsible for employment conditions in the countries where their suppliers were located. But the campaigners persisted. When the *Washington Post* published an article in 1992 on the production of Levi's jeans by Chinese prison labor in Saipan, Levi Strauss responded by adopting a code of conduct for all its overseas suppliers (Shaw and Hale 2002, 103). Other companies followed suit, as activists exposed the sweatshop conditions under which the products of market leaders were produced (Klein 2000, 327–329; Jenkins et al. 2002, 3).

Most of the company codes included child labor and forced labor, because these were seen as emotive issues; very few included freedom of association and the right to collective bargaining or referred to the ILO Core Conventions (Jenkins 2002, 19). This was seen as a danger by campaigning organizations such as the CCC. They developed model codes, based on ILO conventions and highlighting freedom of association and the right to organize and bargain collectively, in order to forestall the adoption of much weaker company codes (Ascoly and Zeldenrust 2002, 174). Another model code was developed in Nicaragua by the Movimiento de Mujeres Trabajadoras y Desempleadas Maria Elena Cuadra (MEC) (Prieto et al. 2002). These model codes were much stronger than corporate codes, and they were developed in consultation with the workers who would be affected by them and therefore included issues affecting women workers (such as sexual harassment and lack of protection for pregnant women), which were absent from most other codes (Pearson and Seyfang 2002). A parallel development was the emergence of multistakeholder codes agreed upon by companies, unions, and NGOs that had worked on model codes. For example, the Ethical Trading Initiative (ETI) was established in Britain in 1998 and later experimented with tripartite pilot projects for monitoring suppliers (Blowfield 2002). A similar initiative was the Fair Wear Foundation (FWF), established in the Netherlands in 1999 (FWF 2003).

While codes of conduct were becoming popular in First World countries, however, most of the workers they were supposed to protect were not even aware of their existence. The WWW education and consultation project on codes of conduct was an attempt to fill this gap (Hale and Shaw 2001).

Responses to Codes of Conduct from Workers—and Researchers—in India

The first step was a preliminary consultation with three small groups of workers, none of whom knew anything about codes other than what we presented.[10] This was followed by a series of educational workshops with larger groups, over the course of which workers were taken through a Marathi-language version of the WWW education pack (WWW 1998a). Part of the exercise was to build up a picture of the production chains they were involved in, by collating information collected by the women with information that we, the researchers, could gather through our contacts, the Internet, and so on. The workers in one factory, Go Go International, did excellent detective work, getting office staff to photocopy a list of the factory's sixty-four buyers, located in twelve different countries. Others knew very little about whom they were producing for or where their production went, although they were eager to collect and show us labels from the garments they worked on. Discussions were in small groups, and one person in each group wrote down responses that were then shared with everyone.

Most felt that workers could get something out of codes of conduct; as one of them put it, "*Anything* which can help us is welcome." Others were more skeptical. "If a company abides by these rules, it would lose orders!" said Kusum. "They won't be much use," said Tanuja, "because no one will come to check. It's more important to have good legislation."[11] Bhanu agreed, and when we asked, "Suppose there is some agency here that *will* inspect regularly?" replied, "Then the owners won't allow them inside the factories!" We asked, "What if that too could be arranged?" Tanuja felt that then it would be important to train workers, because they *could* monitor the codes. A homeworker felt that "most of these rules are not applicable to homeworkers." All the women felt that codes could not work unless there were penalties for violating them, such as boycotts of retailers/brand-name companies and loss of contracts for suppliers. Usha, a homeworker, said that "maybe codes would result in some small units closing down and the workers losing their jobs, but that is already happening anyway."[12] At a discussion on codes of conduct organized by the CCC in Bombay, formal-sector unionists belonging to both central unions and employees' unions felt that codes could help to defend the rights of garment workers (CCC and CEC 2002, 16–18).

Even those who were in general positive about codes felt that effective monitoring was crucial and that codes could work only if there were inspections every two or three months. "Would they have to visit every homeworker?" we asked, to which Manisha replied, "No, the workers should have a place where they can go and complain." There was a general consensus that workers needed to be involved in monitoring and for that purpose should be informed about the codes through the notice board, television, and training programs. At the same time, they feared that if management came to know about the involvement of workers in training programs or monitoring, they would lose their jobs. Therefore they felt that if workers were involved in training about codes of conduct, management should not know about it and that any information supplied by workers should be completely confidential. The place where they gave information or made complaints should not be too near their place of work, otherwise they might be seen by informers and reported to management, nor should workers be involved in putting pressure on management, because it would expose them to dismissal. The women felt the need for help with obtaining information about production chains and for a group to mediate between themselves and consumer organizations. All felt that improving and implementing legislation was as important as codes, if not more so (WWW 1998b, 2002).

Over the course of our project, there were in fact two occasions during which the efficacy of codes was tested. One was when the workers of Go Go International joined a union in 1999; they were dismissed and their workplace was closed down. Since two of the companies buying from them—Carrefour and Kappahl—had codes of conduct, we tried to put pressure on Go Go through CCC. But this did not result in reinstatement of the workers, although threats of bad publicity did persuade the company to give them their unpaid dues and retrenchment compensation. In this case, we could understand why pressure failed to work, because even if two out of Go Go's sixty-four buyers threatened to cancel orders, the company could afford to let them go.

The case of Prakash Garments at first seemed more promising, because one of its major buyers, the Dutch company Zeeman, was participating in the FWF pilot project. When 151 of the two hundred and fifty workers in Prakash Garments joined the SSS in 2002, the company first threatened that the officeholders would be dismissed and the workers thrashed by goons. The union responded by filing a complaint under the MRTU and PULP Act in the Industrial Court, appealing that no worker should be dismissed unlawfully and that the employer should not be allowed to shift or sell machinery, outsource production, or employ a new group of workers to replace those who had joined the union. But the company defiantly started subcontracting production to smaller units, declared a partial lockout affecting these workers, and effectively made it clear that they had been dismissed. When it received this information, FWF requested Zeeman to put pressure on Prakash Garments to reinstate the workers, but Zeeman first prevaricated and then, apparently, withdrew from FWF (for details, see WWW 2003a, 90–103).

The case of Fibres and Fabrics International Pvt. Ltd. (FFI) and its subsidiary Jeans Knit Pvt Ltd. (JKPL) in Bangalore demonstrated the lengths to which Indian companies were prepared to go to sabotage codes of conduct. FFI and JKPL were producing for the Dutch label G-Star and the U.S.-based brands Tommy Hilfiger, GUESS, and Ann Taylor. Workers told the Garment and Textile Workers' Union (GATWU), NTUI, Women

Garment Workers' Front (Munnade), and Civil Initiatives for Development and Peace (CIVIDEP) that they were being subjected to verbal and physical abuse; forced to meet high production targets with unpaid overtime; not being issued appointment letters or identity cards; deprived of the mandated crèche, canteen, and restroom facilities; and fired without warning. In July 2006, these local unions and NGOs were issued with a restraining order by the court, preventing them from circulating information about labor conditions in FFI and JKPL to organizations abroad. Despite this gag order, reports based on the information supplied by workers were sent through the CCC to companies sourcing from FFI /JKPL.

G-Star showed an inclination to dump these suppliers—that is, to "cut and run." Ann Taylor sent third-party monitors who confirmed the complaints and requested FFI/JKPL to take remedial steps. Tommy Hilfiger said they had already stopped sourcing from these companies. GUESS did not respond. Meanwhile, management met with GATWU and NTUI, and some changes, including the cessation of unpaid overtime, took place. But other abuses continued, and the company threatened the CCC, the India Committee of the Netherlands (ICN), and two Dutch Internet providers with legal proceedings, for offenses including criminal defamation and cybercrime, should they fail to remove all articles referring to the denial of workers' rights in FFI/JKPL from their Web sites, and to refrain from appealing to buyers to put pressure on these companies. In June 2007, the CCC, ICN, and the Dutch Internet providers Antenna and Xs4stall were summoned to appear in a Bangalore court, and in September the court issued arrest warrants against seven activists of the CCC and ICN and a representative of Antenna. Amnesty International took up the case, a solidarity campaign for the Dutch activists was launched, FFI's main buyer G-Star stopped sourcing from FFI/JKPL, and the Dutch government stepped in to mediate. The case was finally settled in January 2008, with FFI agreeing to drop all cases against the local and Dutch unions, NGOs, and Internet companies and to respect the workers' right to join a union of their choice. A local ombudsperson was appointed to handle complaints. Based on this agreement, G-Star resumed orders (CCC 2008).

As these examples show, making codes work is not easy. From the standpoint of researchers and monitors, there were two major problems. First, research into long subcontracting chains is extremely difficult. Workers at one factory were able to get a full list of buyers, but this was an exception. At the other end of the spectrum were homeworkers who got their work through a contractor and did not know where it came from. Others could identify the small "job work" unit from which they got work but had no idea where it went from there. These were sweatshops that subcontracted work from different factories at different times, and the factories, likewise, shifted work between different subcontractors, so the chains were constantly shifting at the lower levels. Establishing which small sweatshops and homeworkers were working for which brand-name company or retailer would have required an army of full-time researchers. Second, monitoring, likewise, would be a time-consuming activity if done conscientiously. As the women workers said, it would require unannounced inspections at the production units every two or three months, plus a constant presence so that homeworkers (and others) could come and make complaints.

Indeed, all the country-based studies found that as a result of these problems, monitoring was carried out only for first-tier suppliers. Suppliers also complained that (1) it was confusing and a waste of time to have multiple codes: standard compliance norms would be better (cf. Sabarinath 2003); (2) buyers put contradictory pressures on them, for example insisting they pay minimum wages while paying prices that were too low to allow for that, or saying that there should not be compulsory overtime while imposing impossibly stringent delivery schedules; and (3) they were afraid that if they invested in improvements—for example, better working conditions—their buyers would abandon them for cheaper suppliers.

Problems with Codes

These difficulties are common to other situations where codes of conduct have been endorsed by companies. For example, research in South Africa and Kenya found that worker interviews, though crucial, were hard to get, since workers might fear losing jobs, be exhausted or busy with housework in the evenings, or have changed employment, and that mapping supply chains required "the skills of a detective as much as a researcher" (Barrientos 2002, 72, 61). Perhaps the most vexed issue was that of monitoring. When buyers did it themselves or hired audit firms to do it, the results were dismal. The Hong Kong Christian Industrial Committee (HKCIC) found that audits carried out for McDonald's and Disney in China by a major audit company, Société Générale de Surveillance, were announced beforehand, so that management had plenty of time to prepare: "HKCIC researchers have routinely talked to workers producing for Disney and McDonald's who have been coached on the 'correct' answers to give visitors, have participated in factory clean-up, and have been given personal protective equipment for the first time on the eve of an audit" (Kwan and Frost 2002, 128). A study of audits carried out in Shanghai and Seoul by the world's largest private monitor PricewaterhouseCooper found that the president of the factory selected workers for interview and that the auditor skipped crucial questions. "Audit reports glossed over problems with freedom of association and collective bargaining, overlooked serious violations of health and safety standards, and failed to report common problems with wages and hours" (O'Rourke 2002, 207; see also Yanz and Jeffcott 2001).

Private monitoring in the United States failed equally spectacularly. In the early 1990s, "GUESS? boasts about its pioneering role in monitoring and claims that its program is a model for the industry, yet violations of basic labor rights remain rampant not only in GUESS contractors but also in its own factory" (Esbenshade 2004, 2–3). Even in the rare cases where inspectors were conscientious and competent, it still did not make a difference. In an account that would make one cry if it were not so hilarious, a young sweatshop inspector describes his experience of monitoring a Calvin Klein supplier in Taiwan along with his trainer, whom he nicknames "Heart Attack":

> Heart Attack hands me the previous inspection team's violation list. It has some pretty damning violations. . . . I ask Heart Attack if he thinks the client will pull out of this factory soon, and he snorts derisively. "We've been here five times already, and every time the factory gets a high risk," says Heart Attack. "Calvin Klein won't pull out of this factory until we find 9-year-olds chained to arc welders and strung out on speed. The boss knows that we're only paper tigers."
>
> (Brown 2004, 211)

Shoddy monitoring fails to prevent ghastly tragedies: the Spectrum-Shahriar factories in Dhaka collapsed on April 11, 2005, killing seventy-four workers and injuring more than one hundred, despite the fact that they were supplying companies with codes (MSN 2005).

The fundamental problem here is a conflict of interest: the companies that do the monitoring, or hire audit firms to do it, are precisely the ones that profit most from violations of labor rights; in the words of one commentator, it is a case of "the fox guarding the chicken coop" (Dubinsky 2002). Even with an excellent code like that of Social Accountability 8000 (CEPAA 1998), the problem of effective monitoring remains. Labor Rights in China found that neither trainer nor trainees for SA 8000 had experience in labor rights; consequently, the accreditation of monitors as capable of verifying implementation of the code was highly suspect (LARIC 1999). Finally, if suppliers are not in compliance with the code, who pays for the improvements that are required? A disturbing yet predictable outcome is that suppliers make cosmetic improvements and pass the cost on to workers (Yimprasert and Candland 2000).

One solution is a completely different model: independent monitoring by labor-rights groups. The first instance of this occurred in El Salvador in 1995, when women and girls working at Mandarin International, a Taiwanese-owned *maquila* producing mainly for the Gap, responded to verbal and physical abuse, bathroom restrictions, and compulsory overtime by forming a union. When they were dismissed, the union federation appealed to the National Labor Committee in New York, which launched a large-scale publicity and solidarity campaign. A parallel campaign was organized in El Salvador. Eventually, both Gap and Mandarin agreed to independent monitoring by GMIES, a group formed by four religious and academic groups with expertise in labor rights. The sacked workers were reinstated, the union revived, and conditions in the factory improved. Similar initiatives in Honduras and Guatemala followed (Esbenshade 2004, 169–177).

In the United States, the Workers' Rights Consortium (WRC) was formed by United Students Against Sweatshops in opposition to the Clinton administration–sponsored Fair Labor Association (FLA), which was in theory tripartite but had a dominant employer presence. The WRC saw its role as verification of workers' complaints rather than monitoring, and unlike the FLA's reports, which were confidential, its reports were accessible to the public and could be used for campaigning (Esbenshade 2004, 177–197). Thus when workers in Kukdong, a Korean-owned factory in Mexico supplying college apparel to Nike and Reebok, were dismissed in 2001 after going on strike against poor employment conditions and denial of their right to form an independent union, the WRC produced a report and used it to press universities to reconsider their ties with Nike and Reebok. These companies then pushed Kukdong to reinstate the sacked workers, recognize the independent union, and negotiate with it (Armbruster-Sandoval 2005, 21–22).

What is the distinction between monitoring, verification, and campaigning? Monitoring is a long-term, sustained operation that can be done by companies, workers, unions, and/or NGOs; verification has to be done from time to time by some agency that is accepted by both sides as being impartial; and CCC and MSN are campaigning organizations, which may be consumer based, take up solidarity campaigns requested by workers, or both (Marshall 2005). Clearly, campaigning and independent monitoring and verification do not suffer from the same drawbacks as private monitoring, and their record in helping workers to win their rights has been much better. Their main disadvantage, according to a former activist of the WRC, is that their coverage is so small: a mere drop in the ocean compared to what is needed.[13]

Codes of conduct have been criticized for leading to loss of employment for informal workers, especially homeworkers, because companies shorten supply chains in order to monitor production more easily (Brill 2002). There is evidence that this has happened in India, with more than five hundred small exporting firms shutting down over the course of a year due to "global players . . . enforcing strict compliance for areas like social audits. . . . Most employees of these small firms, mainly workers, are being absorbed by their bigger brethren" (Sabarinath 2004). However, this could be seen as a positive development. The workers who suffer the worst employment conditions are those at the bottom of long supply chains (Hurley 2005, 96, 116); shortening them is therefore a condition for strengthening workers' rights. This need not mean that homeworkers cease to be employed: they could be employed by first-tier factories and organized effectively, as in Australia, provided legislation supports their rights and unions take up the task (HomeNet 1999a).

Perhaps the most serious criticism of codes of conduct is that making companies responsible for implementing ILO conventions, which are addressed to states, is inappropriate, because firms do not have the capacity to carry out the range of actions required to implement them (Murray 2002, 31). This is clearly true if we take, for example, the abolition of child labor. Companies can ensure that their suppliers do not employ underage workers, but this will not result in the abolition of child labor—indeed, it may result in driving child workers into more hazardous occupations. Abolishing child labor depends on ensuring that all children have access to a livelihood and education, which is the responsibility of governments, not companies.

Is It Worth Pursuing Voluntary Codes as a Way of Defending Workers' Rights?

There are skeptics who feel that "workers are protected only by the application of good labour laws and through their self-organization and collective bargaining" (Justice 2002, 93), and that therefore "it may be more productive to ensure that regulation is effective and applies to everyone . . . through strengthening existing regulatory mechanisms" (Dent 2002, 144). Yet a complete dismissal of codes of conduct risks ignoring the problem from which they arose in the first place. In India, for example, where violations of basic labor rights were rampant, the very fact that retailers and brand-name companies were demanding minimum standards from their suppliers served to counteract employer propaganda that being globally competitive meant undermining workers' rights (cf. Bheda 2002; Subramaniam 2003b).

A better strategy is to reshape codes and their implementation mechanisms so as to build on their limited strengths. For example, WWW activists had been pointing out for years that while codes of conduct specified standards that suppliers would have to meet, they did not recognize that the purchasing practices of retailers and brand-name companies could also be a source of violations (Hale 2000, 353). Thus a woman worker in India, protesting against compulsory overtime resulting from the reduction of delivery times from a month to fifteen days, asked, "What's the hurry? Will people in Europe and America have to go without clothes if we take a month to complete the order?"[14] This issue was brought up repeatedly at ETI meetings, was eventually taken up at a workshop in the biennial conference of 2003 (ETI 2003, 50–53), and had moved to center stage by the 2005 conference (ETI 2005). Codes could be reshaped to include purchasing practices, specifying that companies adopting them undertake to pay prices that enable suppliers to abide by them, rule out delivery schedules that cannot be met without compulsory overtime, and build stable relationships with suppliers so that they can invest in upgrading labor standards without fearing that their buyers will shift to cheaper suppliers. This would result in pressure to change being brought to bear on the companies that profit most from the labor of production workers yet are inaccessible to collective bargaining by them. Including these issues, as well as workers' rights, in binding contracts between buyers and suppliers would enable both sides to take legal action in the event of violation by the other and would also allow unions to intervene (Ashim Roy; cit. CCC and CEC 2002, 16).

The problem of monitoring and verifying compliance with codes also needs to be addressed. One workshop at the 2005 ETI conference sought to deal with the confusion and waste of resources arising from a multiplicity of codes by bringing together the key multistakeholder and model codes, and in another there was a mention of the ILO getting involved in monitoring and verification (ETI 2005). Having a common code with common guidelines for assessing compliance is crucially important if codes are to be at all meaningful (Posner and Nolan 2003, 212–214). Having a single organization with acknowledged expertise in workers' rights—the ILO— being paid by companies to carry out the audits would solve most of the existing difficulties in implementing codes. They would still be only one tool among many for protecting and extending workers' rights, but they would be a much better tool than they are at present.

A Social Clause Protecting Workers' Rights in WTO Agreements

The desirability of a social clause protecting workers' rights in multilateral trade agreements of the WTO has been the subject of heated debate within the trade union movement internationally, with institutions such as the ICFTU, GUFs, and unions in North America and Western Europe strongly in favor (Monks 1994). Others, such as all the party-affiliated national unions in India, are just as strongly opposed (Central Trade Union Organisations of India 1995).

Trade union bodies demanding a link between world trade and workers' rights claim that in its absence, trade liberalization *undermines* workers' rights by removing all obstacles to companies shifting production to (or importing products from) countries or sectors where workers' rights are weakest. This causes a "race to the bottom," with the average level of workers' rights globally falling lower and lower (Stone 1996; Lambert 1997). Hence, some trade unions have seen it as crucial to fix a minimum level below which labor rights will not be allowed to sink by inserting a workers' rights clause incorporating the ILO Core Conventions into WTO agreements.

Arguments for the Social Clause

Two distinct arguments inspire this demand, although it is not always easy to disentangle them. One might be called "employment protectionism" (the desire to protect jobs in one's own country) or the "social-dumping defense," which defines the violation of basic workers' rights as an unfair trade practice; the other is a straightforward human-rights argument (Chin 1998). Two examples illustrate this dichotomous reasoning. According to the initial social-clause proposal of the ICFTU, a joint WTO-ILO advisory committee would be set up to examine complaints of violations and formulate recommendations (such as implementation of laws and improvement of labor-inspection systems) to the erring government. The ILO might offer technical and possibly financial support for carrying out the recommendations. After two years, the advisory committee would draw up a second report. If the government was taking steps to tackle the problem but needed more time, an extension of one or two years could be granted. But if no "appropriate efforts" had been made, trade sanctions against the member state would be enforced, taking the form of "increased custom duties which shall be imposed on all exports of the defaulting state by all the GATT member states" (Haas 1999, 17–18). Here the procedure to be adopted in the case of a complaint seems to be inspired by concern for the human rights of workers in the country where the violation is alleged, but the unexpectedly savage penalty—which punishes not just the guilty but also the innocent (companies and industries where violations are not taking place, as well as their employees)—is clearly motivated by employment protectionism.

Another example makes this even clearer. In March 2004, the AFL-CIO lodged a petition alleging that "China's brutal repression of internationally recognized workers' rights constitutes an unfair trade practice" that was responsible for the loss of 268,345 to 727,130 jobs in the United States. It called on the U.S. trade representative and the president to impose commensurate trade sanctions against China and "to negotiate a binding agreement with the Chinese government to come into compliance with internationally recognized workers' rights" (AFL-CIO 2004; cit. Alston 2004, 474). Here, the concern for Chinese workers was indistinguishable from the preoccupation with saving jobs in the United States. The protectionist measures proposed in both cases—imposing wide-ranging trade sanctions—echoed the demands of U.S. employers with a domestic production base, suggesting a nationalist alliance between unions and a section of domestic capital rather than internationalist solidarity between workers (cf. Haworth and Ramsey 1988, 321).

Trade sanctions can help to combat human-rights violations in some cases. The sanctions against apartheid in South Africa are the best-known example; another was trade sanctions against slave-grown produce encouraged by the British and Foreign Anti-Slavery Society (now Anti-Slavery International), formed in 1839, as part of its campaign to abolish slavery (Ould 1995). But sanctions will not work if they fail to address the root cause of the violations. For example, when in 1994 the newly elected People's Alliance government in Sri Lanka announced that workers in free-trade zones would have the right to form unions and bargain collectively, strong pressure from foreign investors forced them to retreat (CCC 2001). Again, it has been observed that stabilization and structural-adjustment programs imposed by the World Bank and IMF often undermine basic workers' rights (cf. Gibbons 1999). Many Third World governments are simply too weak to resist powerful corporations, the IMF, or the World Bank, and weakening them further with sanctions would not help protect workers' rights. It is also relevant to ask: is the country that is asking for sanctions against another WTO member implementing all the ILO Core Conventions itself? Or is it, too, violating them? According to the ICFTU, the United States has been guilty of large-scale violations of the Core Conventions (Blackburn 1999): how, then, could it ask for sanctions to be imposed against another country for doing the same thing?

The worst consequence of this protectionist element in arguments for the social clause is that it has provided credibility to neoliberal arguments against it. By contrast, the human-rights argument—according to which the rights protected by the Core Conventions are fundamental and universal and should, therefore, be protected by all international treaties, including those of the WTO—has much greater moral force. Recasting the proposal in this framework would mean changing the language of the "social clause," and even "labor standards," which have been interpreted as including wage levels and working hours (cf. Brett 1995). Working out implementation procedures that are universally acknowledged by workers as being fair—and that cannot be used for protectionist purposes—would require inputs from Third World unionists who are willing to extend critical support to the proposal.

Debate on a Workers' Rights Clause by Unionists and Labor-Rights Activists in India

It is important to begin by noting that all the unionists and labor-rights activists participating in this debate agreed in principle that the human rights embodied in the ILO Core Conventions should be implemented in India.[15] This distinguished the position of even those who rejected the social-clause proposal from the position of employers, the government, and those who felt that it embodied "Western morality" (Lal 1999).[16]

The most popular argument against the workers' rights clause was that it was a protectionist measure and therefore against the national interest. According to P. K. Ganguly of CITU, "the attempt to include social clause in multilateral trade is essentially to introduce unilateral non-tariff protectionist barriers to multilateral trade" (Ganguly 1996, 45). K. L. Mahendra of AITUC observed: "The introduction of the social clause is to prevent exports from developing countries with a view to protect their own industry at home" (Mahendra 1996, 49). The HMS and INTUC, both affiliated to the ICFTU, also subscribed to these views. Vandana Shiva expressed the view that the social clause "is a one sided protectionist measure favouring developed countries without giving developing countries the right to protect their economies in specific areas which needed protection" (cit. Vivekanandan 1996, 152). The general reasoning behind this position was that "relatively cheap labour is one area where developing countries have a clear comparative advantage. . . . The objective of the developed countries [in introducing the social clause] seems to be to deprive the developing countries of this comparative advantage" (Dubey 1996, 24).

This argument received sharp rejoinders. According to Thomas Mathew of the Delhi General Mazdoor Front, "the question . . . arises as to why labour standards should be decided by individual countries while matters of trade and capital flows are decided globally or bilaterally" (Mathew 1996, 67). Sujata Gothoskar of the Workers' Solidarity Centre said: "This competitive edge is supposedly the miserable wage levels of the workers, the bad living and working conditions and the denial to them of basic human rights. Is it not shameful for us to argue about 'our advantages' in such a cynical manner? . . . With this argument, every struggle by the workers for a better life may be argued as eroding the competitive edge of our country" (Gothoskar 1996, 62). Srilata Swaminadhan of the Rajasthan Kisan Sangathan asked, "is 'national interest' to be decided by what benefits the minority or what benefits the majority?" She advocated, among other things, that labor activists should "insist on the linkage of the social clause with multilateral trade agreements" (Swaminadhan 1996, 55–58). Murlidharan of the Boehringer-Mannheim Employees Union observed, "it may be true that there are protectionist interests behind the social clause proposal. But the protectionist interests of the Lancashire millowners were behind most of our labour legislation, yet we have been able to use it to our advantage" (cit. Hensman 1998, 82–83). This position was endorsed by the journalist Praful Bidwai, who concluded that "given the pitiable performance of the government in safeguarding the interest of labour," trade unionists should see the social clause "as an opportunity to bargain with the government" (cit. Vivekanandan 1996, 161).

A striking characteristic of antiprotectionist arguments against the social clause is that they club together employers, workers, and governments in developed countries as having a common interest, and they do the same for developing countries. It was even alleged that "trade linked labour standards will function in the interest of MNCs" (Roy 1996, 181). Yet multinational corporations did not support the social-clause proposal; on the contrary, the exclusion of labor rights from the WTO agenda "suits the corporate interests of multinationals just fine" (Soros 2002). Indeed, as Bennet D'Costa of the HLEU pointed out: "Most of world trade consists of MNC products, so they will be hardest hit by the social clause" (cit. Hensman 1998, 83).

What this bizarre allegation revealed was a strong belief in a "national interest" that overrides class divisions. By contrast, supporters of the clause recognized divergent class interests and that "the suggestion for the inclusion of the social clause in the multilateral trade agreements has emanated from the workers' organisations in the developed countries" (Mathew 1996, 67). Harish Pujari of the Otis Elevator Employees' Union suggested that while it might be opposed to the interests of employers, "the social clause can't be used against workers, and we may be able to use it to our advantage, so why should we oppose it?" (cit. Hensman 1998, 83). The potential for using it to abolish child labor was also emphasized. Kailash Satyarthi of the South Asian Coalition Against Child Labour took the position that "a social clause is necessary that would not permit the trading of goods (use, sale, purchase, export, import) made by children" (Satyarthi 1996, 86), while Joseph Gathia of the Centre of Concern for Child Labour felt that "we need to support the inclusion of a social clause, but should not allow the developed countries to use it in their favour" (cit. Vivakanandan 1996, 167). Women garment workers felt that a workers' rights clause in WTO trade agreements, like codes of conduct, could be a tool in the struggle for their rights.

The second major argument against the social clause—that it is merely a cover for the attack on workers' rights that is inevitable under globalization—is based on the mistaken notion that globalization is responsible for the havoc wrought by antiunion government policies and neoliberalism. Thus N. Vasudevan of the Blue Star Employees' Federation advocated abrogation of the WTO because

> the Northern governments talk about the social clause, but it is the same governments which through the institutions they dominate such as the IMF, World Bank and WTO impose on every poor country in the world cuts in social subsidies, like welfare, education, housing, agriculture. . . . Globalisation of trade has created several export processing zones in different countries where even minimum labour standards are non-existent. In order to generate profit in a competitive market, investors relocate firms in the most destructive manner. The workforce is kept at the minimum level, contracting and sub-contracting of manufacturing and services become the rule.
>
> (Vasudevan 1996, 73–75)

However, others who opposed globalization felt that it did not follow that the social clause should be rejected; thus M. J. Pande of the Bombay Union of Journalists asked, "we all know that the UN is an organisation dominated by imperialist interests, yet we support its Human Rights Declaration: couldn't we therefore support the social clause while rejecting the exploitative world order represented by the WTO?" (cit. Hensman 1998, 83).

The third argument against a workers' rights clause is that labor is not a trade-related issue and therefore should not be included in trade agreements (John 2000). This is also the position of the Indian government (*ET* 1999b) and the World Bank (World Bank 1995, 6). The claim that there is no link (which ignores the fact that the items traded are produced by labor) seems to be inspired by the need to provide a theoretical basis for the argument that labor rights are the province of the ILO and should be kept out of the WTO, as the national trade unions argue. Yet the child-rights activist Joseph Gathia "felt that the ILO had no teeth and our governments have not been listening to ILO" (cit. Vivekanandan 1996, 167); many unions too felt that the ILO was "toothless" (John and Chenoy 1996, 188). Bennet D'Costa reiterated that the social clause "must be linked to trade, otherwise there will be no way of enforcing it. But Third World workers must have a say in defining the social clause and putting what we want into it; we can't just accept what trade unions in the imperialist countries suggest" (cit. Hensman 1998, 83).

Making Sense of a Confused Debate

It is clear that unions and labor-rights activists in India were very far from having a unified position on a workers' rights clause. In general, the central trade unions were against it, informal workers and activists working with them were in favor of it, and employees' unions were somewhere in the middle, with some in favor and some against. The position of those who supported it was relatively consistent: workers' rights are being undermined due to globalization, domestic employers and the government are party to this attack, and therefore we need an enforceable international agreement to help us protect those rights. Many were opposed to globalization and the WTO but recognized them as a reality that had to be dealt with. Some suspected protectionist intentions on the part of First World unionists but were prepared to negotiate with them on the issue.

Opposition to the clause, on the other hand, came from a variety of standpoints, some incompatible with one another. The characterization of linkage as a protectionist measure was shared by the governments of most developing countries, which declared that it would be too expensive for them to implement: "At the WTO ministerial meeting in Seattle in 1999, more than one hundred WTO members from the developing world opposed international labour standards saying that they can't afford them" (Fields 2004, 70). But this argument was not consistent with a trade union perspective, given that the rights incorporated in the proposed clause "were struggled for and won by the blood of thousands of men and women workers all over the world" (Swaminadhan 1996, 57). If wages were being discussed, the argument might have made sense, but they were not. Even if the clause were enforced, wage costs in Third World countries would still be much lower than those in the First World: the former would not have lost their "comparative advantage."

What such a clause would do is prevent corporations from blackmailing both governments and workers by threatening to shift production elsewhere if minimum rights were enforced. It would also prevent governments in developing countries from competing with one another by denying minimum rights to workers, a strategy that "tends to attract investment in low-skill, highly mobile production methods by peripatetic industries that invest little in skills development within the country and move constantly in search of lower-wage production sites." Protecting basic workers' rights, on the contrary, would "encourage states to compete through skills development and productivity." Higher wages would raise domestic demand, creating more employment. Far from undermining development, enforcement of workers' rights would promote it (Cleveland 2004, 139).

The suggestion that defining the social clause as a protectionist measure is a neoliberal position (van Roosendaal 2001, 287) is confirmed by its coincidence with the views expressed by Arthur Dunkel (cit. Ferguson 1994, 4) and the World Bank (1995, 6). It recognizes the advantages of international trade liberalization for developing countries but opposes any corresponding international regulation of labor. One of the main proponents of this position, Jagdish Bhagwati, argued strongly that labor was not a trade-related issue and that the WTO should concentrate on trade issues while the ILO concentrated on labor (Bhagwati 2002, 79–80). Yet the fact that there was already an institution dealing with intellectual-property rights—the World Intellectual Property Organization—did not lead to a similar outcry against coverage of this issue by WTO rules (Elliott and Freeman 2003, 24–25; Alston 2004, 473–474). What was being advocated by Bhagwati and others, therefore, was enforceable protection for capital without enforceable protection for labor. Sections of the labor movement arguing against the inclusion of labor rights in the WTO tried to distinguish themselves from these ideologues, but the practical outcome of their stand was identical. Nothing they proposed would have prevented WTO rules from forcing governments to import products made in violation of the Core Conventions or prohibiting governments from favoring imports made in compliance with them (Arthurs 2002, 484).

The antiglobalization argument against the social clause was based on the assumption that the WTO is the same kind of institution as the World Bank and IMF, whereas it is not (see chapter 2). What would be the result of abrogating the WTO? There are two possibilities. One is no foreign trade whatsoever, which would mean that if a life-saving drug was not being manufactured domestically, those who needed it would be allowed to die rather than importing it. No one was advocating this. What was being advocated, rather, was that the nation-state should retain control over its foreign trade. Yet foreign trade is, by definition, an activity in which at least two nation-states are involved. In the absence of a global organization like the WTO, bilateral and regional treaties would govern trade: indeed, this was already happening, and the United States was among the most enthusiastic in promoting such deals. Why?

A study of such agreements found that "in several countries, social movements and trade unions have launched campaigns opposing the bilateral agreements." For example, the Korean trade union federations opposed the Japan-Korea bilateral agreement because it sought to protect Japanese investors at the expense of Korean citizens and workers. The Vietnam-U.S. bilateral agreement gave U.S. companies enforceable protection against expropriation (Choudry 2002, 6). The provision protecting companies from expropriation, or measures with a "similar" or "equivalent" effect, were also part of both a New Zealand–Hong Kong bilateral agreement and the North American Free Trade Agreement (NAFTA), and they covered anything that reduced profitability: environmental regulations, for example, could result in award of compensation (Choudry 2002, 26). In all these cases and many more, the imbalance of power between the parties to the agreement resulted in the weaker party or parties being forced to accept conditions and procedures detrimental to their interests. The poorest countries tended to suffer most from a shift to bilateral and regional agreements (Wheatley 2003).

There certainly might have been the intention to use the WTO in the same way. At Seattle, for example, "the developing countries predictably focused on the lack of transparency in the negotiating process. . . . Their objections took on an angry edge when . . . security personnel were used to keep delegates from developing countries out of the Green Room" (*ET* 1999c). But over time, the governments of developing countries learned how to fight back. By 2001, in Doha, they were able to get an agreement that countries with their own domestic drug industries could waive patents and issue compulsory licences to generic manufacturers during a health emergency (*BS* 2003b). Paragraph 6 of the Doha Declaration added: "We recognise that WTO members with insufficient or no manufacturing capacities in the pharmaceutical sector could face difficulties in making effective use of compulsory licence under the TRIPS agreement. We instruct the council of TRIPS to find an expeditious solution to this problem and report it to the General Council." Finally, in August 2003, a deal was struck, allowing countries such as India and Brazil, which were producing cheap generic versions of patented drugs, to export them to poor countries suffering a health emergency (*ET* 2003d).

Recognition by the WTO that the right to life can take priority over property patents was an important step. When the Swiss pharmaceutical company Novartis appealed against the refusal by the Chennai Patents Office to grant a new patent to a slightly different form of its antileukemia drug imatinib mesylate (Glivec) and that appeal was turned down by the Chennai High Court, the Swiss government indicated it had no intention of taking the matter to the WTO. One reason could have been the bad publicity generated by the case, as Glivec was too expensive to be afforded by over 99 percent of leukemia patients in India, but another could be that the Indian government had the option of issuing a compulsory license to domestic manufacturers of imatinib mesylate in order to save thousands of lives per year, and this procedure would have been TRIPS-compliant (Srinivasan 2007).

Another example of concerted action was over the issue of agricultural subsidies by the United States and European Union. What is of interest here is the process by which developing countries became a force to be reckoned with. When a draft that was circulated prior to the Cancun ministerial conference was discovered to have left out the concerns of developing countries, a group of twenty-one developing countries including Brazil, China, India, and South Africa promptly circulated an alternative draft stating these concerns, thus forcing a discussion of them at the meeting (Arun 2003a). "For the first time in any WTO ministerial, the developing countries managed to stay united in the face of pressure and allurement by the rich countries. Further, for the first time, developing countries stayed engaged in the process of the negotiations with properly drafted alternative texts and language" (Arun 2003b). Despite the collapse of the talks when African delegates walked out, the outcome was seen as a significant step forward: "The developing countries got their act together much better this time. . . . Cancun will be remembered for the ability of developing countries to hold together till the end despite heavy pressure exerted by the world's biggest economic and political powers. It heralds a new beginning for the multilateral trade negotiations" (Kumar 2003). At a meeting in India in March 2005, the coalition of Third World countries reiterated its determination not to give way on the issue of agricultural subsidies (*ET* 2005c).

This is language that should be familiar to trade unionists: the language of collective bargaining. Demanding that the WTO should be abrogated and that the world should go back to bilateral agreements because developing countries are weaker is analogous to saying that collective bargaining should be abandoned and workers should negotiate individual agreements with management because workers are weaker. It is precisely *because* developing countries are weaker that they need the WTO, just as it is precisely *because* workers are weaker that they need collective bargaining. "Institutions like the WTO are rule-based and they are meant to protect the weak against the strong. Developing countries would be at a disadvantage against the developed countries in the absence of an organisation like the WTO" (Srinivasan 1999); "weaker trading nations stand to gain from global rules on world trade which apply uniformly to weak and strong trading countries" (Acharya 2003). Third World countries potentially have an advantage because the "WTO is an international body that functions on a 'one country-one vote' principle. Indeed, there is a standard American complaint that GATT and WTO have been highjacked by the developing countries" (*BS* 1998b). Apart from the cases referred to in chapter 2, the WTO ruled in favor of Venezuela and Brazil when they complained that U.S. gasoline standards discriminated against imports (Ghei 1996), in favor of India in three cases on textiles (two against the United States and one against the European Union) (*ET* 1999d), and in favor of India and against the European Union in two cases involving bed linen (Vyas 2001; *ET* 2003e).[17]

In some cases, the anti-WTO position seeks to reverse the increased economic power of the more industrialized Third World countries, because one of its results has been the loss of jobs in First World countries (Kishwar 2004).[18] But this fails to recognize that the attack on workers' rights worldwide is able to succeed not because of globalization and the WTO as such but because capital has a global perspective and the labor movement has not. Thus companies put pressure on their governments to press for inclusion of clauses protecting property rights and exclusion of clauses protecting labor rights, while unions have been too disastrously divided even to agree on a clause that protects workers' rights. The rejection of a social clause by antiglobalizers reinforces the position of the most vicious Indian employers, which finds its political expression in the far right. The RSS-affiliated organizations, which demonstrated in January 2000 against then Director-General of the WTO Mike Moore, used almost identical language: "We will not allow a global system, which actually protects and supports the rich and powerful at the cost of the lives of millions of poor and hungry" (SJM et al. 2000).

Antiglobalization ideology also underlies the seemingly neoliberal argument of other unions that a trade-labor linkage is protectionist. In the background of both arguments lies the fear of surrendering national sovereignty by allowing a multilateral agency to interfere in what are seen as the internal affairs of a nation. But the notion of "national sovereignty" conceals two contradictory ideas. One is the idea of *state sovereignty*, the right of a state to do what it likes within its own borders without interference from outside, which was used by the NDA government to protest against the international concern that was voiced when genocidal violence was unleashed against Muslims in Gujarat. The other is the idea of *democracy*, the fundamental rights and freedoms of the people of a nation, which enable them to control their own lives and govern their own affairs. International law, as embodied in the ILO Core Conventions, may indeed undermine state sovereignty: the right of the state to violate, or allow violations of, the human rights of workers. But it can only strengthen democracy, by protecting the fundamental rights of the overwhelming majority of the population, which has been seen as both the precondition and goal of development (Sen 1999; Langille 2002).

The draft report of a government Commission on Labour Standards and International Trade, which was appointed by the Ministry of Commerce in 1994 to study the issue and chaired by Subramaniam Swamy, strongly supported linkage. The thousand-page report, submitted in January 1996, said that "there are some desirable core labour standards, which deserve to be uniformly enforced internationally, for which trade sanctions are ultimately necessary to obtain serious compliance" (cit. *Times of India* 1996; Gupta and Voll 1999, 121). It concluded that this would have positive implications for sustaining high levels of global economic growth in the long run and that "global labour standards are important for ensuring equity in the new global order" (cit. *LF* 1996). However, instead of seizing the chance to raise the abysmal level of labor standards in India, the only central trade union member (from INTUC) who had participated in the exercise dissociated himself from these conclusions (van Roozendaal 2001, 165–166). It certainly appears that despite the objective interest of unions in the enforcement of workers' rights, "their ideological rhetoric forces the unions, instead, to the forefront of those opposing the effective implementation of international labour standards" (Pani 2003).

The limited experience gained from the supplementary labor agreement to NAFTA—the North American Agreement on Labor Cooperation—and the U.S.-Cambodia Bilateral Textile Trade Agreement, which contained a labor-standards clause, shows that despite the unequal nature of these trade agreements, the labor-rights provisions that went with them were used successfully to defend workers' rights (Compa 2001; Kolben 2004).

Is it possible to formulate a clause in WTO agreements that will do the same, or better?

Crafting a Workers' Rights Clause for the WTO

Proponents and opponents of the social clause in the international labor movement agree that universal protection of certain basic labor rights is desirable,[19] and thus arguably it is possible to formulate a workers' rights clause that would meet the objections of opponents and strengthen the hand of genuinely democratic Third World governments (Barry and Reddy 2005). A minimum condition for making such a clause acceptable to governments and unions in the Third World is that it would have to be formulated in such a way that it could not be used in a discriminatory fashion. This means that an equal standard would have to be applied to all countries, which in turn implies that the vagueness of the 1998 ILO declaration's language would have to be replaced by the more precise language of the conventions. If the United States, which is guilty of widespread violations of the core conventions, could claim to be protecting labor rights, so could the Chinese government. After all, the ACFTU succeeded in forcing Wal-Mart, which is notoriously antiunion in North America, to agree to the establishment of workplace unions at all its outlets in China (Adams 2005; Chan 2005, 19). To ensure an equal standard, ratification of the relevant conventions, their incorporation in national legislation, and genuine efforts to implement the laws should be required of a member state before it has a right to make a complaint against another state.

Unbiased application of the standard would also have to be ensured. The innovative Cambodian example, where the ILO was prevailed upon to monitor the implementation of agreed-upon standards despite its initial reluctance to do so, points to an obvious solution to this problem. Indeed, making the ILO responsible for implementing the clause would dovetail neatly with the solution to the problem of monitoring codes of conduct proposed above. Brand-name companies such as Nike and Gap were already asking the companies they sourced from in Cambodia to provide them with an ILO monitoring report. The fact that the ILO was simultaneously training government labor inspectors held out the possibility that in the long run, monitoring could be handed over to them, although the ILO would still need to verify implementation and look into complaints (Kolben 2004, 97–107). The reports would have to be public and available to workers, employers, and governments in order to ensure transparency, and, as in the original ICFTU proposal, countries should be given time and technical assistance to correct violations. They might also be offered financial assistance in inverse proportion to their per capita GDP. Member states of the WTO could pay for this service by making financial contributions to the ILO at the rate of some percentage of their GDP. Empowering unions and labor-rights NGOs to make complaints would help to democratize the procedure. Companies who were implementing codes of conduct would not have to fear unfair competition from those who were not. The fact that the clause would be applicable globally would allay fears of Third World governments that if they upgraded labor rights, they would be undercut by others. It would thus help developing countries "by decreasing the costs they face at present when pursuing policies to enhance labor standards" (Barry and Reddy 2008, 86).

Second, the ILO would need to ascertain the cause of violations. If a supplier is violating labor rights in order to comply with price and time pressures from buyers, then the ILO would have to put pressure on the buyers. Again, an ILO study found that IMF and World Bank stabilization and structural-adjustment programs were inimical to the protection of labor standards:

> In practice, the main issues at stake have related to minimum wage protection, employment security and severance pay, and restrictions on hiring and firing. But the paradigm is naturally hostile to trade unionism. . . . The neoclassical paradigm is clearly antithetical to ILO philosophy, in that it essentially ignores the value of labour standards as instruments of social justice. It has also been subjected to sharp criticism by a school of economists, broadly referred to as the "neo-institutionalists," who defend labour standards and institutions by the criteria of productive efficiency as well as social justice.
>
> (Plant 1994, 9)

The long-standing ILO demand for a say in framing IMF and World Bank programs in order to ensure that they are consistent with ILO standards would have to met if this source of violations is to be eliminated (Plant 1994, 50). This was also part of the social-clause proposal put forward by the Deutscher Gewerkschaftsbund (Haas 1999, 19).

Third, it would be necessary to agree on procedures and penalties in cases where violations continued and a state made no effort to stop them. A minimum requirement would be that WTO rules should not permit it to force a country that had implemented the core conventions to import products made in violation of them or prevent that country from giving preference to imports produced in compliance with basic labor rights. One suggestion is that article XX(e) of the WTO agreement, which permits countries to ban the import of goods produced using prison labor, should be expanded to include goods and services produced in violation of any of the core human-rights conventions (Elliott and Freeman 2003, 90–91). This would prevent the clause from being used in a protectionist manner to exclude products where no violation was involved. At the same time, it would provide substantial support to workers producing for export—especially in "free-trade zones" or "special economic zones"—in their struggle for basic rights.

However, this very limited interpretation of a workers' rights clause has been criticized. One objection is that it will not protect informal workers in international subcontracting chains, the majority of whom are women (*Asian Labour Update* 1995–1996, 3; Hale 1995–1996). This criticism can be addressed by including in the ILO Core Conventions the right of workers to registration and an employment contract. Another criticism, which has also been made of codes of conduct, is that if children are simply expelled from export production, they are likely to end up in even worse occupations; indeed, this is what initially happened in Bangladesh when the Child Labour Deterrence Act (Harkin Bill) was enacted in the United States, until international agencies stepped in to protect the children (Kabeer 2001, 368–371).

Addressing these problems would involve extending the reach of the Core Conventions beyond export production and requiring the member states of the WTO to protect the fundamental rights of all their workers. This would be necessary from the standpoint of protecting human rights but would also make sense from the standpoint of ensuring fair trade practices, since the way in which the costs of *inputs* into items traded internationally are affected by the violation of workers' rights in *their* production is not taken into account if only production of the exported items themselves is monitored. Here, too, the ILO would be the appropriate monitoring body—indeed, it is already involved in such monitoring, and it would only need to intensify and extend its activities. It is also involved in running programs to assist in the implementation of some of the Core Conventions—IPEC is an obvious example—and such activities could be expanded.

However, international trade sanctions would not be an appropriate penalty for violations of workers' rights in production for domestic consumption. Instead, putting pressure on offending governments could, for example, take the form of fines. The fines could then be used by the ILO to implement the Core Conventions (e.g., take children out of employment and provide for them; set up machinery to deal with cases of bonded labor, union busting, or discrimination; help with the registration of informal-sector workers and employers and regulation of informal employment, etc.). Participating in this labor-rights monitoring regime could be made mandatory for WTO members. It must be emphasized that this would *not* be an intrusion of the WTO onto the territory of labor standards nor of the ILO onto the territory of world trade but would simply be a way of ensuring that world trade rules are compatible with human rights at work.

The prediction that the use of the social-dumping argument by First World unions would lead to a stalemate in discussions around the workers' rights clause has been borne out (Chin 1998). The divisions were not simple North-South ones, as some have argued; there were many Third World unions that supported the proposal (Griffin et al. 2003), while others opposed it. Even within India, unions and labor-rights activists were divided on the issue. Yet it is potentially "the strategy best placed to unify the world's workers" (Munck 2003, 128). It can facilitate the working of international framework agreements as well as codes of conduct. Most importantly, by bringing about an international harmonization of labour law (Stone 1995)—since ILO conventions take the form of "international legislation or draft national laws" (Leary 2004, 183)—it can counteract the inadequacy of national labor law to protect the rights of a globalized labor force. A consensus on this issue among unions and labor activists is possible, but there are two basic requirements for it: genuine dialogue, in which the protagonists actually listen to each other (Waterman 2001, 24), and the abandonment of nationalism in favor of an internationalist outlook (Hensman 2001).

Building Solidarity

A realist would have to admit that the most common attitude of workers toward their counterparts in other countries is indifference based on ignorance. Yet this is easy to change, provided their interest can be aroused.

Often information, presented in an imaginative form, is sufficient. When women workers in a free-trade zone in Sri Lanka read about the struggle at Mandarin in El Salvador, there was instant identification with these workers from a completely different culture. Face-to-face contact is even better, as the tour of the Bhopal gas victims showed. Second World workers are an unknown quantity to most workers in both the First and Third Worlds, but this ignorance can be dispelled very quickly if they have a chance to meet— as, for example, during the struggle of Solidarnosc, when a Polish labor activist came to speak at a public meeting in Bombay, and in the course of the WWW project on subcontracting chains, in which Bulgarian unionists and labor activists participated.

Yet there could be underlying tensions despite shared problems. These could surface in circumstances such as the phase-out of the Multi-Fibre Agreement, when some Third World workers felt that their jobs were under threat from others. In the case of workers from India and Pakistan, it seems at first sight that they are ideally placed to build solidarity: they are contiguous geographically, able to speak what is virtually the same language (Hindi/Urdu)—although the script is different—and suffer similar problems, especially the large-scale informalization of labor. Yet the decades-old hot-cold war between the two countries has created obstacles to their meeting (including, at times, a ban on travel between the two countries) and— perhaps even more importantly—erected psychological barriers between them. Information exchange and contact can certainly counteract some of these tensions, but they are not sufficient as a basis for common action.

In the case of First and Third World workers, the tensions are even greater. For many unionists in India, First World workers constitute a labor aristocracy whose prosperity has been built on imperialism. On the other side, there is often palpable rage against Third World workers on the part of workers in developed countries, who believe that the passivity and docility of the former are responsible for their own loss of jobs. Here, again, concrete information can combat these stereotypes and lead to solidarity action, as in the cases of the campaign to support the Guatemalan Coke workers and the Patel Hosiery workers supporting union rights at Brylane. However, national consciousness and competition for jobs could still undermine any solidarity based on economic interests alone, and "international solidarity . . . will therefore only be achieved (struggled for) by an international politics which deliberately develops the common political interests of an economically differentiated global workforce" (Southall 1988,

26). This chapter and the foregoing ones give us some clues as to what that international politics might be. Among other things, it would have to be based on an understanding that imperialism, which has inflicted poverty and undermined democracy in the Third World, has resulted in the recent growth of poverty and undermining of workers' rights in the First World. This awareness is growing. The activities of U.S. Labor Against the War, and the letter of AFL-CIO president John Sweeney to the prime minister of Iraq, condemning the prohibition of government agencies and departments from dealing with Iraqi oil unions and the declaration of unions in the public sector illegal, exemplify the emergence of a new cross-border solidarity between unions in opposition to imperialism.[20] Giving international solidarity a central place in trade union politics would be essential if unions are to defend workers from the negative consequences of neoliberal policies and the global economic crisis.

[10]

Conclusion

Toward Global Solidarity

"Globalization" has become a catchword, but often its usage is so vague and undefined that it becomes meaningless. In other cases, it appears redundant because the meaning attributed to it is the same as, for example, "capitalism," "imperialism," or "neoliberalism." With both supporters and opponents of globalization concurring that it is linked inextricably to impe-rialism and neoliberalism, the choice appears to be one between a world of discrete national economies on one side and a world dominated by the "Washington consensus" and military might of the United States on the other (T. Friedman 1999).

However, it is far more useful to define globalization as a new stage of capitalism emerging out of imperialism and distinguished from all previous epochs by (a) a capitalist world economy covering more or less the entire globe; (b) large-scale decolonization and the emergence of key Second and Third World countries as powerful players in the world econ-omy; (c) a dynamic sector of capital that depends not on the support of a nation-state for its expansion, nor on rigid national borders to protect it from imports, but on porous borders and global regulation that will allow it to expand globally; (d) the emergence of information and communication technologies, both as a new and increasingly dominant branch of produc-tion in itself and as a factor affecting manufacturing, services, and finance;

(e) the growing dominance of new financial institutions, including pension funds; and (f) new institutions of global governance. Globalization, according to this definition, began to emerge in the middle of the twentieth century with the struggles for independence and national liberation in the Third World, and it progressed further as some of the largest of these countries industrialized. This did not mean the end of imperialist military and political intervention in other countries, which continued into the twenty-first century, but it did mean that the military spending required for being an imperialist power became increasingly incompatible with a strong economy.

The aftermath of the global meltdown of 2008 presents workers and unions with a potent threat as well as an opportunity. The threat comes not just from the immediate loss of millions of jobs and downward pressure on employment conditions, although this is serious enough (ILO 2009). If unions respond to the crisis in the wrong way, by failing to fight against protectionism and hostility to immigrants, there could be a resurgence of right-wing groups that could crush the labor movement for many years to come. Avoiding this danger requires unions to have a strong, well-argued alternative response to the crisis. If they can come up with one, then the crisis presents an opportunity to push governments to abandon a failed model of globalization, clear away the debris of militarist imperialism and nationalism, and adopt a different model in which workers and unions have far greater power to shape the global order.

A Global Working Class

For labor, globalization meant a rapid expansion worldwide: "the global proletariat doubled in numbers between 1975 and 1995 to reach 2.5 billion workers" (Munck 2003, 8). By 2007, the number of workers had grown to three billion in work, with 189.9 million unemployed (ILO 2008). The bulk of this growth occurred in the developing countries, where the annual growth rate of the number of workers between 1985 and 2000 was 2.1 per cent, as against 0.5 per cent in the OECD countries (Munck 2003, 7). However, most of the new jobs were insecure and poorly paid; by 2005, there was a large and persistent deficit of "decent work" available (ILO 2005).

The formation of a "global" working class progressed considerably, despite labor's relative immobility compared to capital. One way in which this occurred was through a convergence of employment conditions in different countries. In First World countries, this tended to involve a lowering of labor standards to levels closer to those prevailing in the Third World. One example was the pressure to lengthen working hours (Thornhill 2005); another was the proliferation of sweatshops and homeworkers laboring under substandard conditions. As the Eastern Bloc and Soviet Union fell apart, their workforces began to be subjected to employment conditions more closely resembling those in the rest of the world; many unions joined the ICFTU and later the ITUC. In China, too, the "iron rice pot" guaranteeing economic security was smashed (Leung 1988), and workers were still struggling for the right to form independent unions in the early twenty-first century.

From the nineteenth century onward, it has been possible to argue that "workers and workers' movements located in different states/regions are linked to each other by the world-scale division of labor and global political processes" (Silver 2003, 26). The link has taken a variety of forms, including the shifting of production by capital from one part of the world to another following labor unrest and the transmission of labor strategies from one country to another by migrant workers (Silver 2003). In the epoch of globalization, given the development of information and communication technologies, the shifting of jobs from one country to another has become easier and more rapid, and the transmission of labor strategies can take place even without the physical migration of workers. The labor movement needs global links more urgently, and at the same time it has acquired the means by which they can be built more quickly and easily.

The Effects on Labor in India

What impact has globalization had on labor in India? For informal workers, who constitute over 90 percent of the labor force, the answer is "very little." They have not joined the "race to the bottom" for the simple reason that they were already there. Employment expanded in export-oriented sectors such as the garment industry, but it was insecure and irregular. Only in a few rare instances did the expansion of export production allow workers to become owners of workshops. However, pressure for basic labor rights from unions and consumers in developed countries can be used to support the struggles of informal workers for better employment conditions.

At first sight, it appears that the small minority of formal workers has taken the brunt of the effects of globalization. They have lost hundreds of thousands of jobs, and the losses have been concentrated in major industrial centers, especially Bombay, where the trade union movement was strongest. However, on closer examination, it is evident that large-scale job losses began before the liberalization policy was announced in 1991 and were fueled by government policies encouraging relocation of production to nonunionized workers in the informal sector or to industrially backward areas. Job losses accelerated after 1991, especially due to the privatization of public-sector industries, yet overall there was a significant expansion of formal-sector employment in the first half of the 1990s. New forms of irregular labor based on information and communication technologies expanded rapidly and posed new problems for the union movement (Remesh 2004). In formal employment, there has indeed been a "race to the bottom," but the prime motor of this descent has been government policy, not globalization. Indeed, by creating international union and consumer pressure for labor rights, globalization has the potential to strengthen the labor rights of formal workers.

The case of India shows that the facile attribution of job losses in the formal sector and the spread of informal and casualized labor to "globalization" is dangerously misleading. In India, widespread poverty and low living standards were a legacy of colonialism, and while British rule did leave behind a small formal sector protected by strong legislation, it also left a large, unprotected, informal labor force. Subsequently, Indian government policy not only retained this discriminatory legal framework but actually encouraged the transfer of jobs from formal to informal workers at a time when it was under no external pressure to informalize employment. Some of this background is common to other Third World countries, but the informal sector is unusually large in India. Other countries have employed policies such as the creation of free-trade or export-processing zones where labor laws do not apply, or they systematically use state security forces to smash independent unions. In First World countries, especially the United States and Britain, governments have implemented antilabor policies in the absence of any external political or economic compulsion to do so (Scipes 2007). These are policy choices that cannot be blamed directly on globalization. "Seen from this perspective, the rhetoric surrounding globalization . . . is a purposefully created shield guarding governments and corporations from political responsibility for policies that favor the massive redistribution of benefits from labor to capital" (Silver 2003, 7).

The Failure of Neoliberalism

However, there are instances where external forces were indeed responsible for the denial of labor rights. In the numerous cases where the United States aided in the overthrow of progressive, prolabor governments, imperialism can be blamed for the resulting repressive regimes. In other cases, policies imposed by the IMF and World Bank resulted in the undermining of labor standards and, in the case of Russia, a catastrophic descent into lawlessness and criminality. Here the culprit was neoliberalism's claim that the market can solve all problems if only the state withdraws. But in fact, capitalism needs the state; it depends, for example, on the enforcement of contracts. Indeed, this was precisely the purpose of most structural-adjustment programs: to enforce the repayment of loans with interest. Thus, contrary to ideology, neoliberalism is not a regime of unregulated capital but of regulation in the interest of capital (Hardt and Negri 2004, 280).

However, the state fails in its duty even to capitalism if it simply implements policies demanded by capital, whether domestic or international. As Marx showed in his discussion of the struggle around the working day, capitalists are shortsighted in their greed and quite capable of killing the goose that lays the golden eggs: namely, they tend to superexploit the working class, their source of profit, to such a degree that labor power is reproduced only in a crippled form. An additional danger is that overexploitation restricts the expansion of the market, which is a necessary condition for capitalist accumulation. It is a paradox of the capitalist system that struggles for workers' rights may actually stimulate capitalist accumulation, as occurred when the struggle for the ten-hour day was won. Neoliberalism contributed to the crisis of 2008 because it failed to take this into account. While it may have enhanced profits in the short term, in the long term it had a negative effect on accumulation by inhibiting the growth of mass markets and undermining the quality of the labor force.

So long as there are sectors or countries within the global economy where labor power is cheaper and workers more easily subordinated due to the denial of their rights, there is a tendency for production to gravitate to those sectors or countries, unless they lack adequate infrastructure and education or suffer from extreme political instability. This has happened within India and also internationally. The way in which globalization exerts a downward pressure on labor standards is by removing barriers to imports and facilitating the shifting of production to countries with lower standards, which tempts governments to boost exports and attract capital by pushing down labor standards in their own countries. But this would not occur unless there were already sectors and countries with low labor standards. To put the blame on globalization is to ignore the real causes of poor labor standards and thus allow them to continue.

Deglobalization: A Reactionary Utopia

Although it makes little sense to be "for" or "against" globalization (Munck 2003, 6) if it is in fact a new phase of capitalism, a large part of what the media inaccurately call the "antiglobalization movement" (inaccurate because not everyone in it is wholly "anti" globalization) is indeed opposed to globalization. The hallmark of these antiglobalizers is their opposition to the WTO. Those who equate globalization with capitalism bemoan the fact that many small capitalists and petty producers (especially farmers) are driven out of business by competitive pressures that intensify with trade liberalization. They want to retain private property in the means of production, which is the basis of the capitalist system, but prevent the capitalist processes of concentration and centralization from eliminating producers who are uncompetitive.

This is an example of what Marx and Engels described in the *Communist Manifesto* as "petty-bourgeois socialism," which criticizes capitalism with great astuteness but sees the remedy in "cramping the modern means of production and exchange within the framework of the old property relations" (Marx and Engels 1973, 89–90). The means by which this is attempted—protection and subsidies—are directly opposed to the interests of the proletariat, as they drive up prices of essential commodities to a point where they are unaffordable by the poor and eat up funds that could be used to develop a comprehensive social-security system. Where they are practiced by developed nations, they are also opposed to the interests of more competitive farmers in developing countries. Support for small-scale capital involves, in addition, the suppression of labor rights. In the long run, this is, as the *Communist Manifesto* puts it, the pursuit of a reactionary utopia. Capitalism can only be superseded by a system with superior productivity, which implies cooperative as opposed to individualistic production. Therefore, sustaining petty production through protection and subsidies only postpones the transition from capitalism to a more equitable society.

Those who equate globalization with imperialism bemoan the loss of sovereignty that occurs when functions formerly performed by the state are handed over to multilateral bodies such as the WTO. With the state presupposed to be a democratic institution and the WTO an imperialist one, this is seen as a loss of democracy. If this is the case, however, how is it that the imperialist U.S. state so persistently came into conflict with the WTO? Furthermore, developing and least-developed countries, health NGOs, and others have negotiated successfully to get their concerns addressed by the WTO. The assumption that the smaller and more local a body, the greater the chances of democratic control over it, is questionable. As feminists and child-rights activists know very well, the smallest social institution, the family, can also be the least democratic.

In fact, the state is often the institution responsible for violating the human rights of its subjects. The most notorious example is the Nazi genocide, and there have been many other instances of ethnic cleansing and genocide in the twentieth century. If the nation-state is presumed to be the highest court of appeal, there can be no redress for victims of these horrific crimes. Recognizing this, special tribunals were set up to try perpetrators of such crimes in Rwanda and the former Yugoslavia, and the ICC was set up as a permanent court to deal with them. However, less egregious crimes committed or permitted by the state within its borders, including violations of the human rights of workers, women, Dalits, indigenous peoples, and ethnic, religious, and sexual minorities, continue to occur, and the principle of sovereignty is all too often invoked to prevent interventions by the international community to end them.

Whether an institution is democratic or not depends on the existence of safeguards for equality and the way in which decisions are made and carried out. The modern bourgeois form of sovereignty, defined in the dictionary as "supreme and unrestricted power, as of a state," has more in common with monarchy and aristocracy than with true democracy. Such power can be exerted only by a monolithic entity. "It should be clear, however, that this mandate of political thought that only the one can rule undermines and negates the concept of democracy" (Hardt and Negri 2004,

328). One example of the consequences of this kind of sovereignty, which identifies the interests of the powerful as the "national interest," is the imposition, in both India and the United States, of antidumping duties, which benefit powerful industrial lobbies at the expense of weaker sections. The requirement of genuine democracy—that all participants in all their diversity should have equal ability to represent themselves—must be fought for at all levels, from the household to the global community. There is no point in privileging one level—the national—above all others, nor is there a contradiction between democratization at one level and democratization at others; on the contrary, they reinforce one another (Brecher et al. 2000, 40–41).

In fact, antiglobalizers who advocate national sovereignty, if they wish to be consistent, would have to support the right of the United States and European Union to subsidize their agriculture and impose protectionist barriers against imports. This is one example of where nationalism leads when it is a matter of regulating relationships in an interdependent world. Autarchy is another. But "we cannot say 'stop the world, we want to get off.' Some countries have tried that, for example, the Democratic People's Republic of Korea, Myanmar and Albania, and they made a mess of their economies" (Bardhan 2001, 479). U.S. exceptionalism—the belief that rules are meant for others while the United States itself is exempt from having to follow them—is also a way of circumventing global regulation. Those who subscribe to it have used the sovereignty argument to refuse to accept the monitoring regimes required by the CTBT or Chemical and Biological Weapons Conventions. The only alternatives to either autarchy or regulation of international trade by a multilateral body like the WTO are bilateral and regional trade agreements, where the stronger or strongest power can impose its agenda on weaker partners. Thus nationalism in international trade favors the strong at the expense of the weak.

Once we see that there is no necessary link between sovereignty and democracy, the reactionary nature of arguments that counterpose national sovereignty to global regulation become clear. The sovereignty of nation-states is the sine qua non of imperialism (in which a strong nation-state imposes political and military control over others) and fuels competitive militarism and war, which has negative consequences for public spending on infrastructure and the social sector in both developing and developed countries. India had a border war with China in 1962, over a remote, uninhabited stretch of territory through which the Chinese had built a road, and tension on the border with Pakistan resulted in a continuous hot-cold war for over half a century. The cost in lives and money was immense and helped to keep human-development indices there among the worst in the world. In the United States, with the subprime-mortgage crisis, credit crunch, job losses, declining value of the dollar, and national debt growing at a rate of $1.4 billion per day by the end of 2007, it has become clear that even the richest country in the world cannot indefinitely spend trillions of dollars on militarism without ruining its economy and debilitating its labor force (Raum 2007; Johnson 2008).

The Right to Mobility as an Element of Human Freedom

Human mobility is the only type of mobility that has not been enhanced by globalization. For refugees fleeing persecution, poverty-stricken migrant workers seeking a livelihood, and families divided by national borders, the impermeability of these borders has been an additional source of anguish and danger. This is not a negligible problem. At the beginning of the twenty-first century, it was estimated that "over 25 million people are international refugees while an estimated similar number are economic migrants—mostly undocumented and generally lacking civil rights" (Brysk 2002, 10). In 2009, the Human Development Report estimated that there were around two hundred million international migrants and took up their cause, arguing that being able to decide where to live is a key element of human freedom as well as being a potential source of human development for the migrants, their home communities, and the host countries (UNDP 2009).

The troubles of these migrants are not over once they manage to cross borders, because "citizenship as an idea and as an institution is not always emancipatory. In fact, it often works to exclude people from the enjoyment of rights and recognition" (Bosniak 2002, 343). The assumption that only citizens have a right to rights means that refugees and migrants can be treated as "aliens" and deprived of basic human rights, including labor rights. "These oppositions between citizens and aliens pose obstacles for migrants' claims to rights based on universal personhood, even within a state that formally supports international human rights norms" (Maher 2002, 21).

The deprivation of rights and brutal treatment at the hands of border-control personnel are justified by the assumption that attempts to cross national borders by migrant workers are illegal, indeed criminal. "In popular media, these efforts have been reported haphazardly as targeting 'criminal aliens,' 'criminal illegal aliens,' and 'illegal aliens,' representing what is arguably a discursive blurring between a 'criminal' status and an 'illegal' status" (Maher 2002, 29). In other words, an activity that has been going on since human beings first began to inhabit the earth—migration in search of a livelihood—becomes classified as "criminal." Yet many economies have come to depend on rightless migrant workers, and some employers even seek them out. Employees who have the threat of deportation hanging over them are not likely to unionize or demand better employment conditions.

The combination of stringent border controls with the covert encouragement of the very activity that is defined as illegal has been seen as characteristic of First World countries and as being fueled by racism: after all, the United States has been a country of immigrants since its original inhabitants were all but exterminated, yet there is a palpable difference between the way that European migrants and Third World migrants are treated. However, Third World countries are by no means innocent of victimizing immigrants. In 1948 and 1949, Sri Lanka passed legislation depriving Tamil plantation workers of recent Indian origin—descendents of indentured laborers brought over under British rule—of their citizenship and franchise, a gross injustice that took over half a century to reverse. In India, Muslims accused of being Bangladeshis have been deported and, in Nellie (Assam) in 1983, massacred. Given the fact that most Indians do not have birth certificates or passports to prove their citizenship, the danger that Indian Muslims were being expelled led human-rights groups to criticize the Foreigners Act, 1946 (which placed the onus of proof of citizenship on the person accused of being a noncitizen), and to oppose the repeal of the Illegal Migrants (Determination by Tribunals) Act (1983) (applicable only to Assam), which placed the responsibility for proving noncitizenship on those who alleged it. Yet even these groups said nothing about the rights of Bangladeshi immigrants, implying tacitly that they had no rights in India (Fernandes 2005; CCPD 2005).[1]

A Global Agenda for Labor

Given all the negative consequences of the nation-state system, those who really oppose globalization could justifiably be seen as conservative or reactionary, attempting to hold still or roll back the wheel of history. To the extent that this opposition is successful, it retards the transition from imperialism to a world order marked by more egalitarian and peaceful relationships between peoples. And even if unsuccessful, it distracts attention from the task of shaping the new global order, leaving the field open for advocates of traditional authoritarian labor relations and modern neoliberal policies to impose their own agendas on it. If globalization has weakened the ability of the nation-state to protect employment and workers' rights, this problem is more than offset by the potential for much stronger protection of labor rights on a global scale. But only international solidarity can ensure that workers are able to make use of these new opportunities. By pitting workers in different countries against one another, nationalism deprives the working class of its most powerful weapon in the struggle to ensure that workers' rights are protected in the new global order: global solidarity.

On the other hand, while globalization does open up the *possibility* of social justice for the poor in the Third World (Kitching 2001), it does not follow that this potential will be realized automatically. On the contrary, only a coordinated struggle can ensure that the new world order is not shaped by neoliberalism, which has its own dire consequences for the poor and excluded. Fortunately, a large section of those who are characterized by the media as "antiglobalization activists" are not actually opposing globalization but, rather, attempting to ensure that the new global order is more equitable, democratic, and caring than the old one. Others may not have a global vision, but they struggle for the same values locally and nationally. This is not a unified program by any means, but if all the elements concerned with workers' rights are put together, they do add up to a coherent agenda.

Starting with the exclusion of noncitizens or the denial of their human rights, there have been two suggestions for dealing with this problem. "One political and scholarly response to migration's challenges to the administration of rights has been to turn to international law to establish and protect a more equal and universal basis for rights than membership of the territorial nation-state"; this includes the enactment by the ILO and United Nations of conventions protecting the rights of migrant workers and their families (Maher 2002, 24). The argument is that "rights and recognition should be based on an individual's personhood or her social participation, rather than on citizenship." Alternatively, according to the cosmopolitan outlook, the locus of citizenship would be displaced from the nation-state to make us "citizens of the world" (Bosniak 2002, 343, 348; Nussbaum 1996a, 1996b).

Another response has been the proposal to abolish immigration controls. Contradicting fears that this would lead to a flood of Third World immigrants pouring into Europe and North America, it has been pointed out that before immigration controls for Commonwealth citizens were imposed in Britain, the tendency was for single young people to come, work for a while, and then return home, possibly to be replaced by another family member. After the imposition of controls, by contrast, the majority of immigrants were dependants coming to join working people, since there was no other way to ensure both family reunion and access to a job (Hayter 2000, 48–49). Similarly, immigration controls imposed on Mexicans coming to work in the United States converted temporary migrants into longer-term settlers (Harris 2005, 4593).

Both these suggested changes would undermine the nation-state—the first by replacing citizenship rights with universal human rights, the second by making national borders even more porous—and therefore could be seen as pushing forward the agenda of globalization. The advantages from the standpoint of migrant workers are obvious: they would not have to risk their lives to cross borders illegally and would have the right to join unions and fight to improve their employment conditions without fear of deportation. The advantage for workers in the host country is that they would not find their own employment conditions threatened by cheap unorganizable workers, and the country too would benefit from the labor, taxes, and social-security contributions of the migrants. For the home countries of migrants, it is estimated that official and unofficial remittances received from them are already many times greater than official development aid; if these inflows were to increase and were channeled appropriately, they could spur development (Harris 2005, 4592). Overall, "the opening of borders could make the world a more harmonious and peaceful and less racist place, and make possible cooperation and democracy and greater mutual understanding worldwide" (Hayter 2000, 172).

This is not a new vision. In 1795, Kant wrote of the cosmopolitan right to universal hospitality, which "belongs to all human beings by virtue of the right of possession in common of the earth's surface" (Kant 1996, 329). Nor is it particularly esoteric. The enduring popularity of John Lennon's "Imagine," in which he invited listeners to "imagine there's no countries," suggests that working for a world without borders might not be a hopelessly utopian exercise. Borders act as mental barriers between "us" and "them," facilitating at best indifference and at worst xenophobia and cruelty. By contrast, "a cosmopolitan ethical perspective . . . provides us with a morally compelling view of how our many worlds may meet . . . on terms of humanity, justice, and tolerance, which are the foundations of perpetual peace and friendship, rather than on terms of cruelty, inequity, and violence, the foundations of perpetual war and animosity" (Lu 2000, 265).

It is not irrelevant that the only solution to the Kashmir dispute acceptable to many Indians, Pakistanis, and the majority of Kashmiris was the idea of a "soft border" between the Indian-controlled and Pakistani-controlled parts of the region, with relative freedom of movement across it (Koithara 2005). The tragedy of the Kashmir earthquake in October 2005—which, like the Asian tsunami of December 2004, showed that nature respects no borders—helped to move the peace process forward. More points were opened up on the Line of Control to facilitate relief operations and help divided families to ascertain the fate of relations across the border (Navlakha 2005). If a soft border between India and Nepal has worked well for so many years, it could work equally well along the rest of the borders in South Asia. This would increase revenues from tourism and pilgrimage in all the countries concerned and be a boon to the relations, friends, and colleagues scattered across them. The absurdity of regarding borders as god-given in a region where migration has been taking place from time immemorial—and where, like many other parts of the Third World, most borders were drawn by colonizers for their own interests—should be obvious.

A phase-out of nuclear-weapons programs and slashing of military budgets in all countries would release an immense volume of funds. Part of these funds could be used for developing green energy and infrastructure in both rural and urban areas, thus creating employment, minimizing the huge losses currently inflicted by floods and droughts, slowing and eventually halting global warming, and raising productivity. The rest could be used to develop the social sector: free health care; free, compulsory, quality formal education for all children; pensions that would eliminate penury in old age; income security; subsidized social housing; shorter working hours; well-paid part-time jobs to accommodate caring work; extension of paid parental leave for both women and men; good-quality childcare; and assistance with caring for sick, disabled, and old people who need care, so that the burden does not fall entirely on the family and especially on the women in it. Apart from engendering a more humane and democratic society, these measures would lead to a far higher quality of labor power, which is required for the new jobs created by globalization.

One of the most urgent tasks from the standpoint of unions is the elimination of informal labor, which would require the registration of all employers, employees, and labor providers and a record to be kept of all employment. This would entail the enactment of employment-regulation laws that, among other things, define an "employee" in such a manner that employers cannot pass off their employees as self-employed persons. Moves by the South African Department of Labour to evolve such an inclusive definition of employees could help in carrying out this task, which becomes all the more important because it affects not just traditional occupations but also new ones created by globalization (Benjamin 2002). Trade union legislation should make it easier to register unions, make it obligatory for employers to recognize representative unions and engage in collective bargaining, make it an unfair labor practice to victimize employees for union membership or activities, and make the provision of time off for union activities mandatory. All legislation should cover all employees regardless of their place of work or the number of workers employed in it. All forms of child labor should be banned. Employment created by public-works schemes should be supplemented by government assistance for cooperatives. In the aftermath of the current economic crisis, these measures are required in both developing and developed countries.

These changes, if accompanied by progressive taxation covering everyone except those earning less than the minimum taxable income, would expand revenue and social-security contributions, making a welfare state sustainable and eliminating extreme poverty. Well-meaning attempts to "make poverty history" cannot possibly succeed unless they empower the poor, and the main way in which the poor are disempowered is by informalizing their work and depriving them of employment and social-security rights. Formalizing all employment would guarantee basic rights and should be accompanied by legislation that prohibits discrimination against irregular workers and makes it impossible to hire irregular workers for regular jobs, thus providing the maximum degree of employment stability possible in a capitalist economy.

In India, many of these reforms would benefit employees who already have formal jobs; a new Trade Union Act, especially, would eliminate the "nonbargainable category" and remove current obstacles to union organizing. Revision of the Companies Act to strengthen information and consultation rights of employees would save many companies from sickness and bankruptcy, safeguarding both the jobs of employees and the interests of small shareholders and the public. State support for cooperatives would also help formal workers, as would other income-security measures that ensure survival if workers lose their jobs. The higher living standards resulting from all these reforms would expand the domestic market and encourage investment. Combined with the strengthening of trade ties with other Asian, Third World, and Second World countries, this would reduce dependence on First World markets and especially on the United States, which has led Asian countries to pour money into the U.S. Treasury, effectively offsetting that country's current account deficits and underwriting its imperial adventures. Expanding domestic markets, reorienting trade, and shifting away from the U.S. dollar as a reserve currency would remove this source of support for imperialism, speeding its decline (Palat 2004; Kumar 2005).

Success in achieving these goals depends on their becoming part of a global agenda. Eliminating informal labor would require the ILO to incorporate the right to proof of identity as a worker and proof of employment in its core conventions and to assist in the registration of employers, employees, and labor providers and the regulation of employment. A campaign to incorporate the provisions of ILO core conventions and a few others in the labor legislation of all countries would lead to the guarantee of basic labor rights worldwide. The harmonization of legislation and emergence of a body of international labor law would also facilitate international collective bargaining and union solidarity action, to which national law often poses obstacles (Atleson 2002). Solidarity campaigns and codes of conduct have raised the issue of global subcontracting chains and the responsibility of companies at the top of the chain for the conditions of workers at the bottom of it. In some cases, this has resulted in workers being successful in claiming their rights. The weakness of voluntary codes has been the lack of pressure on governments to support these rights, without which there is a limit to how much they can achieve.

A labor-rights clause in WTO trade agreements would solve this problem, and crafting such a clause so that it cannot be abused for protectionist purposes is another item on the agenda of the global labor movement. The enormous emphasis given to the need for protection of intellectual-property rights in the WTO, despite the fact that an international organization for this purpose already existed, suggests that workers cannot rely on the ILO alone to protect their rights: unless workers' rights are inscribed on the global trade agenda, the field will be left open for the owners of capital to shape it in their own interests. NGOs and campaigners on issues connected with the WTO have highlighted the need to give equal weight to developing countries and protect the interests of the least developed, and this has been extremely useful in redressing the power imbalance between First and Third World nations. But these campaigners have shown less interest in measures that would redress the disparity in power between employers and workers; indeed, their support for the demands of farmers could in some cases have a negative impact on agricultural workers. Protection of workers' interests has been left to unions, but they, too, have failed to evolve a consensus on what needs to be done.

The key to finding solutions to the challenges confronting the labor movement both within India and internationally is the emergence of a more inclusive and democratic movement. Two questions are relevant:

> First, in what respects and in what circumstances do unions act as private interest organisations, concerned exclusively with their actual members, as against identifying with a broader constituency? Second, how far do unions frame and pursue the interests of their memberships in ways which exclude and contradict those of other constituencies (whether unionised or not); and how do unions—particularly those with heterogeneous memberships—reconcile internal differences of interest?
>
> (Hyman 1996, 55)

In India, the traditional conception of unions was that they existed exclusively to serve their members, and whenever "unity" was invoked, it meant a subordination of the interests of underprivileged sections to those of the dominant section. This is changing. There is an emerging notion of equality and solidarity in the NTUI constitution, but it still needs to be made more concrete, for example in proposals for nondiscrimination and equal-opportunities legislation.

Formulating a country's agenda will involve a complex and difficult process of synthesizing the interests of different groups that may seem to be incompatible with each other: for example, equal opportunities for sections currently discriminated against would mean fewer formal jobs for men of the dominant community. Resolving this problem would involve adopting strategies to expand formal employment and convincing those who feel they would be losing out that discrimination divides and weakens the working-class movement as a whole. "Transformation involves a wider range of structural and cultural organisational change such as extensive and innovative diversity structures and a reallocation of union resources, whereby representing the interests of diversity groupings becomes central to campaigning and collective bargaining agendas" (Ledwith and Colgan 2002, 18).

The same problem is reproduced on a larger scale in the global context. How can the interests of workers losing jobs in developed countries due to outsourcing be reconciled with those of Third World workers employed to do those jobs? A similar process of convincing First World workers that global inequality weakens the labor movement and of working toward a strategy that will expand the total amount of formal employment in all countries would have to be followed; "the future of trade unionism rests on its capacity to construct a global project around which can be built alliances to render partially contradictory interests sufficiently convergent" (Ledwith and Colgan 2002, 23). Part of the solution, both in India and globally, can be seen in terms of building "cosmopolitan unions" where "particular groups or individuals need not relinquish their identities for the common good, but the common good necessarily includes the preservation of identity" (Selmi and McUsic 2002, 440).

Thus the creation of an egalitarian, democratic labor movement that respects diversity goes hand in hand with the search for common goals and strategies that synthesize the interests of workers from diverse backgrounds and different countries. This book has attempted to document and analyze the process as it has occurred among formal and informal workers in India and elsewhere in the world, in the hope that the labor movement can learn both from its successes (like the MV Foundation's drive to take children out of employment and put them into schools) and from its failures (like the Kamani cooperatives), to build a stronger movement, based on global solidarity, which will be successful in meeting the challenges of globalization and economic crisis.

Notes

Introduction

1. Since the name of the city was officially changed to "Mumbai" in 1997, I should explain why I continue to use the older name. The origin of the name "Bombay" is somewhat obscure, but it has been used for the past four hundred years by most of its multifarious inhabitants. For roughly the same length of time, its Marathi name has been "Mumbai," derived from the Hindu goddess Mumba Devi (*ai* is Marathi for "mother"). The campaign to change the official name to Mumbai was spearheaded by the Shiv Sena, an extreme right-wing Hindu and Marathi chauvinist organization. One plank of its platform was the replacement of "Bombay Hindi," which has evolved spontaneously as the link language for people from all over India who have settled in Bombay, by Marathi. Another was the stoking of anti-Muslim sentiment. In 1992 and 1993, the Shiv Sena was involved in the demolition of the Babri Mosque and pogroms against Muslims in Bombay, and at various times it has carried out brutal attacks on south Indians, communists, Muslims, Christians, and others. I have no objection to the Marathi name being Mumbai, but I and many others feel that the official change of name to Mumbai is associated with an attack on the ethnic, religious, and political diversity of the city and with ethnic-cleansing drives against minorities.

2. This describes my "method" in the broader sense, encompassing philosophical outlook and theoretical framework as well as techniques for collection of material, and not in the narrow sense of techniques alone (Harding 1987).

1. Emancipatory Action Research Into Workers' Struggles

1. Geographical definitions of former or currently imperialist countries and former or current colonies (excluding settler-colonies), such as "North" and "South," simply do not work; for example, Japan and Australia cannot be seen as belonging to the "West" or "North" in a geographical sense. It also leaves the countries of the former Soviet Union and Eastern bloc in limbo. This is why I have used the terms "First World," "Second World," and "Third World" as terms that refer to the history of these groups of countries, which has left its mark on them even today.

2. Debates in the Comintern on strategies for the working class in India and other Third World countries assumed that proletarian revolution meant the seizure of state power (Comintern 1971, 138–139; Banaji 1977). They did not include the position that workers could struggle for a bourgeois revolution against imperialism and simultaneously struggle against the bourgeoisie with whom they were allied.

3. Of course it is also true that it is not possible to fight against the oppression of women unless the particular oppression of some sections of women—as workers, *Dalits*, or Muslims, for example—is opposed simultaneously.

4. "Bombay" in this case refers to Bombay Presidency, set up under British rule, which included what are now Maharashtra and Gujarat.

2. Defining Globalization

1. Nathuram Godse, the Hindu fanatic who murdered Mahatma Gandhi, was associated with the Sangh Parivar. The BJP is affiliated with the RSS, but while in power it was forced to take a more open position on globalization, thus coming into conflict with its parent and sibling organizations.

2. Emmanuel started his book by quoting Marx's "Address on the Question of Free Trade" (1848)—"If the free traders cannot understand how one nation can grow rich at the expense of another, we need not wonder, since these same gentlemen also refuse to understand how within one country one class can enrich itself at the expense of another"—and went on to cite Marx's explanation of the equalization of the rate of profit to form an average rate. According

to Marx, if we look at different branches of production with different organic compositions of capital (see chapter 3) but equal rates of surplus value, their individual rates of profit will differ, with those branches with the lower organic composition—i.e., more labor and therefore more surplus value—having a higher rate of profit. However, this does not happen in practice: "These different rates of profit are balanced out by competition to give a general rate of profit which is the average of all these different rates" (Marx 1981, 257). The price at which the product sells will therefore not be the cost price plus the surplus value produced in that particular branch of production but the cost price plus the portion of the total profit at the average rate that would accrue to a capital of that size. Consequently, commodities produced by capitals in branches that are above the average organic composition (less labor intensive) will sell above their value, while those produced by capitals in branches below the average organic composition (more labor intensive) will sell below their value, and there will be a transfer of value from the latter to the former (see Marx 1981, chap. 9). It follows that there will be an "unequal exchange" between these branches of production, whether they are located in the same country or different countries, provided capital can move between them. Thus far, Emmanuel followed Marx's argument quite closely, as well as the arguments of Marxists like Bauer, whom he quoted (Emmanuel 1969, 175). Where he departed from them was in making the statement that it is the workers of the West, as consumers, who are the chief beneficiaries of low wages in Third World countries, and therefore "class is not a form of integration that takes precedence over the nation" (Emmanuel 1969, 183).

3. *Adivasi* = indigenous inhabitant; *Dalit* = oppressed, i.e., people from the "untouchable" castes.

4. Under capitalism, what is produced, and how much of it, is not decided by anyone but is the outcome of a process by which capitalists go into branches of production that are more profitable and leave branches of production that are less profitable (the "law of value"; see Marx 1981, 774, 1020). State ownership and centralized planning would certainly interfere with the capitalist law of value, but so long as the aim was to catch up and compete with capitalist economies, the law would still exert an influence over the way in which labor time was allocated between different branches of production. This is very different from a situation where society decides what to produce in order to satisfy social need, when the law of value would genuinely be abolished (Marx 1981, 288–289).

5. "The machine, which is the starting-point of the industrial revolution, replaces the worker, who handles a single tool, by a mechanism operating with a number of similar tools and set in motion by a single motive power, whatever the form of that power" (Marx 1976, 497).

6. Moves by the Obama administration to end the use of the term "war on terror" suggested that this phase might have ended by 2009 (Burkeman 2009).

3. Four Sources of the Global Crisis of 2008

1. I am indebted to Jairus Banaji for this reference.

4. Capital, the State, and Trade Union Rights

1. There was an eerie echo of their demands, which included nationalization of the oil industry and punishment of corrupt government officials, in the demands of striking workers of the General Union of Oil Workers in Basra in July 2005. See http://www.basraoilunion.org.
2. I shared a platform with a young unionist from Brazil at the 2004 WSF in Bombay, and it was evident that there was widespread disillusionment among unionists with what they had thought was their regime; statements by South African unionists reflected the same feeling.
3. I use this more universally accepted term for a sector that is unregulated by the state in preference to the Indian term "unorganized sector," because the latter can be misinterpreted as referring to nonunionized workers.
4. It has been pointed out that debates on post-Fordism in the 1980s tended to suffer from insufficient attention to the labor-control aspects of decentralized production (Rowbotham 1990; Mitter 1994). In the vast majority of cases, decentralization of production—both high-tech and low-tech—has been accompanied by the erosion of workers' rights.
5. In India, "contract labor" means workers hired through a labor contractor, who have no contracts at all.
6. 1 lakh = 100,000; 1 crore = 10 million.
7. URG interview with Metal Box Workers' Union, March 1985.
8. URG interviews with R. G. Michael of Abbott Laboratories Employees' Union, R. R. Mishra of Philips Workers' Union, and address by Bennet D'Costa of Hindustan Lever Employees' Union to the Get-Together of Hindustan Lever Workers at Nagpur in 1993.
9. URG interviews with union committee members in 1985.
10. At a Knitwear, Footwear, and Allied Trades Union (KFAT) conference workshop in Bridlington (United Kingdom), in 2003, where we were both speaking about organizing garment workers, I asked how long he reckoned it would

take for independent unions to get legal recognition in China. He replied, "Give us ten years!"

5. Employees' Unions: An Experiment in Union Democracy

1. URG interview with D. B. Patil, Metal Box Workers' Union, February 1982. See also BGG (1951, 3117–3121).

2. URG interview with A. W. Noronha, Hoechst Employees' Union, June 1984, and C. C. Mendes, Pfizer Employees' Union, March 1984.

3. URG interview with N. Vasudevan, February 1985.

4. URG interview with Kamala Karkal, May 1984.

5. This is why most of the unions which interacted with the URG were employees' unions. We made our services available to all unions, but it was employees' unions that were most willing to give us information, read our bulletin, and organize interunion workshops jointly with us.

6. URG interview with a Goodlass Nerolac activist of the Paints Employees' Union, February 1980.

7. Most of this information is from collective agreements, which are analyzed in more detail in URG (1983a).

8. Interviews with S. Raghavan of the Voltas and Volkart Employees' Federation and A. W. Noronha of the Hoechst Employees Union, 1981.

9. This account is based on collective agreements, charters of demands (including management "charters"), and numerous interviews with union leaders, activists, and workers in the companies mentioned. Some of the findings are presented in URG (1983b).

10. One would have thought that the company would then have taken "exclusive" responsibility for the disaster, but of course it did not. One of the accusations that enraged workers most was the company's claim that workers were responsible for the leak (*MP Chronicle* 1985).

11. I use the word "victims" or "gas victims" (*gas peedith*) because that is how survivors of the tragedy described themselves.

12. Interviews with Asha Mokashi, convenor of the Women's Wing of AIBEA, 1996. See also Hensman (2002).

13. Interviews with Ilina Sen and other members of MMM in 1995. See also Hensman (2002).

14. There is seething anger among Dalits on this score. At the National Conference on Human Rights, Social Movements, Globalisation and the Law, Panchgani, December 26, 2000–January 1, 2001, when I argued for provisional support to a workers' rights clause in WTO agreements to combat discrimination

against underprivileged sections of the labor force and abolish child labor, my position was attacked by the social activist Medha Patkar and a trade union leader. A Dalit activist counterattacked, alleging that it was because union leaders were all from the upper castes that they did not care about Dalit workers being abused and discriminated against and their children deprived of education and forced to labor. A very heated discussion followed!

15. Named after Shivaji, the warrior-king of sixteenth-century Maharashtra, and asserting the superiority of Maharashtra's culture and history of resistance to Mughal and British invaders. Its founder and leader, Bal Thackeray, organized it on the lines of the RSS, of which he was once a member (Gupta 1982, 73).

16. The SLS claims to be working for the rights of local people (defined as native Marathi speakers, even if they come from outside Bombay, as opposed to people from outside Maharashtra, even if their families have been living in Bombay for generations).

17. I use "communal" and "communalism" in the Indian sense, to mean an overwhelming emphasis on religious identity and a hostility of varying degrees toward people of other religious communities.

18. The quotations below are from workers in the companies mentioned, a union activist from GKW Sankey Division, A. W. Noronha and Raj Khalid from the Hoechst Employees' Union, V. A. Nayampally from the Pfizer Employees' Union, and S. K. Padlia from the Glaxo Laboratories Employees' Union.

19. Interviews with activists of the Paints Employees' Union and Parke-Davis Employees' Union, October 1993.

20. Reported in the bulletin of the Boehringer-Knoll Employees' Union (March 11, 1983).

21. Memorandum dated November 25, 1992, signed by C. C. Mendes, Pfizer Employees' Union; letter dated August 15, 1993, from All-India Chemical and Pharmaceutical Employees' Federation to member unions, signed by C. C. Mendes.

22. Quoted in *The Union's Lever* (1999, 20, 22).

23. Interview with R. G. Michael, Abbott Laboratories Employees' Union, December 1993.

24. Quoted in *The Union's Lever* (1999, 19).

25. Interviews with officeholders in the Paints Employees' Union; Bennet D'Costa and Franklyn D'Souza (Hindustan Lever Employees' Union); R. R. Mishra (Philips Workers' Union); Kiron Mehta (Philips Employees' Union); and Harish Pujari (Otis Elevator Employees' Union); 1985–1994. See also Banaji and Hensman (1995).

26. The account below is based on D'Costa (1997). HLEU simultaneously supported the struggle of the TOMCO Employees' Union and All-India Federation

against forced voluntary retirement schemes and for implementation of HLL's promise upon amalgamation that their employment and service conditions would be protected (TOMCOEU 1995a, 1995b).

27. The account below is based on CWM (1997a).

28. Announced at a TUSC meeting in December 2005 by Abhyankar.

29. Circular of AICAPEF dated February 11, 1994, signed by D. N. Mayekar and R. G. Michael; circular of FOFWUF dated December 17, 1994, signed by R. G. Michael; minutes of AICAPEF meeting, May 26, 1999.

30. Based on interviews with D. Thankappan (Kamani Employees' Union), N. Vasudevan, Bennet D'Costa, Suhas Abhyankar (Hindustan Lever Research Centre Employees' Union), Babu Mathew, Gautam Mody, and Ashim Roy, in July–October 2004.

6. Informal Labor: The Struggle for Legal Recognition

1. Based on a report filed by C. C. Stanley and Raja Kamarajah of Hindustan Lever Employees' Federation, *The Union's Lever* (1999, 6–7).

2. Names have been changed. The interviews, discussions, and workshops in this section were undertaken with Chanda Korgaokar and Apoorva Kaiwar as part of the research and education projects of Women Working Worldwide into codes of conduct and subcontracting chains in the garment industry between 1998 and 2003. For more details, see sections on India in WWW (1998b, 2003a, and 2003b).

3. 100 paise = 1 rupee.

4. This article also makes it clear that India was not the only country where garment exports boomed in the first half of the 1990s and declined just as precipitously in the second half: this was a trend in most developing countries that went into garment exports.

5. The *Dharmashastra* of Manu (popularly known as *Manu Smriti*) was composed some time during the first two centuries A.D. and divided society into four estates or *varnas* (literally, a distinction of color): Brahmans (priests), Kshatriyas (warriors and nobles), Vaishyas (traders), and Shudras (laborers). According to Manu, "One occupation only the lord prescribed to the Shudra, to serve meekly even these other three castes." But below them was a fifth estate, the *Achchoot* (the "Untouchables," renamed Harijans by Gandhi and Dalits by themselves), usually considered to be outside the *varna* system altogether (Upadhyay 2005, 4–5). Castes are subdivisions of these *varnas* and are further subdivided into subcastes.

6. "Fair price shops" sell rations under the Public Distribution System.

7. Shantha Sinha shows how official government statistics are doctored to show figures that are a small fraction of the real number of working children (Sinha 2005a).

8. The description is reminiscent of glass works in the nineteenth century (Marx 1976, 374–375).

9. I should make it clear I agree completely with these arguments. This does not mean that I rule out allowing children to work under all circumstances. Children are often eager to help their parents with household tasks, and I feel that both boys and girls should be encouraged to do so. Nor is it necessary to rule out all paid work; for example, children may want to earn pocket money if their parents cannot afford to give them an adequate amount. So I would not object to children working provided (1) their health and safety is assured, (2) it does not interfere with their education, and (3) it is entirely voluntary and they can quit whenever they want—which means that neither their own livelihood nor that of other family members should depend on it.

10. I am indebted to Janine Almeida for this point.

11. I have the deepest sympathy for parents who give up their children for adoption when they cannot feed or care for them, doing so in the expectation that the children will be well fed, cared for, loved, and educated. But using children solely as a source of income surely cannot be justified under any circumstances, no matter how dire.

12. Marx denounced similar schemes introduced by the Factory Acts, supposedly to enable working children to get an elementary education, as being farcical (Marx 1976, 523–526).

7. Working Women and Reproductive Labor

1. Engels supports his description by quoting from an account by an unemployed male worker. But when I interviewed women workers from SEWA, some of whom were sole breadwinners, there were depressing accounts of unemployed husbands who not only did no housework but sometimes also beat their wives and children.

2. The information in this section was obtained in group interviews with women workers by Sujata Gothoskar and me between 1981 and 1986 as part of our work for the URG and in interviews with Kamala Karkal of the Pfizer Employees' Union and Philo Martin of the Glaxo Wellcome Union in 1994.

3. Information in this section was obtained in group interviews with women workers by Chanda Korgaokar and me between 1998 and 2003 as part of our work for WWW.

4. *Bastis* are shantytowns. *Chawls* originally meant the housing built for work-ers by mill owners—three- or four-story buildings with one-room apartments going off a common corridor, with shared bathrooms and toilets—but today they can also mean apartments with more than one room and an internal bath-room and toilet or, conversely, something closely resembling a *basti*. The lack of an internal water supply in *bastis* means that often the washing of clothes and dishes is done on the doorstep, with wastewater going straight into the drains outside, so it is not an isolated occupation.

5. In case this is doubted by anyone, one way of demonstrating the point would be to ask: is it possible for someone else to substitute for a person in this particular activity or not? If someone else *eats* all my meals for me, I would die of starva-tion. But if someone else *cooks* all my meals for me, I would not suffer at all and may even enjoy them more than if I cooked them myself. Thus, in general, if it is possible to substitute one person for another in some activity, it is a process of production, while if that is not possible, it is a process of individual consumption.

6. The one-child policy, combined with preference for boys, led to the same prob-lem being faced in an even more acute form in China (BBC 2007).

7. However, it is important that the cooperatives should provide adequate wages, benefits, and facilities for their members. On one occasion when I arrived at SEWA very early in the morning and was invited to sit inside while the place was being cleaned, I was taken aback when the woman who was doing the cleaning, herself a member of the SEWA cleaning cooperative, started com-plaining bitterly about how low her wages were. After that, I was not surprised to hear from a local trade unionist that SEWA members had joined other unions to fight for higher wages!

8. A woman's right to control her own fertility also partially protects a child's right to be wanted, loved, and adequately cared for by at least one parent. This is absolutely essential, given the huge amount of time and effort that is involved in this work. Advocates of the socialization of childcare often forget that this presupposes a much larger number of people who love children and wish to spend time on childcare than do so at present.

9. This applies to schoolchildren too. Teachers are responsible for pastoral care as well as education, and therefore even a ratio of twenty-five to thirty children to one teacher—never mind the usual Indian ratio of fifty to seventy children to one teacher!—is not low enough.

8. Employment Creation and Welfare

1. When Arundhati Roy contemptuously dismissed the NREGA as "just throw-ing some crumbs to the creatures under the table" (Sampath 2009), she

demonstrated a complete failure to connect with the lives and aspirations of the rural poor. In fact, much of the violence in the forest belt of India in 2009 was initiated by the brutal state repression of nonviolent mass movements of Adivasis protesting the deprivation to which they had been subjected and demanding their legal rights under NREGA and the Forest Rights Act. Once the CPI(Maoist), which was committed to armed struggle to capture state power—a completely different agenda—infiltrated and hijacked these mass movements, the violence escalated (Bhattacharya 2009).

2. Based on interviews with Thankappan in 1987 and on Fernandez (1986); Subramaniam (1987); participation in a CWM workshop on "A Critical Analysis of Kamani Tubes Ltd. and KMA Ltd," December 28–29, 1998 (report of the workshop dated January 11, 1999); and NTUI (n.d.)

3. A SAL (*Sociedad Anónima Laboral*, or labor company) is like an ordinary limited company (SA), but at least 85 percent of the permanent employees must be shareholders and own at least half the shares. Workers leaving the firm must sell their shares to other employees (Holmström 1993, 2–3).

4. Interview with Roma at CWM, Delhi, July 2004.

5. From the October 20, 2003, report of a joint fact-finding committee (consisting of a retired High Court judge, trade unionists, and human-rights activists) into the deaths of Anant Dalvi and Akhtar Khan.

6. There are many other issues relating to pension funds, which are still a new phenomenon in India. For example, unions can influence the investment policies of pension funds, encouraging corporate social responsibility, albeit in the guise of risk reduction (Minns 2001, 204; also mentioned by Bill Dempsey, deputy director of the Capital Stewardship Program, Service Employees International Union, at a talk to the TUSC in Bombay, December 2005).

9. International Strategies

1. The finding that openness to the world economy can go with high labor standards in any particular country is not incompatible with the proposition that globalization, as a process, undermines labor rights globally.

2. The number of GUFs has been reduced by mergers to ten.

3. Employers at that time used the same argument that they use today to oppose protective legislation: namely, that it would put them at a disadvantage in international competition. Hence the necessity for unions to press for the eight-hour day internationally.

4. The International Union of Food, Agricultural, Hotel, Restaurant, Catering, Tobacco, and Allied Workers Associations.

5. These are no. 87, the Freedom of Association and Protection of the Right to Organize Convention, 1948; no. 98, the Right to Organize and Collective Bargaining Convention, 1949; no. 29, the Forced Labour Convention, 1930; no. 105, the Abolition of Forced Labour Convention, 1957; no. 138, the Minimum Age Convention, 1973; no. 100, the Equal Remuneration Convention, 1951; and no. 111, the Discrimination (Employment and Occupation) Convention, 1958. It is generally considered that no. 182, the Convention Concerning the Prohibition and Immediate Action for the Elimination of the Worst Forms of Child Labour, 1999, is also one of the core conventions.

6. By 2004, the United States had ratified only two out the eight Core Conventions; only four of the ILO's 177 members had ratified fewer, and the United States stood fifth from the bottom, along with Myanmar and Oman. From 1953 to 1988, the United States did not ratify a single convention (Alston 2004, 467–468).

7. At that time, the rupee was worth approximately four times what it was worth in 2005.

8. I helped organize the tour and meetings with members of groups, which included the Kings Cross Families Action Group, Community Action Against Toxic Waste, the Herald Families Association, Parents Against Cancer Environment, Stop Toxic Waste Incinerators in Cleveland, the Belvedere and District Campaign Against Pollution, the Womanagh Valley Protection Association, and the Limerick Environmental Health Protection Group. The delegation also addressed public meetings in London and Cork City (see Hensman and BGJB 1991).

9. At one time, I used to think that Esperanto was the answer, but experience has shown that idea to be impractical. Today, I feel that English—at least for those of us who come from former British colonies—would be far more realistic, because it is already known to enough people to ensure a supply of teachers and there is a demand for it from workers.

10. See chapter 6 for a description of the workers who participated in this exercise.

11. Names have been changed.

12. This conflicts with the position of some consumer campaigners that boycotts should not be contemplated and terminating contracts with suppliers should be avoided because they lead to loss of jobs. But the workers are right: what is the alternative if companies are persistent violators?

13. Ashwini Sukthankar, personal communication.

14. Padmini Swaminathan, personal communication.

15. This debate owes much to two consultations organized by CEC in 1995, in Delhi (March) and Bangalore (November), and discussions of the TUSC in Bombay, in April and May 1995 and August 2000.

16. This is a strange position, given that all the rights in the proposed social clause are also included in the Indian constitution and were adopted by all ILO members—a majority of whom are from developing countries—in the form of the declaration! Moreover, not a single worker whom I have interacted with—formal or informal, male or female—thinks that he or she should not be entitled to the rights embodied in these conventions.

17. It has been suggested that the idea of abrogating the WTO "reflects a 'creationist' view of institutions rather than an 'evolutionary' view"—i.e., the belief that unless an institution emerges perfect, it has to be an instrument of oppression (Rodrigo 2007)—whereas there is considerable scope for pushing for the incorporation of human rights and environmental concerns in it.

18. One reason why the number of protesters at Seattle was about ten times the number protesting against the IMF and World Bank could be that the effects of the Washington institutions' policies were not felt in the developed countries (Kaushal 2002).

19. The opinion has been expressed (e.g., Alston 2004) that the rights embodied in the Core Conventions are too restricted and that basic human rights at work are broader. This is true, but from a practical point of view, it is much easier to start with rights that have already been agreed to in principle by all ILO members as being universal.

20. Letter dated August 2, 2007. http://www.uslaboragainstwar.org/article.php?id= 14248.

10. Conclusion: Toward Global Solidarity

1. In India, there is no such thing as permanent residence for foreigners, and citizens of neighboring countries have an even harder time. As a citizen of Sri Lanka married to an Indian, I still had to extend my visa every year after being settled in India for thirty-seven years. My first citizenship application was lost in the bureaucratic labyrinth, and the second was rejected on the grounds that I had not been resident in India for 365 days during the year prior to the application. In 2010, Home Minister P. Chidambaram initiated a process to make the residence requirement for citizenship less inflexible.

References

Abolition 2000. 2007. Press release, August 14. *Peace Now*. New Delhi: Coalition for Nuclear Disarmament and Peace.

Acharya, Shankar. 2003. Wanted: A trade policy. *BS* (September 23).

——. 2005. Thirty years of tax reform in India. *EPW* 40, no. 20 (May 14): 2061–2070.

Adams, Roy. 2004. Wal-Mart's anti-unionism and human rights, recent developments in Canada. *IUR* 12, no. 1: 13.

Adler, Max. 1978. The ideology of the world war. In *Austro-Marxism*, ed. Tom Bottomore and Patrick Goode, 125–135. Oxford: Clarendon Press, Oxford. Excerpted from Zur Ideologie des Weltkrieges, *Der Kampf* 8 (1915): 123–130.

Adve, Nagaraj. 2005. Living to fight another day: The attack on Honda's workers. *EPW* 40, no. 37 (September 10): 4015–4019.

AFL-CIO. 2004. When China represses workers' rights, US workers lose jobs. http://www.aflcio.org/issuespolitics/globaleconomy/ExecSummary301.cfm.

——. 2008. 2007 trends in CEO pay. http://www.aflcio.org/corporatewatch/paywatch/pay/index.cfm.

Agarwal, Bina. 2010. Rethinking agricultural production collectives. *EPW* 45, no. 9 (February 27): 64–78.

Aggarwal, Aradhana. 2004. Pleading for the public. *BS* (November 5).

Aggarwal, Smita. 2009. Sacking of two jet pilots illegal, says labour commissioner. *YAHOO! India News* (September 11). http://in.news.yahoo.com/48/20090911/1238/tbs-sacking-of-two-jet-pilots-illegal-sa.html.

Ahmed, Iftikhar. 1999. Getting rid of child labour. *EPW* 34, no. 27 (July 3): 1815–1822.

Ahya, Chetan. 2001. India: Pension systems—Time to reform. http://www.morganstanley.com/GEFdata/digests/20010705-thu.html.

Aiyar, Swaminathan. 1996. India, 14 others rebut non-trade issues. *Economic Times* (December 10).

Alden, Edward. 2002. US divided on EU levy issue. *BS* (September 17).

——. 2004. US white-collar job losses touch a raw nerve. *BS* (January 29).

Alden, Edward, and Guy De Jonquieres. 2002. Washington declares it will stand by US producers. *BS* (March 12).

Allen, Sheila, and Carol Wolkowitz. 1986. The control of women's labour: The case of homeworking. *Feminist Review* 22 (February): 25–51.

Alston, Philip. 2004. "Core labour standards" and the transformation of the international labour rights regime. *European Journal of International Law* 15, no. 3: 457–521.

Ambasta, Pramathesh. 2009. Programming NREGS to succeed. *The Hindu* (October 31).

Ambasta, Pramathesh, P. S. Vijay Shankar, and Mihir Shah. 2008. Two years of NREGA: The road ahead. *EPW* 43, no. 8 (February 23): 41–50.

Amin, Samir. 1964. *Accumulation on a world scale: A critique of the theory of underdevelopment.* New York: Monthly Review Press.

——. 1990. *Delinking: Towards a polycentric world.* London: Zed Books.

——. 1998. Towards a progressive and democratic new world order. *EPW* 33, no. 23 (June 6): 1385–1390.

Anderson, Michael. 1990. Periodizing law and labour in India c.1918–1952. Paper presented at postgraduate seminar, University of London Institute of Commonwealth Studies (January 19).

Andreas, Joel. 2004. *Addicted to war: Why the U.S. can't kick militarism.* Oakland, Calif.: AK Press.

Anti-Fascist Forum, ed. 2000. *My enemy's enemy: Essays on globalization, fascism, and the struggle against capitalism.* Toronto: Anti-Fascist Forum.

Antony, M. J. 2001a. Casual staff cannot be kept permanently. *BS* (January 24).

——. 2001b. Bid to dilute contract labour law fails. *BS* (February 21).

——. 2003. The ambit of labour contracts. *BS* (July 23).

Armbruster-Sandoval, Ralph. 2005. *Globalization and cross-border labor solidarity in the Americas: The anti-sweatshop movement and the struggle for social justice.* New York: Routledge.

Arokiasamy, P., Kirsty McNay, and Robert H. Cassen. 2004. Female education and fertility decline: Recent developments in the relationship. *EPW* 39, no. 41 (October 9): 4503–4507.

Arora, Rashme. 2003. Adverse sex ratio results in no brides in Rohtak. *InfoChange News and Features* (February). http://www.infochangeindia.org/features76.jsp.

Arrighi, Giovanni. 1994. *The long twentieth century.* London: Verso.

Arrighi, Giovanni, and John S. Saul. 1974. Nationalism and revolution in sub-Saharan Africa. In *Essays on the political economy of Africa,* ed. Giovanni Arrighi and John S. Saul, 44–102. Nairobi: East African Publishing House.

Arthurs, Harry. 2002. Private ordering and workers' rights in the global economy: Corporate codes of conduct as a regime of labour market regulation. In *Labour law in an era of globalization: Transformative practices and possibilities,* ed. J. Conaghan, R. M. Fischl, and K. Klare, 471–487. Oxford: Oxford University Press.

Arun, T. K. 2002. Excise, customs duty rationalisation can weave success for textile sector. *ET* (January 15).

——. 2003a. G-21 proposal puts onus on developed world. *ET* (September 11).

——. 2003b. After a lot of ho hum, comes the anti-climax: Meet collapses without a pact. *ET* (September 16).

Ascherson, Neal. 1981. *The Polish August.* Harmondsworth: Penguin.

Ascoly, Nina. 2004. Meissen brings together garment industry labour rights activists and informal economy experts. Report of IRENE/CCC Seminar on Campaigning Strategies on Informal Labour in the Global Garment Industry (September 23–25), at the Evangelische Akademie Meissen.

Ascoly, Nina, and Ineke Zeldenrust. 2002. Working with codes: Perspectives from the Clean Clothes Campaign. In *Corporate responsibility and labour rights: Codes of conduct in the global economy,* ed. R. Jenkins, R. Pearson, and G. Seyfang, 172–183. London: Earthscan.

Ashwin, Sarah. 2007. Russian trade unions: Stuck in Soviet-style subordination? In *Trade union revitalisation: Trends and prospects in thirty-four countries,* ed. Craig Phelan, 319–333. Berne: Peter Lang.

Asian Labour Update. 1995–1996. The social clause: Will it work for workers? *Asian Labour Update* 20 (November–March).

ASK. 2001. *Report on pre-study: Basic information on labour conditions in the garment industry in the region of Mumbai.* New Delhi: ASK.

Atleson, James. 2002. The voyage of the *Neptune Jade*: Transnational labour solidarity and the obstacles of domestic law. In *Labour law in an era of globalization: Transformative practices and possibilities,* ed. J. Conaghan, R. M. Fischl, and K. Klare, 380–399. Oxford: Oxford University Press.

Atzeni, Maurizio, and Pablo Ghiliani. 2007. The resilience of traditional trade union practices in the revitalisation of the Argentine labour movement. In *Trade union revitalisation: Trends and prospects in thirty-four countries,* ed. Craig Phelan, 105–199. Berne: Peter Lang.

Avineri, Shlomo, ed. 1969. *Karl Marx on colonialism and modernization.* New York: Anchor.

Bagchi, Amiya Kumar. 1972. *Private investment in India, 1900–1939.* Cambridge: Cambridge University Press.

Bajpai, Asha. 1996. *Women's rights at the workplace: Emerging challenges and legal interventions.* Mumbai: Tata Institute of Social Sciences.

Balasubramanyam, V. N., and V. Mahambare. 2001. *India's economic reforms and the manufacturing sector.* Lancaster University Management School Working Paper 2001/010, Lancaster University Management School, Lancaster.

Ball, Chris. 1990. *Trade unions and equal opportunities employers.* London: MSF.

Banaji, Jairus. 1977. The Comintern and Indian nationalism. *International* 3, no. 4 (Summer): 25–41.

——. 1996. Globalisation and restructuring in the Indian food industry. In *Agrarian questions: Essays in appreciation of T. J. Byres,* ed. Henry Bernstein and Tom Brass, 191–210. London: Frank Cass.

——. 2001a. Workers' rights in a new economic order. *Biblio* 4, nos. 1–2 (January–February).

——. 2001b. Corporate governance and the Indian private sector. In *Corporate governance and the Indian private sector,* by Jairus Banaji and Gautam Mody, 5–33. Oxford: Queen Elizabeth House.

——. 2005. Thwarting the market for corporate control: Takeover regulation in India. Paper presented to the QEH Fiftieth Anniversary Conference (July 4–5).

Banaji, Jairus, and Rohini Hensman. 1990. *Beyond multinationalism: Management policy and bargaining relationships in international companies.* New Delhi: Sage.

——. 1995. India: Multinationals and the resistance to unionised labour. *IUR* 2, no. 2: 5–6.

Banaji, Shakuntala, and Ammar Al-Ghabban. 2006. "Neutrality comes from inside us": British-Asian and Indian perspectives on television news after 11 September. *Journal of Ethnic and Migration Studies* 32, no. 6 (August): 1005–1026.

Banerjee, Debabrata. 2006. Changing labour relations, informalization, conditions of struggle of labour under real subsumption by capital: A historical perspective in India and Delhi. *Scribd.* http://www.scribd.com/doc/21250364/Changing-Labour-Relations-Hegel-Marx-Distinction.

Banerjee, Nirmala. 1981. Is small beautiful? In *Change and choice in Indian industry,* ed. A. Bagchi and N. Banerjee, 177–295. Calcutta: Centre for Studies in Social Sciences.

——. 1985a. Women's work and discrimination. In *Tyranny of the household: Investigative essays on women's work,* ed. D. Jain and N. Banerjee, 146–191. New Delhi: Shakti.

——. 1985b. *Women workers in the unorganized sector.* Hyderabad: Sangam.

Banerji, Rukmini. 2003. Revitalising government provision: Partnership between Pratham and municipal primary schools in Mumbai. In *Child labour and the right to education in South Asia: Needs versus rights?*, ed. N. Kabeer, G. Nambissan, and R. Subrahmanian, 267–291. New Delhi: Sage.

Baran, Paul A., and Paul M. Sweezy. 1966. *Monopoly capital: An essay on the American economic and social order.* Harmondsworth: Penguin.

Bardhan, Pranab. 2001. Social justice in the global economy. *EPW* 36, nos. 5–6 (February 3): 467–480.

Barman, Abheek. 1998. Integral ignorance. *ET* (December 9).

Barratt Brown, Michael. 1972. A critique of Marxist theories of imperialism. In *Studies in the theory of imperialism,* ed. Roger Owen and Bob Sutcliffe, 35–70. London: Longman.

——. 1974. *The economics of imperialism.* Harmondsworth: Penguin.

Barrett, Michele. 1980. *Women's oppression today: Problems in Marxist feminist analysis.* London: Verso.

Barrett, Michele, and Mary McIntosh. 1980. The "family wage": Some problems for socialists and feminists. *Capital and Class* 11 (Summer): 51–72.

Barrientos, Stephanie. 2002. Mapping codes through the value chain: From researcher to detective. In *Corporate responsibility and labour rights: Codes of conduct in the global economy,* ed. R. Jenkins, R. Pearson, and G. Seyfang, 61–76. London: Earthscan.

Barrios De Chungara, Domitila, and Moema Viezzer. 1978. *Let me speak: Testimony of Domitila, a woman of the Bolivian mines.* New York: Monthly Review Press.

Barry, Christian, and Sanjay G. Reddy. 2005. Promoting poor countries' interests in the international trading system: A proposal. http://www.alternatefutures.org.

——. 2008. *International trade and labor standards: A proposal for linkage.* New York: Columbia University Press.

Basu, Dipak. 2000. Children as slaves. *ET* (April 9).

Basu, Kaushik. 2003. International labour standards and child labour. In *Child labour and the right to education in South Asia: Needs versus rights?*, ed. N. Kabeer, G. Nambissan, and R. Subrahmanian, 95–106. New Delhi: Sage.

Baud, Isa. 1983. *Women's labour in the Indian textile industry.* Research project IRIS report no. 23. Tilburg: Tilburg Institute of Development Research.

——. 1987. Industrial subcontracting: The effects of the putting-out system on poor working women in India. In *Invisible hands: Women in home-based production,* ed. Andrea Menefee Singh and Anita Kelles-Viitanen, 69–91. New Delhi: Sage.

Bauer, Otto. 1913. The explanation of imperialism. *Neuer Zeit* 24.

Bayat, Assef. 1987. *Workers and revolution in Iran.* London: Zed.

Bayly, C. A. 2004. *The birth of the modern world, 1780–1914.* Malden, Mass.: Blackwell.

BBC News. 2000. Tetley bagged by India's Tata. http://www.news.bbc.co.uk/1/hi/business/658724.stm.

——. 2007. Chinese facing shortage of wives. http://news.bbc.co.uk/2/hi/asia-pacific/6254763.stm.

Beechey, Veronica. 1977. Some notes on female wage labour in the capitalist mode of production. *Capital and Class* 3: 45–66.

——. 1978. Women and production: A critical analysis of some sociological theories of women's work. In *Feminism and materialism*, ed. A. Kuhn and A. Wolpe, 155–195. London: Routledge & Kegan Paul.

Bello, Walden. 2000. Prague 2000: Toward a deglobalized world. *Focus Dossiers* 3 (September). http://www.focusweb.org.

——. 2006. Introduction: George Bush's rollback economics. In *Destroy and Profit: Wars, Disasters and Corporations*. Bangkok: Focus on the Global South.

——. 2009. The virtues of deglobalization. *Foreign Policy in Focus* (September 3). http://www.fpif.org/fpiftxt/6399.

Ben Barka, Mehdi. 1969. Resolving the ambiguities of national sovereignty. In *From Gandhi to Guevara*, ed. C. R. Hensman, 405–410. London: Allen Lane.

Bendiner, B. 1987. *International labour affairs: The world trade unions and the multinational companies*. Oxford: Clarendon.

Benjamin, Paul. 2002. Who needs labour law? Defining the scope of labour protection. In *Labour law in an era of globalization: Transformative practices and possibilities*, ed. J. Conaghan, R. M. Fischl, and K. Klare, 75–92. Oxford: Oxford University Press.

Benston, Margaret. 1969. The political economy of women's liberation. *Monthly Review* 21, no. 4 (September): 13–27.

Berger, Iris. 1992. *Threads of solidarity*. Bloomington: Indiana University Press.

Bergman, David. 1993. *Disasters—Where the law fails: A new agenda for dealing with corporate violence*. London: Herald Families Association.

Bettelheim, Charles. 1978. *Class struggles in the USSR*. New York: Monthly Review Press.

BGG. 1949a. Part I-L (October 6): 1413ff.

——. 1949b. Part I-L (December 29): 2458ff.

——. 1949c. Part I-L (December 8): 2095ff.

——. 1951. Part I-L (June 26): 3117ff.

——. 1952a. Part I-L (August 28): 2818ff.

——. 1952b. Part I-L (March 27): 1255ff.

Bhaduri, Aditi. 2007. This act falls short. *Boloji.com* (September 9). http://www.boloji.com/wfs5/wfs995.htm.

Bhaduri, Amit. 2005. First priority: Guaranteeing employment and the right to information. *EPW* 40, no. 4 (January 22): 267–269.

Bhagwati, Jagdish. 2002. *Free trade today*. Princeton, N.J.: Princeton University Press.

Bhargava, Anjuli. 1996. India softens stand on labour standards, investment. *BS* (December 13).

Bhatt, Ela, and Renana Jhabvala. 2004. The idea of work. *EPW* 39, no. 48 (November 27): 5133–5140.

Bhattacharjea, Aditya. 2005. Predatory pricing and anti-dumping revisited. *EPW* 40, no. 5 (January 29): 482–484.

Bhattacharjee, Debashish. 1999. *Organized labour and economic liberalization India: Past, present, and future*. Geneva: International Institute for Labour Studies.

Bhattacharya, Santwana. 2009. This land is my land. . . . *Asia Times Online* (June 25). http://www.atimes.com/atimes/South_Asia/KF25Df03.html.

Bhaumik, T. K. 2004. Debate: Will new US law on outsourcing affect India? *ET* (February 3).

Bheda, Rajesh. 2002. Beware! Labour standards are already here. *ET* (January 12).

Bidwai, Praful. 2004. Hopes for Indo-Pak peace in '05. http://www.antiwar.com/bidwai/?articleid=4204.

——. 2005. Anti-labour violence isn't random. *ET* (August 5).

——. 2008. World's cheapest car environmentally costly. *Inter-Press Service* (January 17). http://ipsnews.net/news.asp?idnews=40805.

Bidwai, Praful, and Achin Vanaik. 1999. *South Asia on a short fuse: Nuclear politics and the future of global disarmament*. New Delhi: Oxford University Press.

Birnbaum, David. 2000. *Birnbaum's global guide to winning the great garment war*. Hong Kong: Third Horizon.

——. 2001. The coming garment massacre. http://just-style.com/features_print.asp?art=453.

Bissell, Susan. 2003. The social construction of childhood: A perspective from Bangladesh. In *Child labour and the right to education in South Asia: Needs versus rights?*, ed. N. Kabeer, G. Nambissan, and R. Subrahmanian, 49–72. New Delhi: Sage.

Black, William K. 2009. Those who forget the regulatory successes of the past are condemned to failure. *EPW* 44, no. 13 (March 28): 80–86.

Blackburn, Daniel. 1999. ICFTU slams US standards. *IUR* 6, no. 4: 27–28.

Blackburn, Robin. 1999. The new collectivism: Pension reform, grey capitalism, and complex socialism. *New Left Review* 233 (January–February): 3–65.

Blowfield, Mick. 2002. ETI: A multi-stakeholder approach. In *Corporate responsibility and labour rights: Codes of conduct in the global economy*, ed. R. Jenkins, R. Pearson, and G. Seyfang, 184–195. London: Earthscan.

Bombay Journalist. 1993. Pension scam! *Bombay Journalist* 7 (September).

Boraston, Ian, Hugh Clegg, and Malcolm Rimmer. 1975. *Workplace and union: A study of local relationships in fourteen unions*. London: Heinemann.

Bosniak, Linda. 2002. Critical reflections on "citizenship" as a progressive aspiration. In *Labour law in an era of globalization: Transformative practices and possibilities*, ed. J. Conaghan, R. M. Fischl, and K. Klare, 339–349. Oxford: Oxford University Press.

Boston, Sarah. 1980. *Women workers and the trade union movement*. London: Davis-Poynter.

Brahm, Laurence. 2009. China moves into reserve position. *Asia Times Online* (October 1). http://www.voxeu.org/index.php?q=node/3672.

Braverman, Harry. 1964. *Labor and monopoly capitalism*. New York: Monthly Review Press.

Brecher, Jeremy, Tim Costello, and Brendan Smith. 2000. *Globalization from below: The power of solidarity*. Cambridge, Mass.: South End Press.

Breman, Jan. 1990. "Even dogs are better off": The ongoing battle between capital and labour in the cane-fields of Gujarat. *Journal of Peasant Studies* 17: 546–608.

——. 1995. Labour, get lost: A late-capitalist manifesto. *EPW* 30, no. 37 (September 16): 2294–2300.

——. 1996. *Footloose labour*. Cambridge: Cambridge University Press.

——. 2004. *The making and unmaking of an industrial working class: Sliding down the labour hierarchy in Ahmedabad, India*. New Delhi: Oxford University Press.

——. 2007. *The poverty regime in village India*. New Delhi: Oxford University Press.

——. 2009. The myth of the global safety net. *New Left Review* 59 (September–October): 29–36.

Brett, Bill. 1995. The ILO and the WTO. *IUR* 2, no. 1: 4–5.

Brill, Lucy. 2002. Can codes of conduct help home-based workers? In *Corporate responsibility and labour rights: Codes of conduct in the global economy*, ed. R. Jenkins, R. Pearson, and G. Seyfang, 113–123. London: Earthscan.

Briskin, Linda. 1993. Union women and separate organizing. In *Women challenging unions: Feminism, democracy, and militancy*, ed. Linda Briskin and Patricia McDermott, 89–108. Toronto: University of Toronto.

——. 2002. The equity project in Canadian unions: Confronting the challenge of restructuring and globalisation. In *Gender, diversity, and trade unions: International perspectives*, ed. F. Colgan and S. Ledwith, 28–47. London: Routledge.

Briskin, Linda, and Patricia McDermott. 1993. Introduction: The feminist challenge to the unions. In *Women challenging unions: Feminism, democracy, and militancy*, ed. Linda Briskin and Patricia McDermott. Toronto: University of Toronto Press.

Brown, Joshua Samuel. 2004. Confessions of a sweatshop monitor. Reprinted in *Monitoring sweatshops: Workers, consumers, and the global apparel industry*, by J. Esbenshade, 209–213. Philadelphia: Temple University Press.

Broyelle, Claudie. 1977. *Women's liberation in China*. Sussex: Harvester.

Brysk, Alison. 2002. Introduction: Transnational threats and opportunities. In *Globalization and Human Rights*, ed. A. Brysk, 1–16. Berkeley: University of California Press.

——, ed. 2002. *Globalization and Human Rights.* Berkeley: University of California Press.

BS. 1985. Union Carbide to close down Bhopal factory. *BS* (April 12).

——. 1994. RSS asks Left to join swadeshi stir. *BS* (November 21).

——. 1995. RSS to continue attack on globalisation, MNCs. *BS* (March 28).

——. 1996. ILO chief barred from speaking at meet. *BS* (December 7).

——. 1998a. RSS plans stir against govt today. *BS* (November 30).

——. 1998b. Turtle hawks. *BS* (October 16).

——. 1999a. Tarapore flays exchange control rules. *BS* (November 25).

——. 1999b. Factory jobs keep growing. *BS* (November 12).

——. 2000a. Anti-dumping duty slapped on optical fibre from Korea. *BS* (June 22).

——. 2000b. Dumping duty imposed on China soda ash. *BS* (July 15–16).

——. 2001a. Bandh brings Maharashtra to a halt. *BS* (April 26).

——. 2001b. Labour law changes nullified, assures CM. *BS* (May 11).

——. 2001c. PM snubs BMS, says PSU disinvestment is a reality. *BS* (May 19–20).

——. 2001d. Garment exports register four per cent decline. *BS* (April 21–22).

——. 2002a. EU files formal complaint with WTO. *BS* (March 8).

——. 2002b. Japan retaliates against US steel tariffs. *BS* (May 18–19).

——. 2002c. US under fire at WTO over steel tariffs. *BS* (March 9–10).

——. 2002d. Sops required for textile exports. *BS* (February 25).

——. 2002e. India losing low labour cost edge. *BS* (January 9).

——. 2002f. Minimum pay for casual staff. *BS* (November 25).

——. 2003a. Dabur to buy UK firm Redrock in $5m deal. *BS* (July 24).

——. 2003b. African states plead for drug deal. *BS* (August 30–31).

——. 2003c. Employment levels fall 1.5% in organised sector. *BS* (May 16).

——. 2004a. Jobs outsourced to local firms won't come home. *BS* (September 3).

——. 2004b. Policy hurting job creation. *BS* (December 28).

——. 2004c. India can be a global apparel player. *BS* (April 27).

——. 2004d. Need for flexibility in labour market: FM. *BS* (September 29).

——. 2005a. TCS, Infosys bag $400-m ABN outsourcing deal. *BS* (September 2).

——. 2005b. M&M set to buy Romania firm. *BS* (September 17–18).

——. 2005c. Bharat Forge now snaps up Swedish firm. *BS* (September 22).

——. 2005d. Ranbaxy to set up JV in Mexico. *BS* (February 21).

——. 2005e. Jubilant buys US R&D unit for $33 mn. *BS* (October 6).

——. 2008. Modi's Gujarat bags Tata's Nano. *BS* (October 8).

Bukharin, Nikolai. 1972. Imperialism and the accumulation of capital. In *Imperialism and the accumulation of capital*, ed. Kenneth Tarbuck, 151–270. London: Penguin.

Burawoy, Michael. 1979. *Manufacturing consent.* Chicago: University of Chicago Press.

Bureau of Economic Analysis. 2008. National income and product accounts table. http://www.bea.gov/national/nipaweb/TableView.asp?SelectedTable=55&View Series=NO&Java=no&Request3Place=N&3Place=N&FromView=YES&Freq=Qtr& FirstYear=2006&LastYear=2008&3Place=N&Update=Update&JavaBox=no#Mid.

Burkeman, Oliver. 2009. Obama administration says goodbye to "war on terror." *Guardian* (March 25). http://www.guardian.co.uk/world/2009/mar/25/ obama-war-terror-overseas-contingency-operations.

Burra, Neera. 1999. Social mobilization strategies for child labour elimination. In *Against child labour: Indian and international dimensions and strategies,* ed. Klaus Voll, 261–269. New Delhi: Mosaic.

——. 2001. Cultural stereotypes and household behaviour: Girl child labour in India. *EPW* 36, nos. 5–6 (February 3): 481–488.

——. 2003. Rights versus needs: Is it in the "best interest of the child"? In *Bangladeshi women workers and labour market decisions: The power to choose,* ed. N. Kabeer, 73–94. New Delhi: Vistaar.

——. 2005. Causes and consequences of children's work. *Children and Poverty,* UNDP India (December 14). http://hdrc.undp.org.in/childrenandpoverty/ CHILDPOV/CAUSESC.htm.

Business Week. 1963. Multinational companies. *Business Week* (April 20).

Cairo Conference. 1969. Peace and international cooperation. In *From Gandhi to Guevara,* by C. R. Hensman, 128–134. London: Allen Lane.

Callahan, Kevin. 2000. "Performing inter-nationalism" in Stuttgart in 1907: French and German socialist nationalism and the political culture of an international socialist congress. *International Review of Social History* 45, no. 1 (April): 51–87.

Carew, Anthony. 1976. *Democracy and government in European trade unions.* London: Allen & Unwin.

Cartier, Jan. 1989. The experience at Ford. In *Solidarity for survival: The Don Thomson reader on trade union internationalism,* ed. Mike Press and Don Thomson, 59–64. Nottingham: Spokesman.

Castells, Manuel. 2003. Global informational capitalism. In *The global transformations reader: An introduction to the globalization debate,* ed. David Held and Anthony McGrew, 311–334. Cambridge: Polity Press. Excerpted from Castells, Manuel. 2000. *The rise of the network society.* Oxford: Blackwell.

CCC. 2001. Campaign to support the free trade zone workers' union of Sri Lanka. http://www.cleanclothes.org/urgent/01-09-23.htm.

——. 2008. FFI "Case Closed." http://www.cleanclothes.org/urgent/ffi.htm.

CCC and CEC. 2002. *Trade union–Clean Clothes Campaign interface: A brief report on meetings at Delhi, Mumbai, and Thiruppur.* New Delhi: CEC.

359
References

CCPD. *Democracy, citizens, and migrants: Nationalism in the era of globalization.* Delhi: CCPD.

Central Trade Union Organisations of India. 1995. Appeal from the Central Trade Union Organisations of India to the fifth conference of labour ministers of non-aligned and other developing countries. New Delhi. Mimeograph.

CEPAA. 1998. *Guidance document for social accountability 8000.* London: CEPAA.

Chakravarty, Chaitali. 2002. FMCG heads north-east for a holiday. *ET* (February 1).

Chakravarty, Manas. 2004. The spectre of outsourcing. *BS* (February 3).

Chan, Anita. 2005. China says no to developed countries' corporate social responsibility. *IUR* 12, no. 1: 18–19.

Chanda, Rupa. 2004. Debate: Will new US law on outsourcing affect India? *ET* (February 3).

Chandavarkar, Rajnarayan. 2003. *The origins of industrial capitalism in India: Business strategies and the working classes in Bombay, 1900–1940.* Cambridge: Cambridge University Press.

Chandra, Pankaj, and P. R. Shukla. 1994. Manufacturing excellence and global competitiveness. *EPW* 39, no. 9 (February 26): M2–11.

Chandrasekhar, C. P. 1997, The economic consequences of the abolition of child labour: An Indian case study. *Journal of Peasant Studies* 24, no. 3 (April): 137–179.

Chang, Ha-Joon. 2007. *Bad Samaritans: The myth of free trade and the secret history of capitalism.* London: Bloomsbury.

Chatterjee, Sumeet. 2004. Now, US, UK techies try their luck in India. *ET* (January 21).

Chatterji, Saubhadra. 2008. Unorganised sector bill: Govt junks Left proposals. *BS* (January 28).

Chauhar, Paro. 1998. Living on the edge. *LF* 4, no. 8 (August): 17–20.

Chhachhi, Amrita. 1983. The case of India. In *Of common cloth: Women in the global textile industry,* ed. Wendy Chapkis and Cynthia Enloe, 39–45. Amsterdam: Transnational Institute.

——. 2005. *Eroding citizenship: Gender and labour in contemporary India.* Amsterdam: Academisch Proefschrift, Universiteit van Amsterdam.

Chhachhi, Amrita, and Renee Pittin. 1996. Multiple identities, multiple strategies. In *Confronting state, capital, and patriarchy: Women organizing in the process of industrialization,* ed. Amrita Chhachhi and Renee Pittin, 93–130. Basingstoke: Macmillan; New York: St. Martin's Press.

——, ed. 1996. *Confronting state, capital, and patriarchy: Women organizing in the process of industrialization.* Basingstoke: Macmillan; New York: St. Martin's Press.

Chibber, Vivek. 2003. *Locked in place: State-building and late industrialization in India.* Princeton, N.J.: Princeton University Press.

Chikarmane, Poornima, and Lakshmi Narayan. 2000. Formalising livelihood: Case of wastepickers in Pune. *EPW* 35, no. 41 (October 7): 3639–3642.

Chikkatur, Ananth, and Sunita Dubey. 2009. Black to green: The carbon debate and beyond. *Himal Southasian* 22, no. 6 (June): 24–35.

Chin, David. 1998. The social clause: Dumping the "social dumping defence." *IUR* 5, no. 8: 24–25.

Chodorow, Nancy, and Susan Contratto. 1982. The fantasy of the perfect mother. In *Rethinking the family: Some feminist questions,* ed. B. Thorne with M. Yalom, 54–75. New York: Longman.

Choudry, Aziz. 2002. *Bilateral trade and investment agreements.* Colombo: TIE-Asia.

Christensen, Paul T. 1999. *Russia's workers in transition: Labor, management, and the state under Gorbachev and Yeltsin.* DeKalb: Northern Illinois University Press.

CINI-ASHA. 2003. Family adjustments for mainstreaming child labourers into formal schools in Calcutta: The experience of CINI-ASHA. In *Child labour and the right to education in South Asia: Needs versus rights?,* ed. N. Kabeer, G. Nambissan, and R. Subrahmanian, 335–348. New Delhi: Sage.

Clark, Andrew. 2009. Report: Regulator was tipped off about Madoff fraud as early as 1992. *Guardian* (September 2).

Clarke, Ian. 1999. *Globalization and international relations theory.* Oxford: Oxford University Press.

Clarke, Martin. 1977. *Antonio Gramsci and the revolution that failed.* New Haven: Yale University Press.

Clarke, William. 2004. Revisited: The real reasons for the upcoming war with Iraq: A macroeconomic and geostrategic analysis of the unspoken truth. A revised version of his January 2003 essay. http://www.ratical.org/ratville/CAH/RriraqWar.html.

Clawson, Dan, and Mary Ann Clawson. 2007. US unions and revitalisation strategies in the neo-liberal era. In *Trade union revitalisation: Trends and prospects in thirty-four countries,* ed. Craig Phelan, 39–57. Berne: Peter Lang.

Cleveland, Sarah H. 2004. Why international labor standards? In *International labor standards: Globalization, trade, and public policy,* ed. R. J. Flanagan and William B. Gould IV, 129–178. Stanford, Calif.: Stanford University Press.

Cliff, Tony. 1974. *State capitalism in Russia.* London: Pluto.

Cockburn, Cynthia. 1983. *Brothers: Male dominance and technological change.* London: Pluto.

——. 1985. *Machinery of dominance: Women, men, and technical know-how.* London: Pluto.

Cohen, Joshua, ed. 1996. *For love of country: Debating the limits of patriotism.* Boston: Beacon.

Cohen, Robin. 1987. Theorizing international labour. In *International labour and the third world: The making of a new working class,* ed. Rosalind E. Boyd, Robin Cohen, and Peter C. W. Gutkind. Aldershot: Avebury Press.

Colgan, Fiona, and Sue Ledwith, ed. 2002. *Gender, diversity, and trade unions: International perspectives.* London: Routledge.

Comintern. 1971. Theses on the national and colonial question adopted by the second Comintern congress. In *The communist international 1919–1943: Documents*, ed. Jane Degras, 1:138–144. London: Frank Cass.

Comisso, Ellen Turkish. 1979. *Workers' control under plan and market: Implications of Yugoslav self-management.* New Haven, Conn.: Yale University Press.

Communalism Combat. 2002. *Genocide Gujarat 2002* 77–78 (March–April).

Compa, Lance. 2001. NAFTA's labor side agreement and international labor solidarity. In *Place, space, and the new labour internationalisms*, ed. Peter Waterman and Jane Wills, 147–163. Oxford: Blackwell.

Conaghan, Joanne. 2002. Women, work, and family: A British revolution? In *Labour law in an era of globalization: Transformative practices and possibilities*, ed. J. Conaghan, R. M. Fischl, and K. Klare, 53–73. Oxford: Oxford University Press.

Conaghan, Joanne, R. M. Fischl, and K. Klare, eds. 2002. *Labour law in an era of globalization: Transformative practices and possibilities.* Oxford: Oxford University Press.

Cooke, Shamus. 2009a. Workers rights in America: Unraveling the card check debate—the Employee Free Choice Act (EFCA). *Global Research* (March 30). http://www.globalresearch.ca/index.php?context=va&aid=12964.

——. 2009b. Global warming accelerating while the US backpedals. *OpEdNews* (October 18). http://www.opednews.com/articles/2/Global-Warming-Accelera-tin-by-shamus-cooke-091018–498.html.

Cooley, Mike. 1980. *Architect or bee? The human/technology relationship.* Comp. and ed. by Shirley Cooley. London: Hand and Brain Publications.

——. 1985. After the Lucas plan. In *Very nice work if you can get it: The socially useful production debate*, ed. Collective Design/Projects. Nottingham: Spokesman.

Coulson, Margaret, Branka Magas, and Hilary Wainwright. 1975. The housewife and her labour under capitalism: A critique. *New Left Review* 89 (January–February): 59–71.

Cripps, Francis, John Eatwell, and Alex Izurieta. 2005. Financial imbalances in the world economy. *EPW* 40, no. 52 (December 24): 5453–5456.

Crotty, James. 2009. Profound structural flaws in the US financial system that helped cause the financial crisis. *EPW* 44, no. 13 (March 28): 127–135.

Crotty, James, and Gerald Epstein. 2009. Avoiding another meltdown in the US financial system. *EPW* 44, no. 13 (March 28): 87–93.

CSO. 1999. CSO's comments: How good are India's industrial statistics? *EPW* 34, no. 23 (June 5): 1461–1463.

Cunnison, Sheila, and Jane Stageman. 1993. *Feminizing the unions: Challenging the culture of masculinity.* Aldershot: Avebury.

CWM. 1997a. Lack of transparency and accountability: The case of KEC International Ltd. Delhi: Centre for Workers' Management.

——. 1997b. Analysis of and recommendations on Sick Industrial Companies (Special Provisions) Bill, 1997. Delhi: Centre for Workers' Management.

dalla Costa, Mariarosa, and Selma James. 1972. *The power of women and the subversion of the community*. Bristol: Falling Wall Press.

Dangl, Benjamin. 2005. Occupy, resist, produce: Workers' cooperatives in Argentina. http://upsidedownworld.org/main/content/view/21/32/.

Daniel, W. W., and N. Millward. 1983. *Workplace industrial relations in Britain*. London: Heinemann.

D'Antona, Massimo. 2002. Labour law at the century's end. In *Labour law in an era of globalization: Transformative practices and possibilities*, ed. J. Conaghan, R. M. Fischl, and K. Klare, 31–49. Oxford: Oxford University Press.

Das, Keshab. 2003. Income and employment in informal manufacturing. In *Informal economy centrestage: New structures of employment*, ed. Renana Jhabvala, Ratna M. Sudarshan, and Jeemol Unni, 62–103. New Delhi: Sage.

Datta, Kanika. 2001. Employers of India may lose their chains. *BS* (March 2).

Datta, Rumi. 2003. Clariant AG in local outsourcing plan. *BS* (September 18).

Dawn. 2005. Malaysia too ends dollar peg. *Dawn* (July 22).

Day, Richard B. 1973. *Leon Trotsky and the politics of economic isolation*. Cambridge: Cambridge University Press.

Dayal, Raghu. 2004. We failed to stitch in time, but. . . . *ET* (December 27).

D'Costa, Bennet. 1997. Trade unions and mergers: The case of the HLL-TOMCO merger. CWM.

——. 1999. VRS: Unions must act. *The Union's Lever* 1, no. 2 (November): 18–23.

——. 2000. Will Maharashtra government turn the clock back? Labour law amendments: charter for new slavery. *Angdai*, Trade Union Solidarity Committee (November 15).

——. 2001. The imperative of globalization: Changes in labour laws restricted to amendments. Paper presented to Conference of Labour Law Practitioners' Association, Pune, August.

——. 2006. The legal regulation of contract labour: Objectives and reality. Synopsis of thesis for LL.M, University of Mumbai.

De, Arjit. 2001. CII proposes voluntary closure of potentially sick companies. *BS* (May 4).

De Beauvoir, Simone. 1997. *The second sex*. Trans. H. M. Parshley. London: Random House.

Deccan Herald. 2009. Trade unions extend support to Jet Airways pilots. *Deccan Herald* (September 9).

De Jonquieres, Guy. 2002a. WTO ruling opens new chapter in US-EU dispute. *BS* (January 16).

——. 2002b. US attacked over trade curbs. *BS* (May 18–19).

——. 2004. Pessimists should not blame offshoring. *BS* (March 13–14).

De Jonquieres, Guy, and Frances Williams. 2002. World Bank attacks US, EU "hypocrisy" on subsidies. *BS* (November 21).

De Neve, Geert. 2005. *The everyday politics of labour: Working lives in India's informal economy.* Delhi: Social Science Press.

De Ryck, Koen. 1998. Asset allocation, financial market behaviour and impact of EU pension funds on European capital markets. In *Institutional Investors in the New Financial Landscape,* 267–276. Paris: OECD.

Delaney, Annie. 2007. Can campaigns support homeworker recognition, rights and organising? *We Work at Home–Newsletter of Homeworkers Worldwide* no. 2 (November).

Dent, Kelly. 2002. The contradictions in codes: The Sri-Lankan experience. In *Corporate responsibility and labour rights: Codes of conduct in the global economy,* ed. R. Jenkins, R. Pearson, and G. Seyfang, 135–145. London: Earthscan.

Desai, Mihir. 2005. Sexual harassment at the workplace: Starting the battle. *Combat Law* 4, no. 1 (January).

Desai, Sapna. 2009. Keeping the "health" in health insurance. *EPW* 44, no. 38 (September 19): 18–21.

Deshpande, Rajeshwari. 1999. Organising the unorganised: Case of Hamal Panchayat. *EPW* 34, no. 39 (September 25): L-19–L-26.

Deshpande, R. S., and Nagesh Prabhu. 2005. Farmers' distress: Proof beyond question. *EPW* 40, nos. 44–45 (October 29): 4663–4665.

Dewan, Meera. 1999. "The leaves that are green turn to brown": Shared moments with working children. In *Against child labour: Indian and international dimensions and strategies,* ed. Klaus Voll, 293–298. New Delhi: Mosaic.

Dhar, Sujoy. 2007. Communists turn unpopular over SEZ plans. *Inter-Press Service* (November 12).

Dickenson, Mary. 1982. *Democracy in trade unions: Studies in membership participation and control.* St. Lucia: University of Queensland Press.

DN. 2005. Microfinance: Transforming the economic ethic. *EPW* 40, no. 4 (January 22): 275–278.

Dollar, D., and A. Kraay. 2001a. Growth is good for the poor. Mimeo, Development Research Group, World Bank, Washington, D.C.

——. 2001b. Trade, growth and poverty. Mimeo, Development Research Group, World Bank, Washington, D.C.

Drake, Barbara. 1984. *Women in trade unions.* London: Virago.

Drèze, Jean. 2009. Employment guarantee or slave labour? *The Hindu* (September 19).

Drèze, Jean, and Amartya Sen. 1999. Public action for social security: Foundations and strategy. In *Social security in developing countries*, ed. Ehtisham Ahmad, Jean Drèze, John Hills, and Amartya Sen, 1–40. New Delhi: Oxford University Press.

Drèze, Jean, and Aparajita Goyal. 2003. Future of mid-day meals. *EPW* 38, no. 44 (November 1): 4673–4683.

Drèze, Jean, and Reetika Khera. 2009. The battle for employment guarantee. *Frontline* 26, no. 1 (January 3): 4–25.

D'Souza, Radha Iyer. 1996. Industrialization, labour policies, and their impact on the labour movement: A historical overview. In *Class formation and political transformation in postcolonial India*, ed. T. V. Sathyamurthy, 105–126. Delhi: Oxford University Press.

Dubashi, Jagannath. 1985. Executive cornucopia. *India Today* (May 31): 142–143.

Dubey, Muchkund. 1996. Social clause: The motive behind the method. In *Labour, environment, and globalisation—Social clause in multilateral trade agreements: A southern response*, ed. J. John and Anuradha M. Chenoy, 19–28. New Delhi: CEC.

Dubinsky, Laura. 2002. The fox guarding the chicken coop: Garment industry monitoring in Los Angeles. In *Corporate responsibility and labour rights: Codes of conduct in the global economy*, ed. R. Jenkins, R. Pearson, and G. Seyfang, 160–171. London: Earthscan.

Du Boff, Richard B., and Edward S. Herman. 2002. Mirror, mirror on the wall, who is the biggest rogue of all? *Philadelphia Inquirer* (February 25).

Dunayevskaya, Raya. 1996. On the family, love relationships, and the new society. Excerpts from a radio interview by Katherine Davenport on March 8, 1984. In *Dialectics of women's liberation*, by Raya Dunayevskaya and Olga Domanski, 72–82. Nagpur: Spartacus Publications.

Eashvaraiah, P. 2000. *Workers' cooperatives: Exploring new perspectives on socialism.* Report on National Seminar, University of Hyderabad, January 3–4, 1997, University of Hyderabad.

Economist. 2004. By how much has the dollar fallen? *ET* (September 27).

Education International. 2009. Education now a right for Indian children. http://www.ei-ie.org/en/news/show.php?id=1089&theme=educationforall&country=india.

Edwards, Richard. 1979. *Contested terrain: The transformation of the workplace in the twentieth century.* London: Heinemann.

Edwards, Tony. 1998. The industrial relations impact of cross-border mergers and acquisitions. http://www.eiro.eurofound.eu.int/1998/12/feature/uk9812164f.html.

Edwin, Tina. 2003. Govt may allow cos to hire labour for short projects. *ET* (March 17).

Elliott, Kimberly Ann, and Richard B. Freeman. 2003. *Can labor standards improve under globalization?* Washington, D.C.: Institute for International Economics.

Elson, Diane. 1994. People, development and international financial institutions: An interpretation of the Bretton Woods system. *Review of African Political Economy* 62: 511–524.

Elson, Diane. 1995. Male bias in macro-economics: The case of structural adjustment. In *Male bias in the development process*, ed. Diane Elson, 164–190. Manchester: Manchester University Press.

Elson, Diane, and Ruth Pearson. 1981. The subordination of women and the internationalisation of factory production. In *Of marriage and the market: Women's subordination in international perspective*, ed. Kate Young, Carol Wolkowitz, and Roslyn McCullagh, 144–166. London: CSE.

Emirates Business. 2009. GCC nations to hold poll for naming new currency. http://www.business24-7.ae/Articles/2009/10/Pages/03102009/10042009_1aea2963 48564336bda538cae2180ec4.aspx.

Emmanuel, Arghiri. 1969. *Unequal exchange: A study of the imperialism of trade.* Trans. Brian Pearce. London: New Left Books.

Engels, Frederick. 1975. The condition of the working-class in England. In *Collected works*, by Karl Marx and Frederick Engels, 4:295–583. Moscow: Progress Publishers.

Engels, Frederick. 1987. Letter to Lafargue, October 17, 1889. In *Marx and Engels on the trade unions*, ed. Kenneth Lapides. 149–150. New York: Praeger.

EPFO. N.d. Employees' pension scheme 1995. http://www.epfindia.com/pension.htm.

EPW. 1997. Bihar: More bloodshed. *EPW* 32, no. 13 (March 29): 622.

——. 1999. Bihar: Fratricidal politics. *EPW* 34, no. 6 (February 6): 308.

Esbenshade, Jill. 2004. *Monitoring sweatshops: Workers, consumers, and the global apparel industry.* Philadelphia: Temple University Press.

ET. 1996. Globalisation causes social tension in the north. *ET* (February 2).

——. 1999a. BMS joins left in slamming govt's economic policies. *ET* (January 14).

——. 1999b. WTO must not take up labour norms: Maran. *ET* (December 2).

——. 1999c. Seattle round of talks hit by lack of transparency. *ET* (December 5).

——. 1999d. India used WTO rules to settle textile disputes. *ET* (October 29).

——. 2000a. Garments off SSI list, FDI can flow. *ET* (November 3).

——. 2000b. 90m working children in India: ILO. *ET* (April 29).

——. 2001. Import of Chinese batteries below Rs 3.50 to be banned. *ET* (January 25).

——. 2002a. US excludes [additional] 116 steel products from tariffs. *ET* (June 26).

——. 2002b. Split Cabinet gives in-principle nod to promised labour reforms. *ET* (February 23).

——. 2002c. Vajpayee hints at tough labour laws. *ET* (February 24).

——. 2003a. Export of electronic parts jumps 200% in 6 yrs on outsourcing. *ET* (December 29).

——. 2003b. Ranbaxy buys out RPG Aventis. *ET* (December 14).

——. 2003c. Just slash tariffs—Steel does not need protection. *ET* (September 23).

——. 2003d. What's para. 6 of Doha Declaration? *ET* (September 2).

——. 2003e. WTO ruling to smoothen bedlinen exports. *ET* (April 10).

——. 2004a. Curbs on outsourcing can backfire on US: Greenspan. *ET* (March 13).

——. 2004b. EU lifts sanctions on US goods after Bush repeals export sops. *ET* (October 26).

——. 2004c. EU seeks sanctions against US over dumping duty move. *ET* (January 16).

——. 2004d. US appetite for foreign stock takes toll on $. *ET* (December 20).

——. 2004e. CalPERS gets going, pumps in $100m here. *ET* (November 3).

——. 2004f. Rethink food strategy: Time we junked traditional MSP. *ET* (November 5)

——. 2005a. RBI may diversify into Chinese yuan. *ET* (March 12).

——. 2005b. Infosys, TCS walk away with $400m ABN Amro contracts. *ET* (September 2).

——. 2005c. G-20 flexes muscles on market access for farm goods. *ET* (March 20).

——. 2008. BPO rape case: Supreme Court puts onus on Som Mittal. *ET* (February 24).

ETI. 2003. *Key challenges in ethical trade: Report on the ETI biennial conference 2003.* London: Ethical Trading Initiative.

——. 2005. *Ethical trade: Shaping a new agenda (ETI biennial conference 2005).* London: Ethical Trading Initiative.

Evans-Pritchard, Ambrose. 2007. Is China quietly dumping US Treasuries? http://www.telegraph.co.uk/money/main.jhtml?xml=/money/2007/09/05/bcnchina105.xml.

Fabre, Guilhem. 2009. The twilight of "Chimerica"? China and the collapse of the American model. *EPW* 44, nos. 26–27 (June 27): 299–307.

Fallon, Peter, and Zafiris Tzannatos. 1998. *Child labor: Issues and directions for the World Bank.* Social Protection Human Development Network, World Bank/IBRD, Washington, D.C.

Farooq, Omer. 2005. Indian girl, 14, wins a divorce. *BBC News* (June 22). http://www.bbc.co.uk/2/hi/south_asia/4120238.stm.

Ferguson, Ann, and Nancy Folbre. 1981. The unhappy marriage of patriarchy and capitalism. In *Women and revolution: A discussion of the unhappy marriage of Marxism and feminism*, ed. Lydia Sargent, 313–317. London: Pluto.

Ferguson, Martin. 1994. International trade and workers' rights. *IUR* 1, no. 7: 3–5.

Ferguson, Niall. 2008. The age of obligation. *Financial Times* (December 18).

Fernandes, Walter. 2005. IMTD act and immigration in northeastern India. *EPW* 40, no. 30 (July 23): 3237–3240.

Fernandez, Aloysius. 1986. Kamani tubes: Employees' takeover. *Update* (October 31): 14–21.

Fields, Gary. 2004. Labor standards and decent work. Why international labor standards? In *International labor standards: Globalization, trade, and public policy*, ed. R. J. Flanagan and William B. Gould IV, 61–79. Stanford, Calif.: Stanford University Press.

Fimmen, Edo. 1922. *The International Federation of Trade Unions: Development and aims*. Amsterdam: IFTU. http://library.fes.de/pdf-files/netzquelle/01299.pdf.

Firestone, Shulamith. 1970. *The dialectic of sex: The case for feminist revolution*. New York: Bantam.

Firodia, Arun. 2003. Debate: Labour reforms for global competitiveness. *ET* (February 4).

Fischer, Bernhard. 1998. The role of contractual savings institutions in emerging markets. In *Institutional investors in the new financial landscape*, 235–263. Paris: Organisation for Economic Cooperation and Development.

Flanagan, Robert J. 2004. Labor standards and international competitive advantage. In *International labor standards: Globalization, trade, and public policy*, ed. R. J. Flanagan and William B. Gould IV, 15–59. Stanford, Calif.: Stanford University Press.

Flanagan, Robert J., and William B. Gould IV, eds. 2004. *International labor standards: Globalization, trade, and public policy*. Stanford, Calif.: Stanford University Press.

Fontes, Paulo. 2000. The "strike of 400,000" and the organisation of workers in São Paulo, Brazil 1957. *International and Comparative Labour History, Socialist History* 17.

Foster, Bellamy, and Robert W. McChesney. 2009. Monopoly-finance capital and the paradox of accumulation. *Monthly Review* (October).

Fox, Michael. 2009. ALBA summit ratifies regional currency, prepares for Trinidad. *Venezuelanewsanalysis.com* (April 17). http://www.venezuelanalysis.com/news/4373.

Frank, Andre Gunder. 1966. The development of underdevelopment. *Monthly Review* (September).

————. 1969a. *Capitalism and underdevelopment in Latin America.* New York: Monthly Review Press.

————. 1969b. *Latin America: Underdevelopment or revolution.* New York: Monthly Review Press.

————. 1998. *ReOrient: Global economy in the Asian Age.* Berkeley: University of California Press.

Freeman, Caroline. 1982. When is a wage not a wage? In *The politics of housework,* ed. Ellen Malos, 166–173. London: Allison and Busby.

Friedman, Milton. 1999. Social security socialism. *Wall Street Journal* (January 26).

Friedman, Thomas L. 1999. *The Lexus and the olive tree: Understanding globalization.* New York: Farrar, Straus and Giroux.

————. 2005. *The world is flat: A brief history of the twenty-first century.* New York: Farrar, Straus and Giroux.

————. 2009. Mother nature's Dow. *New York Times* (March 28).

Froebel, F., J. Heinrichs, and O. Kreye. 1980. *The new international division of labour.* Cambridge: Cambridge University Press.

Fuentes, Carlos. 1963. The argument of Latin America: Words for the North Americans. *Monthly Review* (January).

FWF. 2003. *Fair Wear Foundation annual report 2003.* Amsterdam: FWF.

Gallie, Duncan. 1978. *In search of the new working class: Automation and social integration within the capitalist enterprise.* Cambridge: Cambridge University Press.

Gallin, Dan. 2001. Propositions on trade unions and informal employment in times of globalisation. *Place, space and the new labour internationalisms,* ed. Peter Waterman and Jane Wills, 227–245. Oxford: Blackwell.

————. 2002. Labour as a global social force: Past divisions and new tasks. In *Global unions? Theory and strategies of organized labour in the global political economy,* ed. Jeffrey Harrod and Robert O'Brien, 235–250. London: Routledge.

Ganguly, P. K. 1996. Labour rights and national interests. In *Labour, environment, and globalisation—Social clause in multilateral trade agreements: A southern response,* ed. J. John and Anuradha M. Chenoy, 43–46. New Delhi: CEC.

Gardiner, Jean, Susan Himmelweit, and Maureen Mackintosh. 1982. Women's domestic labour. In *The politics of housework,* ed. Ellen Malos, 198–216. London: Allison and Busby.

Gatehouse, Mike. 1989. Soft drink, hard labour. In *Solidarity for survival: The Don Thomson reader on trade union internationalism,* ed. Mike Press and Don Thomson, 51–58. Nottingham: Spokesman.

The Gavel. 2008. Oversight committee holds hearings on the causes and effects of the AIG bailout. *The Gavel* (October 7). http://speaker.house.gov/blog/?p=1538.

Ghei, Nita. 1996. WTO ruling against US gives a ray of hope to Third World. *ET* (January 21).

Gibbons, Steve. 1999. The IMF and labour rights. *IUR* 6, no. 2: 19.

Giugni, G. 1969. Articulated bargaining in Italy. In *Collective bargaining*, ed. A. Flanders, 267–285. London: Penguin. Excerpted from G. Giugni. Recent developments in collective bargaining in Italy. *International Labour Review* 91, no. 4 (April 1965): 273–291.

Glendon, Mary Ann. 1989. *The transformation of family law: State, law, and family in the United States and Western Europe.* Chicago: University of Chicago Press.

Global Business Policy Council. 2001. *FDI confidence audit: India.* A. T. Kearney, Inc.

——. 2008. *New concerns in an uncertain world: The 2007 A. T. Kearney FDI confidence index.* A. T. Kearney, Inc. http://www.atkearney.com/images/global/pdf/FDICI_2007.pdf.

GlobalSecurity.org. 2007. World wide military expenditures. http://www.globalsecurity.org/military/world/spending.htm.

——. 2009. Arihant: Advanced technology vessel (ATV). http://www.globalsecurity.org/military/world/india/atv.htm.

Gluck, Caroline. 2002. North Korea embraces the euro. *BBC News* (December 1).

Godoy, Julio. 2009. CLIMATE CHANGE: Set that 110 limit. *IPS* (October 30). http://www.ipsnews.net/news.asp?idnews=49072.

GOI. 1951. The Industries (Development and Regulation) Act. http://www.vakilno1.com/bareacts/industriesdevact/industriesdevact.htm.

——. 1964. *Women in employment.* Labour Bureau Pamphlet Series 8. New Delhi: Ministry of Labour and Employment.

——. 1977. Industrial policy statement. In *India's Industrial Policies from 1948 to 1991.* December. http://www.laghu-udyog.com/policies/iip.htm.

——. 1979. *Report of the committee on child labour.* New Delhi: Ministry of Labour.

——. 1980. Industrial policy statement. In *India's Industrial Policies from 1948 to 1991.* July. http://www.laghu-udyog.com/policies/iip.htm.

——. 1990. Industrial policy 1990: Policy measures for the promotion of small scale and agro-based industries and changes in procedures for industrial approvals. In *India's Industrial Policies from 1948 to 1991.* http://www.laghu-udyog.com/policies/iip.htm.

——. 2005a. *SEZ Act, 2005.* http://sezindia.nic.in/HTMLS/SEZ%20Act,%202005.pdf.

——. 2005b. Pension fund regulatory and development authority: Discussion paper on pension reforms and new pension system (NPS). Ministry of Finance. http://finmin.nic.in/the_ministry/PFRDA/dispaper.pdf.

Goldar, Bishwananth. 2000. Employment growth in organised manufacturing in India. *EPW* 35, no. 14 (April 1): 1191–1195.

Goodrich, Carter L. 1975. *The frontier of control: A study in British workshop politics.* London: Pluto.

Goodman, Peter S. 2005. China ends fixed-rate currency. *Washington Post* (July 22).

Gordon, Linda. 1982. Why nineteenth-century feminists did not support "birth control" and twentieth-century feminists do: Feminism, reproduction, and the family. In *Rethinking the family: Some feminist questions*, ed. B. Thorne with M. Yalom, 40–53. New York: Longman.

Gothoskar, Sujata. 1996. The social clause: Whose interest is it serving? In *Labour, environment, and globalisation—Social clause in multilateral trade agreements: A southern response*, ed. J. John and Anuradha M. Chenoy, 59–65. New Delhi: CEC.

Gothoskar, Sujata, R. Athavale, S. Bangera, H. Pujari, V. Kanhere, M. J. Dalal, and S.Mehdi. 1998. *Neither bread nor roses: A study of women and men workers in the 'galas' of industrial estates in Mumbai.* Bombay: Workers' Solidarity Centre.

Gould, William B. 2003. Labor law for a global economy: The uneasy case for international labor standards. In *International labor standards: Globalization, trade, and public policy*, ed. R. J. Flanagan and William B. Gould IV, 81–128. Stanford, Calif.: Stanford University Press.

Gowan, Peter. 2001. The American campaign for global sovereignty. Deutscher Memorial Lecture.

Goyal, Arun. 2001. No let-up in dumping notices, industry not unduly hurt either. *ET* (February 5).

———. 2004. DGFT imposes port curbs on copper from Sri Lanka. *ET* (November 20).

GPRS. 1985. Press release (November 17).

Gramsci, Antonio. 1971. The intellectuals. In *Selections from the Prison Notebooks*, trans. Quintin Hoare and Geoffrey Nowell Smith, 3–23. London: Lawrence and Wishart.

———. 1977. Unions and councils. In *Selections from Political Writings, 1910–1920*, 98–102. London: Lawrence and Wishart.

Griffin, Gerard, Chris Nyland, and Anne O'Rourke. 2003. Trade unions and the trade–labour rights link: A north-south union divide? *International Journal of Comparative Labour Law and Industrial Relations* 19, no. 4: 469–494.

Grimshaw, Chris. 1997. The arms conversion programme. *Corporate Watch* 3 (Spring). http://archive.corporatewatch.org/magazine/issue3/cw3fi.html.

Groendahl, Boris. 2003. Sony, Bertelsmann seal music merger deal. *ET* (December 13).

Grossmann, Henryk. 1992. *The law of accumulation and breakdown of the capitalist system.* Trans. Jairus Banaji. London: Pluto.

Grote, Ulrike. 2000. Impact of trade sanctions and social labeling on labor standards. *Bridges Between Trade and Sustainable Development* 4, no. 1: 11–16.

Gupta, A. K. 2008. NREGA activists who paid with their lives: Lalit Mehta (Jharkhand). *Down to Earth*. http://www.cse.org.in/full6.asp?foldername=2008 0630&filename=news&sec_id=50&sid=48.

Gupta, Dipankar. 1982. *Nativism in a metropolis: The Shiv Sena in Bombay*. Delhi: Manohar.

Gupta, Indrani, and Mayur Trivedi. 2005. Social health insurance redefined: Health for all through coverage for all. *EPW* 40, no. 38 (September 17): 4132–4140.

Gupta, Manju. 1999. A situational analysis and strategies to combat child labour in the carpet industry in India. In *Against child labour: Indian and international dimensions and strategies*, ed. Klaus Voll, 176–187. New Delhi: Mosaic.

Gupta, Manju, and Klaus Voll. 1999. Child labour in India: An exemplary study. In *Against child labour: Indian and international dimensions and strategies*, ed. Klaus Voll, 85–144. New Delhi: Mosaic.

Gupte, Vasant. 1981. *Labour movement in Bombay: Origin and growth up to independence*. Bombay: Institute of Workers Education.

Gurung, Madhu. 1999. Mumbai's Annapurna. *Financial Express* (March 7).

Haas, Daniel. 1999. Social clauses and global trade: Instruments of a global social policy? In *Against child labour: Indian and international dimensions and strategies*, ed. Klaus Voll, 11–30. New Delhi: Mosaic.

Hakeem, M. A. 2000. Labour flexibility for competitive edge. *ET* (November 30).

Hale, Angela. 1995–1996. We need a woman's perspective on the social clause. *Asian Labour Update* 20 (November–March): 8.

——. 2000. What hope for "ethical" trade in the globalised garment industry? *Antipode* 32, no. 4: 349–356.

Hale, Angela, and Linda M. Shaw. 2001. Women workers and the promise of ethical trade. In *Place, space, and the new labour internationalisms*, ed. Peter Waterman and Jane Wills, 206–226. Oxford: Blackwell.

Hale, Angela, and Jane Wills, eds. 2005. *Threads of labour: Garment industry supply chains from the workers' perspective*. Oxford: Blackwell.

Hall, Susan. 1996. Reflexivity in emancipatory action research: Illustrating the researcher's constitutiveness. In *New directions in action research*, ed. Ortrun Zuber-Skerritt, 28–48. London: Falmer Press.

Hansen, Joseph, and William F. Warde. 1970. Introduction to *In defence of Marxism*, by Leon Trotsky. New York: Pathfinder Press.

Hardt, Michael, and Antonio Negri. 2000. *Empire*. Cambridge, Mass.: Harvard University Press.

——. 2004. *Multitude: War and democracy in the age of empire*. London: Hamish Hamilton.

Harding, Sandra. 1987. Introduction: Is there a feminist method? In *Feminism and methodology*, ed. Sandra Harding, 1–14. Bloomington: Indiana University Press.

Harris, Nigel. 2005. Migration and development. *EPW* 40, no. 43 (October 22): 4591–4595.

Harriss-White, Barbara. 2003. *India working: Essays on society and economy.* Cambridge: Cambridge University Press.

———. 2005. India's socially regulated economy. Paper presented at Fiftieth Anniversary Conference at Queen Elizabeth House, July 4–5.

Harriss-White, Barbara, and Nandini Gooptu. 2000. Mapping India's world of unorganized labour. In *Working classes global realities: Socialist register 2001*, ed. Leo Panitch and Colin Leys, 89–118. London: The Merlin Press.

Harrod, Jeffrey, and Robert O'Brien. 2002a. Organized labour and the global political economy. In *Global unions? Theory and strategies of organized labour in the global political economy*, ed. Jeffrey Harrod and Robert O'Brien, 3–28. London: Routledge.

———, eds. 2002b. *Global unions? Theory and strategies of organized labour in the global political economy.* London: Routledge.

Hartmann, Heidi. 1981. The unhappy marriage of Marxism and feminism: Towards a more progressive union. *Women and revolution: A discussion of the unhappy marriage of Marxism and feminism*, ed. Lydia Sargent, 2–41. London: Pluto.

Harvey, David. 1982. *The limits to capital.* Oxford: Blackwell.

———. 2003. *The new imperialism.* Oxford: Oxford University Press.

Hawkins, Julia. 2005. Codes of labour practice: Revisiting the debate. *IUR* 12, issue 1: 9–10.

Haworth, Nigel, and Harvie Ramsey. 1988. Workers of the world untied: International capital and some dilemmas in industrial democracy. In *Trade unions and the new industrialisation of the Third World*, ed. Roger Southall, 306–331. London: Zed Books.

Hayter, Teresa. 1971. *Aid as imperialism.* Harmondsworth: Penguin.

———. 2000. *Open borders: The case against immigration controls.* London: Pluto.

Held, David, and Anthony McGrew, eds. 2003. *The global transformations reader: An introduction to the globalization debate.* Cambridge, Mass.: Polity Press.

Held, David, Anthony McGrew, David Goldblatt, and Jonathan Perraton. 1999. *Global transformations: Politics, economics, and culture.* Stanford, Calif.: Stanford University Press.

Henderson, Hazel. 2002. Beyond Bush's unilateralism: Another bi-polar world or a new era of win-win? *Inter-Press Service* (June).

Hensman, C. R. 1969. *From Gandhi to Guevara: The polemics of revolt.* London: Allen Lane.

———. 1971. *Rich against poor: The reality of aid.* London: Allen Lane.

Hensman, Rohini. 1988. The gender division of labour in manufacturing industry: A case study in India. IDS Discussion Paper 253. Institute of Development Studies, University of Sussex, Brighton.

——. 1996a. The impact of industrial restructuring on women, men, and trade unions. In *Class formation and political transformation in postcolonial India*, ed. T. V. Sathyamurthy, 80–104. Delhi: Oxford University Press.

——. 1996b. Urban working-class women: The need for autonomy. In *Confronting state, capital, and patriarchy: Women organizing in the process of industrialization*, ed. Amrita Chhachhi and Renee Pittin, 183–204. Basingstoke: Macmillan; New York: St. Martin's Press.

——. 1998. How to support the rights of women workers in the context of trade liberalisation in India. In *Trade myths and gender reality: Trade liberalisation and women's lives*, ed. Angela Hale, 71–88. Sweden: Global Publications Foundation and International Coalition for Development Action.

——. 2000. Organising against the odds: Women in India's informal sector. In *Working classes global realities: Socialist register 2001*, ed. Leo Panitch and Colin Leys, 249–257. London: The Merlin Press.

——. 2001. World trade and workers' rights: In search of an internationalist position. In *Place, space, and the new labour internationalisms*, ed. Peter Waterman and Jane Wills, 123–146. Oxford: Blackwell.

——. 2002. Trade unions and women's autonomy: Organisational strategies of women workers in India. In *Gender, diversity, and trade unions: International perspectives*, ed. F. Colgan and S. Ledwith, 95–111. London: Routledge.

Hensman, Rohini, and BGJB. 1991. A common cause. *Studies for Trade Unionists* 16, no. 63.

Hensman, Rohini, and Jairus Banaji. 1998. A short history of the employees' unions in Bombay, 1947–1991. Paper presented at the First Annual Conference of the Association of Indian Labour Historians in association with V. V. Giri National Labour Institute, March 16–18.

Henwood, Doug. 1993. *Wall Street*. London: Verso.

Herod, Andrew. 2001. *Labor geographies: Workers and the landscapes of capitalism*. New York: The Guilford Press.

——. 2002. Organizing globally, organizing locally: Union spatial strategy in a global economy. In *Global unions? Theory and strategies of organized labour in the global political economy*, ed. Jeffrey Harrod and Robert O'Brien, 83–99. London: Routledge.

Hilferding, Rudolf. 1981. *Finance capital: A study of the latest phase of capitalist development*. Trans. Morris Watnick and Sam Gordon. London: Routledge and Kegan Paul.

References

Himmelweit, Susan. 1984. The real dualism of sex and class. *Review of Radical Political Economics* 16, no. 1: 167–183.

Himmelweit, Susan, and Simon Mohun. 1977. Domestic labour and capitalism. *Cambridge Journal of Economics* 1: 15–31.

The Hindu. 2006. Big rise in trade union membership. *The Hindu* (December 31).

Hinton, James. 1973. *The first shop stewards' movement.* London: Allen & Unwin.

Hirst, Paul, and Grahame Thompson. 2003. The limits to economic globalization. *The global transformations reader: An introduction to the globalization debate,* ed. David Held and Anthony McGrew, 335–348. Cambridge: Polity Press.

Hitler, Adolf. 1943. *Mein Kampf.* Trans. Ralph Manheim. Boston: Houghton Mifflin.

Hobson, J. A. 1938. *Imperialism: A study.* London: Allen & Unwin.

Holmström, Mark. 1976. *South Indian factory workers: Their life and their world.* Cambridge: Cambridge University Press.

———. 1984. *Industry and inequality: The social anthropology of Indian labour.* Cambridge: Cambridge University Press.

———. 1989. *Industrial democracy in Italy: Workers' co-ops and the self-management debate.* Aldershot: Avebury.

———. 1993. *Spain's new social economy: Workers' self-management in Catalonia.* Oxford: Berg.

HomeNet. 1999a. The Textile, Clothing, and Footwear Union of Australia (TCFUA). In *New ways of organising in the informal sector: Four case studies of trade union activity.* Leeds: HomeNet International.

HomeNet. 1999b. *The HomeNet guide: Using the ILO convention on home work.* Leeds: HomeNet International.

Hughes, Jennifer. 2003. Dollar gets sinking feeling as investor confidence fades. *BS* (May 24–25).

Humphries, Jane. 1980. Class struggle and the persistence of the working-class family. In *The economics of women and work,* ed. Alice H. Amsden, 140–165. Harmondsworth: Penguin. Reproduced from *Cambridge Journal of Economics* 1 (September 1977): 241–258.

Hurley, Jennifer. 2005. Unravelling the web: Supply chains and workers' lives in the garment industry. In *Threads of labour: Garment industry supply chains from the workers' perspective,* ed. Angela Hale and Jane Wills, 95–132. Oxford: Blackwell.

Hyman, Richard. 1971. *Marxism and the sociology of trade unionism.* London: Pluto.

———. 1979. The politics of workplace trade unionism. *Capital and Class* 3, no. 2: 54–67.

———. 1996. Changing union identities in Europe. In *The challenges to trade unions in Europe: Innovation or adaptation,* ed. Peter Leisink, Jim Van Leemput, and Jaques Vilrokx, 53–73. New York: Edward Elgar.

ICFTU. 1997. *"Search and destroy": Hunting down free trade unions in China.* Brussels: ICFTU.

———. 1999. *Building workers' human rights into the global trading system.* Brussels: ICFTU.

ICJ. 1996. Communique regarding "Legality of the Threat or Use of Nuclear Weapons (Request for Advisory Opinion by the General Assembly of the United Nations) Advisory Opinion." July 8. http://www.icj-cij.org/docket/files/95/10407.pdf.

ILO. 1996a. Multinational corporations. http://www.itcilo.it/actrav-english/telearn/global/ilo/multinat/multinat.htm.

———. 1996b. *Child labour: The impact of early employment on productivity and wages. An exploratory study in four unorganised-sector industries in India by the Administrative Staff College of India and ILO.* Delhi.

———. 1998. *ILO declaration on fundamental principles and rights at work and its follow-up.* Geneva: ILO.

———. 2002. *Resolution concerning decent work and the informal economy.* Geneva: ILO.

———. 2005. *World employment report 2004–05: Employment, productivity, and poverty reduction.* Geneva: ILO.

———. 2007. Global employment trends for women. March. http://209.85.175.104/search?q=cache:IHTAyV8GylcJ:www.ilo.org/public/english/employment/strat/download/getw07.pdf+ilo+women+proportion+global+labor+force&hl=en&ct=clnk&cd=3&gl=i.

———. 2008. Global employment trends—2008. Geneva: ILO. http://www.ilo.org/wcmsp5/groups/public/---dgreports/---dcomm/documents/publication/wcms_090106.pdf.

———. 2009. Unemployment, working poor and vulnerable employment to increase dramatically due to global economic crisis. Geneva: ILO. http://www.ilo.org/global/About_the_ILO/Media_and_public_information/Press_releases/lang---en/WCMS_101462/index.htm.

ILO-CFA. 1995. Case no. 1651: Complaint against the government of India presented by the International Union of Food and Allied Workers' Association (IUF). In *295th Report, Reports of the Committee on Freedom of Association*, 185–191. Geneva: ILO.

India Post. 2009. Maharashtra gives recognition, incentives to domestic workers. *India Post* (January 5). http://www.theindiapost.com/2009/01/05/maharastra-gives-recognition-incentives-to-domestic-workers/.

International Labour Reports. 1984. Things get worse with Coke. *International Labour Reports* 3: 8–10.

Iran Financial News. 2002. Forex fund shifting to euro. *Iran Financial News* (August 25).

IUF. 2000. Report on activities (e) Transnational company activities. Executive Committee, May 10–11, IUF, Geneva.

IUR. 1998. March against child labour begins in Manila, culminates in Geneva. *IUR* 5, no. 2: 30.

Iyengar, Vishwapriya L. 1986. Where children labour and fathers despair. *Indian Express* (February 16).

Jacobs, Michael. 1985a. Bhopal victims join workers against Carbide. *New Statesman* (July 12).

——. 1985b. Building hope on Bhopal's ashes. *New Socialist* (November).

Jaipuria, R. 2001. There are no economies of scale in textile sector. Interview with Sunanda Sanganeria. *BS* (December 24).

Janardhan, V. 2007. Depoliticisation of trade unions: The need of the hour? *LF* 5, nos. 1–2 (January–April): 34–38.

Jang Jip Choi. 1989. *Labor and the authoritarian state: Labor unions in South Korean manufacturing industries, 1961–1980.* Seoul: Korea University Press.

Jans, Marc. 2004. Children as citizens: Towards a contemporary notion of child participation. *Childhood* 11, no. 1: 27–44.

Jayadev, Arun. 2009. A blueprint for a fairer and more stable global economy. *EPW* 44, no. 36 (September 5): 26–31.

Jenkins, Rhys. 2002. The political economy of codes of conduct. In *Corporate responsibility and labour rights: Codes of conduct in the global economy,* ed. Rhys Jenkins et al., 13–30. London: Earthscan, 2002.

Jenkins, Rhys, Ruth Pearson, and Gill Seyfang, eds. 2002. *Corporate responsibility and labour rights: Codes of conduct in the global economy.* London: Earthscan.

Jenkins, Rob, and Anne Marie Goetz. 2002. Civil society engagement and India's public distribution system: Lessons from the Rationing Kruti Samiti in Mumbai. Paper presented at World Development Report 2003/04 Workshop, Oxford, November 4–5.

Jhabvala, Renana. 2003. Bringing informal workers centrestage. In *Informal economy centrestage: New structures of employment,* ed. R. Jhabvala, 258–275. New Delhi: Sage, 2003.

Jhabvala, Renana, Ratna M. Sudarshan, and Jeemol Unni, eds. 2003. *Informal economy centrestage: New structures of employment.* New Delhi: Sage.

Jhingran, Dhir. 2003. Universalisation of elementary education: Government policies and perspectives. In *Child labour and the right to education in South Asia: Needs versus rights?,* ed. N. Kabeer, G. Nambissan, and R. Subrahmanian, 195–215. New Delhi: Sage.

John, J. 1998. Dollar city in tiffin box. *LF* 4, no. 8 (August): 3–13.

——. 2000. *Fair trade and standard setting: A labour rights perspective*. New Delhi: CEC.

——. 2005a. Umbrella legislation: A deception on Indian working people. *LF* 3, no. 2 (March–April): 1–5.

——. 2005b. Brutality beneath the veneer of industrial excellence and retail opulence. *LF* 3, no. 4 (July–August): 1–5.

——. 2008. Social security act: The great Indian *tamasha* on unorganised workers. *LF* 6, no. 6 (November–December 2008): 5–11.

John, J., and Anuradha M. Chenoy, eds. 1996. *Labour, environment, and globalisation—Social clause in multilateral trade agreements: A southern response*. New Delhi: CEC.

Johnson, Chalmers. 2007. *Nemesis: The last days of the American republic*. New York: Metropolitan Books.

——. 2008. Going bankrupt: The US's greatest threat. *Asia Times Online* (January 24). http://www.atimes.com/atimes/Middle_East/JA24Ak04.html.

Johnson, Steve. 2005. Asian banks cut exposure to dollar. *ET* (March 11).

Joseph, Anto T. 2002. Garment exports give fillip to logistics. *ET* (February 26).

Joshi, Chitra. 2003. *Lost worlds: Indian labour and its forgotten histories*. Delhi: Permanent Black.

Joshi, Heather, and Vijay Joshi. 1976. *Surplus labour and the city: Study of Bombay*. Delhi: Oxford University Press.

Jumani, Usha. 1987. The future of home-based production. In *Invisible hands: Women in home-based production*, ed. Andrea Menefee Singh and Anita Kelles-Viitanen, 251–266. New Delhi: Sage.

Justice, Dwight W. 2002. The international trade union movement and the new codes of conduct. In *Corporate responsibility and labour rights: Codes of conduct in the global economy*, ed. R. Jenkins, R. Pearson, and G. Seyfang, 90–100. London: Earthscan.

Kabeer, Naila. 2001. *Bangladeshi women workers and labour market decisions: The power to choose*. New Delhi: Vistaar.

Kabeer, Naila, Geetha B. Nambissan, and Ramya Subrahmanian. 2003. Needs versus rights? Child labour, social exclusion, and the challenge of universalising primary education. In *Child labour and the right to education in South Asia: Needs versus rights?* ed. Naila Kabeer, Geetha Nambissan and Ramya Subrahmanian, 1–48. New Delhi: Sage.

——, eds. 2003. *Child labour and the right to education in South Asia: Needs versus rights?* New Delhi: Sage.

Kachru, Seema Hakhu. 2004. Accounting, finance, BPOs may eclipse IT in 5 years. *ET* (April 24).

Kakatkar, Manasi. 2009. India launches nuclear submarine. *Foreign Policy Blogs* (July 29). http://india.foreignpolicyblogs.com/2009/07/29/india-launches-nuclear -submarine.

Kalpana, K. 2004. *The shifting trajectories in microfinance discourse: A critical reading of the anti-poverty dimensions of microfinance programmes.* Working paper no. 189. Chennai: Madras Institute of Development Studies.

Kannabiran, Vasanth. 2005. Marketing self-help, managing poverty. *EPW* 40, no. 34 (August 20): 3716–3719.

Kannan, K. P. 2005. Linking guarantee to human development. *EPW* 40, no. 42 (October 15): 4518–4530.

Kant, Immanuel. 1996. Towards perpetual peace. In *Practical philosophy*, trans. and ed. Mary J. Gregor, 315–351. Cambridge: Cambridge University Press.

Kapur, Naina. 1996. Equal but different: Sexual harassment in India. In *Women's rights at the workplace: Emerging challenges and legal interventions*, ed. Asha Bajpai, 95–103. Bombay: Tata Institute of Social Sciences.

Karunanithi, G. 1998. Plight of pledged children in beedi works. *EPW* 33, no. 9 (February 28): 450–452.

Kashif-ul-Huda. 2009. Long road to justice: *Franklin Thomas vs. Ministry of Minority Affairs. TwoCircles.net* (September 28). http://www.twocircles.net/2009sep27/ long_road_justice_franklin_thomas_vs_ministry_minority_affairs.html.

Kaushal, Neeraj. 2002. Misdirected anger. *ET* (October 1).

Kawanishi, Hirosuke. 1992. *Enterprise unionism in Japan.* Trans. Ross E. Mouer. London: Kegan Paul International.

Kelkar, Rajas, and Abhinaba Das. 2003. A silent auto revolution is sweeping through India. *ET* (May 9).

Kemp, Tom. 1972. The Marxist theory of imperialism. In *Studies in the theory of imperialism*, ed. Roger Owen and Bob Sutcliffe, 15–33. London: Longman.

Kennedy, James J. 1981. *Women and American trade unions.* Montreal: Eden Press Women's Publications.

Kennedy, Van Dusen. 1966. *Unions, employers, and government: Essays on Indian labour questions.* Bombay: Manaktalas.

Kerr, Ian J. 1997. *Building the railways of the Raj, 1850–1900.* Delhi: Oxford University Press.

Keynes, J. M. 1932. The end of *laissez faire*. In *Essays in Persuasion.* London: Macmillan.

Kgoali, Joyce, et al. 1992. *No turning back: Fighting for gender equality in the unions.* Lacom (Sached), Speak and Cosatu Wits Women's Forum, Johannesburg.

Khan, Shamshad. 1999. Community participation eliminates child labour. In *Against child labour: Indian and international dimensions and strategies*, ed. Klaus Voll, 212–220. New Delhi: Mosaic.

Khanna, Tarun. 2007. Tata-Corus: India's new steel giant. *Harvard Business School Working Knowledge* (February 14). http://hbswk.hbs.edu/item/5634.html.

Khor, Martin. 2006. Failure of WTO Geneva mini-ministerial. *EPW* 41, no. 29 (July 22): 3143–3146.

——. 2007. WTO: Why Potsdam failed. *EPW* 42, no. 26 (June 30): 2487–2490.

Kidron, Michael. 1965. *Foreign investments in India.* Oxford: Oxford University Press.

——. 1967. A permanent arms economy. *International Socialism* 1, no. 28 (Spring). http://www.anu.edu.au/polsci/marx/contemp/pampsetc/perm/perm/htm.

——. 1970. *Western capitalism since the war.* Harmondsworth: Penguin.

Kishwar, Madhu. 2004. Who's afraid of WTO? Not us. *Indian Express* (January 23).

Kitching, Gavin. 2001. *Seeking social justice through globalization: Escaping a nationalist perspective.* State College, Penn.: Penn State University Press.

Klare, Karl. 2002. The horizons of transformative labour and employment laws. In *Labour law in an era of globalization: Transformative practices and possibilities,* ed. J. Conaghan, R. M. Fischl, and K. Klare, 3–29. Oxford: Oxford University Press.

Klein, Naomi. 2000. *No logo.* London: Flamingo.

Koithara, Verghese. 2005. Soft border approach in Kashmir: How it can be made to work. *EPW* 40, no. 18 (April 30): 1804–1806.

Kolasky, William J. 2002. Can the international competition network help tame the growing multinational merger thicket? http://www.usdoj.gov/atr/public/speeches/200123.pdf.

Kolben, Kevin. 2004. Trade, monitoring, and the ILO: Working to improve conditions in Cambodia's garment factories. *Yale Human Rights and Development Law Journal* 7: 79–107.

Kottegoda, Sepali. 2004. *Negotiating household politics: Women's strategies in urban Sri Lanka.* Colombo: Social Scientists' Association.

Kotwal, Manohar. 2000. First national labour commission. *Angdai* (November 15): 3.

Krätke, Michael R. 2001. "Hier bricht das Manuskript ab." (Engels) Hat das *Kapital* einen Schluss? Teil I. *Beiträge zur Marx-Engels-Forschung. Neue Folge:* 7–43.

Krebbers, Eric, and Merjin Schoenmaker. 2000. *De Fabel van de illegaal* quits Dutch anti-MAI campaign. In *My enemy's enemy: Essays on globalization, fascism, and the struggle against capitalism,* ed. Anti-Fascist Forum. Toronto: Anti-Fascist Forum.

Krishnakumar, Asha. 2004. Unsafe motherhood. *Frontline* 21, no. 16 (August 13).

Krishnamoorthy, Sujana. 2004. *Structure of the garment industry and labour rights in India: The post-MFA context.* New Delhi: Centre for Education and Communication.

Krishnaraj, Maithreyi. 2005. Research in women studies: Need for a critical appraisal. *EPW* 40, no. 28 (July 9): 3008–3017.

Kuber, Girish. 2005. Liberal labour laws for garment parks likely. *ET* (March 25).

Kulkarni, Mangesh. 1994. Theories of the Soviet system: A retrospective critique. *EPW* 29, no. 31 (July 30): 2036–2039.

Kumar, Nagesh. 1995. Industrialisation, liberalisation, and two-way flows of foreign direct investments: Case of India. *EPW* 30, no. 50 (December 16): 3228–3237.

——. 2003. Debate: Is it curtains for Doha development agenda? *ET* (September 16).

——. 2004. India should be proactive, not reactive at WTO. *BS* (August 6).

——. 2005. A broader Asian community and possible roadmap. *EPW* 40, no. 36 (September 3): 3926–3931.

Kumar, Radha. 1983. Family and factory: Women in the Bombay cotton textile industry, 1919–1939. *Indian Economic and Social History Review* 20, no. 1: 81–110.

Kumar, V. Phani. 2002. 2-wheeler firms seek duty hike to counter Chinese imports. *BS* (April 18).

Kundu, Amitabh, and Niranjan Sarangi. 2005. Issue of urban exclusion. *EPW* 40, no. 33 (August 13): 3642–3646.

Kurian, Rachel. 2005. *Trade unions and child labour: Challenges for the twenty-first century.* Maastricht: Shaker Publishing. Commissioned by FNV Mondiaal.

Kuron J., and K. Modzelewski. 1969. *An open letter to the party.* London: International Socialist Publications.

Kwan, Alice, and Stephen Frost. 2002. "Made in China": Rules and regulations versus corporate codes of conduct in the toy sector. *Corporate responsibility and labour rights: Codes of conduct in the global economy,* ed. R. Jenkins, R. Pearson, and G. Seyfang, 124–134. London: Earthscan.

Lago, Carmelo Mesa. 1994. Expansion of social security protection to the rural population in Latin America. In *Social security in developing countries,* ed. T. S. Sanakaran et al., 34–62. New Delhi: Social Security Association of India, FES, and Har-Anand Publications.

Lal, Deepak. 1999. India urged to resist WTO's social charter. *ET* (April 6).

——. 2004. Wolfensohn's world bank. *BS* (October 19).

Lal, Vinay. 2005. New Orleans: The Big Easy and the big shame. *EPW* 40, no. 38 (September 17): 4099–4100.

Lambert, Rob. 1997. Globalisation and the new trade union strategies. *IUR* 4, no. 2: 29.

Langille, Brian A. 2002. Seeking post-Seattle clarity—and inspiration. In *Labour law in an era of globalization: Transformative practices and possibilities,* ed. J. Conaghan, R. M. Fischl, and K. Klare, 139–157. Oxford: Oxford University Press.

Lannoo, Karel. 1998. Institutional investors, capital markets, and EMU. In *Institutional investors in the new financial landscape,* 315–329. Paris: Organisation for Economic Cooperation and Development.

LARIC. 1999. *No illusions: Against the global cosmetic SA 8000*. Hong Kong: Labour Rights in China.

Leah, Ronnie. 1993. Black women speak out: Racism and unions. In *Women challenging unions. Feminism, democracy, and militancy*, ed. Linda Briskin and Patricia McDermott, 157–171. Toronto: University of Toronto Press.

Leary, Virginia. 2004. "Form follows function": Formulations of international labor standards—Treaties, codes, soft law, trade agreements. In *International labor standards: Globalization, trade, and public policy*, ed. R. J. Flanagan and William B. Gould IV, 179–205. Stanford, Calif.: Stanford University Press.

Ledwith, Sue, and Fiona Colgan. 2002. Tackling gender, diversity, and trade union democracy: A worldwide project? In *Gender, diversity, and trade unions: International perspectives*, ed. F. Colgan and S. Ledwith, 1–27. London: Routledge.

Lee, Ching Kwan. 1998. *Gender and the south China miracle: Two worlds of factory women*. Berkeley: University of California Press.

——. 2007. *Against the law: Labor protests in China's rustbelt and sunbelt*. Berkeley: University of California Press.

Lee, Eddy, and Marco Vivarelli. 2006. *Globalization, employment, and income distribution in developing countries*. New York: ILO and Palgrave Macmillan.

Lee, Eric. 2005. ILO conventions, the Web, and global trade union organising. *IUR* 12, no. 1: 23.

Leijnse, F. 1980. Workplace bargaining and trade union power. *Industrial Relations Journal* 11.

Leisink, Peter. 1993. Is innovation a management prerogative? Changing employment relationships, innovative unions. Leverhulme Public Lecture, School of Industrial and Business Studies Industrial Relations Research Unit, University of Warwick, Coventry.

Leisink, Peter, Jim Van Leemput, and Jaques Vilrokx, eds. 1996. *The challenges to trade unions in Europe: Innovation or adaptation*. New York: Edward Elgar.

Lenin, V. I. 1964. Imperialism, the highest stage of capitalism. A popular outline. In *Collected Works*, Moscow: Progress Publishers, 22:185–304.

Leung, Wing-Yue. 1988. *Smashing the iron rice pot: Workers and unions in China's market socialism*. Hong Kong: Asia Monitor Resource Center.

Levinson, Charles. 1972. *International trade unionism*. London: Allen & Unwin.

Lewenhak, Sheila. 1977. *Women and trade unions: An outline history of women in the British trade union movement*. London: Ernest Benn.

Lewis, Neil A. 2002. US to renounce its role in pact for world tribunal. *New York Times* (May 5).

Liddle, Joanna. 1988. Occupational sex segregation and women's work in India. *Equal Opportunities International* 7, nos. 4–5: 7–25.

Lindsay, Reed. 2002. Worker control in Argentina. http://www.ainfos.ca/02/nov/ainfos00259.html.

Lipset, Seymour Martin, Martin A. Trow, and James S. Coleman. 1956. *Union democracy*. Glencoe, Ill.: Free Press.

Liu, Henry C. K. 2002. US dollar hegemony has got to go. *Asia Times Online* (April 11). http://www.atimes.com/global-econ/DD11Djo1.html.

LF. 1996. In defence of labour standards. *LF* 2, no. 2: 3–4.

——. 1998. Deaths all the way. *LF* 4, no. 8 (August): 26–27.

Lokshahi Hakk Sanghatana. 2001. Otis contract-labour system claims yet another life. Lokshahi Hakk Sanghatana (June 30).

Lomax, Bill. 1979–1980. The working class in the Hungarian revolution of 1956. *Critique* 12 (Autumn–Winter): 27–54.

Losson, Christian, and Frederic Pons. 2002. Red card for PPR's suppliers. *Libération* (May 22).

Lovasz, A., and S. White. 2007. Dollar slumps to record on China's plans to diversify reserves. http://www.bloomberg.com/apps/news?pid=20601087&sid=aDV6XhaTyJZg&refer=home.

LRD. 1996. *Women's health and safety: A trade union guide*. Labour Research Department Booklets.

Lu, Catherine. 2000. The one and many faces of cosmopolitanism. *Journal of Political Philosophy* 8, no. 2: 244–267.

Luce, Edward. 2004. India waits to pounce as textile quota scheme lapses. *BS* (April 3–4).

Luxemburg, Rosa. 2003. *The accumulation of capital*. Trans. Agnes Schwarzschild. London: Routledge.

——. 1972. The accumulation of capital: An anti-critique. In *Imperialism and the accumulation of capital*, ed. Kenneth Tarbuck, 45–150. London: Allen Lane.

Mackintosh, Maureen. 1981. Gender and economics: The sexual division of labour and the subordination of women. In *Of marriage and the market: Women's subordination in international perspective*, ed. Kate Young, Carol Wolkowitz, and Roslyn McCullagh, 1–15. London: CSE.

Magdoff, Harry. 1972. Imperialism without colonies. In *Studies in the theory of imperialism*, ed. Roger Owen and Bob Sutcliffe, 144–170. London: Longman.

Mahajan, Vijay. 2005. From microcredit to livelihood finance. *EPW* 40, no. 41 (October 8): 4416–4419.

Mahendra Dev, S. 2000a. Economic reforms, poverty, income distribution, and employment. *EPW* 35, no. 10 (March 4): 823–835.

——. 2000b. Economic liberalisation and employment in South Asia—I. *EPW* 35, nos. 1–2 (January 8): 40–51.

Mahendra, K. L. 1996. A protectionist measure. In *Labour, environment, and globalisation—Social clause in multilateral trade agreements: A southern response*, ed. J. John and Anuradha M. Chenoy, 47–50. New Delhi: CEC.

Maher, Kristen Hill. 2002. Who has a right to rights? Citizenship's exclusions in an age of migration. In *Globalization and Human Rights*, ed. A. Brysk, 19–43. Berkeley: University of California Press.

Maitland, Alison. 2002. Sewing a seam of worker democracy in China. *BS* (December 14–15).

Majumdar, Abhik. 1999. The people who died were the lucky ones. *LF* 5, nos. 10–11 (October–November): 32–35.

Majumdar, J. S. 1996. *Why we should oppose pension scheme*. FMRAI.

Majumdar, Pallavi. 2004. Textile industry pessimistic. *BS* (December 31).

Majumdar, Pallavi, and Piyush Pandey. 2005. Dwarfed by the dragon. *BS* (January 18).

Malachevskaya, N. 1979. The mother—Family. Trans. Saral Kumar Sarkar. *Almanac* (Leningrad). Published in March 1980 in the German feminist monthly *Courage*.

Mallet, Serge. 1975. *The new working class*. Nottingham: Spokesman.

Malos, Ellen, ed. 1982. *The politics of housework*. 3rd ed. London: Allison and Busby.

Mansingh, Pallavi. 2005. The people's verdict. *LF* 3, no. 4 (July–August): 18–21.

Mao Tse-tung. 1969a. The Chinese revolution and the Chinese Communist Party. In *The political thought of Mao Tse-tung*, ed. S. Schram, 229–234. Harmondsworth: Penguin.

——. 1969b. We must preserve a rich peasant economy. In *The political thought of Mao Tse-tung*, ed. S. Schram, 342–343. Harmondsworth: Penguin.

——. 1969c. The question of agricultural cooperation. In *The political thought of Mao Tse-tung*, ed. S. Schram, 343–346. Harmondsworth: Penguin.

Marin, Enrique. 2003. How employers sidestep the law. In *From marginal work to core business: European trade unions organising in the informal economy*, 19. Amsterdam: FNV.

Marshall, Shelley. 2005. Outwork in Bulgaria. *IUR* 12, no. 1: 5–6.

Martin, R. M. 1862. *The progress and present state of British India*. London.

Marx, Karl. 1963. *Theories of surplus value, part I*. Moscow: Progress Publishers.

——. 1969a. Parliamentary debate on India. *New York Daily Tribune* (June 25, 1853). In *Karl Marx on colonialism and modernization*, ed. S. Avineri, 81–87. New York: Anchor.

——. 1969b. The East India Company: Its history and results. *New York Daily Tribune* (July 11, 1853). In *Karl Marx on colonialism and modernization*, ed. S. Avineri, 99–108. New York: Anchor.

——. 1969c. Indian affairs. *New York Daily Tribune* (August 5, 1853). In *Karl Marx on colonialism and modernization*, ed. S. Avineri, 128–131. New York: Anchor.

———. 1969d. The future results of British rule in India. *New York Daily Tribune* (August 8, 1853). In *Karl Marx on colonialism and modernization*, ed. S. Avineri, 132–139. New York: Anchor.

———. 1969e. Investigation of torture in India. *New York Daily Tribune* (September 17, 1857). In *Karl Marx on colonialism and modernization*, ed. S. Avineri, 228–234. New York: Anchor.

———. 1969f. Opium and monopoly. *New York Daily Tribune* (September 25, 1858). In *Karl Marx on colonialism and modernization*, ed. S. Avineri, 345–348. New York: Anchor.

———. 1974a. Critique of the Gotha programme. In *The First International and After*, 339–359. Harmondsworth: Penguin.

———. 1974b. The civil war in France. In *The First International and After*, 187–268. Harmondsworth: Penguin.

———. 1974c. Documents of the First International: 1864–70. In *The First International and After*, 73–120. Harmondsworth: Penguin.

———. 1975a. Concerning Feuerbach. In *Early Writings*. Trans. Rodney Livingstone and Gregory Benton, 421–423. Harmondsworth: Penguin.

———. 1975b. Excerpts from James Mill's *Elements of political economy*. In *Early Writings*. Trans. Rodney Livingstone and Gregory Benton, 259–278. Harmondsworth: Penguin.

———. 1976. *Capital, volume 1*. Trans. Ben Fowkes. Harmondsworth: Penguin.

———. 1978. *Capital, volume 2*. Trans. David Fernbach. Harmondsworth: Penguin.

———. 1981. *Capital, volume 3*. Trans. David Fernbach. Harmondsworth: Penguin.

———. 1987. Wages, price, and profit. In *Marx and Engels on the trade unions*, ed. Kenneth Lapides, 90–95. London: Praeger.

Marx, Karl, and Frederick Engels. 1973. Manifesto of the Communist Party. In *The revolutions of 1848*, ed. David Fernbach, 67–98. Harmondsworth: Penguin.

Mather, Celia. 2005. Unions face up to contract/agency labour. *IUR* 12, no. 1: 22.

Mathew, A. F. 2001. Rethinking globalisation. Paper presented at UGC National Seminar on Globalisation and India's Environment, SNDT Women's University, Bombay, February 15–16.

Mathew, Thomas. 1996. The need for a social clause. In *Labour, environment, and globalisation—Social clause in multilateral trade agreements: A southern response*, ed. J. John and Anuradha M. Chenoy, 67–69. New Delhi: CEC.

Mathrani, Sheila. 2000. WTO court rules against US subsidies to blue-chip cos. *ET* (February 28).

Mattick, Paul. 1981. *Economic crisis and crisis theory*. London: The Merlin Press.

Mazumdar, Indrani. 2007. *Women workers and globalization: Emergent contradictions in India*. Kolkata: Stree.

McAuley, Alastair. 1981. *Women's work and wages in the Soviet Union*. London: Allen & Unwin.

McCann, Deirdre. 2005. Sexual harassment at work: National and international responses. Geneva: ILO.

McMonnies, Dave. 1984. Trade unions and co-ops? A Merseyside case study: The Scott Bader synthetic resins saga. Working Paper no. 6, Dept. of Political Theory and Institutions, University of Liverpool, Liverpool.

Mehta, Bhanu Pratap. 2004. Affirmation without reservation. *EPW* 39, no. 27 (July 3): 2951–2954.

Mehta, Pradeep S. 1999. Child labour, social clause, and the WTO. *ET* (June 16).

Melicharova, Margaret. 2000. 100 years of action for peace. *Peace Pledge Union*. http://www.ppu.org.uk/century/century9.html.

Melman, Seymour. 2001. *After capitalism: From managerialism to workplace democracy*. New York: Knopf.

——. 2008. *War Inc. AmeriQuests* 5, no. 2. http://ejournals.library.vanderbilt.edu/ameriquests/viewissue.php?id=11.

Menon, Sindhu. 1999. Spectre of death haunts construction industry. *LF* 5, nos. 1–4 (January–April): 20–24.

——. 2005a. Endorsing an unorganised bill: A game of hide-and-seek. *LF* 3, no. 2 (March–April): 7–20.

——. 2005b. Indian Provident Fund: A systematic denial. *LF* 3, no. 3 (May–June): 5–11.

——. 2005c. Safai Karamcharis: Reinvented untouchables in modern India. *LF* 3, no. 6 (November–December): 5–12.

MGG. 1961. Part I-L (November 2): 2757ff.

——. 1963. Part I-L (July 11): 2357ff.

——. 1965. Part I-L (December 2): 4179ff.

——. 1966. Part I-L (January 6): 34ff.

——. 1981. Part I-L (July 30): 195ff.

Milkman, Ruth. 1987. *Gender at work: The dynamics of job segregation by sex during World War II*. Urbana: University of Illinois Press.

Miller, Doug. 2004. Preparing for the long haul: Negotiating international framework agreements in the global textile, garment, and footwear sector. *Global Social Policy* 4, no. 2: 215–239.

Milmo, Cahal. 2002. Sweatshop allegations leave Gucci under fire. *Independent* (June 7).

Ministry of Labour. 2002. *Report of the National Commission on Labour*. New Delhi: Government of India.

Minns, Richard. 2001. *The cold war in welfare: Stock markets versus pensions*. London: Verso.

Mishra, Lakshmidhar. 2005. Provident Fund for unorganised-sector workers: A mirage. *LF* 3, no. 3 (May–June): 12–13.

Mitra, Ashok, S. Mukerjee, and R. Bose. 1980. *Indian cities: Their industrial structure, in-migration, and capital investment, 1961–71.* New Delhi: ICSSR/JNU.

Mitra, Saumya Kanti. 2001. Capitalise on labour flexibility. *ET* (March 8).

Mitter, Swasti. 1994. On organising women in casualised work: A global overview. In *Dignity and daily bread: New forms of economic organising among poor women in the Third World and the First*, ed. Sheila Rowbotham and Swasti Mitter, 14–52. London: Routledge.

Mody, Gautam. 2001. Governance of the private sector: Regulatory Issues. In *Corporate governance and the Indian private sector*, by Jairus Banaji and Gautam Mody, 51–69. Oxford: Queen Elizabeth House.

Moglen, Eben, and V. Sasi Kumar. 2007. The spectre of free information. *Frontline* 24, no. 20 (October 6): 100–104.

Mohapatra, Prabhu. 1998. Immobilising labour: Indenture laws and enforcement in Assam and the West Indies, 1860–1920. Paper presented at the First Annual Conference of the Association of Indian Labour Historians in association with V. V. Giri National Labour Institute, March 16–18.

Molyneux, Maxine. 1979. Beyond the domestic labour debate. *New Left Review* 116 (July–August): 3–27.

Monks, John. 1994. Linking trade and basic rights. *IUR* 1, no. 7: 2.

Montgomery, David. 1979. *Workers' control in America. Studies in the history of work, technology, and labor struggles.* Cambridge: Cambridge University Press.

Monthly Review. 2004. Notes from the editors. *Monthly Review* (January).

Moody, Kim. 1997. *Workers in a lean world: Unions in the international economy.* London: Verso.

——. 2007. *U.S. labor in trouble and transition: The failure of reform from above, the promise of revival from below.* London: Verso.

Mooij, Jos. 1999. Food policy in India: The importance of electoral politics in policy implementation. *Journal of International Development* 11: 625–639.

Morris, Morris D. 1965. *The emergence of an industrial labor force in India.* Berkeley: University of California Press.

MP Chronicle. 1985. Union carbide staff assail Anderson's statement. *MP Chronicle* (April 4).

MSN. 2005. Garment factory collapse kills 74 workers. *Maquila Network Update* 10, no. 2: 1, 8.

Muhammad, Anu. 2009. Grameen and microcredit: A tale of corporate success. *EPW* 44, no. 35 (August 29): 35–42.

Mukherjee, Krittivas. 2008. Update 1: India's Goa drops contentious industry zones plan. *Reuters* (January 2). http://www.reuters.com/article/rbssHealthcareNews/idUSDEL565820080102.

Mukherjee, Writankar. 2004. India Inc. wants a piece of HR outsourcing pie now. *ET* (April 24).

Munck, Ronaldo. 1988. *New international labour studies: An introduction*. London: Zed Books.

——. 2003. *Globalisation and labour: The new 'great transformation.'* Delhi: Madhyam Books.

Munck, Ronaldo, Ricardo Falcón, and Bernardo Gallitelli. 1987. *Argentina, from anarchism to Peronism: Workers, unions, and politics 1855–1985*. London: Zed Books.

Mundlek, Guy. 2002. The limits of labour law in a fungible community. In *Labour law in an era of globalization: Transformative practices and possibilities*, ed. J. Conaghan, R. M. Fischl, and K. Klare, 279–298. Oxford: Oxford University Press.

Muralidharan, Sukumar. 2005. Development deficit agenda of Doha round. *EPW* 40, no. 2 (December 24): 5450–5453.

Murray, Jill. 2002. Labour rights/corporate responsibilities: The role of ILO labour standards. In *Corporate responsibility and labour rights: Codes of conduct in the global economy*, ed. R. Jenkins, R. Pearson, and G. Seyfang, 31–42. London: Earthscan.

Murray, Robin. 1971. Internationalization of capital and the nation state. *New Left Review* 67 (May–June): 84–109.

Nagaraj, R. 1999a. How good are India's industrial statistics? An exploratory note. *EPW* 34, no. 6 (February 6): 350–355.

——. 1999b. Reply. *EPW* 34, no. 23 (June 5): 1463–1464.

——. 2003. Industrial policy and performance since 1980: Which way now? *EPW* 38 (August 30): 3707–3715.

——. 2004. Fall in organised manufacturing employment: A brief note. *EPW* 39, no. 30 (July 24): 3387–3390.

Nagarjuna, M., and Shantha Sinha. 2004. The poverty argument. http://www.mvfindia.org/pdf/poverty.pdf.

Nair, Arvind, Bennet D'Costa, and Sanober Keshwar. 1999. The new units of HLL: "Subsidized" exploitation. *The Union's Lever* 1, no. 2: (4–11).

Nambissan, Geetha B. 2003. Social exclusion, children's work, and education: A view from the margins. In *Child labour and the right to education in South Asia: Needs versus rights?*, ed. N. Kabeer, G. Nambissan, and R. Subrahmanian, 109–142. New Delhi: Sage.

Narayanan, M. S. 1994. Industrial sickness: Review of BIFR's role. *EPW* 39, no. 7 (February 12): 362–376.

Nath, Surendra. 2003. Labour reforms: Tips from China. *ET* (July 4).

National Commission for Enterprises in the Unorganised Sector. 2007. *Report on conditions of work and promotion of livelihoods in the unorganised sector*. http://nceus.gov.in/Condition_of_workers_sep_2007.pdf.

Navlakha, Gautam. 2005. Crisis as an opportunity. *EPW* 40, no. 47 (November 19): 4874–4876.

Nayak, Gayatri. 2005. Dragon raises its head in the forex market too. *ET* (March 28).

NCL. N.d. *A Call to the unorganised workers to unite against oppression and marginalisation, to struggle for protective legislation and social security: From the margin to the centre.* Bangalore: National Centre for Labour.

Nederveen Pieterse, Jan. Delinking or globalisation? *EPW* 34, no. 5 (January 29): 239–242.

Neetha, N. 2001. *Gender and technology: Impact of flexible organisation and production on female labour in the Tiruppur knitwear industry.* Noida: V. V. Giri National Labour Institute.

New Age Weekly. 2002. TU convention demand sack of Narendra Modi. *New Age Weekly* (August 11–17).

Nicholas Employees' Union. 2003. Trade union rally jams capital. *Samvaad* (March): 1.

Norris, Pippa. 2003. Global governance and cosmopolitan citizens. In *The global transformations reader: An introduction to the globalization debate,* ed. David Held and Anthony McGrew, 287–297. Cambridge: Polity Press.

NTUI. N.d. Worker cooperatives: A force resisting industrial closure. New Delhi: NTUI.

——. 2001. For a new initiative. Delhi: New Trade Union Initiative.

——. 2004. Minutes of meeting on February 14–15 at Shramik union office, Bombay.

——. 2006. *Constitution.*

——. 2007a. New workers and unions join the strike. *Union Power* 1, no. 1 (January).

——. 2007b. Special article: Sexual harassment bill 2007. *Union Power* 1, no. 3 (March): 4–5.

——. 2007c. Hindustan Lever employees' union's long-standing struggle at the Sewri plant. *Union Power* 1, no. 4 (April): 3–5.

——. 2009. *Union Power* (June).

Nussbaum, Martha C. 1996a. Patriotism and cosmopolitanism. In *For love of country: Debating the limits of patriotism,* ed. Joshua Cohen, 2–17. Boston: Beacon.

——. 1996b. Reply. In *For love of country: Debating the limits of patriotism,* ed. Joshua Cohen, 131–144. Boston: Beacon.

OECD. 1998. *Institutional investors in the new financial landscape.* Paris: Organization for Economic Cooperation and Development.

Olle, Werner, and Wolfgang Schoeller. 1977. World market competition and restrictions upon international trade union policies. *Capital and Class* 2: 56–75.

Onaran, Özlem. 2009. A crisis of distribution. *EPW* 44, no. 13 (March 28): 171–178.

O'Rourke, Dara. 2002. Monitoring the monitors: A critique of corporate third-party labour monitoring. In *Corporate responsibility and labour rights: Codes of conduct in the global economy*, ed. R. Jenkins, R. Pearson, and G. Seyfang, 196–208. London: Earthscan.

Ould, David. 1995. Is free trade fair? *IUR* 2, no. 2: 17.

Owen, Roger, and Bob Sutcliffe, eds. 1972. *Studies in the theory of imperialism*. London: Longman.

Padhi, Ranjana. 2009. On women surviving farmer suicides in Punjab. *EPW* 44, no. 19 (May 9): 53–59.

Padmapriya, J., and V. Balasubramanian. 2004. Outsourcing of auto parts revs up Job St. *ET* (September 24).

Palat, Ravi Arvind. 2004. Flailing eagle, crouching tigers: Decline of U.S. power and new Asian regionalism. *EPW* 39, no. 32 (August 7): 3620–3626.

Pani, Narendar. 2003. The do-nothing trap. *ET* (August 15).

Panitch, Leo, and Colin Leys, eds. 2000. *Working classes, global realities: Socialist register 2001*. London: The Merlin Press.

Papola, T. S. 2005. A universal programme is feasible. *EPW* 40, no. 7 (February 12): 594–599.

Patel, B. B. 1988. *Workers of closed textile mills: Patterns and problems of their absorption in a metropolitan labour market*. Ahmedabad: Oxford and IBH Publishing Co.

———. 2001. Socio economic marginalisation of displaced textile mill workers in Ahmedabad, Gujarat, India. Paper presented to IDPAD workshop on Collective Care Arrangements Among Workers and Nonworkers in the Informal Sector, Centre for Economic and Social Studies, Hyderabad, March 1–2.

Patel, Freny. 2005. Part-time hiring, full-time job. *BS* (January 3).

Patel, Pravin. 2009. NREGA: Vice president of Paschim Banga Khet Majoor Samiti (PBKMS) has been brutally attacked and has been hospitalized on 2.4.2009. (April 9). http://www.mail-archive.com/jharkhand@yahoogroups.co.in/msg04339.html.

Patel, Shanti G. 1999. Political parties and trade unions. Paper presented at conference on Industry-Labour Relations in the Twentieth Century, Mumbai, March 7–8.

Patnaik, Prabhat. 1972. Imperialism and the growth of Indian capitalism. In *Studies in the theory of imperialism*, ed. Roger Owen and Bob Sutcliffe, 210–230. London: Longman.

Pearson, Ruth, and Gill Seyfang. 2002. "I'll tell you what I want . . .": Women workers and codes of conduct. In *Corporate responsibility and labour rights: Codes of conduct in the global economy*, ed. R. Jenkins, R. Pearson, and G. Seyfang, 43–60. London: Earthscan.

Pelikan, Jiri. 1972. The struggle for socialism in Czechoslovakia. *New Left Review* 71 (January–February): 3–35.

Pelletier, D. L, E. A. Frongillo Jr., D. G. Schroeder, and J. P. Habicht. 1995. The effects of malnutrition on child mortality in developing countries. *Bulletin of the World Health Organization* 73, no. 4: 443–448.

Petras, James. 1999. Globalisation: A socialist perspective. *EPW* 34, no. 8 (February 20): 459–464.

Phadnis, Aditi. 2001. Workers of the country, nothing to cheer. *BS* (May 1).

Phelan, Craig. 2007a. Worldwide trends and prospects for trade union revitalisation. In *Trade union revitalisation: Trends and prospects in 34 countries*, ed. Craig Phelan, 11–38. Berne: Peter Lang.

——, ed. 2007b. *Trade union revitalisation: Trends and prospects in 34 countries*. Berne: Peter Lang.

Philip, Lijee. 2004. Dragon may run away with auto outsourcing. *ET* (September 21).

Philips Employees' Union. 1985. *One owl will suffice to send the garden to seed. What fate awaits it with an owl on every branch?* Bombay: Philips Employees' Union.

Pinchbeck, Ivy. 1930. *Women workers and the industrial revolution, 1750–1850*. London: Routledge.

Pittsburgh Summit. 2009. Leaders' statement: Pittsburgh summit, 24–25 September. http://www.pittsburghsummit.gov/mediacenter/129639.htm.

Plant, Roger. 1994. *Labour standards and structural adjustment*. Geneva: ILO.

Pollert, Anna. 1981. *Girls, wives, factory lives*. London: Macmillan.

——. 1996. "Team work" on the assembly line: Contradiction and the dynamics of union resilience. In *The new workplace and trade unionism: Critical perspectives on work and organization*, ed. Peter Ackers, Chris Smith, and Paul Smith, 178–209. London: Routledge.

Posner, Michael, and Justine Nolan. 2003. Can codes of conduct play a role in promoting workers' rights? In *International labor standards: Globalization, trade, and public policy*, ed. R. J. Flanagan and William B. Gould IV, 207–226. Stanford, Calif.: Stanford University Press.

Press, Mike. 1984. The lost vision: Trade unions and internationalism. In *For a new internationalism*, ed. Peter Waterman, 88–107. The Hague: International Labour Education Research and Information Foundation.

——. 1989a. The people's movement. In *Solidarity for survival: The Don Thomson reader on trade union internationalism*, ed. Mike Press and Don Thomson, 26–47. Nottingham: Spokesman.

——. 1989b. International trade unionism. In *Solidarity for survival: The Don Thomson reader on trade union internationalism*, ed. Mike Press and Don Thomson, 17–24. Nottingham: Spokesman.

Press, Mike, and Don Thomson, eds. 1989. *Solidarity for survival: The Don Thomson reader on trade union internationalism*. Nottingham: Spokesman.

Prieto, Marina. 2002. Thoughts on feminist action research. Working paper, New Academy of Business, Bath.

Prieto, Marina, Angela Hadjipateras, and Jane Turner. 2002. The potential of codes as part of women's organizations' strategies for promoting the rights of women workers: A Central American perspective. In *Corporate responsibility and labour rights: Codes of conduct in the global economy*, ed. R. Jenkins, R. Pearson, and G. Seyfang, 146–159. London: Earthscan.

PROBE Team. 1999. *Public report on basic education in India*. Delhi: Oxford University Press.

PUCL Bulletin. 2001. Rajasthan PUCL writ in Supreme Court on famine deaths. *PUCL Bulletin* (November). http://www.pucl.org/reports/Rajasthan/2001/starvation-writ.htm.

Punekar, S. D. 1950. *Social insurance for industrial workers in India*. New Delhi: Oxford University Press.

Purcell, John, and Robin Smith. 1979. *The control of work*. London: Macmillan.

Radice, Giles, ed. 1972. *Working power*. Fabian Society Tract 43.

Raghu, Sunil. 2002. SEZs seek "more freedom," separate labour laws. *ET* (January 9).

Rai, Asha. 2004. Garment makers rope in expats to man shopfloors. *ET* (February 1).

Rajagopalan, T. N. C. 2004. WTO ruling against US to help poor nations. *BS* (May 3).

Rajanala, Sunil. 2003. Outsourcing HR: The next big thing. *ET* (May 18).

Rajesh, R., and Depinder Singh. 2003. The brick-layer's plight. *Humanscape* 10, no. 1 (January).

Rajwade, A. V. 2004a. The BPO backlash? *BS* (January 12).

———. 2004b, 'Globalisation and offshoring – I,' *BS*, 12 April

———. 2004c. Asia's dollar dilemma. *BS* (December 20).

Ram Mohan, T. T. 2009. The impact of the crisis on the Indian economy. *EPW* 44, no. 13 (March 28): 107–114.

Ramachandran, Vimla. 2005. Reflections on the ICDS programme. *Seminar* 546. http://www.india-seminar.com/2005/546/546%20vimla%20ramachandran.htm.

Ramalho, José Ricardo. 2007. Trade unions and politics in Brazil. In *Trade union revitalisation: Trends and prospects in thirty-four countries*, ed. Craig Phelan, 91–104. Berne: Peter Lang.

Ramaswamy, E. A. 1988. *Worker consciousness and trade union response*. Delhi: Oxford University Press.

——. 1999. Child labour in the larger context of industrial relations. In *Against child labour: Indian and international dimensions and strategies*, ed. Klaus Voll, 53–61. New Delhi: Mosaic.

Ramaswamy, K. V. 1994. Small-scale manufacturing industries: Some aspects of size, growth and structure. *EPW* 29, no. 9 (February 26): M-13–23.

Ramaswamy, Uma. 1983. *Work, union, and community: Industrial man in South India*. Delhi: Oxford University Press.

Rao, Rukmini, and Sahba Husain. 1987. Women in home-based production in the garment export industry in Delhi. In *Invisible hands: Women in home-based production*, ed. Andrea Menefee Singh and Anita Kelles-Viitanen, 51–67. New Delhi: Sage.

Rappaport, Alan. 2009. Surprise fall in US trade deficit. *Financial Times* (October 10).

Raum, Tom. 2007. National debt grows $1 million a minute. *ABC News* (December 3). http://abcnews.go.com/Business/wireStory?id=3944576.

Recknagel, Charles. 2000. Iraq: Baghdad moves to euro. *Radio Free Europe* (November 1).

Reisen, Helmut. 2009. Shifting wealth: Is the US dollar empire falling? *VOX* (June 20). http://www.voxeu.org/index.php?q=node/3672.

Remesh, Babu. 2004. *Labour in business process outsourcing: A case study of call centre agents*. Noida: V. V. Giri National Labour Institute.

Ricardo, David. 1821. *On the principles of political economy and taxation*. 3rd ed. London.

Right to Food Campaign. 2005. Foundation statement. http://www.righttofoodindia.org/foundation.html.

Roberts, Dan. 2004. Outsourcing now widespread in US, Europe. *BS* (April 16).

Roberts, Paul Craig. 2004. The coming currency shock. *Counterpunch*. http://www.counterpunch.org/roberts11162004.html.

Rodrigo, G. Chris. 2007. Globalization and its misconceptions. *Polity* 4, no. 1 (January–March): 25–27.

Rosa, Kumudini. 1994. The conditions and organisational activities of women in free trade zones: Malaysia, Philippines, and Sri Lanka. In *Dignity and daily bread: New forms of economic organising among poor women in the Third World and the First*, ed. Sheila Rowbotham and Swasti Mitter, 73–99. London: Routledge.

Rosenberg, Matt. 2005. Bollywood. http://geography.about.com/od/cultural geography/a/bollywood.htm.

Roubini, Nouriel. 2008. How will financial institutions make money now that the securitization food chain is broken?' *RGE Monitor*. http://www.rgemonitor.com/blog/roubini/252638.

Rowbotham, Sheila. 1974. *Women, resistance, and revolution*. Harmondsworth: Penguin.

———. 1990. Post-Fordism. *Z Magazine* (September): 31–36.

———. 1994. Strategies against sweated work in Britain, 1820–1920. In *Dignity and daily bread: New forms of economic organising among poor women in the Third World and the First*, ed. Sheila Rowbotham and Swasti Mitter, 158–192. London: Routledge.

Rowbotham, Sheila, and Swasti Mitter, eds. 1994. *Dignity and daily bread: New forms of economic organising among poor women in the Third World and the First*. London: Routledge.

Roy, A. K. 1994. Kamani to Kanoria: Marxists workers' co-operatives. *EPW* 29, no. 39 (September 24): 2533–2535.

Roy, Aruna, and Nikhil Dey. 2009. NREGA: Breaking new ground. *The Hindu* (June 21).

Roy, Ashim. 1996. Labour standards in multilateral trade agreements: An overview. In *Labour, environment, and globalisation—Social clause in multilateral trade agreements: A southern response*, ed. J. John and Anuradha M. Chenoy, 177–186. New Delhi: CEC.

Roy, Tirthankar. 1998. Development or distortion? "Powerlooms" in India, 1950–1997. *EPW* 33, no. 16 (April 18): 897–911.

Roy, William G. 1997. *Socializing capital: The rise of the large industrial corporation in America*. Princeton: Princeton University Press.

Rubin, Gayle. 1977. The traffic in women: Notes on the "political economy" of sex. In *Towards an anthropology of women*, ed. Rayna Reiter. New York: Monthly Review Press.

Ruddick, Sara. 1982. Maternal thinking. In *Rethinking the family: Some feminist questions*, ed. B. Thorne with M. Yalom, 76–94. New York: Longman.

Sabarinath, M. 2003. Apparel exporters want govt to push for standard compliance norms. *ET* (December 12).

———. 2004. Small garment exporters are frayed at the edges. *ET* (August 9).

Sabarinath, M., and Arun Iyer. 2001. Garment cos want dumping duty on Lanka, Bangladesh. *ET* (February 17).

Sabarinath, M., and R. Sriram. 2005. Pension funds are next. *ET* (September 12).

Sachar committee chaired by Justice Rajindar Sachar. 2006. *Social, economic, and educational status of the Muslim community of India: A report*. http://www.sabrang.com/sachar/sacharreport.pdf.

Sakai, J. 1989. *Settlers: The mythology of the white proletariat*. Chicago: Morningstar Press.

———. 2000. Aryan politics and fighting the WTO. In *My enemy's enemy: Essays on globalization, fascism, and the struggle against capitalism*, ed. Anti-Fascist Forum, 7–23. Toronto: Anti-Fascist Forum.

Samant, Dada. 2000. *Angdai*. Trade Union Solidarity Committee.

Sampath, G. 2009. Bachchan was the coolie, but now, in movies, he only lives in villas. Interview with Arundhati Roy. *DNA* (October 11).

Sargent, Lydia, ed. 1981. *Women and revolution: A discussion of the unhappy marriage of Marxism and feminism*. London: Pluto.

Satpathy, Anoop. 2005. *Size, composition, and characteristics of informal sector in India*. NLI Research Study Series 56. Noida: V. V. Giri National Labour Institute.

Sathyamurthy, T. V., ed. 1996. *Class formation and political transformation in postcolonial India*. Delhi: Oxford University Press.

Satyarthi, Kailash. 1996. Perceptions with child labour in focus: Rugmark as an alternative. In *Labour, environment, and globalisation—Social clause in multilateral trade agreements: A southern response*, ed. J. John and Anuradha M. Chenoy, 83–87. New Delhi: CEC.

Satyarthi, Kailash. 1999. The struggle against child labour: International donors, practical steps, political and social networking. In *Against child labour: Indian and international dimensions and strategies*, ed. Klaus Voll, 270–280. New Delhi: Mosaic.

Savara, Mira. 1986. *Changing trends in women's employment*. Bombay: Himalaya Publishing House.

Scheu, Hildegard. 1999. The "T-shirt city" of South India: Child labour in Tiruppur. In *Against child labour: Indian and international dimensions and strategies*, ed. Klaus Voll, 228–237. New Delhi: Mosaic.

Schram, Stuart. 1969. *The political thought of Mao Tse-tung*. Harmondsworth: Penguin.

Scipes, Kim. 2007. Neoliberal policies in the United States: The impact on American workers. *Z Magazine* (February 2). http://www.zmag.org/content/showarticle.cfm?sectionID=19&itemID=12018.

Seccombe, Wally. 1973. The housewife and her labour under capitalism. *New Left Review* 83 (January–February): 3–24.

——. 1975. Domestic labour: Reply to critics. *New Left Review* 94 (November–December): 85–96.

Sehgal, Rakhi. 2005. Gurgaon, July 25: Police brutality not an aberration. *EPW* 40, no. 35 (August 27): 3796–3797.

Seidman, Gay W. 1994. *Manufacturing militance: Workers' movements in Brazil and South Africa, 1970–1985*. Berkeley: University of California Press.

Selmi, Michael, and Molly S. McUsic. 2002. Difference and solidarity: Unions in a postmodern age. In *Labour law in an era of globalization: Transformative practices and possibilities*, ed. J. Conaghan, R. M. Fischl, and K. Klare, 429–446. Oxford: Oxford University Press.

Sen, Amartya. 1999. *Development as freedom*. New York: Alfred A. Knopf.

Sen, Bulbul. 2006. The significant downside of SEZs. *ET* (February 21).

Sen, Sukomal. 1979. *Working class of India: History of emergence and movement 1830–1970.* Calcutta: K. P. Bagchi.

Sengupta, Padmini. 1960. *Women workers of India.* Bombay: Asia Publishing House.

Sethuraman, S. V. 1998. *Gender, informality, and poverty: A global review—Gender bias in female informal employment and incomes in developing countries.* Geneva: ILO.

Shah, Mihir. 2005. Saving the employment guarantee act. *EPW* 40, no. 7 (February 12): 599–602.

Shah, Suresh. 2001. Textile imports seen crossing Rs 4,000 cr. *ET* (March 30).

Shanbagh, A. N. 1995. *Selected articles on the employees' pension scheme.* Bombay.

Shankar, Kripa. 2004. How efficient is TPDS in tribal areas? *EPW* 39, no. 21 (May 22): 2093–2096.

Sharma, D. P. 1999. Fishing and aquaculture policies debates continue. *LF* 5, nos.1–4 (January–April): 68–71.

Sharma, Kalpana. 2005. Viewing health as an inalienable right. *India Together* (October 7). http://www.indiatogether.org/2005/oct/ksh-health.htm.

Sharma, Mukul. 1998. Voice of memory/silence of pain. *LF* 4, no. 8 (August): 21–25.

Shaw, Linda, and Angela Hale. 2002. The emperor's new clothes: What codes mean for workers in the garment industry. In *Corporate responsibility and labour rights: Codes of conduct in the global economy,* ed. R. Jenkins, R. Pearson, and G. Seyfang, 101–112. London: Earthscan.

Shrivastava, Aseem. 2008. The problem. *Seminar* 582 (February).

Silver, Beverley J. 2003. *Forces of labor: Workers' movements and globalization since 1870.* Cambridge: Cambridge University Press.

Simeon, Dilip. 1995. *The politics of labour under late colonialism.* New Delhi: Manohar.

Singhal, Arvind. 2003. Lessons from China. *BS* (November 1–2).

Singh, Andrea Menefee, and Anita Kelles-Viitanen, ed. 1987. *Invisible hands: Women in home-based production.* New Delhi: Sage.

Singh, Gayatri, and P. A. Sebastian. 1989. *The right to be recognised: The TELCO strike.* Bombay: Committee for the Protection of Democratic Rights.

Singh, Gurbir. 2004. Industrial tribunals to cover workmen only, rules SC. *ET* (April 28).

Singh, Samir Kumar. 2005. An analysis of anti-dumping cases in India. *EPW* 40, no. 11 (March 12): 1069–1074.

Sinha, Shantha. 2000. Re: Equity in national education policies. http://www.edc .org/GLG/edudemoc/hypermail/0074.html.

———. 2003. Schools as institutions for the elimination of child labour: The experience of the M. V. Foundation in the Ranga Reddy district. In *Child labour and the right to education in South Asia: Needs versus rights?,* ed. N. Kabeer, G. Nambissan, and R. Subrahmanian, 321–334. New Delhi: Sage.

——. 2005a. The missing children. http://www.mvfindia.org/The_%20miss-ing%20children.doc.

——. 2005b. Appeal for total abolition of child labour. http://www.pagalguy.com/index.php?categoryid=13&p2_articleid=75.

——. 2005c. Emphasising universal principles towards deepening of democracy: Actualising children's right to education. *EPW* 40, no. 25 (June 18): 2569–2576.

Sinha, Vivek. 2004. Made in India brands are now globe trotters. *ET* (January 31).

SJM, BMS, ABVP, and Bharatiya Kisan Sangh. 2000. Open letter to Mike Moore. Quoted in full in J. Singh. Resisting global capitalism in India. In *My enemy's enemy: Essays on globalization, fascism, and the struggle against capitalism*, ed. Anti-Fascist Forum, 84–85. Toronto: Anti-Fascist Forum.

Smith, Adam. 1776. *An inquiry into the nature and causes of the wealth of nations*. London.

Soboul, Albert. 1977. *A short history of the French revolution*. Berkeley: University of California Press.

Soman, Mangesh. 2001. Organised sector sheds flab, but there's work elsewhere. *ET* (May 9).

——. 2002. Casual labour spurts in last decade. *ET* (February 20).

——. 2003. India Inc cuts more jobs in '01–02 than in past three years. *ET* (May 6).

Soros, George. 1998. *The crisis of global capitalism*. PublicAffairs.

——. 2002. WTO's labour lost? *BS* (May 21).

South Asian. 2005. Indian laws against bonded labour. *South Asian* (March 15). http://www.thesouthasian.org/archives/000327.html#000327.

Southall, Roger, ed. 1988. *Trade unions and the new industrialisation of the Third World*. London: Zed Books.

Spalding Jr., Hobart A. 1988. US labour intervention in Latin America: The case of the American Institute for Free Labor Development. In *Trade unions and the new industrialisation of the Third World*, ed. Roger Southall, 259–286. London: Zed Books.

Spiegel Online. 2007. Strikes against pension reform hit France. *Business Week* (November 14).

Spiro, David E. 1999. *The hidden hand of American hegemony: Petrodollar recycling and international markets*. Ithaca, N.Y.: Cornell University Press.

Srinivasan, S. 2007. Battling patent laws: The Glivec case. *EPW* 42, no. 37 (September 15): 3686–3690.

Srinivasan, T. N. 1999. Anti-dumping is not in India's interest. *BS* (January 1).

Stalker, P. 1996. *Child labour in Bangladesh*. Dhaka: UNICEF.

Standing, Hilary. 1991. *Dependence and autonomy: Women's employment and the family in Calcutta*. London: Routledge.

Stapleton, G. P. 1996. *Institutional shareholders and corporate governance*. Oxford: Oxford University Press.

Steinherr, Alfred. 2000. *Derivatives: The wild beast of finance*. Chichester: John Wiley & Sons.

Stevis, Dimitris. 2002. Unions, capitals, and states: Competing (inter)nationalisms in North American and European integration. In *Global unions? Theory and strategies of organized labour in the global political economy*, ed. Jeffrey Harrod and Robert O'Brien, 130–150. London: Routledge.

Stiglitz, Joseph. 2000. The insider: What I learned at the world economic crisis. *New Republic Online* (April 17). http://www.thenewrepublic.com/041700/stiglitz041700.html.

——. 2002. *Globalization and its discontents*. London: Penguin.

——. 2009. Thanks to the deficit, the buck stops here. *Washington Post* (August 30).

Stoleroff, Alan, and Reinhard Naumann. 1996. Unions and the restructuring of the public sector in Portugal. In *The challenges to trade unions in Europe: Innovation or adaptation*, ed. Peter Leisink, Jim Van Leemput, and Jaques Vilrokx, 205–222. New York: Edward Elgar.

Stone, Katherine van Wezel. 1996. Labour in the global economy: Four approaches to transnational labour regulation. In *International regulatory competition and coordination: Perspectives on economic regulation in Europe and the United States*, ed. William Bratton et al., 445–477. Oxford: Clarendon Press.

Subramaniam, Arun. 1987. Kamani Tubes: Workers mean business. *Business India* (February 9): 63–67.

Subramaniam, G. Ganpathy. 2001a. Anti-dumping wrangles keep Indian firms occupied. *ET* (May 14).

——. 2003a. Dark secret: Who killed the Cancun conference? *ET* (September 20).

——. 2003b. Exporters adopt "clean" labour norms. *ET* (April 28).

Subramanian, K. N. 1977. *Wages in India*. New Delhi: Tata McGraw-Hill.

Subramanya, R. K. A. 2005. The importance of employment regulation and unorganised sector workers' bill. *LF* 3, no. 2 (March–April): 26–30.

Subramanyam, R. 2004. Outsourcing: The leveller. *ET* (December 30).

Sudarshan, Ratna M., and Jeemol Unni. 2003. Measuring the informal economy. In *Informal economy centrestage: New structures of employment*, ed. Renana Jhabvala, Ratna M. Sudarshan, and Jeemol Unni, 19–38. New Delhi: Sage.

Suroor, Hasan. 2008. Marx is back. *The Hindu* (October 22).

Surya, Vasantha. 1985. Learning to live with fear. *Indian Express* (August 4).

Sutcliffe, Bob. 1972. Imperialism and industrialisation in the Third World. In *Studies in the theory of imperialism*, ed. Roger Owen and Bob Sutcliffe, 171–192. London: Longman.

Swaminadhan, Srilata. 1996. Towards international solidarity. In *Labour, environment, and globalisation—Social clause in multilateral trade agreements: A southern response*, ed. J. John and Anuradha M. Chenoy, 55–58. New Delhi: CEC.

Swaminathan, Padmini. 2002. *Labour-intensive industries but units without "workers": Where will ILO's dialogue begin?* Working Paper 168. Chennai: Madras Institute of Development Studies.

Swann, Christopher. 2004. Economists retaliate in spat over US protectionism. *BS* (April 3–4).

Sykes, Alan. 2003. *International trade and human rights: An economic perspective.* John M. Olin Law and Economics Working Paper 188 (2nd series). Chicago: University of Chicago Law School.

Taibbi, Matt. 2007. The great Iraq swindle: How Bush allowed an army of for-profit contractors to invade the US Treasury. *Rolling Stone* (September 6). http://www.rollingstone.com/politics/story/16076312/the_great_iraq_swindle/print.

Taylor, Andrew. 2005. MNCs face higher wage costs in China than India: Study. *BS* (November 16).

Teerink, Rensje. 1995. Migration and its impact on Khandeshi women in the sugar cane harvest. In *Women and seasonal labour migration*, ed. Loes Schenk-Sandbergen, 210–300. New Delhi: Sage.

Tehelka. 2007. Gujarat 2002: The truth in the words of the men who did it. *Tehelka* (November).

Teltumbde, Anand. 2007. Reverting to the original vision of reservations. *EPW* 42, no. 25 (June 23): 2383–2385.

Terry, Michael. 1993. Workplace unions and workplace industrial relations. *Industrial Relations Journal* 24: 2.

Thankappan, D. 1999. The informal sector and child labour. In *Against child labour: Indian and international dimensions and strategies*, ed. Klaus Voll, 62–71. New Delhi: Mosaic.

Thompson, E. P. 1966. *The making of the English working class.* Harmondsworth: Penguin.

Thomson, Don, and Rodney Larson. 1978. *Where were you, brother?* London: War on Want.

Thorat, Sukhadeo. 1999. Poverty, caste, and child labour in India: The plight of Dalit and Adivasi children. In *Against child labour: Indian and international dimensions and strategies*, ed. Klaus Voll, 154–175. New Delhi: Mosaic.

Thorat, Sukhadeo, and Joel Lee. 2005. Caste discrimination and food security programmes. *EPW* 40, no. 39 (September 24): 4198–4201.

Thorat, Sukhadeo, Aryama Negi, and Prashant Negi, eds. 2005. *Reservations and private sector: Quest for equal opportunity and growth.* New Delhi: Indian Institute of Dalit Studies and Rawat Publications.

Thorne, Barrie. 1982. Feminist rethinking of the family: An overview. In *Rethinking the family: Some feminist questions*, ed. B. Thorne with M. Yalom, 1–24. New York: Longman.

Thorne, Barrie, with Marilyn Yalom, eds. 1982. *Rethinking the family: Some feminist questions*. New York: Longman.

Thornhill, John. 2005. France firm on longer work hours. *BS* (February 8).

Ticktin, Hillel. 1979–1980. The Afghan war: The crisis in the USSR. *Critique* 12 (Autumn–Winter): 13–25.

Times of India. 1996. Trade sanctions, social clause linkage needed: Swamy commission submits draft report. *Times of India* (February 3).

——. 2008. Budget 2008: Farmers all over are loving it. *Times of India* (March 1).

TOMCOEU. 1995a. DHARNA: Public appeal to the management of HLL. Bombay: TOMCO Employees' Union.

——. 1995b. Press release: DHARNA by employees of erstwhile Tata Oil Mills all over India supported by workers of Hindustan Lever. Bombay: TOMCO Employees' Union.

Tomkins, Richard. 2002. Big Mac gives way to a little more goodness. *BS* (December 23).

Tribune. 2005. Punjab differs with Centre on workers' bill. *The Tribune* (December 10).

Trotsky, Leon. 1923. *Voina i Revolyutsiya*. Vol. 1. Moscow: Gosudarstvennoe Izdatel'stvo.

——. 1970. The USSR in war. In *In Defense of Marxism*, by Leon Trotsky. New York: Pathfinder Press.

Tulpule, Bagaram. 1996. Segmented labour, fragmented trade unions. In *Class formation and political transformation in postcolonial India*, ed. T. V. Sathyamurthy, 127–150. Delhi: Oxford University Press.

TURF. 1985. Press statement, July 11.

TUSC. N.d. Time-off and trade union rights: The management attack and our response.

——. 1992. Circular signed by N. Vasudevan and Franklyn D'Souza, September 11.

——. 1993. The aftermath of the Marathwada earthquake: A TUSC survey.

Tyabji, Nasir. 1998. What the bosses should have done: Unlearnt lessons from Mumbai's interwar textile industry. Paper presented at the First Annual Conference of the Association of Indian Labour Historians in association with the V. V. Giri National Labour Institute, March 16–18.

United Nations. 1997–2007. *General recommendations made by the Committee on the Elimination of Discrimination Against Women*. http://www.un.org/womenwatch/daw/cedaw/recommendations/recomm.htm.

——. 2009a. *Report of the Commission of Experts of the President of the United Nations General Assembly on Reforms of the International Monetary and Financial System*. http://www.un.org/ga/econcrisissummit/docs/FinalReport_CoE.pdf.

———. 2009b. Historic summit of Security Council pledges support for progress on stalled efforts to end nuclear weapons proliferation. http://www.un.org/News/Press/docs/2009/sc9746.doc.htm.

UNDP. 2009. *Human development report 2009: Overcoming barriers: Human mobility and development.* New York: UNDP. http://www.undp.org.in/content/pub/HDR/HDR_2009_EN_Complete.pdf.

Undy, Roger, and Roderick Martin. 1984. *Ballots and trade union democracy.* Oxford: Blackwell.

UNICEF. 2004. State of the world's children. http://www.unicef.org/sowc04_contents.html.

Union's Lever. 1999. Magazine of the All-India Council of Unilever Unions. *Union's Lever* 1, no. 2 (November).

Unni, Jeemol, and Namrata Bali. 2002. Subcontracted women workers in the garment industry in India. In *The hidden assembly line,* ed. Radhika Balakrishnan, 115–144. Connecticut: Kumarian Press.

Unni, Jeemol, and Uma Rani. 2003. Employment and income in the informal economy. In *Informal economy centrestage: New structures of employment,* ed. Renana Jhabvala, Ratna M. Sudarshan, and Jeemol Unni, 39–61. New Delhi: Sage.

Upadhyay, Deen Dayal. 1965. *Integral humanism.* New Delhi: Bharatiya Jan Sangh.

Upadhyay, Shashi Bhushan. 2005. Meaning of work in Dalit autobiographies. Paper presented at the SEPHIS Conference, "Towards Global Labour History: New Comparisons," Noida, November 10–12.

URG. 1983a. Dearness allowance schemes and ceilings on DA. *Bulletin of Trade Union Research and Information* 2 (July).

———. 1983b. Automation and redeployment on packing lines: Need for a union strategy. *Bulletin of Trade Union Research and Information* 3 (December).

———. 1984a. Women's employment in industry: A challenge for unions? *Bulletin of Trade Union Research and Information* 4 (February).

———. 1985a. The Bhopal MIC disaster: The beginnings of a case for workers' control. Bombay: URG.

———. 1985b. Workers allege company negligence and official callousness. *Health and Safety at Work* (May).

———. 1985c. A workers' perspective on Bhopal. Bombay: URG.

———. 1986. Leave and working hours. *Bulletin of Trade Union Research and Information* 9 (November).

———. 1996. Relative pay in large concerns. In *Company restructuring and the unions.* Sydney: IUF-Asia and Pacific.

U.S. Labor Against the War. N.d. http://uslaboragainstwar.org/index.php.

Vakulabharanam, Vamsi. 2009. The recent crisis in global capitalism: Towards a Marxian understanding. *EPW* 19, no. 13 (March 28): 144–150.

van der Linden, Marcel. 1988. The rise and fall of the First International: An interpretation. In *Internationalism in the labour movement 1830–1940*, ed. F. van Holthoon and M. van der Linden, 1:323–335. Leiden: E. J. Brill.

van Holthoon, Frits, and Marcel van der Linden, eds. 1988. *Internationalism in the labour movement 1830–1940*. Leiden: E. J. Brill.

van Roosendaal, Gerda. 2001. *Social challenges to trade: Trade unions and the debate on international labour standards*. Amsterdam: Academisch Proefschrift, Universiteit van Amsterdam.

van Tijn, Th. 1988. Nationalism and the socialist workers' movement. In *Internationalism in the labour movement 1830–1940*, ed. F. van Holthoon and M. van der Linden, 1:611–623. Leiden: E. J. Brill.

van Voss, Lex Heerma. 1988. The International Federation of Trade Unions and the attempt to maintain the eight-hour working day. In *Internationalism in the labour movement 1830–1940*, ed. F. van Holthoon and M. van der Linden, 1:518–542. Leiden: E. J. Brill.

van Wersch, Huub. 1992. *The Bombay textile strike 1982–83*. Oxford: Oxford University Press.

Varadarajan, W. R. 2005. Provident Fund administration in India: Needs reassessment not reforms. *LF* 3, no. 3 (May–June): 21–23.

Vasudeva, P. K. 2001. Food for us is cattlefeed for them. *BS* (April 27).

Vasudevan, N. 1996. Workers should demand abrogation of WTO. In *Labour, environment, and globalisation—Social clause in multilateral trade agreements: A southern response*, ed. J. John and Anuradha M. Chenoy, 71–75. New Delhi: CEC.

Venu, M. K. 2004. Armageddon in stars and stripes. *ET* (December 28).

Verma, Samar. 2003. Battle won, but too early to celebrate. *BS* (September 22).

Vester, Michael. 1975. *Die Entstehung des Proletariats als Lernprozess: die Enstehung antikapitalistischer Theorie und Praxis in England 1792–1848*. Frankfurt: Europaischer Verlagsanstalt. Extracts translated by Jairus Banaji, in *Bulletin of the Communist Platform* 2 (1978).

Vijayraghavan, Kala. 2000. If you can't beat Chinese imports, source from them. *ET* (November 30).

Vijayraghavan, Kala, and Chaitali Chakravarty. 2004. The enemy within: Detergent war hurts almost all. *ET* (August 13).

Vivekanandan, V. 1996. Outright rejection or strategic use? A report. In *Labour, environment, and globalisation—Social clause in multilateral trade agreements: A southern response*, ed. J. John and Anuradha M. Chenoy, 151–175. New Delhi: CEC.

Voll, Klaus, ed. 1999. *Against child labour: Indian and international dimensions and strategies*. New Delhi: Mosaic Books.

Vyas, Devendra. 2001. Bed linen dumping: WTO rules in favour of India. *BS* (March 5).

Waddington, Richard. 2002. EU gets WTO nod for $4-bn sanctions on US. *ET* (August 31).

——. 2005. US loses battle in WTO court on cotton subsidies. *ET* (March 3).

Wade, Robert. 2009. Steering out of the crisis. *EPW* 44, no. 13 (March 28): 39–46.

Wainwright, Hilary, and Dave Elliot. 1982. *The Lucas plan: A new trade unionism in the making?* London: Allison and Busby.

Wall, Derek. 2005. *Babylon and beyond: The economics of anticapitalist, antiglobalist, and radical green movements.* London: Pluto.

Warren, Bill. 1973. Imperialism and capitalist industrialization. *New Left Review* 81 (September–October): 1–44.

——. 1980. *Imperialism: Pioneer of capitalism.* London: New Left Books and Verso.

Watanabe, S. 1972. International sub-contracting, employment, and skill promotion. *International Labour Review* 105, no. 3.

Waterman, Peter. 1988. Needed: A new communications model for a new working-class internationalism. In *Trade unions and the new industrialisation of the Third World*, ed. Roger Southall, 351–378. London: Zed Books.

——. 2001. Trade union internationalism in the age of Seattle. In *Place, space, and the new labour internationalisms*, ed. Peter Waterman and Jane Wills, 8–32. Oxford: Blackwell.

Waterman, Peter, and Jane Wills, eds. 2001. *Place, space, and the new labour internationalisms.* Oxford: Blackwell.

Wazir, Rekha. 2002. "No to child labour, yes to education": Unfolding of a grass roots movement in Andhra Pradesh. *EPW* 37, no. 52 (December 28): 5225–5229.

Webster, Edward, and Sakhela Buhlungu. 2007. The state of trade unionism in South Africa. In *Trade union revitalisation: Trends and prospects in thirty-four countries*, ed. Craig Phelan, 415–430. Berne: Peter Lang.

Weinbaum, Batya. 1978. *The curious courtship of women's liberation and socialism.* Boston: South End Press.

Weiskopf, Richard, and Stephan Laske. 1996. Emancipatory action research: A critical alternative to personnel development or a new way of patronising people? In *New directions in action research*, ed. O. Zuber-Skerritt, 121–136. London: Falmer Press.

Weissman, Robert. 2009. The financial crisis one year later: The more things change, the more they stay the same. http://www.multinationalmonitor.org/editorsblog/index.php?/archives/118-The-Financial-Crisis-One-Year-Later-The-More-Things-Change,-the-More-They-Stay-the-Same.html.

Westwood, Sallie. 1991. Gender and the politics of production in India. In *Women, development, and survival in the Third World*, ed. Haleh Afshar, 288–308. London: Longman.

Wheatley, Alan. 2003. Cancun spawns flurry of one-on-one trade pacts. *ET* (October 21).

Wheen, Francis. 2005. Why Marx is man of the moment. *The Hindu* (July 22).

White, Gordon. 1995. *Chinese trade unions in the transition from socialism: The emergence of civil society or the road to corporatism?* Working Paper 18. Brighton: Institute of Development Studies.

WIEGO. N.d. *Addressing informality, reducing poverty: A response to the informal economy.* Cambridge, Mass.: WIEGO.

Williams, Frances. 2004. WTO rejects textile quota reprieve. *BS* (April 30).

Wills, Jane. 2001. Uneven geographies of capital and labour: The lessons of European works councils. In *Place, space, and the new labour internationalisms*, ed. Peter Waterman and Jane Wills, 180–205. Oxford: Blackwell.

——. 2002. Bargaining for the space to organize in the global economy. *Review of International Political Economy* 9, no. 4: 675–700.

Wills, Jane, and Jennifer Hurley. 2005. Action research: Tracing the threads of labour in the global garment industry. In *Threads of labour: Garment industry supply chains from the workers' perspective*, ed. Angela Hale and Jane Wills, 69–94. Oxford: Blackwell.

Windmuller, J. P. 1969. *Labor relations in the Netherlands.* Ithaca, N.Y.: Cornell University Press.

Winter, Richard. 1996. Some principles and procedures for the conduct of action research. In *New directions in action research*, ed. Ortrun Zuber-Skerritt, 13–27. London: Falmer Press.

Wolf, Martin. 2004. Sweep away the barriers to growth. *Lounsbury* (October 5). http://lounsbury.aqoul.com/archives/2004/10/debt_and_corrup.html.

Wolffe, Richard. 2002. US ready to abide by WTO tax-break ruling. *BS* (January 28).

Wood, Ellen Meiksins. 2004. The historical specificity of capitalist empire. Paper presented at the conference on "The Rise and Fall of Empires," organized by the London Socialist Historians' Group, London, May 8.

——. 1999. Unhappy families: Global capitalism in a world of nation-states. *Monthly Review* 51, no. 3 (July–August): 1–12.

Workers' Solidarity Movement. 1988. The alternative plan: What the Lucas plan proposed. *Workers' Solidarity Movement* (Summer). http://flag.blackened.net/revolt/ws88_89/ws29_lucas_plan.html.

World Bank. 1995. *World development report: Workers in an integrating world.* Washington, D.C.: World Bank/IBRD.

World Conference Against A & H Bombs. 2009. Declaration of the international meeting (5 August). *Peace Now* 7, no. 3 (October): 20–21.

Wright, Melissa W. 2001. A manifesto against femicide. In *Place, space, and the new labour internationalisms*, ed. Peter Waterman and Jane Wills, 246–262. Oxford: Blackwell.

WWW. 1991. *Common interests: Women organising in global electronics.* London: Women Working Worldwide.

———. 1998a. *Company codes of conduct: What are they? Can we use them?* Manchester: Women Working Worldwide.

———. 1998b. *Women workers and codes of conduct: Report of preliminary research and consultation exercise.* Manchester: Women Working Worldwide.

———. 2002. *Company codes of conduct and worker rights: Report of an education and consultation programme with garment workers in Asia.* Manchester: Women Working Worldwide.

———. 2003a. *Subcontracting in the garment industry: Women Working Worldwide project workshop, Bangkok.* Manchester: Women Working Worldwide.

———. 2003b. *Garment industry subcontracting and workers' rights: Report of Women Working Worldwide action research in Asia and Europe 2003.* Manchester: Women Working Worldwide.

Yanz, Linda, and Bob Jeffcott. Bringing codes down to earth. *IUR* 8, no. 3: 8–10.

Yasmeen, Summiya. 2004. Swelling support for common schools. *India Together* (July). www.indiatogether.org/2004/jul/edu-kothari.htm.

Yimprasert, Junya, and Christopher Candland. 2000. *Can corporate codes of conduct promote labor standards? Evidence from the Thai footwear and apparel industries.* Bangkok: Thai Labor Campaign.

Young, Kate, Carol Wolkowitz, and Roslyn McCullagh, eds. 1981. *Of marriage and the market: Women's subordination in international perspective.* London: CSE Books.

Zaretsky, Eli. 1982. The place of the family in the origins of the welfare state. In *Rethinking the family: Some feminist questions*, ed. B. Thorne with M. Yalom, 188–244. New York: Longman.

Zielenziger, David. 2003. US quietly moves more tech jobs to India. *ET* (December 25).

Zhu, Xiaohua. 1997. Anti-dumping measures: Time to roll them back. *EPW* 32, no. 18 (May 13): 936–937.

Zoll, Rainer. 1996. Modernization, trade unions, and solidarity. In *The challenges to trade unions in Europe: Innovation or adaptation*, ed. Peter Leisink, Jim Van Leemput, and Jaques Vilrokx, 77–104. New York: Edward Elgar.

Zuber-Skerritt, Ortrun. 1996. Introduction: New directions in action research. In *New directions in action research*, ed. Ortrun Zuber-Skerritt, 3–9. London: Falmer Press.

Zuber-Skerritt, Ortrun, ed. 1996. *New directions in action research.* London: Falmer Press.

Index

International Labour Organization (ILO),
10, 113, 302, 321, 330, 347; and child
labor, 190–191, 197, 200; Committee on
Freedom of Association, 287; Core Conventions, 208, 284–285, 289, 292, 293,
313, 334, 347, 348; Convention on Home
Work, 189, 206, 242, 291; Conventions
on Freedom of Association and Right to
Organize and Collective Bargaining, 144;
Declaration on Fundamental Principles
and Rights at Work and Its Follow-up,
284–285; Discrimination (Occupation
and Employment) Convention, 121, 242;
Equal Remuneration Convention, 242;
formation, 57, 281; Forty-Hour Week
Convention, 242; and informal employment, 164, 187, 207–208, 334; and
International Labour Parliament, 284;
international program on the Elimina-
tion of Child Labour (IPEC), 200, 316;
Maternity Protection Convention, 242;
Minimum Age Convention, 196, 228;
Part-Time Work Convention, 242; Resolution Concerning Decent Work and
the Informal Economy, 207; on sexual
harassment, 242; and social clause, 111,
302–305, 307, 309, 314–317; and women
workers, 209; Workers' with Family
Responsibilities Convention, 242
International Labour Parliament, 284
International Metalworkers' Federation
(IMF), 285, 286
International Monetary Fund (IMF), 1, 6,
42–43, 52, 66, 74, 75, 76, 112, 304, 307,
309, 315, 324, 348
International Restructuring Education Net-
work Europe (IRENE), 208
International Textile, Garment and Leather
Workers' Federation (ITGLWF), 283
International Trade Secretariat (ITS),
280–281, 282
International Trades Union Secretariat
(ITUS), 281
International Trade Union Confederation
(ITUC), 4, 291, 322
International Union of Food, Agricultural,
Hotel, Restaurant, Catering, Tobacco,

and Allied Workers' Associations (IUF),
283, 286, 287
International Working Men's Association.
See First International
Iran, 36, 60, 90
Iraq, 36, 58, 59, 60, 77–78, 81, 319
irregular work/workers, 170, 178, 189–190,
220, 271–272, 322, 323, 333
Italy, 93–94, 116, 261

Janata Party, 101, 102
Japan, 35, 40, 49, 51, 52, 61, 74–75, 77, 90,
133, 310, 338
job losses, 10, 26, 48, 66, 84, 115, 124–127,
161, 244–245, 276, 281, 323, 328
job security, 5, 173, 182, 244
job segregation, 214, 233

Kaleen label, 200
Kamani Employees' Union (KEU), 151–152,
155, 157–158, 253–257, 261, 343, 346
Kerala Agricultural Workers Act, 184–185
Kerala Head Load Workers' Act, 184–185
Keynes, J. M., 41–42
Korea, 3, 49, 52, 54, 61, 75, 90, 94, 174, 299,
310

labor contractor/provider, 100, 166, 188,
333–334, 340
labor laws/legislation, 5, 21, 94–99, 101,
105, 107, 110–112, 149, 153, 165, 172, 174,
175, 179–184, 190, 191, 204, 206, 207,
278–280, 281, 283, 285, 317, 323, 334
labor-rights clause. See social clause
Labor Rights in China (LARIC), 299
Labour Behind the Label, 23
Labour Research Department, 121, 286
large-scale sector, 32, 101, 102, 103, 110, 166,
168, 174, 175, 182, 204. See also formal
sector
leave, 143, 182, 183, 189, 229, 234, 241, 332
Lenin, V. I., 27–29, 31, 38, 40, 45, 46, 65, 80,
92, 280
leverage ratios, 71, 73
Liebknecht, Karl, 80
lockout, 105, 124, 140, 145, 146, 147, 148, 157,
254, 255, 295

Printed in the USA
CPSIA information can be obtained
at www.ICGtesting.com
JSHW020639080624
64421JS00008B/16/J